# Introduction

These are the earliest court minutes I have found for Pulaski County KY. This volume covers the years 1804 to 1809. Will Fox was the clerk of court, and fortunately his handwriting is usually clear and legible. His entries are often narratives of the back and forth of the court procedure, so students of legal history can see the progress of a case. There are many cases of interest. We see inquiries into a person's mental health, a hotly contested claim of arson, disputes about horses, and bear and deer skins (reminding us that the frontier has not completely passed away), legal and illegal sales of spirituous liquor, assaults with battery, and quarrels over land. The whole panoply of life in the early West appears sooner or later before the Courts.

There is no indication of a settled currency. Amounts are as likely to be given in pounds as in dollars.

There is a pronounced interest in the minutia of the legal system. Objections and appeals run to great lengths, with occasional recourse to the state Court of Appeals. It seems as if any decision could be contested indefinitely if the loser was willing to pay for another round of trial. Women appear very infrequently in these pages. Kizziah Chappel had a long running legal battle over a defamation of her character. Slaves are mentioned, but not extensively. The case of Negro Jack, suing to prove his freedom, is perhaps the most interesting. The many names appearing in this document provide a cross check on the population of the county, as indicated in the publications of the Pulaski County Historical Society, such as the 1799-1800 Tax Lists; 1810, 20, 30, 40 Census and Marriage Records Vol I 1799 - 1850 and Index to Wills, 1800 - 1950. I have transcribed this to the best of my ability; I do not claim it is completely accurate, because there are smudges and tears in the pages, as well as the less legible hand of a second clerk. Still, I offer it with hopes that it may be useful to students of family and local history. I dedicate this to the memory of my brother, Michael Allan Wagner, 1945 - 1984, basketball player, Viet Nam veteran, policeman, and Army recruiter. He died too young, but his ancestors, as my own, lived in Pulaski County, KY.

Karen Wagner Treacy
Charlottesville VA
karent100@embarqmail.com

[page 1] March the 26th 1804

At a Circuit Court Composed of the Counties of Pulaski and Wayne, at the Courthouse in the Town of Sommerset on the twenty sixth day of March 1804

Present the honourable **James G Hunter, John Smith**, and **John Prather** Gentlemen

– A Grandjury were sworn for the Circuit aforesaid to Wit, **John Mitchell**, foreman, **John Evans, John Tully, Isaac Ingram, Reubin Hill, Andrew Turner, James Kerr, Samuel Cornbes, James Horrell, Samuel Neal, David Buster, John Martin, Edward Cooper, Jonas Irvine, David Puckett, Peter Pettyjohn, John Evans, Henry James, Nathaniel Forbis**, and **Robert Modrel**, who having received their charge retired to consider of their presentments

– **William Owens** and **William Davis**, Esquires each took the necessary Oaths as Attornies at Law in this Court, which was ordered to be entered of Record

– **Kizziah Chapple** by her next friend **Jesse Chapple** Plts
against In Case
**Jesse Burton** Deft

On the motion of the Plaintiff **Jesse Chapple**, who made Oath as the law directs, this case made and provided, that he had reason to believe the Defendant would remove himself & [page 2] whereupon the Sheriff is directed to take Bail of said Defendant in the sum of one hundred Pounds

– **Stephen Coyle** & **Mary** his wife Plts
against In Case
**Alexander Roberson** Deft

On the Motion of the Plaintiff **Stephen** who made Oath as the law directs, in such cases made & provided, that he had reason to believe that the Defendant was about to remove himself, & therefore the sheriff is directed to take Bail of said Defendant, as the law directs in the sum of One hundred Pounds.

– **Abner Muirheed** by his next friend **Daniel Muirheed** Plts
against In Case
**John Brooks** Deft

This day came the Parties aforesaid by their attornies, and by their Consent all matters in difference between them respecting this suit is refered to the Arbitration and determination of **William Penit** and **Philip Williams**, whose award or the award of any one of them, with an umphire by them chosen in case of their disagreement be the Judgment of the Court, and the same is Ordered Accordingly.

– The Commonwealth Plt
against Upon Presentment, for not keeping the Road in Repair
**Willis Embry**

– The Same Plt
against The Same
**John Dick** Deft

[page 3] The Commonwealth Plt
against The Same
**Micajah Hogan** Deft

This day came as well the attorney for the Commonwealth, as the said Defendants in their Proper Persons, and for reasons appearing to the Court It is Ordered that these Presentments be Dismissed

– The Grand jury returned into Court an Indictment the Commonwealth against **William Evans** a true Bill, Also the following Presentments to wit, We of the Grand jury for the Circuit Composed of the Counties of Pulaski and Wayne, do present **Thomas McElwen**, for profanely swearing twice, by God, On Monday the 26th day of March 1804 in the Street of Sommerset and County of Pulaski by the Information of **David Puckett**, and **James Herrell**, both of the Grand jury aforesaid

**John Mitchell** foreman

– We of the Grand jury for the Circuit aforesaid do present **John Troxall** for profanely swearing three times by God the 25th day of February 1804, also eight times 24th day of March 1804 at the house of **John Fitzgerald** in the County of Pulaski by the Information of **Jesse Burton**, of the County of Pulaski not of the Grand jury

**John Mitchell** foreman

– We of the Grand jury for the Circuit aforesaid do present **Ephraim Churchwell**, of the County of Pulaski for Profanely swearing by the great god almighty twice 25th day of February 1804 in the street of Sommerset & County of Pulaski by the [page 4] Information of **Reubin Hill**, and **John Mitchell**, both of this Grand jury

**John Mitchell** foreman

– The Grand jury having nothing further to present were discharged by the Court, and Delinquents Ordered to be Summoned

– **Robert Modrel** Plt
against Upon Attachment 2nd case
**Alexander McFarling** & Als Deft

On the motion of Plaintiff by his attorney, an Alias Summons is awarded him against **David Hays** of Lincoln County as a Garnishe herein, And It is Ordered that he appear here on the third day of the next Term to shew Cause if any he can why he shall not be fined, for failing to attend, as a Witness herein, on this Present day

– Ordered that the Court be adjourned until Tommorrow morning ten OClock

**J G Hunter**

At a Circuit Court Composed of the Counties of Pulaski and Wayne continued and held at the Courthouse in the Town of Sommerset on the twenty seventh day of March 1804

Present **James G Hunter John Smith** and **John Prather** Gentlemen

– **Martin Turpin** came into Court and on his motion acknowledged himself Indebted to **William Sharp**, in the sum of [page 5] fifty three Dollars and fifty cents, agreeable to an Act of the General Assembly of Kentucky in that case made and provided, the said **Sharp** being in Court accepted the Confession for the sum aforesaid It is therefore Considered by the Court that he recover of the said **Turpin** the sum Confessed as aforesaid and his Costs by him in this behalf expended, with legal Interest thereon from this present day until paid & Costs & execution to be stayed until May next

– On the motion of **Thomas McElwee**, who was presented by the Grand jury yesterday for Profanely swearing twice by God paid ten Shillings as his fine to the Sheriff, agreeable to the directions of the Court and Process is Ordered not to Issue against said **Thomas**

– On the Motion of **John Chesney**, an Injunction is granted him to stay all further Proceedings on a Judgment in ejectment Obtained against him in this Court at Common law by **Tunstall Qualls** he having filed his bill for that purpose, and entered into and acknowledged bond with **John Gee** his security in the sum of thirty pounds conditioned as the law directs

– **Celia Taylor** by her next friend **George Taylor** Prosecutor for the Commonwealth Plts
against upon an Indictment
**Robert Smith** Constable Deft

[page 6] This day came as well the attorney for the Commonwealth as the said Defendant by his attorney, and thereupon came also a Jury, to wit, **William Barnes, John Tully, Samuel Neal, Malcom McCown, Henry Sage, David Richardson, George Modrel, John Evans, Isaac Mayfield** Senr, **Daniel McKinsey, George McWhorter** & **Jonas Irvine**, who being elected tryed and sworn the truth to speak upon the Issue Joined upon their Oaths do say that the said Defendant is not guilty in manner and form as the attorney for the Commonwealth in the Indictment against him hath alleged It is therefore Considered by the Court that they take nothing by their bill but for their false clamor be in mercy &c and that the Defendant go thereof without day and recover of the said Prosecutors his Costs by him about his defense in this behalf expended

– **Joseph Oatman** Plt
against In Debt
**Jeremiah Elrod** Deft

**Samuel Newell** of Wayne County came into court and undertook for the said Defendant that if he shall be cast in the action aforesaid that he shall satisfy and pay the condemnation of the Court or render his body to Prison in execution for the same or on falure thereof that he the said Samuel shall do it for him

[page 7] **Robert Modrel** Plt
against upon Attachment
**Alexander McFarling** &c Deft

This day came the Plaintiff by his attorney, and **Robert Modrell** a Garnishee, herein came into Court and declared upon Oath that he had in his possession property belonging to the said Defendants to wit, One bay roan Horse about nine or ten years old fourteen hands high which was Ordered to be entered of Record

– **Holkum Roberson** Plt
against The Same
**George Etherington** Deft

– **Zachariah Price** & wife Plts
against In Case
**John Scott** & wife Defts

Ordered that these suits be Continued untill the next Court

– **George Saunders** Plt
against upon Attachment
**Samuel Saunders** Deft

This day came the parties aforesaid by their attornies, and on the motion of the said Defendant by his attorney It is Ordered by the Court that the said Attachment be dismissed by reason of Informality in the Attachment, and that the Defendant recover against the said Plaintiff his costs by him about his defense in this behalf expended &c

– **Samuel Kindal** Plt
against upon Attachment
**William Hardgrove** Deft

This day came the Plaintiff by his Attorney and **John Jasper** a Garnishee, herein declared upon Oath that he was Indebted to the Defendant the sum of nine pence and no more and on the motion of the Plaintiff by his attorney Judgment is granted him against the said Defendant for fifty five Dollars sixty six and a half Cents, besides his costs It is therefore Ordered that the Plaintiff recover against the said Defendant the sum of fifty five Dollars & sixty six and a half cents & his Costs by him about his suit in this behalf expended

– **James Eastham** Junr by his next friend **James Eastham** Senr Plts
against In Case
**Daniel Hill** Deft

Ordered that this suit be Dismissed at the Defendants Costs

– **John Eastham** Plt
against In Trespass assault and Battery
**Daniel Hill** Deft

– The same Plt
against The Same
The Same Deft

Ordered that these suits be dismissed it being agreed by the parties

[page 9] Ordered that **John January** pay **William Floyd** one hundred and sixty seven pence for attending and travelling seventy one miles as a witness for him at the suit of **Joseph Casky**

– **Valentine Hardgrove** Plt
against In Case
**Absolem Bridges** Deft

Ordered that this suit be Continued untill the next Court at the Defendants Costs

– **James Clark** Plt
against In Case

**Daniel McKinsey** Deft

This day came the parties aforesaid by their attornies and thereupon came also a Jury, to wit, **Frederick Williams, Charles Neal, Jonas Irvine, John Wilkerson, William Barns, Smith Williams, Henry Sage, William Owens, Jesse Williams, Samuel Neal, Jonathan Smith** & **David Richardson**, who being elected tryed & Sworn the truth to speak upon the Issue Joined, Afterward One of the Jurors, to wit, **Frederick Williams**, by Consent of the Parties was withdrawn by the Court, and the cause Continued until the next Court

– The Same Plt
against In Case, Or on Motion
The Same Deft

The Defendant by his attorney moved for a nonsuit in this [page 10] cause, which motion being over ruled by the Court, It is Ordered that the Plaintiff recover against the said Defendant his Costs by him about this motion expended

– Absent **John Smith** Gent

– On the motion of **George Saunders** by his attorney for an Injunction against **Samuel Saunders** the said Defendant by his attorney moved that the said motion be Over ruled After hearing the arguments of the Counsel on both sides It is the Opinion of the Court that the same be over ruled with Costs &c

– **Robert Brown** Plt
against In Case
**Charles Stewart** Deft

– **Edward Cooper** Plt
against In Case
**Charles Richardson** Deft

Ordered that these suits be Discontinued

– **James Cowen** Plt
against In Case
**Henry Willis** Deft

This day came the Parties aforesaid by their attornies and By their Consent all matters in difference between them respecting this suit is refered to the arbitration and determination [page 11] of **Philip A Sublette, Nicholas Jasper** & **William Barnes**, whose award or the award of any two of them, be the Judgment of the Court and the same is Ordered Accordingly

– **Ephraim Churchwell** Plt
against In Case
**Henry Francis** Deft

This day came the Parties aforesaid by their attornies and thereupon came also a Jury to wit, **Richard Hill, Aaron Lawson, Daniel Hill, Andrew Jasper, Thomas McGuire, Peter Lee, Edward Cooper, Micajah Hogan, Jonathan Stephens, John McCullough, George Modrel**, & **Robert Anderson**, who being elected tryed and Sworn the truth to speak upon the Issue Joined, upon their Oaths do say, that the said Defendant is guilty in manner and form as the Plaintiff against him hath declared and they do assess the Plaintiffs Damages by Occasion thereof to six Pounds eighteen Shillings, besides his costs, It is therefore Considered by the Court that the Plaintiff recover against the said Defendant his Damages aforesaid by the Jurors in their Verdict aforesaid assessed and his costs by him about his suit in this behalf expended and the said Defendant in mercy &c

– **John Hunt** Plt
against In Case
**David Johnson** Deft

[page 12] This day came the Parties aforesaid by their attornies, and It is Ordered that this suit be continued until the next Court at the Defendants Costs And on the motion of the said Defendant by his attorney a Commission is awarded him to take the Deposition of **George Willis** Debenesse, of the state of North Carolina before any person of said State Authorized to administer an Oath

– Ordered that the Court be adjourned "till Tommorrow morning ten OClock

**J G Hunter**

At a Circuit Court Composed of the Counties of Pulaski and Wayne Continued and held at the Courthouse in the Town of Sommerset on the 28th day of March 1804

Present **James G Hunter, John Smith & John Prather** Gentlemen

– **Alexander Moore** Plt
against In Debt
**Micah Taul** Deft
– **Alexander Hambliton** Plt
against In Debt
The Same Deft

**Joshua Jones** of Wayne County came into court, and undertook for the said Defendant, that if he shall be cast in the Actions aforesaid that he shall satisfy and pay the Condemnation of the Court, or render his body to Prison in execution for the Same Or on falure thereof that the he the said **Joshua** shall do it for him

[page 13] **John Ashley** Plt
against In Debt
**Jonathan Stephens & James Alderson** Defts

**Joseph Evans** of Pulaski County came into Court and undertook for the Defendant **Stephens** that if he shall be cast in the Action aforesaid that he shall satisfy and pay the condemnation of the Court or render his body to prison in execution for the same, or on falure thereof that he shall do it for him

– **Johnson Vaughn** by his next **Joseph Lewis** Plts
against In Trespass Assault and Battery
**Samuel Caughron** Deft

Ordered that this suit be Dismissed at the Defendants Costs

– **John Kennedy** Plt
against
**James Smith** Deft

Ordered that this suit be discontinued, it being by Order of the Plaintiffs Attorney

– **Alexander Hambleton** Plt
against In Covenant
**Arch^d E Mills** & Al^s Defts

**Philip A Sublette**, of Pulaski County came into Court and undertook for the Defendant **Mills**, that he shall satisfy and pay the Condemnation of the Court, or render his body to Prison in execution for the same or on falure thereof that he the said **Philip** shall do it for him

[page 14] **Joseph Casky** Plt
against In Case
**John January** Deft

This day came the Parties aforesaid by their Attornies, and on the motion of the Defendants Attorney It is ordered that this suit be remanded to the rule Dockett &c

– **Samuel Kindal** Plt
against In Trespass Assault & Battery
**William Hardgrove** Deft

This day came the Parties aforesaid by their attornies and thereupon came also a Jury, to wit, **Israel Hart, John McCullough, Thomas Whites, Bazil Meek, Jeremiah Meek, Micajah Hogan, John Gee, Francis Stephens, Jesse Williams, Andrew Turner, William Denham** & **Hugh Logan**, who being elected tryed and sworn the truth to speak upon the Issue Joined upon their Oaths do say that the said Defendant is guilty in manner and form as the Plaintiff against him hath declared, and they do assess the Plaintiffs damages by Occasion thereof to four pounds ten Shillings besides his Costs, it is therefore considered by the Court, that the Plaintiff recover against the said Defendant his Damages aforesaid by the Jurors in their Verdict aforesaid assessed and his Costs by him about his suit in this behalf expended, and the said Defendant in mercy &c

– **Alexander Hambleton** Plt
against In Covenant
**William Dodson** Deft

[page 15] **Allin Burton** came into Court and undertook for the said Defendant that if he shall be cast in the Action aforesaid that he shall satisfy and pay the condemnation of the Court, or render his body to Prison in execution for the same or on falure thereof he the said **Allin** shall do it for him

– **Thomas Owsley** Plt
against In Case
**Joseph Knox** & Others Deft

This day came the Parties aforesaid by their attornies, and on the motion of the said Defendants by their attorney It is Ordered that this suit be continued until the next Court, at the Defendants Costs

– Ordered that **Thomas Owsley** pay **Thomas McGuire, Samuel Neal, James Smith** Junr fifty pence each for attending two days each also **Zachariah Owsley** One hundred pence for attending four days as a witness for him against **Knox** & Others

– Ordered that **Joseph Casky** pay **James Smith, Charles Neal, Matthew Hickson, Linsey Hardgrove, Thomas Owsley, James Kelly,** & **Ambrose Mayfield** fifty pence each for attending two days each as witnesses for him against **John January**

– Ordered that **James Clark** pay **Thomas Owsley** fifty pence for attending two days as a Witness for him against **Daniel McKinsey**

– Ordered that **John January** pay **Philip A Sublette** fifty pence for attending two days as a witness for him at the suit of **Joseph Casky**

[page 16] Ordered that **Samuel Kindal** pay **William Williams** one hundred pence for attending four days as a Witness for him against **William Hardgrove**

– Ordered that **Valentine Hardgrove** pay **Robert Anderson** and **John Hardgrove** twenty five pence each for attending one day each as a Witness for him against **Bridges**

– Ordered that **John Wilkerson** pay **Andrew Evans & Frederick Williams** fifty pence each for attending two days each also **Edward Turner** two hundred and ninety pence for attending two days and traveling One hundred and ninety pence for a Witness for him against **Joseph Casky**

– **John Chesney** Plt
against In Case
**John Hardgrove** Deft

This day came Parties aforesaid by their attornies, and thereupon came also a Jury, to wit, **Edward Cooper, John Charney, John Wilkerson, Matthew Hickson, John Newby, John Blacklidge, Abraham Smith, David Dodson, Robert Scott, William Barnes, John McCullough,** and **George Modrel** who being elected tryed and sworn the truth to speak upon the Issue Joined upon their Oaths do say that the said Defendant is not guilty in manner and form as the Plaintiff against him hath declared, It is therefore Considered by the Court that the Plaintiff take nothing for his Bill but for his false clamour be in mercy &c And [page 17] that the Defendant go thereof without day and recover of the said Plaintiff his costs by him about his defence in this behalf expended

– Ordered that **Joseph Casky** pay **Arthur Moore** fifty pence for Attending two days also One hundred pence to **James Kerr** for attending four days as Witnesses for him against **John January**

– **John Wilkerson** Plt
against In Case
**Joseph Casky** Deft

This day came the parties aforesaid by their attornies, and the Demurer of the said Defendant to the Plaintiffs Declaration herein being argued at the last Term of this Court, The Court took time to consider thereof, It is therefore the Opinion of the Court that the said Demurer be Over ruled &c and the said Defendant by his attorney comes and defends the wrong and Injury when and where &c and saith that he is not guilty in manner and form as the Plaintiff against him hath declared, and this he prays may be inquired off by the County, and the said Plaintiff likewise, and the said Defendant for further plea herein says that he was Justifiable in speaking of and Concerning the Plaintiff the words [page 18] as laid in the Declaration & of this he puts himself upon the County and the said Plaintiff likewise, therefore It is commanded the Sheriff that he cause to come here Immediately twelve good and lawful men by whose &c and thereupon came also a Jury, to wit, **Edward Cooper, John Singleton, Jacob Smith, Samuel Cowpenheifer, Joel Jackson, John Tully, Ambrose Mayfield, Apolis Hess, Joseph Ellis, John Chesney, George McWhorter** and **John Ashley** who being elected tryed and sworn the truth to speak upon the Issue Joined upon them upon their Oaths do say that the said Defendant is guilty in manner and form as the Plaintiff against him hath alleged, and that he was not Justifiable in speaking of an Concerning the Plaintiff the words laid in the Declaration, and they do assess the plaintiffs Damages by Occasion thereof to thirty Pounds besides his Costs It is therefore Considered by the Court that the Plaintiff recover against the said Defendant, his Damages aforesaid by the Jurors in their Verdict aforesaid assessed, and his Cost by him about his defence in this behalf expended, and the said Defendant may be taken &c

– Ordered that **John Chesney** pay **Winston Walker** two hundred and twelve pence for attending two days, travelling seventy three miles, and two ferriages as a witness for him against **John Hardgrove**

[page 19] **John Fitzgerald** &c Plt
against In Debt
**W<sup></sup>m Addison** & **John Chesney** Deft

**John McWhorter** of Pulaski County came into Court and undertook for the Defendant **Chesney** that if he shall be cast in the action aforesaid that he shall satisfy and pay the Condemnation of the Court or render his body to Prison, in Execution for the same or on falure thereof that he the said **John**, shall do it for him

– Ordered that **John January** pay **Jesse Williams** & **John Newby** fifty pence each for attending two days each as Witnesses for him at the suit of **Joseph Clasky**

– Ordered that **John Hardgrove** pay **Philip A Sublette, Israel Hart** & **Richard Churchwell** Senr fifty pence each for attending two days each as Witnesses for him at the suit of **John Chesney**

– Ordered that **John Chesney** pay **Issabella** Sublette fifty pence for attending two days as a Witness for him against **John Hardgrove**

– Ordered that **Ephraim Churchwell** pay **Richard Churchwell** Senr fifty pence for attending two days as a Witness for him against **Henry Francis**

[page 20] On the Motion of the Attorney for the Circuit Court composed of the Counties of Pulaski and Wayne, It is Ordered that a writ of De Idista Inquirendo Issue directed to the Sheriff commanding him to summon a Jury Immediately to meet at some Convenient place in the Town of Sommerset, and then and there Inquire whether **Nancy Mize** is a person of unsound mind &c and do such other things as the Act of Assembly is Such cases made and provided directs, and make report thereof to the Court

– Ordered that **Ephraim Churchwell** pay **Richard Churchwell** Senr fifty pence for attending two days as a witness for him at the suit of **Robert Whitehead**

– Ordered that **John Hardgrove** pay **Richard Churchwell** Senr fifty pence for attending two days as a witness for him at the suit of **John Chesney**

– **John Fitzgerald** &c Plt
against In Debt
**William Addison** & Als Deft

This day came the Parties aforesaid by their attornies & It is ordered that this suit be dismissed at the Defendants Cost (excepting an attornies fee)

– Ordered that **Robert Whitehead** pay **Jacob Smith,** and **Dianah Burnham** one hundred pence each for attending four days each as Witnesses for him against **Ephraim Churchwell**

[page 21] **Robert Whitehead** Plt
against In Trespass Assault & Battery
**Ephraim Churchwell** Deft

On the motion of the Defendant It is Ordered that the Judgment and Writ of Inquiry awarded against him in the clerks Office be set a side, and the said Defendant by his attorney maintains and defends the wrong and Injury when and where &c and says that if he did assault the Plaintiff it was Occasioned by the Plaintiffs giving the first assault, and this he prays may be enquired of the Country, and the said Plaintiff likewise and the said Defendant for further plea here in says that he is not guilty in manner and form as the plaintiff against him hath declared, and this he prays may be enquired of by the Country and the said Plaintiff likewise, Therefore It is Commanded the Sheriff that he cause to come here Immediately twelve good and lawfull men by whom &c and thereupon came also a Jury, to wit, **Joel Jackson, George McWhorter, George Allcorn, Ambrose Mayfield, Jn° Willis, John McWhorter, James Kelly, John Wilkerson, Jesse Williams, Smith Williams, William Barns & Peleg Baker** who being elected tryed and sworn the truth to speak upon the Issue Joined upon their Oaths do say that the Plaintiff did not give the first assault as in pleading the Defendant hath alledged, but that the Defendant [page 22] said Defendant is guilty in manner and form as the Plaintiff against him hath declared, and they do assess the Plaintiff damages by Occasion thereof to twenty five Dollars, besides his Costs It is therefore considered by the Court that the Plaintiff recover against the said Defendant his Damages aforesaid by the Jurors in their Verdict aforesaid assessed and his Costs by him about his defence in this behalf expended and the said Defendant may be taken &c

– Ordered that the Court be adjourned until tomorrow morning ten OClock

**J G Hunter**

At a Circuit Court Continued and held for the Counties of Pulaski and Wayne at the Courthouse in the Town of Sommerset on the twenty ninth day of March 1804

Present **James G Hunter, John Smith** and **John Prather** Gentlemen

– On the motion of **Nicholas Jasper John Jasper** and **Andrew Jasper** It is ordered that an Injunction be granted them to stay all further procedings on a Judgment in Ejectment Obtained against them at Common Law by **Tunstall Qualls** they having filed their bill for that purpose on their entering into bond in the clerks Office, within twenty days from the present day, with **John Hardgrove** Senr their security in the Penalty of sixty pounds Conditioned as the law directs

[page 23] **John Chesney** Plt
against In Case
**John Hardgrove** Deft

This day came the parties aforesaid by their attornies, and on the motion of the Plaintiff by his attorney It is Ordered that a new Trial be granted him in this Case, On the Verdict of the Jury herein Obtained yesterday, and that he pay unto the said Defendant his costs &c and the cause Continued till the next Court

– **Robert Whitehead** Plt
against In Trespass Assault and Battery
**Ephraim Churchwell** Deft

This day came the Parties aforesaid by their Attornies and On the motion of said Defendant by his attorney for a new trial On the Judgment Obtained against him in this Case yesterday, It is Ordered by the Court that the said motion be Over ruled, and that the Plaintiff recover against the said Defendant his Costs by him about this motion expended &c

– The Commonwealth Plt
against upon Writ of Idista Inquirendo
**Nancy Mize**

Inquisition returned in the words and figures following, to wit, In Obedience to the within writ of de Idista Inqurendo, we have after being sworn examined into the state of **Nancy Mize** mind & Capacity and do find her to be insane, and that her insanity is not from her nativity, but from some cause to us unknown also that she has no lucid intervals also that she has a husband [page 24] now living with her **Jeremiah Mize**) and from the best proof we have of his estate we suppose it to be worth about forty pounds

**James Kerr, Frederick Williams, William Owens, William Allison, John Dollihide, John Singleton, Joseph Reaney, Malachi Cooper, Hansford Price, Andrew Evans, John Tully, David Evans**

Whereupon it is decreed and Ordered that **Frederick Williams, John Dollihide** & **Andrew Evans** be appointed a committee for the restraint & safe keeping of the said **Nancy Mize** and further that they have full power & authority to appropriate so much of the state of her Husband mentioned in the said Inquisition aforesaid as will be sufficient to support the said **Nancy Mize** &c

– **James Beazly** Plt
against In Debt
**George Allcorn** Deft

This day came the parties aforesaid by their attornies, and It is Ordered that the said Defendants Plea herein be waved, and the said Defendant says he cannot gainsay that Plaintiffs Action against him for the Debt in the Declaration mentioned It is therefore considered by the Court that the Plaintiff recover against the said Defendant the said Debt in the Declaration mentioned & his Costs by him about his suit in this behalf expended, and the said Defendant in mercy &c. [page 26] Note this Judgment is to be discharged by the payment of eighteen pounds with legal Interest thereon from the twenty fifth day of December One thousand eight hundred and two until paid & Costs

– **James Beazly** Assce of **Charles Hutcheson** Plt
against In Covenant
**George Allcorn** Deft

This day came the Parties aforesaid by their Attornies, and It is Ordered that the Defendants Plea herein be waved and the said Defendant Acknowledged the Plaintiffs Action against him for seventeen pounds. It is therefore considered by the Court that the Plaintiff recover against the said Defendant the sum Confessed as aforesaid with Legal Interest thereon from the first day of May One thousand eight hundred and two until paid & Costs by him about his suit in this behalf expended and the said Defendant in Mercy &c. Note this Judgment is to have credit for four pounds nine Shillings paid the on the first day of June One thousand eight hundred and two

– **Dolly George** Plt
against In Case
**Joshua Jones** Senr & **Saml Banks** Defts

– **William George,s** administratrix Plt
against In Trespass with fource & arms
**Zachariah Saunders** Deft

On the motion of the said Defendants It is Ordered that the Judgment and Writ of Inquiry awarded against them in the [page 26] Clerks Office be set a side and the said Defendants by their Attornies now Come and defend the wrong and Injury when and where &c and said that they are not guilty in manner and form as the Plaintiff against them hath declared and of this they put themselves upon the Country and the said Plaintiff likewise. Therefore let a Jury come here &c and the Cause is continued untill the next Court

– **John Hill** Plt
against In Trespass Assault & Battery
**Micajah Hogan** Deft

On the Motion of the Defendant It is Ordered that the Judgment and Writ of Inquiry awarded against him in the Clerks Office be set a side, and the said Defendant by his Attorney comes and defends the force and Injury when & where &c. and says the plaintiff his action aforesaid against him ought not to have and maintain because he says that after the Commission of the Trespass Assault and battery in the Declaration mentioned to wit, on the ___ day of ___ in the year ____ at the County of Pulaski it was agreed by the Plaintiff with the Defendant that if the

Defendant would recant a Contract which before that time the Defendant had made with the Plaintiff father, for a certain bay mare he the Plaintiff would dismiss the action aforesaid and pay the costs of the suit, to which the Defendant assented and he avers that he did in conformity to the said agreement to wit on the day and year aforesaid & at the County aforesaid deliver up the said Mare and this is he ready to Verify wherefore he [page 27] prays Judgment &c. and the said Defendant for further plea herein say that he is not guilty in manner and form as the Plaintiff against him hath declared, and this he prays may be enquired of by the Country and the said Plaintiff likewise therefore let a Jury Come here &c. and the Cause is continued until the next Court

- **Edward Flowers** Plt
against In Covenant
**Henry Francis** Deft
- **William Buford** Plt
against In Debt
The Same Deft

This day came the Parties aforesaid by their attornies, and It is ordered that these suits be remanded to the rule Dockett

- **Drewry Lee** Plt
against In Case
**Smith & Sublette** Defts

This day came the Plaintiff by his attorney, and on his motion It is Ordered that the Objections filed in this case as to the Defendant Bail be waved, and It is ordered that this suit be prosecuted no further against the Defendant **Sublette**, And thereupon came also a Jury, to wit, **David Buster, Apolis Hess, Andrew Jasper, William Salley, John McWhorter, John Willis, Samuel** [page 28] **Kindal, Golfin Minor, William Brock & Micajah Hogan, John Fitzjerald** & **Jeremiah Meek** who were sworn well and truly to enquire what Damages the Plaintiff hath sustained in premise upon their Oath do say that the Plaintiff hath sustained Damage by Occasion thereof to sixty seven Dollars and eighty four Cents besides his costs. It is therefore Considered by the Court that the plaintiff recover agains the said Defendant his Damages aforesaid by the Jurors in their Verdict aforesaid assessed and his Costs by him about his suit in this behalf expended and the said Defendant in mercy &c.

- **William Buford** Plt
against In Debt
**Joseph Beard** Deft

This day came the Plaintiff by his attorney, and thereupon came Also a Jury, to wit, **Bazil Meek, William Barns, George Taylor, Andrew Russell, William Evans, John Hardgrove, John Bushey, Micajah Hogan, Henry Willis, John Fitzgerald, Drewry Lee**, and **Andrew Jasper**, who were sworn well and truly to enquire what Damages the plaintiff hath sustained in the premises upon their Oaths say that the plaintiff hath sustained Damages by Occasion thereof to twenty four pounds ten Shillings and nine pence, and they do also find for the plaintiff the Debt in the Declaration mentioned and his Costs by him about his suit in this behalf expended and the said Defendant in mercy &c. Note this Judgment is to be Discharged by the payment of One hundred and sixty two pounds six shillings and two pence [page 29] together with the Damages aforesaid & Costs

- **Joseph Oatman** Plt
against In Debt
**Jeremiah Elrod** Deft

This day came the Plaintiff by his attorney and thereupon came Also a Jury, to wit, **Bazil Meek, William Barns, George Taylor, Andrew Russell, William Evans, John Hardgrove, John Bushey, Micajah Hogan, Henry Willis, John Fitzgerald, Drewry Lee** and **Andrew Jasper** who were sworn well and truly to enquire what Damages the plaintiff hath sustained in the premises, upon their Oaths do say that the plaintiff hath sustained Damages by Occasion thereof to seventeen shillings and three pence besides his Costs [ ] we do find for the plaintiff sixteen pounds two shillings the Debt in the Declaration mentioned, It is there Considered by the Court that the Plaintiff recover against the said Defendant his Damages and Debt aforesaid by the Jurors in their Verdict aforesaid assessed and his Costs by him about his suit in this behalf expended. and the said Defendant in Mercy &c.

– **William Burton** Plt
against In Case
**Frederick & John Troxwell** Defts

On the motion of the Defendants It is Ordered that the Judgment and Writ of Inquiry awarded against them in the clerks Office be set a side, and the said Defendants by their attornies now comes and defends the wrong and Injury when and [page 30] where &c and says that they are not guilty in manner & form as the Plaintiff against them hath declared and they pray may be enquired of by the Country and the said Plaintiff likewise therefore it is commanded the Sheriff that he cause to come here Immediately twelve good and lawfull men by whom and so forth, and thereupon came also a Jury, to wit, **William Evans, Bazil Meek, John Wilkerson, Matthew Hickson, Abram Smith, Robert Smith, John Jasper, Frederick Williams, William Barns, John Eastham, Jonathan Richardson & Lewis Richardson,** who being elected tried and sworn the truth to speak upon the Issue Joined upon their Oaths do say that the Defendants are guilty in manner and form as the plaintiff against them hath declared, and they do Assess the plaintiffs Damages by Occasion thereof to seven pounds ten shillings, besides his Costs, It is therefore Considered by the Court that the Plaintiff recover against the said Defendant his Damages aforesaid by the Jurors in their Verdict aforesaid assessed and his Costs by him about his suit in this behalf expenses and the said Defendant in mercy &c

– **Alexander Hambleton** Plt
against In Covenant
**James Berry, Arch^d E Mills & Andrew McCaslin** Deft

**Ephraim Churchwell** of Pulaski County Came into Court and undertook for the Defendant **McCaslin,** that if he shall be cast [page 31] in the action aforesaid that he shall satisfy and pay the condemnation of the Court Or render his body to Prison in execution for the same Or on falure thereof that he the said **Ephraim** shall do it for him

– **John January** Plt
against In Case
**Joseph Casky** Deft

– The Same Plt
against In Case
The Same Deft

– The Same Plt
against In Trespass Assault & Battery
**Ephraim Churchwell** Deft

– The Same Plt
against In Trespass Vict Armis
**George Agnue** Deft

– **James Garrard** &c Plts
against In Debt
**Robert Smith** Deft

– **George Taylor** Jun Plts
against In Trespass Assault & Battery
**Robert Smith** Deft

Ordered that these suits be Continued until the next Court

– **Joseph Wright** Plt
against On Motion
The County Court of Wayne County Defts

Ordered that this motion be Dismissed by Order of the Plts Attorney

[page 32] **Benjamin Burton** Plt
against In Case
**Fred: & John Troxwell** Defts

This day came the Parties aforesaid by their Attornies & the said Defendant. Acknowledges the plaintiffs action against them for three Dollars. There with assent of the Plaintiff It is Considered by the Court that the Plaintiffs recover against the said Defendants the sum acknowledged as aforesaid, and his Costs by him about his suit in this behalf expended and the said Defendant in mercy &c

– **Grissom** against **Roberson** Dismissed agreed

– Ordered that the Court be adjourned untill Tomorrow morning twelve OClock

**John Smith**

At a Circuit Court composed of the Counties of Pulaski & Wayne Continued and held at the courthouse in the Town of Sommerset On the 31th day of March 1804

Present **John Smith & John Prather** Gentlemen

– Ordered that the Court be adjourned untill Court in Course

**John Smith**

[page 33] At a Circuit Court holden for the Counties of Pulaski & Wayne at the Courthouse of Pulaski County in Sommerset on Monday the 25th day of June 1804

Present the Honourable **James G Hunter, John Smith & John Prather** Gentlemen

– A Grand jury was sworn for the Circuit composed of the Counties of Pulaski and Wayne, to wit, **John Singleton**, foreman, **Robert Anderson, Samuel Stewart, William Hill, George Saunders, Stephen Lee, George Dougherty, John Martin, Daniel Matthews, Andrew Turner, Israel Hart, John Kelly, Joseph Erwin, Isaac Ingram, James Noflett, Matthew Hickson & Isaac Mayfield**, who after having received their charge retired to consider of their Presentments

– The Commonwealth Plt
against Upon Presentment
**Ephraim Churchwell** Deft

– **Jesse Burton** pros: for The Commonwealth Plt
against The Same
**John Troxell** Deft

This day came as well the attorney for the Commonwealth against the said Defendants by their attornies. And on the motion of said Defendants by their attorneys It is Ordered that their Presentments be Quashed, and that the Defendant **Troxell** recover of the said Prosecutor his costs by him about his defence in this behalf expended

[page 34] **Robert Modrell** Plt
against upon Attachment
**Alexander McFarling** &c Deft

– The Same Plt
against The Same
The Same Deft

Ordered that these attachments be continued untill the next Court

– The Grandjury returned into Court, an Indictment the Commonwealth against **Obediah Richardson** a true Bill

**John Singleton** foreman

– The Grand jury having nothing further to present was discharged and Process Ordered to Issue against the said **Richardson**

– **Holkum Robertson** Plt
against upon Attachment
**George Etherington** Deft

This day came the Plaintiff by his attorney, and **Jonathan Stephens** a Garnishee herein

declared in court, that he was Indebted to the Defendant a second rate Cow & Calf, which property the said Garnishee, is ordered to retain in his Possession until the further order of the Court, and the cause is Continued "till the next Term
[page 35] **James Clark** Plt
against In Case
**Daniel McKinsey** Deft

This day came the Parties aforesaid by their attornies, and by their consent all matters in difference between them respecting this suit in refered to the arbitration and determination of **Samuel McKee, William Owsley, John James, & Samuel Gilmore,** whose award or the award of their umpire in case of their disagreement be the Judgment of the Court & the same is Ordered Accordingly

– **James Cowen** Plt
against In Case
**Henry Willis** Deft

Ordered that this suit be continued for award

– **Zachariah Price** & wife Plt
against In Case
**John Scott** & wife

This day came the Plaintiffs by their Attorney, and thereupon came also a Jury, to wit, **Samuel Stewart, Isaac Ingram, George Allcorn, David Puckett, Thomas McGuire, Stewart Clark, Samuel Allin, John Kelly, David Dodson, George Dougherty, George Hanks** & **William Williams**, who were sworn well and truly to inquire what Damages the Plaintiffs have sustained in the premises upon their Oaths do say the Plaintiffs have sustained Damages by Occasion thereof to one penny besides their Costs It is therefore Considered by the Court that the Plaintiffs recover against the [page 36] said Defendants their Damages aforesaid by the Jurors in their Verdict aforesaid assessed and their Costs by them about their suit in this behalf expended, and the said Defendants may be taken &c

– **Elizabeth Sharp** Complt
against In Chancery
**Michael Stoner** Deft

This day came the Parties aforesaid by their attornies and by their Consent all matters in difference between them respecting this suit is refered to the arbitration and determination of **Joshua Jones, John Francis, & James Allcorn,** whose award or the award of any two of them, be the Judgment of the Court, and the same is Ordered Accordingly,

– **Thomas Owsley** Plt
against In Case
**Joseph Knox** & **Wm Eoff** Deft

This day came the Parties aforesaid by their attornies, and thereupon came also a Jury to wit, **John Ping, Reubin Hill, John Blacklidge, Barnard Houseman, Daniel Hill, Joseph Porter, Gilmore Cowen, Elias Kelly, Daniel Matthews, William Hill, George Dingins, Jacob Blacklidge**, who being elected tryed and sworn the truth to speak upon the Issue Joined afterwards One of the Jurors by Consent of the Parties to wit, **John Ping**, is withdrawn & the Cause is Continued till the next Court

[page 37] **Dolly George** Plt
against In Trespass
**Joshua Jones** & **Saml Banks** Defts

This day came the Parties aforesaid by their attornies, and thereupon came also a Jury, to wit, **Peter Troxell, John Kelly, Stephen Condry, Robert Williams, Andrew Jasper, Edward Cooper, William Ussery, Henry James, Jonathan Smith, John Green, Temple Sargent** & **John Hardgrove** who being elected tryed and sworn the truth to speak upon the issue Joined upon their Oaths do say that the Defendant **Joshua Jones** is Guilty in manner and form as the Plaintiff against him hath declared, and they do assess the Plaintiffs Damages by Occasion thereof to eighteen pounds besides his costs & find the Defendant **Banks** not Guilty, It is therefore Considered by the Court that the Plaintiff recover against the said Defendant **Jones** her Damages aforesaid by the Jurors in their Verdict aforesaid assessed and her Costs by her about her suit in this behalf expended and the said Defendants may be taken &c.

– Ordered that the Court be adjourned "till Tomorrow morning ten OClock

**J G Hunter**

At a Circuit Court Continued and held for the Circuit comprised of the Counties of Pulaski and Wayne, On Tuesday the 26th day of June 1804 Present the same Judges as yesterday

– **James Cowen** Plt
against In Case
**Henry Willis** Deft

[page 38] The Persons appointed to settle all matters in difference between the Parties aforesaid, returned into Court, their award in the words and figures following, to wit, Agreeable to an Order of the Circuit Court of Pulaski & Wayne, at March Term we **P A Sublette, Nicholas Jasper** & **William Barns,** who being appointed as referrees to determine the case between **James Cowen** Plt vs **Henry Willis** Deft do find for said Plaintiff eight pounds ten Shillings & all costs in the said suit expended given under our hands this 26th day of May 1804

**P A Sublette**
**Nicholas Jasper**
**Wm Barnes**

and the same is made the Judgment of the Court

– **Abner Muirheid** &c Plts
against In Case
**John Brooks** Deft

Ordered that this suit be dismissed It being agreed

– **Thomas Owsley** Plt
against In Case
**Joseph Knox** & Als Deft

Ordered that this suit be Dismissed at the Defendants Costs, by consent (excepting an Attorneys fees)

– **Dolly George** Plt
against In Case
**Joshua Jones** Deft

On the motion of the defendant by his attorney for a new trial On the Judgment Obtained against him yesterday in this Case After hearing the Arguments of the Counsel on both sides It is Ordered [page 39] by the Court that said Motion be Over ruled and that the Plaintiff recover her Costs in this case expended

– **William Beard** Complt
against In Chancery
**Joseph Georns** Admor of **Hiram Georn** Decd Deft

This day came the Parties aforesaid by their Attornies, and the Complainant by his Counsil moved the Court to file an amended Bill in this Cause

[page 40] **James Clark** Plt
against In Case
**Daniel McKinsey** Deft

This day came the Parties aforesaid by their attornies, and the Persons appointed to settle all matters in difference between them respecting this suit returned into Court their award in the words and figures following, to wit, We **John James, Samuel Gilmore**, **Samuel McKee** and **William Owsley**, being appointed by the Worshipfull Circuit Court of Pulaski and Wayne, to settle and determine the matters of Controversy as in this Order Contained, did meet at the Town of Sommerset this 25th day of June 1804 after being sworn do award that the Deft pay unto the Plt ten pounds and all legal Costs Given under Our hands and seals the above day and date

**John James**
**Sam[l] Gilmore**
**Sam[l] McKee**
**W[m] Owsley**

By Consent of Parties the above award is this day returned into Court and the same is made the Judgment of the Court

– **John Chaney** Plt
against In Case
**John Hardgrove** Deft

Ordered that this suit be continued untill the next Term at the Plaintiffs Costs

[page 41] **William Buford** Plt
against In Debt
**Henry Francis** Deft

This day came the Parties aforesaid by their attornies, and the said Defendant acknowledged the Plaintiffs Action against him for twenty four pounds the Debt in the Declaration mentioned, Therefore with assent of the Plaintiff It is considered by the court that the Plaintiff recover against the said Defendant the sum acknowledged afores[d] and his costs by him about his suit in this behalf expended and the said Defendant in mercy &[c]. Note this Judgment is to have credit for eight pounds three shillings and six pence & the residue of said Judgment to bare legal Interest from the first day of September One thousand eight hundred and two But to have a credit for seven pounds ten shillings paid the first day of November One thousand eight hundred and three

– **John Hill** Plt
against In Trespass Assault & Battery
**Micajah Hogan** Deft

This day came the Parties aforesaid by their attornies and thereupon came also a Jury to wit, **George Saunders, Israel Hunt, Lewis Singleton, Airs Dors, Henry Willis, John Tully, William Bridges, James Kerr, Jeremiah Boone, Vincent Smith, Abram Smith & John Black**, who being elected tryed and sworn the truth to speak upon the Issue Joined upon their Oaths do say that the Plaintiff his Action aforesaid against the said Defendant Ought not to have and maintain as in pleading the Defendant hath alledged and that the s[d] Defendant is not guilty in [page 42] manner and form as the Plaintiff against him hath declared It is therefore considered by the Court that the Plaintiff take nothing by his suit but for his false clamour be in mercy &[c] & that the Defendant go thereof without a day and recover against the said Plaintiff his Costs by him about his defence in this behalf expended

– **Valentine Hardgrove** Plt
against In Case
**Absolem Bridges** Deft

On the motion of the Defendant, It is ordered that the Judgment and Writ of Inquiry awarded against them in the clerks Office be set a side. and the said Defendant by his Attorney now comes and defends the wrong and Injury when & where &[c]. and saith that he did not assume upon himself in the manner and form as the Plaintiff against him has declared and of this he puts himself upon the Country and the said Plaintiff likewise therefore let a Jury come here &[c]. and the Cause Continued "till the next Court

– **John Hunt** Plt
against In Case
**David Johnson** & ux Deft

This suit abates the Plaintiff being dead

– **Dolly George** Adm[or] of **William George** Dec[d] Plt
against In Trespass with force & Arms
**Zachariah Saunders** Deft

Ordered that this suit be continued until the next Court

[page 43] **John January** Plt
against In Case
**Joseph Casky** Deft

On the motion of the Defendant It is Ordered that the Judgment and writ of Inquiry awarded against him in the Clerks Office be set a side and the said Defendant by his attorney now comes and defends the wrong and Injury when and where &c and saith that he is not guilty in manner and form as the plaintiff against him has declared, and of this he puts himself upon the Country and the Plaintiff likewise Therefore It is commanded the Sheriff that he cause to come here Immediately twelve good and lawfull men by whom &c and thereupon came also a Jury, to wit, **James Hardgrove, Jesse Williams, Wm Barns, John McCullough, Stephen Dubois, Charles Neal, Matthew Hickson, Jonathan Smith, Joseph Ewin, Smith Williams, Wm Mayfield** & **Robert Williams**, who being elected tried and Sworn the truth to speak upon the Issue Joined upon their Oaths do say that the sd Defendant is guilty in manner and form as the plaintiff against him has declared and they do assess the Plaintiffs Damages by Occasion thereof to four pounds ten Shillings besides his Costs It is therefore Considered by the Court that the Plaintiff recover against the said Defendant his Damages aforesaid by the Jurors in their Verdict aforesaid assessed and his Costs by him about his suit in this behalf expended and the said Defendant in mercy &c.

[page 44] **John January** Plt
against In Case
**Joseph Casky** Deft

On the motion of the Defendant It is Ordered that the Judgment and writ of Inquiry awarded against him in the Clerks Office be set a side and the said Defendant by his attorney now comes and defends the Wrong & Injury when & where &c and says that he did not assume upon himself in manner & form as the Plaintiff against him has declared and of this he puts himself upon the Country, and the said Plaintiff likewise therefore It is commanded, the Sheriff that he cause to come here Immediately twelve good and lawfull men by whom &c and thereupon came also a Jury, to wit, **Archibald Moore, Frederick Williams, Aaron Lawson, Obediah Denham, David Richardson, John Williams, James Kerr, John McWhorter, Saml Kelly, Edward Cooper, Andrew Jasper** & **Ambrose Mayfield**, who being elected tried and sworn the truth to speak upon the Issue Joined upon their Oaths do say that the Defendant did not assume upon himself in manner and form as the Plaintiff against him hath declared, It is therefore Considered by the Court that the Plaintiff take nothing by his bill but for his false Clamour be in mercy &c. and that the Defendant go thereof without day & recover of the said plaintiff his costs by him about his defence in this behalf expended.

[page 45] **John Roberts** Plt
against In Debt
**Martin Barrier** Deft

Ordered that this suit be dismissed at the Defts Costs

– **John January** Plt
against In Trespass Assault & Battery
**Ephraim Churchwell** Deft

Ordered that this suit be dismissed

– **John January** Plt
against In Trespass Vict armis &c
**George Agnew, George Humphreys, James Doolin, Lewis Farris** & **William Doolen** Defts

This day came the Plaintiff by his attornies, and thereupon came also a Jury, to wit, **John McCullough, William Barns, William Patterson, Abraham Smith, Robert Modrel, Robert Smith, Stephen Dubois, Jonathan Smith, George Allcorn, Reubin Hill, Robert Adams** & **Joseph Erwin**, who were sworn well and truly to inquire what Damages the Plaintiff has sustained in the premises upon their Oaths do say that the Plaintiff has sustained Damages by Occasion thereof to twenty two pounds ten Shillings besides his costs. It is therefore Considered by the Court that the plaintiff recover against the said Defendant his Damages aforesaid by the Jurors in their

Verdict aforesaid assessed and his costs by him about his suit in this behalf expended and the said Defendant may be taken &c

[page 46] **William Beard** Complt
against On Motion In Chancery
**Joseph Georn** adm[or] of **Hiram Georn** Dec[d]

This day came the Parties aforesaid by their attornies, and on the motion of the complainant by his attorney for leave to amend his Bill in this cause, after hearing the arguments of the Counsel on both sides It is considered by the Court that said motion be Over ruled, and on the motion of the Defendant by his attorney It is Ordered that the Complainants Injunction Obtained here [ ] be desolved by reason of Irregularity in the Proceedings and that the Defendant recover against the said Complainant, his costs by him about his defence in this behalf expended

– **Joseph Casky** Plt
against In Case
**John January** Deft

This day came the Parties aforesaid by their attornies and thereupon came also Jury to wit, **John Tully, Jacob Baker, Andrew Jasper, George Saunders, Reubin Scott, Lewis Singleton, James Cox, Valentine Hardgrove, George Humphreys, Aaron Lawson, Edward Cooper** & **Martin Barrier**, who being elected tried and Sworn the truth to speak upon the Issue Joined, were adjourned "till Tomorrow Morning eight OClock

– Ordered that the Court be adjourned "till Tommorrow morning eight OClock

**J G Hunter**

At a Circuit Court holden for the counties of Pulaski & Wayne at the Courthouse of Pulaski County in Sommerset On Wednesday the 27th day of June 1804

Present **James G Hunter, John Smith** & **John Prather** Gent

– **Alexander Hambleton** Ass[ee] Plt
against In Covenant
**William Dodson** Deft

On the motion of the Defendant It is Ordered that the Judgment and Writ of Inquiry awarded against him in the Clerks Office be set a side, and the said Defendant by **Micah Taul** his attorney now comes and defends the Wrong & Injury when and where &c & saith that the Plaintiff aforesaid his action aforesaid against him Ought not to have & maintain because he says that the writing Obligatory in the Plaintiffs declaration mentioned is not his act & Deed & as this he puts himself upon the Country &c and the said Plaintiff likewise

Pulaski County Sct This day came **William Dodson** before me **Philip A Sublette** a Justice of the Peace for the County aforesaid& under Oath that what he has stated in the within Plea is true Certified under my hand this 26th day of June 1804

**P A Sublette**

and the cause is Continued untill the next Term

– **Joseph Casky** Plt
against In Case
**John January** Deft

The Jury sworn & adjourned in this case yesterday came into Court this day and after hearing the Testimony of each Party &c retired [page 48] to consider of their Verdict, afterward One of the Jurors in this case to wit, **Edward Cooper** by Consent of Parties was withdrawn & the Cause continued "till the next Term

– **John Blacklidge** Ass[ee] Plt
against In Covenant
**James Eastham** Deft

Ordered that this suit be Continued until the next Court

– **Robert Modrel** Plt
against upon Attachment

**Alexander McFarling** & Al[s] Defts

This day came the Plaintiff by his attorney and on his motion a Pluvias Summons awarded him against **David Hays** of Lincoln County as a Garnishee herein returnable to the third day of the next September Term of this court. And It is ordered that the said **David Hays** do appear before this Court on the third day of the Term aforesaid & show cause why he should not be Attached for his Contempt for not attending on this Court at the present Term as a Garnishee in this suit

– **James Garrard** Governor of Kentucky for **George Taylor** Plt
against In Debt
**Robert Smith** &[c] Defts

On the motion of the Defendant It is ordered that the Judgment and Writ of Inquiry awarded against him in the Clerks Office be set a side and the said Defendant by his attorney now comes and defends the Wrong and Injury when and where &[c]. and says the plt his action aforesaid in manner and form aforesaid against him [page 49] Ought not to have and maintain because he says that the bond a copy of which is made profest of the Declaration, is a bond Conditioned for the faithful discharge of the duties of the Office of Constable, and the said Defendant avers he hath kept and performed all the conditions of the said bond agreeable to his undertaking, and of this he prays may be enquired of by the Country, and the said Plaintiff by his attorney says his action aforesaid against the said Defendant he Ought to have and maintain because he says the Defendant has not kept and performed all the conditions of the Bond aforesaid agreeable to his undertaking as a Constable, and this he prays may be Inquired of by the country, and the said Defendant likewise. Therefore let a Jury Come here &[c]. and the cause Continued "till the next Court

– **George Taylor** & wife Plts
against In Trespass assault & Battery
**Robert Smith** Deft

On the motion of the Defendant, It is ordered that the Judgment and Writ of Inquiry awarded against him in the clerks Office be set a side, and the said Defendant by his attorney now comes and defends the wrong and Injury when and where &[c]. and says he is not guilty in manner and form as the Plaintiff against him has declared, and of this he putteth himself upon the Country and the said Plaintiff likewise, Therefore it is commanded the Sheriff that he cause to come here Immediately twelve good and lawfull men by whom &[c]. and thereupon came also a Jury to wit, **Richard Barns, William Gwin, William Clarke, James Green, Ralph Williams, Temple Sargent, David Matthews, William Wyatts, Joel Evans, James Bodle, John Gwin** & **Joseph Irwin** who being elected tried and sworn the truth to speak upon the Issue Joined upon their Oath do say that the said defendant is not guilty in manner and form as the plaintiff against him has declared It is therefore Considered by the Court that the Plaintiff take nothing by his bill but for his false Clamour be in mercy &[c]. and that the Defendant go thereof without day, and recover of the said Plaintiff his costs by him about his defence in this behalf expended

– **Edward Flowers** Plt
against In Covenant
**Henry Francis** Deft

Ordered that this suit be continued untill the next Court

– **David Swope** Plt
against In Covenant
**William Bailey** Deft

This day came the Plaintiff by his attorney and thereupon Came Also a Jury, to wit, **Thomas McGuire, William Gwin, Isaac Ingram, Sam[l] Caughran, Ivy Lankford, John Scott, Ralph Williams, George Dungins, James Campbell, William Fears, John Ashley** and **James Skidmore** who were sworn well and truly to enquire what Damages the plaintiff has sustained in the premises upon their Oaths do say that the Plaintiff has sustained Damages by Occasion thereof to sixty four pounds besides his Costs It is therefore Considered by the court that the [page 51] Plaintiff recover against the said Defendant his Damages afores[d] by the Jurors in their Verdict aforesaid assessed and his Costs by him about his suit in this behalf expended, and the said

Defendant in mercy &c.

– **David Swope** Plt
against In Debt
**William Bailey** Deft

This day came the Plaintiff by his attorney, and thereupon came also a Jury, to wit, **Samuel Caughron, Thomas McGuire, William Gwin, Isaac Ingram, Ivy Lankford, John Scott, Ralph Williams, George Dungins, James Campbell, William Fears, John Ashley, & James Skidmore** who were sworn well and truly to enquire what Damages the Plaintiff has sustained in the Premises, upon their Oaths do find for the Plaintiff the Debt in the Declaration mentioned and do assess the Plaintiffs Damages by Occasion thereof to as much as the Interest amounts to on the Debt aforesaid besides his Costs, and the said Defendants by their attorney sayeth that Judgment on the Verdict herein Ought not to be entered but Ought to be stayed and arrested for the following errors to wit, 1st that an appearance was entered and the Pltffs Declaration was filed on the same rule day whereby the Act of Assembly. the Declaration could not regularly be pled until the next Suceeding Rule day after the appearance was entered &c 2nd that this was an action that required appearance Bail and the Proceeding in the Office has been had and [page 52] the Verdict found against **A E Mills** as appearance Bail when the name of the bail is not returned on the writ as required by the Act of Assembly without which the law doth not authorize or warrant a Judgment against the appearance Bail 3d that the law doth not warrant a Verdict & Judgment against the Defendant **Mills** wherefore an arrest of Judgment is moved for by the Deft

**Bridges** for Deft

– **Daniel Adams** Plt
against In Case
**John McCullough** Deft

This day came the Parties aforesaid by their attornies, and on the motion of the Plaintiff by his attorney a Commission is awarded him to take the Deposition of **John Stuck** Debe nesse to be examined by any Justice of the Peace by Consent, and On the motion of the Defendant It is ordered that the Judgment & Writ of Inquiry awarded against him in the Clerks Office be set a side, and the said Defendant by his attorney now comes and defends the wrong and Injury when & where &c and says that he is not guilty in manner and form as the Plaintiff against him has declared, and of this he putteth himself upon the Country and the said Plaintiff likewise, Therefore let a Jury come here &c and the cause is continued "till the next Court

[page 53] **John Smith** Plt
against In Case
**John Hill, Robert Modrel** & **Richd Hill** Defts

On the motion of the Defendants It is ordered that the Judgment and Writ of Inquiry awarded against them in the Clerks Office be set a side and the said Defendants by their attornies now come and defend the wrong and Injury when and where &c and say that they did not assume upon themselves in manner and form as the Plaintiff against them has declared, and of this they pray may be enquired of by the Country and the said Plaintiff likewise Therefore it is Commanded the sheriff that he cause to come here Immediately twelve good and lawfull men by whom &c. and therefore came also a Jury to wit, **Richard Churchwell** Senr, **David Johnson, Mark Jackson, John Ashley, Isaac Ingram, Stephen Dubois, Joseph Irvine, Jacob Blacklidge, Daniel Hill, William Gwin, John Gwin** & **Ralph Williams**, who being elected tried and Sworn the truth to speak upon the Issue Joined upon their Oaths do say that the Defendants **John Hill**, and **Robert Modrel**, did assume upon themselves in manner and form as the Plaintiff against them has declared, and they for the assess the Plaintiffs Damages by Occasion thereof to twenty seven pounds besides his Costs. and do say that the Defendant **Richard Hill** did not assume upon himself in manner and form as the Plaintiff against him has declared, It is therefore Considered by the Court that the Plaintiff recover against the Defendants **John Hill** & **Robert Modrel** his Damages [page 54] aforesaid by the Jurors in their Verdict aforesaid assessed and his Costs by him about his suit in this behalf expended and the said Defendants in mercy &c.

– **Kizziah Chapple** by her next friend **Jesse Chapple** Plts
against In Case
**Jesse Burton** Deft

**William Burton** & **John Scrimiger**, having Justified & undertook for the Defendant that if he shall be Cast in the action aforesaid that they will satisfy and pay the condemnation of the court or render his body to Prison in Execution for the same Or on falure thereof that they the said **William** and **John** would do it for him

– **Christ**° **Troxell** Plt
against In Case
**William Burton** Deft

On the motion of the Defendant It is Ordered that the Judgment and Writ of Inquiry awarded against him in the Clerks Office be set a side and the said Defendant by his attorney now comes and defends the wrong and Injury when and where &c and says that he did not assume upon himself in manner and form as the plaintiff against him has declared, and this he prays may be Inquired of by the Country. and the said Plaintiff likewise. Therefore it is Commanded the Sheriff that he cause to come here Immediately twelve good and lawfull men by whom &c. Thereupon came also a Jury, to wit, **John Scott, David Puckett, Reubin Scott, Thomas Hanks, David** [page 55] **Matthews, John Gwin, Jonathan Smith, Robert Hunt, W**m **Barns, James Gun, John Black** & **James Kerr** who being elected tried and sworn the truth to speak upon the Issue Joined upon their Oaths do say that the Plaintiff has sustained Damages by Occasion thereof to twenty five pounds besides his Costs It is therefore Considered by the Court that the Plaintiff recover against the said Defendant his Damages aforesaid by the Jurors in their Verdict aforesaid assessed and his Costs by him about his suit in this behalf expended and the said Defendant in mercy &c.

– **Vincent Smith** Assee Plt
against In Debt
**Jacob Flory** & **Sam**l **Gilmore** Defts

This day came the Plaintiff by his attorney, and on his motion It is Ordered that the Judgment and Writ of Inquiry awarded against the said Defendant in the clerks Office be waved and on the motion of the Plaintiff by his attorney Judgment is granted him against the said Defendant for thirty five Dollars the Debt in the Declaration mentioned and his costs by him about his suit in this behalf expended and the said Defendant in mercy &c Note this Judgment is to bare Interest from the first day of September One thousand eight hundred and three until paid & Costs but to have credit for six shillings and nine pence paid the 14th day of September One thousand eight hundred and three, also for thirteen shillings and eleven pence ¼ paid on the eleventh day of October in the same year & thirteen shillings and four pence ¼ paid on the 25th day of the same Instant in sd year

[page 56] Ordered that the Court be adjourned untill tommorrow morning nine OClock

**J G Hunter**

At a Circuit Court holden for the Counties of Pulaski & Wayne at the Courthouse of Pulaski County in Sommerset on Thursday the 28th day of June 1804

Present **James G Hunter, John Smith** & **John Prather** Gent

– **Daniel Adams** Plt
against In Case
**John McCullough** Deft

This day came the Parties by their attornies, and by their consent, all matters in difference between them respecting this suit is refered to the arbitration and determination of **John Smith, John Griffen, Tho**s **McGuire, John Hardgrove, Davis Roper** & **Reubin Hill** whose award or the award of any four of them be the Judgment of the Court and the same is ordered Accordingly

– **James Garrard** for **George Taylor** Plt
against In Debt
**Robert Smith** &c Deft

On the motion of the Defendants a Dedimus is awarded them to take the Deposition of **Abram Smith** Debenesse

– **Joseph** & **Thomas Welch**
against In Debt
**Nathaniel Forbis** Deft

This day came the Plaintiff by their attorney, on their motion It is ordered that the Judgment and Writ of Inquiry awarded against the said Defendant in the clerks [page 57] Office be waved and on the motion of the Plaintiff by their Attorney Judgment is granted them against the said Defendants for twenty two Dollars the Debt in the Declaration mentioned & their Costs by them about their suit in this behalf expended and the said Defendant in mercy &c Note this Judgment is to be discharged by the payment of the said Debt in the Declaration with legal Interest thereon from the twenty ninth day of August One thousand eight hundred and three until paid & Costs

– **Dolly George** Plt
against Second motion
**Joshua Jones** Deft

On the motion of the Defendant by his attorney for a new trial, On the Verdict of the Jury & Judgment of this Court Obtained by the Plaintiff against the said Defendant On the first day of this present June Term in this Case It is Ordered that the said motion be Over ruled & that the Plaintiff recover against the said Defendant her Costs by her in this behalf expended

– **David Swope** Plt
against In Covenant
**William Bailey** Deft

This day came the Parties aforesaid by their attornies Errors filed in this case on this day On the Verdict of the Jury & Judgment Obtained herein yesterday, after hearing the arguments of the Counsil on each side It is the Opinion of the Court that the Errors are adjudged good by reason of the Sheriff of Wayne County failing to endorse on the Writ the name of the appearance Bail &c.

[page 58] **David Swope** Plt
against In Debt
**William Bailey** Deft

This day came the Parties aforesaid by their Attornies, and after hearing the arguments of the Counsil on each side, On the Errors filed in the case yesterday in arrest of Judgment on the Verdict of the Jury Obtained herein, It is the Opinion of the Court that the said Errors be adjudged good, Because the Sheriff failed to name on the Original Writ the name of the appearance Bail &c.

– **Nicholas Jasper** & Als Complt
against In Chancery
**Tunstall Quarles** Deft

– **John Chesney** Complt
against In Chancery
The Same &c Deft

On the motion of the Complainants, It is Ordered that **Saml McKee**, be appointed to go On the lands in controversy between the parties On the ____ day of next if fair if not then on the next fair day, and then survey and lay of the same as either party would have it having regard to all Deeds and Other evidence that may be produced report all matters of fact especially, and return four fair platts & Certificates thereof to the clerks Office before the day of hearing, and the Sheriff of said County is Ordered to attend the said surveyor to remove for a should any be Offered

[page 59] **John Beard** Complt
against In Chancery
**George Saunders** &c Defts

On the motion of the complainant, It is Ordered that the Surveyor of Pulaski County do go on the lands in controversy between the Parties on the ____ day of ____ next if fair, if not then on the next fair day and then survey and lay of the same as either party would have it having regard to all Other evidences that may be produced report, all matters of fact specialty and return four fair platts & Certificates thereof to the Clerks Office before the said hearing, and the Shff is Ord[d] to attend to remove force should any be offered

– **George Dungins** Plt
against In Case
**Reubin Hill** Deft

On the motion of the Defendant, It is ordered that the Judgment and writ of Inquiry awarded against him in the Clerks Office be set a side and the said Defendant by his attorney now comes & defends the wrong & Injury when & where &[c] and says that he is not guilty in manner and form as the Plaintiff against him has declared, and of this he putteth himself up the Country and the said Plaintiff likewise, therefore It is Commanded the Sheriff that he cause to come Immediately twelve good and lawfull men by whom &[c] and thereupon came also a Jury, to wit, **William Fears, Stephen Dubois, Henry Willis, Jacob Baker, William Barns, Jonathan Smith, John McCullough, George Moore, William Hays, James Kerr, William Avery** & **Jacob Blacklidge** who being elected tried and sworn the truth to speak upon the Issue Joined, afterwards One of the Jury, to wit, **Stephen** [page 60] **Dubois** by Consent was withdrawn & the Cause continued "till the next Court

– **Airs Dors** Plt
against In Case
**Henry Willis** Deft

– **Joel Dors** Plt
against In Case
**Henry Willis** Deft

– **Henry Willis** Plt
against In case
**Joel** & **Airs Dors** Defts

– The Same Plt
against In Trespass
The Same Defts

By Consent of Parties all matters in difference between them respecting this suit is refered to the arbitration and determination of **Richard Churchwell** Senr, **George Taylor, William Hays**, & **John Newby**, whose award or the award of any three of them shall be the Judgment of the Court and the same is Ordered Accordingly

– **John Ashley** Plt
against In Debt
**Jonathan Stephens** &[c] Defts

On the motion of the Plaintiff by his attorney It Ordered that the Judgment and Writ of Inquiry awarded against the Defendants in the Clerks Office be waved and on the motion of the Plaintiff by his attorney Judgment is granted him against the said Defendants for thirty three pounds [page 61] the Debt in the Declaration mentioned, & his Costs by him about his suit in this behalf expended & the said Defendant in Mercy. Note this Judgement is to bare Interest from the twenty fifth day of December One thousand eight hundred and three untill paid & Costs

– **James Johnson** &[c] Plt
against In Case
**Moses Hanks** Deft

By Consent of Parties all matters in difference between them respecting ths suit is refered to the arbitration and determination of **John Smith, John Prather** & **John Hardgrove** Senr whose award or the award of any two them be the Judgment of the Court. and the same is Ordered According & returned their award in the words & figures following to wit, We the Arbitrators appointed by the above Order are of Opinion from the Testimony to us delivered that the Plaintiff hath no Cause of Action, therefore no Damages can or ought to accrue but that the Deft recover his costs, and the plaintiff pay the Same in the manner prescribed by law Given under our hands & Seals at Sommerset this 28[th] day of June 1804

**John Smith**
**John Prather**
**John Hardgrove**

and the same is made the Judgment of the Court
– **William Churchwell** Plt
against In case
**Lewis Singleton** Deft
Ordered that this suit be Dismissed
[page 62] **Alexander Hambleton** Plt
against In Debt
**Solomon Brush** Deft
This day came the Plaintiff by his attorney and thereupon came also a Jury to wit **John Williams, Richard Barns, W^m Wyatt, Robert Hunt, David Puckett, Temple Sargent, John Gwin, William Waldon, George McWorter, James Cox, David Dodson** & **Andrew Evans** Junr who were sworn well and truly to enquire what Damages the Plaintiff has sustained in the Premises upon their Oaths do say that the plaintiff has sustained Damages by Occasion thereof to seven pounds, twelve Shillings and four pence besides his Costs It is therefore Considered by the Court that the Plaintiff recover against the said Defendant his Damages aforesaid by the Jurors in their Verdict aforesaid assessed and his Costs by him about his suit in this behalf expended and the said Defendant in mercy &^c.
– The Same Plt
against In Covenant
**James Berry** & Al^s Deft
This day came the Plaintiff by his attorney and thereupon came also a Jury, to wit, **John Williams, Richard Barns, William Wyatt, Rob^t Hunt, David Puckett, Temple Sargent, John Gwin, William Waldon, George McWhorter, James Cox, David Dodson** & **Andrew Evans** Junr who were sworn well and truly to enquire what Damages the Plaintiff has sustained in the premises upon their Oaths do say that the plaintiff [page 63] hath sustained Damage by Occasion thereof to thirty six Pounds fifteen Shillings besides his costs It is therefore Considered by the Court that the Plaintiff recover against the said Defendant his Damages aforesaid by the Jurors in the Verdict aforesaid assessed and his Costs by him about his suit in this behalf expended and the said Defendant in mercy &^c.
– **John Ashley** Plt
against In Case
**Benjamin Taylor** Deft
This day Came the Plaintiff by his attorney, and thereupon came also a Jury, to wit, **John Williams, Richard Barns, W^m Wyatt, Robert Hunt, David Puckett, Temple Sargent, John Gwin, W^m Walden, George McWhorter, James Cox, David Dodson** & **And^w Evans** Junr, who were sworn well and truly to enquire what Damages the Plaintiff has sustained in the Premises upon their Oaths do say the Plaintiff has sustained Damages by Occasion thereof to nine Pounds besides his Costs It is therefore Considered by the Court that the Plaintiff recover against the said Defendant his Damages aforesaid by the Jurors in their Verdict aforesaid assessed and his Costs by him about his suit in this behalf expended & the Defendant in mercy &^c.
[page 64] **Kizziah Chapple** &^c Plt
against In Case
**William Burton** Deft
– **James Johnson** &^c Plt
against In Case
**John Guinn** Deft
On the motion of the Defendants It is Ordered that the Judgments & Writ of Inquirys awarded against them in the clerks Office be set a side and the said Defendants by their attornies now come and defend the wrong & Injury when & where &^c and say that they are not guilty in

manner and form as the Plaintiffs in their Declarations against them has declared and of this they pray may be enquired of by the Country and the said Plaintiffs likewise therefore let a Jury come &c and the cause is continued "till the next Court

– **Bartlett Hillard** Plt
against In Case
**William J Salle** Deft

– **Andrew Evans** Plt
against In Covenant
**John Fitzgerald** Deft

– **Kizziah Chapple** &c Plts
against In Case
**William Burton** Deft

Ordered that these suits be Continued "till the next Court

[page 65] **Samuel Gilmore** late Shff of Pulaski County Plt
against On Motion
**Andrew Russell** his Deputy Deft

This day came the Plaintiff by his attorney & Notice of this motion being admitted, the Defendant Confessed Judgment for £41..7..10 with a credit of £9..10, and **William J Sallee**, came into Court by Consent of the Parties aforesaid and acknowledged that he was Indebted to the Deft in this motion the sum of £10..6 which he agreed to pay for said Deft to the Plt in discharge of the Judgment aforesaid, and **Philip A Sublette** also came into Court as afs^d acknowledged that he was Indebted to the s^d Deft £21..10..4 which he agreed to pay to the Plt for the Deft as afs^d Case [ ] of said [ ] & that the Plaintiff recover his Costs &c. Note these Judgments is for the benefit of **William Fron**

– **Jeremiah Jackson** Plt
against In Case
**Samuel Caughran** Deft

On the motion of the Defendant is Ordered that the Judgment and Writ of Inquiry awarded against him in the clerks Office be set a side and the said Defendant by his attornies now comes and defends the Wrong and Injury when & where &c. and says that he is not guilty in manner and form as the plaintiff against him has declared and of this he putteth himself [page 66] upon the Country and the said Plaintiff likewise therefore It is commanded the Sheriff that he cause to come here &c Immediately twelve good and lawful men by whom &c and thereupon came also a Jury, to wit, **John Williams, John Wilkerson, Richard Barns, Sam^l Stewart, Peter Lee, James Bobbet, Sam^l Lewis, John Williams, William Gwin, Ralph Williams, William Barns** & **Stephen Dubois** who being elected tried & sworn the truth to speak upon the Issue Joined upon their Oaths do say that the s^d Defendant is not guilty in manner and form as the Plaintiff against him hath declared. It is therefore Considered by the Court that the Plaintiff take nothing by his Bill but for his false clamour be in mercy &c and that the Defendant go thereof without day and recover of the said Plaintiff his Costs by him about his defence in this behalf expended

– Commonwealth Plt
against upon an Indictment
**William Evans** Deft

Ordered that the Venerafacies in this Case be quashed & that another Issue agreeable to the Indictment in this case returnable to the next Court.

– **Andrew Evans** Plt
against In Covenant
**John Fitzgerald** Deft

Ordered that this suit be Dismissed

[page 67] **George Dungins** Plt
against In Case
**Reubin Hill** Deft

Ordered that this suit be dismissed at the Defendants costs It being by Consent
– **Bartlett Hillard** Ass[ee] Plt
against In Case
**William J Sallee** Deft

On the motion of the Defendant It is Ordered that the Judgment and writ of Inquiry awarded against him in the clerks Office be set a side and the said Defendant by his attorny now comes and Defends the wrong & Injury when & where &[c] (special plea, statute limitations filed) and the said Defendant for further plea herein says he did not assume upon himself in manner and form as the Plaintiff against him hath Declared and of this he putteth himself upon the Country.

– **Philip A Sublette** Ass[ee] Plt
against In Covenant
**Joseph Casky** Deft

**Matthew Hickson** of Pulaski County came into Court and undertook for the Defendant that if he shall be cast in the action aforesaid that he shall satisfy and pay the Condemnation of the Court Or render his body to prison in execution for the same Or on falure thereof the said **Matthew** shall do it for him and the said Defendant is prayed in Custody of the Sheriff &[c]

[page 68] **Joseph Casky** Plt
against In Case
**John January** Deft

By Consent of the Parties all matters in difference between them respecting this suit is refered to the arbitration and final determination of **Sam[l] McKee**, **William Barns**, **John Wilkerson**, & **Thomas Whites**, whose award or the award of their umpire in Case of their disagreement be made the Judgment of the Court and the same is Ordered accordingly

– **George Saunders** Plt
against In Case
**Sam[l] Stewart** & Al[s] Defts

Ordered that this suit be dismissed and that the Defendant pay the clerks & Sheriffs fees herein

– Ordered that the Court be adjourned until tomorrow morning nine OClock

– The Circuit Judge being this morning absent the Record is Signed

**John Smith**

At a Circuit Court Continued and held for the Counties of Pulaski and Wayne at the courthouse of Pulaski County in Sommerset. On the 29[th] day of June 1804

Present **John Smith** & **John Prather** Gent

– **Alexander Hambleton** Ass[ee] Plt
against In Covenant
**William Dodson** Deft

On the motion of the Plaintiff by his attorney Dedimus [page 69] is awarded him in this Case to take the Deposition of ________ of the state of Tenesee, and the note on which the Action aforesaid brought to accompany the same

– **Philip A Sublette** Plt
against In Covenant
**Joseph Casky** Deft

**George Agnue**, came into Court and Justif[d] as the law directs &[c] and undertook for the Defendant that if he shall be cast in the Action aforesaid that he shall satisfy and pay the condemnation of the Court. Or render his body to Prison in Execution for the Same, Or On falure thereof that he the said **George** shall do it for him

– Ordered that the Court be adjourned untill Court in Course

**John Smith**

At a Circuit Court holden for the Counties of Pulaski & Wayne at the Courthouse of Pulaski County in Sommerset, On the 24th day of September 1804

Present the Honourable **James G Hunter John Smith & John Prather**

– On the Motion of **Tunstall Quarles** Esqr who produced a License Authorizing him to practise law in this Court who took the [page 70] necessary Oaths &c

– A Grand jury was sworn for the Pulaski Circuit, to wit, **John Hardgrove** Senr forman, **Linsey Hardgrove, Jonathan Smith, Jacob Blacklidge, Jeremiah Boone, Nicholas Jones, Townsend Fugate, Matthew Hickson, Nathaniel Forbis, Jonathan Stephens, Israel Hart, David Dodson, James Smith** Senr, **Jonas Irvine, Peter Pettyjohn, James Harril, John H Gee, David Buster, Stephen Lee, John Duncan, Richard Churchwell, Jeremiah Meeks & John Hardgrove** Junr who retired to Consider of their Presentments, and afterwards returned into Court and Indictment the Commonwealth against **John Griffin** a true Bill

**John Hardgrove** foreman

and having nothing further to present were discharged by the Court and Delinquents Ordered to be summoned

– **George Taylor** by Governor Plt
against In Debt
**Robert Smith & Thos White** Defts

**Thomas Owsley & George Agnue** by Consent came into Court and undertook for the Defendants that if they shall be Cast in the Action aforesaid that they shall satisfy and pay the Condemnation of the Court, or render their bodies to Prison in execution for the same. Or on falure thereof that the **Thomas & George** shall do it for him

[page 71] **Robert Modrel** Plt
against upon Attachment
**Alexander McFarling** Deft

– The Same Plt
against the Same
The Same Deft

This day came the Parties aforesaid by their attornies, and It is Ordered that these suits be continued "till the third day of this Present September Term 1804

– The Commonwealth by **William Fears** Plt
against upon an Indictment
**William Evans** Deft

This day came as well the Defendant by his attorney as the Attorney for the Commonwealth likewise, and the said Defendant comes and defends the wrong and Injury when & where &c and says that he is not guilty in manner and form as the Attorney for the Commonwealth in his Indictment against him hath declared, and of this he puts himself upon the Country and the attorney for the Commonwealth likewise, and thereupon came also a Jury, to wit, **Jonas Irvine, Edward Prather, David Richardson, John Singleton, Benjamin Thurman, Jesse Williams, George Allcorn, Isaac Mayfield, Richard Beason, Jeremiah Boone, Edward Cooper & Matthew Hickson** who being elected [page 72] tried and sworn the truth to speak upon the Issue Joined upon their Oaths do say that the said Defendant is guilty in manner and form as the attorney for the Commonwealth in the Indictment against him hath declared, and they do assess the Commonwealths Damages by Occasion thereof to ten Dollars besides Costs It is therefore considered by the Court that the said Defendant make his fine to the Commonwealth by paying the Damages aforesaid, by the Jurors in their Verdict aforesaid assessed and that he pay the Costs of this Prosecution & may be taken &c.

– The Commonwealth
against upon an Indictment
**Obediah Richardson**

Ordered that this Indictment be dismissed, It being by Order of the Commonwealth Attorney

– **James Burton** Senr, **James P Burton, James Burton** Junr, **William, George, Robert, Jesse** &

**John Burton** appeared by their attorney before this Court. On this present Day
– Ordered that the Court be adjourned "till Tomorrow morning ten OClock

**J G Hunter**

At a Circuit Court continued and held for the Pulaski Circuit at the Courthouse of Pulaski County in Sommerset On the 25th day of September 1804.

Present the Honourable **James G Hunter**

[page 73] On the motion of **Frederick Troxwell**, and Injunction is granted him to stay all further Proceedings on a Judgment Obtained against him at common law by **William Burton**, in this Court, who Acknowledged bond with **Nathaniel Black**, his security, Conditioned as the law directs the said **Black** Justified &c Bill Sworn to in Court

– Present the Honourable **John Smith** & **John Prather**

– **Joshua Jones** Complt
against In Chancery
**Dolly George** Deft

This day came the Parties aforesaid by their attornies and on the motion of the said Defendant by her attorney to Discharge & Desolve the Injunction Obtained by the Complainant herein at Common law after hearing the Bill &c and the arguments of the Counsil on both sides on Mature Consideration, being thereon had it the Opinion of the Court that the said Injunction be discharged & Desolved, and that the Deft proceed with her Judgment against the said Complainant at Common law, and that she recover her costs by her about this motion expended, and ten percentum According to the Act of the General Assembly in this case made & provided

– **Airs Dors** Plt
against In Case
**Henry Willis** Deft

– **Joel Dors** Plt
against In Case
**Henry Willis** Deft

[page 74] **Henry Willis** Plt
against In Case
**Joel** & **Airs Dors** Defts

– The Same Plt
against In Trespass &c
The Same Defts

This day came the Parties aforesaid by their attornies, and the person appointed to settle all matters in difference between them respecting their suit, returned into Court their award in the words & figures following, to wit, whereas, a a Court held for the counties of Pulaski and Wayne, last June Circuit Term, a Cause in the said Court depending between **Airs Dors** against **Henry Willis**, also Between **Joel Dors** against **Henry Willis**, against **Joel** and **Airs Dors**, and **Willis** against the same by Consent of Parties refered to **John Newby, George Taylor, Richard Churchwell** Senr and **William Hays** to hear and determine all the said differences now we the said **John Newby, George Taylor, Richard Churchwell**, and **William Hays** in persuant of the said Order, or rule of referance having heard all the said Parties their allegations answers touching matters in differences between them and having thoroughly considered of the same do award Order and adjudge of and upon the premises in manner and form following and of the Opinion that each Person pay their own Costs in the Different suits expended as Witness Our hands this 25 day of September 1804

**John Newby** **George Taylor**
**Richard Churchwell** **William Hays**

[page 75] and the same is made the Judgment of the Court

– **Daniel Adams** Plt
against In Case

**John McCullough** Deft

This day came the Parties aforesaid by their attornies, and by their Consent a former Order of this Court refering all matters in difference between them relative to this Cause is Ordered to be set a side, & It is Ordered that this suit be Dismissed at the Defendants Costs

– **John Chesney** Plt
against In Case
**John Hardgrove** Deft

This day came the Parties aforesaid by their attornies and thereupon came also a Jury, to wit, **Andrew Cowen, David Buster, Jonas Irvine, Jacob Blacklidge, Jeremiah Boone, James Northrip, Lewis Singleton, Micajah Hogan, Henry James, James Taylor, Thomas Whites** & **Bazil Meek**, who being elected tryed and sworn the truth to speak upon the Issue Joined, upon their Oaths do say that the s[d] Defendant is guilty, in manner and form as the Plaintiff against him hath declared, and they do assess the Plaintiffs Damages by Occasion thereof to One Penny besides his Costs It is therefore Considered by the Court that the Plaintiff recover against the said Defendant his Damages aforesaid by the Jurors in their Verdict aforesaid assessed and his costs by him about his suit in this behalf expended and the said Defendant may be taken

– **William Barnett** & **John Adair**, against **W[m] Crawford** & **William Fear**, the Complainant **Adair** made Oath to the [page 76] Bill herein in Court

– **William George's** adm[or] Plt
against In Trespass
**Zachariah Saunders** Deft

This day came the Parties aforesaid by their attornies and It is Ordered that this be Dismissed

– **John Colton** Plt
against In Debt
**Joseph Casky** & **James Smith** Defts

This day came as well the Plaintiff by his attorney as the said Defendants in their proper persons, and the said Defendants say they cannot gainsay the Plaintiffs action against them for the Debt in the Declaration mentioned, therefore with assent of the Plaintiff It is considered by the Court that the Plaintiff recover against the said Defendants the said Debt in the Declaration mentioned, and his costs by him about his suit in this behalf expended and the said Defendants in mercy &[c]. Note this Judgment is to be discharged by the payment of seven pounds eight shillings & six pence with legal Interest thereon from the twenty fourth day of September One thousand eight hundred and three until paid & costs

The Defendants reserves Equity

– **John Adair** & Al[s] Complts
against In Chancery
**W[m] Crawford** & Al[s] Defts

On the motion of the complainants by their Counsil It is Ordered [page 77] that the Defendant **William Fox**, neither pay, Convey away or Conceal the money Or effects which is now in his hands of the property of the said Defendant **Crawford**, unless by Order of this Court, whereupon the said **Fox** acknowledged bond for neither convey &[c] as afs[d] with **Samuel McKee** his security in the penalty of one thousand Dollars conditioned &[c]

– **George Taylor** by the Governor Plts
against In Debt
**Robert Smith** Constable & **Tho[s] Whites** his security Defts

This day came the Parties aforesaid by their attornies and thereupon came also a Jury, to wit, **Thomas Hanks, John Guinn, Ichabud Blacklidge, Hansford Price, Johnathan Smith, David Puckett, Fortunatus Dodson, Robert Williams, James Cox, John Blacklidge, Rich[d] Churchwell**, & **Nathaniel Black**, who being elected tried and sworn the truth to speak upon the Issue Joined, Afterwards one of the Jury **John Guinn**, by consent was withdrawn & the Cause Continued "till the next Court.

– Ordered that the Court be adjourned until Tomorrow morning ten OClock

**J G Hunter**

[page 78] At a Circuit Court Continued and held for the Pulaski Circuit at the Courthouse of Pulaski in Sommerset. On Wednesday the 26th day of September 1804

Present the Honourable **James G Hunter, John Smith & John Prather**

– **Benjamin Upton** Plt
against In Covenant
**Bend & Julious Bunch** Defts

**Moses Francis**, came into Court and Justified and undertook for the said Defendant that if they shall be cast in the action aforesaid that he shall satisfy and pay the Condemnation of the Court Or render his body to Prison in execution for the same, Or on falure thereof that he the said **Moses** shall do it for him, afterwards the said Bail surrendered here in fact the body of the said Defendant, agreeable to his recognizance and undertaking herein & the said Deft was Ordered into the Custody of the Sheriff &c.

– The Same Plt
against In Covenant
The Same Deft

**Rodin Bunch** came into Court, and Justifd &c and undertook for the said Defts that if they shall be cast in the action aforesaid that he shall satisfy and pay the Condemnation of the Court Or render their bodies to Prison [page 79] in Execution for the same or on falure thereof that he the said **Rodin Bunch**, shall do it for them

– **Robert Modrel** Plt
against upon Attachment
**Alexander McFarling** &c Defts

– The Same Plt
against The same
The Same Defts

Ordered that these suits be continued until tomorrow

– **John Blacklidge** Assee Plt
against In Covenant
**James Eastham** Deft

On the motion of the Defendant It is Ordered that the Judgment and Writ of Inquiry awarded against him in the Clerks Office be set a side, and the said Defendant by his attorney now comes and defends the wrong and Injury when and where &c and says that he hath not broken his Covenant in manner and form as the Plaintiff against hath declared, and of this he prays may be enquired of by the Country, and the said Plaintiff likewise, Thereupon It is Commanded the Sheriff that he cause to come here Immediately twelve good and lawful men by whom &c and thereupon came also a Jury, to wit, **George Sanders, Elias Kelly, Jonas Irvine, Thomas Whites, William Barnes, Henry Sage, Robert Scott, James Kerr, John Guinn, Jonathan Smith, Edward Cooper & Jonathan Stephens** who being elected tried and sworn the truth to speak upon the Issue Joined upon their Oaths do say that the said Defendant [page 79] hath not kept and performed his Covenant in manner & form as in pleading he hath alledged but hath broken the same in manner and form as the Plaintiff against him hath declared, and they do assess the plaintiffs Damages by Occasion thereof to seventy five pounds, besides his Costs It is therefore Considered by the Court, that the Plaintiff recover against the said Defendant his Damages aforesaid by the Jurors in their Verdict aforesaid assessed and his costs by him about his suit in this behalf expended, and the said Defendant in mercy &c.

– **Hugh Donigy** Plt
against In Covenant
**Joseph Casky** Deft

**William Hays** came into Court and Justifd and undertook for the said Defendant that if he shall be cast in the action aforesaid that he shall satisfy and pay the Condemnation of the Court Or render his body to prison in execution for the Same or on falure thereof that he the said **William Hays** shall do it for him

– **Alexander Hambleton** Ass[ee] Plt
against In Covenant
**William Dodson** Deft

Ordered that this suit be continued until the next Court at the Plaintiffs Costs

[page 81] **David Swope** Plt
against In Covenant
**William Bailey** & the Shff Wayne Cty Defts

This day came the Plaintiff by his attorney and thereupon came also a Jury, to wit, **John Harmon, Reubin Hill, William Barns, Nathaniel Black, David Dodson, George Hanks, Moses Hanks, Richard Higgins, Richard Beason, John Mitchell, David Puckett** & **Thomas Hanks**, who were sworn well and truly to enquire what Damages the Plaintiff hath sustained in the premises upon their Oaths do say that the Plaintiff hath sustained Damages by Occasion thereof to sixteen pounds twelve shillings besides his Costs It is therefore Considered by the Court that the Plaintiff recover against the said Defendant his Damages aforesaid by the Jurors in their Verdict aforesaid assessed, and his costs by him about his suit in this behalf expended, and the said Defendant in mercy &[c].

– The Same Plt
against In Debt
The Same Deft

This day came the Plaintiff by his attorney, and thereupon came also a Jury to wit, **John Harmon, Reubin Hill, William Barns, Nathaniel Black, David Dodson, George Hanks, Moses Hanks, Richard Higgins, Richard Beason, John Mitchell, David Puckett** & **Thomas Hanks**, who were sworn well [page 82] truly to enquire what Damages the Plaintiff hath sustained in Premises upon their Oaths do find for the plaintiff the Debt in the Declaration mentioned and One Penny in Damages. It is therefore Considered by the Court that the Plaintiff recover against the said Defendant the Debt in the Declaration mentioned his Damages aforesaid by the Jurors in their Verdict aforesaid assessed, and his costs by him about his suit in this behalf expended, and the said Defendant in mercy &[c]. Note this Judgment is to be Discharged by the payment of thirty pounds with legal Interest thereon from the first day of May One thousand eight hundred and three until paid the Damages ass[d] & Costs

– **Robert Modrel** Plt
against upon a Attachment 2[nd] case
**Daniel McFarling, John** & **Alexander McFarling** Defts

This day came the Parties aforesaid by their attornies, & **David Hays** being sworn as a Garnishee declares that he Owed **Alexander McFarling** Or **Daniel McFarling** aforesaid to whom as he has understood his bond passed by ejectment the sum of One hundred & six pounds in Property payable in Hasford Lincoln County in the month of March One thousand eight hundred and three. One hundred Dollars of which he paid shortly after his Contract & before it was due Twenty One Dollars of which he paid at another time before it was due & three Dollars & One half at another time [page 83] & before it was due, he declares further that he executed one Other bond to Col[o] **Alexander McFarling** for One hundred & five Dollars in Property & which had been pawned to a certain **Christopher Singleton**, by one of the **McFarlings** but he does not know which & that he afterwards paid the sum of two Dollars the sum the bond was pawned for and took up the said Bond

– **Kizziah Chappel** by her next friend Plt
against In Case
**William Burton** Deft

On the motion of the Defendant It is Ordered that the Judgment and Writ of Inquiry awarded against him in the Clerks Office be set a side and the said Defendant by his attorney now comes and defends the wrong and Injury, when and where &c. and saith that he is not guilty in manner and form as the Plaintiffs against him hath declared and this he prays may be enquired of b the Country and the said Plaintiff likewise, therefore it is commanded the Sheriff that he cause to come here Immediately twelve good and lawfull men by whom &c. and thereupon came also a Jury, to wit, **John Harmon**, **Reubin Hill**, **William Barns**, **Nathaniel Black**, **David Dodson**, **George Hanks**, **Moses Hanks**, **Richard Higgins**, **Richard Beason**, **John Mitchell**, **David Puckett** & **Thomas Hanks**, who being elected tried and sworn the truth to speak upon the Issue Joined upon their Oaths do say that the said Defendant is guilty in manner and form as the Plaintiff against him hath declared and they do assess the Plaintiffs Damages by Occasion thereof to three pounds twelve shillings besides [page 84] Costs, It is therefore Considered by the Court that the Plaintiff recover against the said Defendant their damages aforesaid by the Jurors in their Verdict aforesaid assessed, and their Costs by them about this suit in this behalf expended, and the said Defendant may be taken &c.

– **Tunstall Quarles** Plt
against In Ejectment
**Andrew Cowen** Deft

This day came the parties aforesaid by their attornies, and the said Defendant says he cannot gainsay the Plaintiffs Action against him, It is therefore Considered by the Court that the Plaintiff recover against the said Defendant his Term yet to Come and unexpired of and in the premises in the declaration mentioned & also his Costs by him in this behalf expended, and on the motion of the plaintiff by his attorney. It is Ordered that the Commonwealths writ of Habeas facias Possessionum be awarded him to cause him to have possession &c and all and singular the matters of equity arrising herein are sent and issued to the said Defendant

– **Andrew Cowen** Complt
against In Chancery
**Tunstall Quarles** Deft

This day came the parties aforesaid by their attornies, and by Consent filed their Bill and answer thereto herein without making affidavit to the same

– Ordered that the Court be adjourned until tomorrow morning ten OClock

**J G Hunter**

[page 85] At a Circuit Court Continued and held for the Circuit composed of the Counties of Pulaski & Wayne, at the Courthouse of Pulaski County in Sommerset. On Thursday the 27th day of September 1804

Present the Honourable **James G Hunter**, **John Smith** and **John Prather**

– **John Weirs** admor Plt
against In Case
**Nathaniel Forbis** Deft
– The Same Plt
against In Case
The Same Deft

Ordered that these suits be continued until the next Court

– **Obediah Paine** Plt
against In Case
**Robert Gillelands** admor Defts
– **Henry Grindstaff** Plt
against In Case
The Same Deft

This day came the Parties aforesaid by their attornies, and On the motion of the Defendant It is Ordered that the Judgments and Writ of Inquiry awarded against them in the Clerks Office be set a side and the said Defendants by their attornies now Come and defend the wrong & Injury when & where &c and saith they did not assume upon themselves in manner and form as the [page

86] Plaintiff against them hath declared, and of this they pray may be enquired of by the Country. and the said Plaintiff likewise, Therefore let a Jury come here &c and the Cause is Continued til the next Court

– **John Adair** & **William Barnett** Complt
against In Chancery
**William Crawford** & **William Fox** Defts

This day came the Complainants by their Counsil, and on their motion, and It appearing to the satisfaction of this Court that the Defendant **Crawford** is not an Inhabitant of this state, It is therefore that unless the said Deft shall appear here on the third day of the next March Term of this Court and answer the complainants bill the same will be taken for Confessed, and that a Copy of this Order to be Published in the Palladium for two months successively agreeable to the Act of Assembly in such cases Provided

– The Commonwealth
against upon an Indictment
**William Evans** Deft

This day came as well the attorney for the Commonwealth as the said Defendant by his attorney, and on motion It is Ordered that the Damages Obtained herein be released & that the said Defendant pay the Costs of this Prosecution &c.

– **Edward Flowers** Plt
against In Covenant
**Henry Francis** Deft

Ordered that this suit be Continued until the next Court

[page 87] **Joseph Casky** Plt
against In Case
**John January** Deft

Ordered that this suit be continued for award

– **Kizziah Chappel** &c Plts
against In Case
**William Burton** Deft

This day came the Parties aforesaid by their attornies, and on the motion of the Plts a new trial is awarded them On the Verdict of the Jury & Judgment Obtained herein yesterday

– **Matthew Hickson** Complt
against In Chancery
**George Taylor** & Als Deft

This day came the Parties aforesaid by their attornies, and on Mo leave is granted to take Depositions & the Cause is continued until next Court

– **Robert Modrel** Plt
against upon Attachment
**Alexander McFarling** & Als Deft

The complainant here now complains against the said Defendant for this that they assumed upon themselves on the ____ day of September, October, or November in the year 1801 at the County of Pulaski, that they would on or before the twenty fifth day of [page 88] December in the year One thousand eight hundred and One pay him a negroe Boy healthy, well grown & sensible & between the age of fourteen or fifteen and twenty years which negroe the Plaintiff avers they have not paid him & that he is injured & prays that his Damages may be enquired of by a Jury to be Summoned by the Coroner of Pulaski County, the Plaintiff being Sheriff of said County and thereupon came a Jury, to wit, **Henry Willis, James Kerr, William Mayfield, Edward Boldin, Matthew Hickson, Asa Dodson, John Evans, Jesse Williams, Tapley Yates, Fortunatus Dodson, George Saunders** & **Robert Williams**, who were sworn well and truly to enquire what Damages the Plaintiff hath sustained in the Premises upon their Oaths do say that the Plaintiff hath sustained Damages by Occasion thereof to One hundred & thirty nine pounds, four shillings besides his costs. It is therefore Considered by the Court that the Plaintiff recover against the said

Defendant his Damages aforesaid by the Jurors in their Verdict aforesaid assessed and his Costs by him, about his attachment expended. and the said Defendant in mercy &c.

– **Frederick Troxwell** Complt
against In Chancery
**William Burton** Deft

The Defendant made Oath to his answer herein, in Court

[page 89] **Alexander Moore** Plt
against In Debt
**Micah Taul** Deft

This day came the Parties aforesaid by their attornies, and on the motion of the Defendant It is Ordered that the Judgment and writ of Inquiry awarded against him in the clerks Office Be set a side, and the said Defendant by his attorney comes and defends the wrong and Injury when &c and prays Judgment of the Plaintiff Writ, Sheriffs return Appearance Bond & Declaration & that the same may be quashed because he says that the said Writ, return, appearance bond, & Declaration, are Insufficient in law for the Plaintiff to have and maintain his action afs[d] against the said Defendant neither is he the said Defendant bound by the Law of the land in any manner to answer thereto, and this he is ready to verify: therefore as before he prays Judgment &c and the said Defendant according to the Act of the general Assembly in such cases made and provided sets down the following causes of Demurer, to wit, 1st It is not Designated on the memorandum endorse on the writ, what kind of bail is to be taken, as directed by the Act of Assembly in such cases made & provided 2nd the Sheriff has returned the Original Bail Bond whereas the act of assembly directs that he shall return a copy thereof, 3d the Declaration is wholy Insufficient wanting both form and Substance, and the said Plaintiff says that his said writ, Sheriffs return and Declaration herein, ought not to be quashed because he says they are sufficient in law for him to have and maintain his said action against the said Defendant, wherefore he prays [page 90] Judgment &c and the said Plaintiff says that It is designated on the writ what kind of bail is to be taken, as directed by the act of Assembly in such cases made and provided, and that his Declaration is sufficient and lacks neither form nor substance, and thereupon the matters of law arrising upon the Defendants said Demurer. It is the Opinion of the Court that the said Demurer and the matter therein contained are not sufficient in law to bar the Plaintiff from having & maintaining his said Action against the said Defendant. and that the same be Over ruled, and the Damages be enquired of by a Jury (and by Consent of the Parties, It is Ordered that the Demurrage be considered as filed at the July rules last past of this Court, and that it have every legal effect, that it would if entered on the Record, at that time, it being admitted that it was left with the Clerk for that purpose previous thereto) The said Defendant refuses to put in any other plea herein. On the motion of the Plaintiff a Writ of Inquiry De novo is awarded him, therefore It is commanded the Sheriff that he cause to come here Immediately twelve good and lawfull men by whom &c. and thereupon came also a Jury, to wit, **Robert Smith, Robert Williams, John Gwin, David Dodson, Asa Dodson, Andrew Evans, Fortunatus Dodson, John Newby, Matthew Hickson, Edward Baldwin, James Pruit** & **David Johnson** who were sworn well and truly to enquire what Damages the Plaintiff hath sustained in the premises upon their [page 91] Oaths do find for the Plaintiff by Occasion thereof to four hundred Dollars the Debt in the Declaration mentioned & do find for the Plt one penny in Damages besides his Costs. It is therefore Considered by the Court that the plaintiff recover against the said Defendant, the said four hundred Dollars the Debt in the Declaration mentioned, his Damages aforesaid by the Jurors in their Verdict aforesaid assessed and his Costs by him about his suit in this behalf expended and the said Defendant in mercy &c. Note this Judgment or the said four hundred Dollars is to have credit for sixty nine Dollars and the residue to bare legal Interest until paid & Costs

– **Roger Carson** Plt
against In Trespass
**William Simpson** Deft

Ordered that this suit be continued until the next Court at the Defendants Costs

– **Bartlett Hillard** Plt
against In Case
**William J Sallee** Deft

This day came the Parties aforesaid by their attornies, and the Plaintiff by his attorney saith that his action aforesaid against the s[d] Deft ought to have and Support because the said Defendant did undertake and assume upon himself or within five years next before the suing [?] Out the Original Writ herein, &[c] (Defendant Demurs to the Plaintiffs Declaration here to be Inserted) which was Over ruled by the Court: and on the motion of the said Defendant leave is [page 92] granted him to amend his plea herein ( here recite the same & Joinder) and the cause is remanded to the Rule Dockette

– **James Johnson** by his next friend **David Johnson** Plt
against In Case
**John Guinn** Deft

On the motion of the Defendant It is Ordered that the Judgment and Writ of Inquiry awarded herein in the Clerks Office be set a side and the said Defendant by his attorney now comes and defends the wrong and Injury when & where &[c] and says he is not guilty in manner and form as the Plaintiff against him hath declared, and of this he prays may be enquired of by the Country and the said Plaintiff likewise therefore It is commanded the Sheriff that he cause to come here Immediately twelve good and lawfull men by whom &[c] and thereupon came also a Jury, to wit, **George Saunders, Lewis Fitzgerald, John Williams, W[m] Mayfield, Robert Smith, Fred: Williams, Joel Jackson, Nathaniel Black, John Irvine, W[m] Barns, Jesse Richardson** & **Jacob Stephens**, who being elected tried and sworn the truth to speak upon the Issue Joined upon their Oaths do say that the said Defendant is not guilty in manner and form as the Plaintiff against him hath declared, It is therefore Considered by the Court that the Plaintiff take nothing by his Bill but for his false Clamour be in mercy &[c] and that the said Deft recover [page 93] against the said Plaintiff his costs by him about his defence in this behalf expended

– **Hugh Donigy** Plt
against In Covenant
**Joseph Casky** Deft

Ordered that this suit be continued until the next Court

– **Robert Modrel** Plt
against upon Attachment 2[nd] Case
**Alexander McFarling** &[c] Defts

This day came the plaintiff by his attorney, and on motion Order of sale of £68-13 the ballance of the One hundred and six pounds confessed in the hands of the Garnishee, and It is further ordered that the Order respecting the appropriation of the One hundred and five Dollars, Confessed as aforesaid by the Garnashee postponed until the next Term of this Court

– **John Long** Ass[ee] Plt
against In Debt
**Julious Bunch** Deft

This day came the Plaintiff by his attorney and on the motion of the said attorney It is ordered that the Judgment and writ of Inquiry awarded against the said Defendant in the Clerks Office be waved. and on his motion Judgment is granted him against the said Defendant for eight pounds the Debt in the Declaration mentioned & his costs by him about his suit in this behalf expended and the said Defendant in mercy &[c]. Note this Judgment is to bare legal Interest [page 94] thereon from the first day of August One thousand seven hundred and ninety eight until paid & Costs

– **Jacob Stephens** Plt
against In Debt
**Jonathan Hopkins** Deft

This day came the Plaintiff by his attorney, and on his motion It is Ordered that the Judgment and Writ of Inquiry awarded against the said Defendant in the Clerks Office be waved and, on the motion of the Plaintiff by his attorney Judgment is granted him against the said Defendant for the Debt in the Declaration mentioned, and his Costs by him about his suit in this behalf expended and the said Defendant in mercy &c. Note This Judgment is to be discharged by the payment of One hundred and fifteen pounds, with legal Interest thereon from the twentyfourth day of September One thousand eight hundred and three until paid & Costs

– **David Swope** Plt
against In Debt
**Roger Oatts** Deft

This day came the Plaintiff by his attorney, and on his motion it is Ordered that the Judgment and Writ of Inquiry awarded against him in the Clerks Office be waved, and on his motion It is ordered that the Plaintiff recover against the said Defendant thirty pounds the Debt in the Declaration mentioned and his Costs by him about his suit in this behalf expended and the said Defendant in mercy &c. [page 95] Note this Judgment is to bare legal Interest from the fourteenth day of October One thousand eight hundred and three until paid & Costs

– **John Moran** Ass[ee] Plt
against In Debt
**William Bailey** Deft

This day came the Plaintiff aforesaid by his attorney and thereupon came also a Jury, to wit, **Robert Williams, Robert Smith, John Guinn, David Dodson, Asa Dodson, Andrew Evans, Fortunatus Dodson, John Newby, Matthew Hickson, Edward Baldwin, James Price** & **David Johnson** who were sworn well and truly to enquire what Damage the Plaintiff hath sustained in the Premises upon their Oaths do say that the Plaintiff hath sustained Damages by Occasion thereof to one penny, and do find for the plaintiff the Debt in the Declaration mentioned besides his Costs It is therefore Considered by the Court that the Plaintiff recover against the said Defendant his Damages aforesaid and the said Debt in the Declaration mentioned & his Costs by him about his suit in this behalf expended, and the said Defendant in mercy &c. Note this Judgment to bare legal Interest from the 25th day of Oct[r] One thousand eight hundred & three until paid & Costs. But to have credit for One pound sixteen shillings paid the 24th day of February 1804

[page 96] **Philip A Sublette** Plt
against In Covenant
**Joseph Casky** Deft

**John Roberson** came into Court and Justified, and undertook for the said Defendant that if he shall be cast in this action aforesaid that he shall satisfy and pay the condemnation of the Court or render his body to prison in execution for the same Or on falure thereof that he the said **John** shall do it for him

– **William J Sallee** Deft
ads In Case
**Bartlett Hillard** Plt

In this Case the Deft **Sallee** by his attorney moved the Court for leave to file the following Demurer, to wit, **Lightfoot** and **Sallee**, at the suit of **Hillard** the Defts by &c here Jurat the Demurer Verbatom, to which a motion of the Deft to file his said Demurer, the Plaintiff by his attorney Objected because the Deft by pleading to the action at the last Term from which the suit was continued until this Term, has in law admitted that the Plaintiff had pursued the right form of action & Precluded from filing this said Demurer which Objection of the Plaintiff by his Attorney was sustained by the Court, and the Court thereupon overruled the motion of the Deft to file said Demurer to which Judgment and Opinion of the Court, in Over ruling said motion the Deft by his attorney, excepts and prays [page 97] that his bill of exception may be signed and sealed by the Court and admitted to Record, in persuance of the act of Assembly in that case made & provided

**J G Hunter**
**John Smith**
**John Prather**

– Ordered that the Court be adjourned until Tomorrow morning ten OClock

At a Circuit Court Continued and held at the Courthouse of Pulaski County in Sommerset. On Friday the 28th day of September 1804

Present the Honourable **James G Hunter, John Smith & John Prather**

– Ordered that it be certified to the County Court of Pulaski County that this Court allowed **Arch[d] Mills** Esq[r] as their attorney the sum of One hundred Dollars, for services performed by him in the execution of his Office for the last year preceeding this date

– Ordered that it be Certified to the Auditor of Publick Accounts that this Court allows to **William Fox** as their Clerk the sum of thirty Dollars for public service performed by him in the execution of his Office for the last year preceeding this date

– The Clerk of this Court exhibited into Court an account for Paper &[c] furnished by him for the use of his Office which was Ordered to be Certified

[page 98] **Robertson Burge** Ass[ee] Plt
against In Debt
**Joshua Jones** Deft

This day came the Plaintiff by his attorney and thereupon came also a Jury, to wit, **Israel Hart, Jacob Stephens, William Barns, Edward Coper, John Willis, Samuel Dick, David Dodson, George Saunders, John Ingraham, Jesse Cundiff, James Eastham** and **James Kerr** who were Sworn well and truely to enquire what damages the Plaintiff hath sustained in the Premises upon their Oaths do say that the Plaintiff hath sustained Damages by Occasion thereof to One Penny. and find for the Plaintiff the sum of One hundred and thirty six Dollars and sixty seven Cents, the Debt in the Declaration mentioned besides his costs It is therefore considered by the Court that the Plaintiff recover against the said Defendant his Damages aforesaid, the sum in the Declaration mentioned & his Costs by him about his suit in this behalf expended, and the said Defendant in mercy & Note this Judgment Or the sum mentioned in the Declaration is to bare legal Interest from the twentieth day of November 1803 until paid & Costs

– **Robertson Burge** Ass[ee] Plt
against In Debt
**Roger Oats** Deft

This day came the plaintiff by his attorney and thereupon came also a Jury to wit, **Israel Hunt, Jacob Hopkins, William Barns, Edward Cooper, John Willis, Samuel Dick, David** [page 99] **Dodson, George Saunders, John Ingram, Jesse Cundiff, James Eastham** and **James Kerr** who were sworn well and truly to enquire what Damage the Plaintiff hath sustained in the premises upon their Oaths to say that the plaintiff hath Sustained Damage by Occasion thereof to One penny and do find for the plaintiff twenty one Dollars the Debt in the Declaration mentioned & his Costs by him about his suit in this behalf expended and the said Defendant in mercy &[c]. Note this Judgment is to have credit for five Dollars and the residue to bare legal Interest from the sixth day of November One thousand eight hundred & three until paid & Costs

– **John Hiatt** Ass[ee] Plt
against In Debt
**James Alderson** Deft

This day came the Plaintiff by his attorney and thereupon came also a Jury, to wit, **Israel Hunt, Jacob Stephens, William Barns, Edward Cooper, John Willis, Samuel Dick, David Dodson, George Saunders, John Ingram, Jesse Cundiff, James Eastham & James Kerr**, who were sworn well and truly to enquire what Damages the plaintiff hath sustained in the Premises upon their Oaths do say that the Plaintiff hath sustained Damages by Occasion thereof to One Penny & do find for the Plaintiff twenty Dollars the Debt in the Declaration mentioned & his Costs by him about his suit in this behalf expended and the said Defen[page 100]dant in mercy &[c]. Note this Judgment is to bare legal Interest from the 25th day of December One thousand eight hundred and three until paid & Costs

– **Philip A Sublette** Plt

against In Covenant
**Joseph Casky** Deft

This day came the parties aforesaid by their attornies and the said Defendant acknowledges the Plaintiffs action against him for sixty six Dollars, Therefore It is Considered by the Court that the Plaintiff recover against the said Defendant the sum confessed as ass[d] and his Costs by him about his suit in this behalf expended and the said Defendant in mercy &[c]. Note the Defendant reserves Equity

– **William Evans** Plt
against In Covenant
**John Roberson** Deft

**John Fitzgerald** came into Court, and Justified, and undertook for the said Defendant that if he shall be cast in the action aforesaid that he shall satisfy and pay the Condemnation of the Court or render his body to Prison in Execution for the same Or on falure thereof that he the said **John Fitzgerald** shall do it for him

[page 101] **Roger Oats**
at the suit In Debt
**David Swope**

And the said Defendant by his attorney saith that Judgment on waving the writ of Inquiry herein Ought not to be entered but ought to be stayed & arrested for the following error to wit, 1[st] that the Judgment is awarded against **James Jones**, as appearance Bail, when the sheriff has not returned & endorsed the name of the appearance Bail on the writ, as required by the act of assembly &[c] that the proceedings herein doth not warrant a Judgment against **Jones**, as appearance Bail, wherefore an Arrest of Judgment is prayed for, after hearing the arguments of the Counsil & mature deliberation being thereon had, It is considered by the Court that said errors be sustained as to the Bail, and the Cause is remanded to the rule Dockette

– **Alexander Hambleton** Plt
against In Debt
**Micah Taul** Deft

This day came the Plaintiff by his attorney and on his motion the Judgment and writ of Inquiry awarded against him in the Clerks Office be waved, and on his motion It is Ordered that the Plaintiff recover against the said [page 102] Defendant fifty nine Dollars & seventy five Cents besides his Costs the Debt in the Declaration mentioned Note this Judgment is to bare legal Interest from the twenty fifth day of February One thousand eight hundred and four until paid & Costs

– **Holkum Robertson** Complt
against In Chancery
**William Renick** Deft

On the motion of the Defendant by his attorney to disolve the Complainants Injunction herein, after hearing the Bill, and the arguments of Counsil on both sides &[c] Mature deliberation being thereon had, It is Ordered by the Court that the said Injunction be desolved and that the said Defendant proceed with his Judgment Obtained against the said Complainant at Common law, and recover his costs by him about this motion expended, and that he recover the percent alloted by law On the Disolution of Injunctions

– **Abraham Price** Plt
against
**Salley A Price** his wife Deft

This day came the plaintiff by his attorney & thereupon came also a Jury, to wit, **William Barns, Thomas Whites, James Montgomery, Henry Sage, John Wilkerson,** [page 103] **James Kerr, John Reynolds, Joseph Rainey, James Eastham, John Ingram, Edward Cooper,** & **Lewis Fitzgerald** who were sworn well and truly to enquire as to the facts stated in the Plaintiffs Declaration upon their Oaths do say that they find said facts as stated in said Declaration to be true therefore On the motion of the said **Abraham Price** by his attorney It is Considered by the Court that the bonds of Matrimony between the said **Abraham** & his said wife, be desolved & that the

said **Abraham** be from henceforth divorced from her
– **Alexander Hambleton** Plt
against In Case
**Samuel Munday** Deft
– **Kizziah Chapple** &c Plt
against In Case
**Jesse Burton** Deft
– **James Arbuckle** Plt
against In Case
**Samuel Kitchens** Deft

Ordered that these suits be continued until the next Court
– **Willis Embry** Plt
against In Case
**John Rogers** Deft

Ordered that this suit be Dismissed
[page 104] **James Kerr** Plt
against In Case
**Andrew Evans** Deft

Ordered that this suit be Continued until the next by Consent of the Parties, now in Court
– The Sheriff Exhibited an account into Court which was Ordered to be Certified to the auditor of Public Accounts
– Ordered that the Court be adjourned "till Court in Course

**John Smith**

At a Circuit Court holden for the Pulaski Circuit, On Monday the 22nd day of April 1805

Present the Honourable **James G Hunter, John Smith,** and **John Prather** Gentlemen
– On the motion **Thomas B Reed** and **Samuel Davis** Esquires, who Produced their licence authorizing them to Practice law &c and took the necessary Oaths &c.
– **William D Irvine** Plt
against In Debt
**John Barrow** Deft

This day came as well the Plaintiff by his attorney, as the said Defendant in his Proper Person and the said Defendant says he cannot gainsay the Plaintiffs action against him for Twenty four Dollars ____ the Debt in the Declaration mentioned, Therefore with assent of the [page 105] Plaintiff It is Considered by the Court that the Plaintiff recover against the said Defendant, the sum acknowledged as aforesaid and his Costs by him about his suit in this behalf expended and the said Defendant in mercy &c. Note this Judgment is to be discharged by the payment of thirty seven Dollars and thirty eight Cents with legal Interest thereon from the Seventh day of July One thousand eight hundred and two until paid & costs. But to have credit for eight Dollars and twenty five cents paid on the fourteenth day of March One thousand eight hundred and three
– A Grand jury were sworn for the Pulaski Circuit, to wit, **James Smith** Senr foreman, **John Evans, Thomas Owsley, Jonathan Smith, William Lynch, Abner McWhorter, John Portman, Ambrose Mayfield, Jeremiah Meek, Israel Hart, James Smith** Junr, **John Puckett, Andrew Turner, Robert Smith, John Russell, Fortunatus Dodson** Senr, **William Worson, Andrew Wolverton** & **George McWhirter,** who having received their charge retired to consider of their Presentments
– **Roger Carson** Plt
against In Case
**William Simpson** Deft

This day came the Parties aforesaid by their attornies, and It is Ordered that this suit be Dismissed at the Defendants Cost
– **William Simpson** Complt

against In Chancery
**Roger Carson** Deft

This day came the Parties aforesaid by their attornies, And by [page 106] their consent It is Ordered that the complainants Bill be Dismissed at the s[d] Complainants Costs, and he hereby relinquishes all claim to the land mentioned therein

– **John Beard** Complt
against In Chancery
**George Saunders** Deft

This day came the Parties aforesaid by their attornies, and on their motion It is Ordered that a former Order of this Court appointing **Samuel McKee** to Survey the lands in Controversy between the Parties aforesaid be set a side,

And On the motion of the said Complainant It is Ordered that **Thomas Whites**, do go On the land in Controversy between the said Parties on the ___ day of ___ next if fair if not then on the next fair day, and then and there Survey and lay of the same as either party would have it having regard to all Deeds, and Other evidence that may be Produced, report all matters of fact especially and return four fair Platts and Certificates thereof to the Clerks Office 20 days before the day of hearing

– The Commonwealth
against upon an Indictment
**John Griffin** Deft

This day came the Attorney for the Commonwealth, and On his motion it is Ordered that an Alias Venerafacias Issue, against the said Defendant &[c] and the cause is continued untill the next Court

[page 107] The Grand jury returned into Court and made the following presentments, to wit, Pulaski County April Circuit Term we of the Grand jury for the body of the County aforesaid do present **Thomas Malone** labourer for selling Spiritous liquors by the half pint, without Ordinary licence in the town of Sommerset in the Streets of the same on the fourth Monday in February 1805 against the peace and dignity of the Commonwealth, by the Information of **Benjamin Cundiff**, not of the Grand jury, and residenter of the County of Pulaski

**James** Senr foreman

Pulaski County April Circuit Term 1805, we of the Grand jury for the body of Pulaski County, **Vinson Goldsmith** labourer for selling spiritous liquors by the half pint without Ordinary licence, on the fourth Monday in March 1805 in the town of Sommerset against the peace and dignity of the Commonwealth of Kentucky by the Information of **Benjamin Cundiff** not of the Grand jury and residenter of Pulaski County

**James Smith** Senr foreman

Pulaski County April Circuit Term 1805 we of the Grand jury for the body of the county aforesaid present **John January** Innkeeper of the Town of Sommerset and County aforesaid for selling Spiritous liquors by the half pint without Ordinary licence on the ___ day of March last and keeping other entertainment for the accomodation of his Customers & Others against the peace and dignity of the Commonwealth by the Information of **Benjamin Cundiff** not of the Grand jury and a residenter of Pulaski County

**James Smith** Senr foreman

[page 108] Pulaski County April Circuit Term 1805, we of the Grand jury for the body of the County aforesaid Present **William Ussery**, Innkeeper, of the County aforesaid for selling Spiritous Liquors by the half pint On the ___ day of March 1805 in the Town of Sommerset, and County aforesaid without Ordinary licence against the peace and dignity of the Commonwealth by the Information of **Benjamin Cundiff** not of the Grand jury & a resider of Pulaski County

**James Smith** Senr foreman

Pulaski County April Circuit Term 1805 we of the Grand jury for the body of the County aforesaid present **William J Sallee**, labourer, of the County aforesaid for selling spiritous Liquors by the half pint without Ordinary license On the day of March 1805 in the Town of Sommerset and County aforesaid against the peace and dignity of the Commonwealth by the Information of **Benjamin Cundiff** not of the Grand jury and a residenter of Pulaski County

**James Smith** Senr foreman of the Grand jury

The Commonwealth against **Isaac Mayfield**, a true Bill, also Commonwealth against **Michael Stoner** a true Bill

**James** Foreman of the Grand Jury

And the Grand jury having nothing further to Present was discharged, and delinquents Ordered to be Summoned

– The Commonwealth
against upon a recognizance
**Jesse Burton** & Deft

[page 109] This day came the said Defendants by their attorney who was bound by a recognizance to appear here on this day, to answer the Complt of **John Scrimiger**, and on the motion of the said Defendant by their attorney It is ordered that this recognizance be dismissed for irregularity therein, and the defendants recover their costs by them about their defence in this behalf expended

– **Robert Modrel** Complt
against upon Attachment
**Alexander McFarland** &c Defts

This day came the Parties aforesaid by their attornies, and the appropriation of the sum of One hundred and five Dollars, as per the note mentioned in the Confession of the Garnishee, being now taken into Consideration, whereupon it is Ordered that the Sheriff do make Sale of One hundred and three Dollars the ballance of said Bond deducting the two dollars paid by the said Garnishee **David Hays**, and that the said **David Hays** do deliver, the same for Sale, according to the Stipulations of his said bond, and that the money arrising from the sale, be applied towards satisfying the Plaintiffs Judgment, and that he recover his Costs &c.

– **Robert Modrel** Complt
against upon Attachment
**Alexander McFarland** & Defts

This day came the Complainant by his attorney, and It is Ordered that this Attachment be dismissed

– **Holkum Robertson** Plt
against upon Attachment
**George Etherington** Deft

Ordered that this Attachment be Continued until the next Court

[page 110] **Daniel Duncan** Plt
against upon a Attachment
**Allin Burton** Deft

– **William Barrow** Plt
against Same
The Same Deft

This day came the said Plaintiffs by their attorney, and It is Ordered that the return made by the Sheriff on said Attachments be set a side And on the motion of the said Plaintiffs by their attorney Alias Attachments are awarded them against the said Defendants &c And if is further ordered that **James Johnson** be summoned as a Garnishee herein to appear here on the first day of the next Term of this Court to declare what estate he has in hands belonging to the said Defendant. and the said Attachments is Ordered to be continued until the next Court

– **William Hill** Plt
against upon Attachment
**Samuel Cole** Deft

This day came the Defendant by his attorney and on his motion It is Ordered that this Attachment be Dismissed for want of Prosecution, and that the Defendant recover of the said

Plaintiff his Costs by him about his defence in this behalf expended
– **William Mayfield** Plt
against upon Attachment
**David Clark** Deft
Ordered that this attachment be Discontinued
[page 111] **Laurence Hutcherson** Complt
against In Chancery
**Mashack Hicks** Deft
On the motion of **Samuel McKee** Esquire, It is Ordered that this suit be refered to the Arbitration and determination of **William Jennings**, **Benjamin Letcher**, and **James Thompson** Gent whose award Or the award of any two of them be the Judgment of this Court and that the award be returned to this Court by the third day of the next Term thereof, and the same is ordered accordingly
– Ordered that the Court be adjourned until Tomorrow morning ten Oclock
**J G Hunter**

At a Circuit Court continued and held for the Pulaski Circuit at the Court house in Sommerset On Tuesday the 23rd day of April 1805,
Present the Honourable **James G Hunter**, **John Smith**, and **John Prather**, Gentlemen
– The Commonwealth Plt
against upon an Indictment
**Michael Stoner** Deft
This day came as well the attorney for the Commonwealth as the said Defendant by his attorney, and on the motion of the said Defendant by his attorney, by consent A Dedimus awarded him to take the Deposition of **Robert Todd**, of Adair County Debeneesse
[page 112] The Commonwealth Plt
against upon Presentment
**William J Sallee** Deft
– The Commonwealth Plt
against The Same
**John January** Deft
– The Same Plt
against The Same
**William Ussery** Deft
This day came as well the Attorney for the Commonwealth as the said Defendants by their attornies, and on the motion of the said Defendants by their attornies to quash the Presentments herein after hearing the arguments of counsil on each side the Court are of Opinion that the said Presentments are Illegal, and be quashed, and that the said Defendants recover their Costs by them about their defence in this behalf expended
– **Alexander Hambleton** Plt
against
**Samuel Monday** Deft
Ordered that this suit be Dismissed
– The Commonwealth Plt
against upon Presentment
**Vincent Godsmith** Deft
– The Same Plt
against upon Presentment
**Thomas Malone** Deft
[page 113] Ordered that these Presentments be quashed, by reason of their having been Illegal, and that the Defendants recover their costs by them about their defence in this behalf expended

– **Elizabeth Sharp** Complt
against In Chancery
**Michael Stoner** Deft

This day came the Parties aforesaid by their attornies, and On the motion of the said Complt by her attorney leave is granted her to amend her bill herein

– On the motion of **John Hill** to Obtain an Injunction to stay all further Proceedings On a Judgment Obtained against him by **John Smith** at common law, motion continued "till tomorrow morning Bill sworn to in Court

– **Elizabeth Sharp** Complt
against In Chancery
**Michael Stoner** Deft

This day came the Parties aforesaid by their attornies, and by their consent It is Ordered that a former Order of this Court refering all matters in difference between the said Parties be set a side.

– **George Taylor**, by Governor Plt
against In Debt
**Robert Smith** Constable & **Thomas Whites** his Security Defts

This day came the Parties aforesaid by their attornies, and thereupon came also a Jury, to wit, **Henry Willis, John Jasper, James Kerr, Reubin Hill, William Ussery, William J** [page 114] **Sallee, Charles Richardson, William Barns, Thomas Price, James Brock, Samuel Hand** and **John Scrimiger** who being elected tried and sworn the truth to speak upon the Issue Joined upon their Oaths do say that the said Deft has not kept or performed the several Conditions of the bond agreeable to his undertaking as a Constable, as in Pleading he hath alledged, and returned into Court their Verdict in these words to wit, we of the Jury find for the Plaintiff the Debt in the Declaration mentioned to be discharged by the payment of Five Pounds, in damages It is therefore Considered by the Court that the Plaintiff recover against the said Defendant his Damages afores[d] by the Jurors in their Verdict aforesaid assessed and his Costs by him about his suit in this behalf expended, and the said Defendant in mercy &[c].

– **Edward Flower** Plt
against
**Henry Francis** Deft

Ordered that this suit be continued until the next Court

– **Alexander Hambleton** Plt
against In Covenant
**William Dodson** Deft

This day came the Parties aforesaid by their attornies and It is Ordered that this suit be Discontinued

[page 115] **Kizziah Chapple** by **Jesse Chapple**, her next friend Plts
against In Case
**Jesse Burton** Deft

**William & Benjamin Burton** came into Court and Justified and undertook for the said Defendant that if he shall be cast in the Action aforesaid that he shall satisfy and pay the Condemnation of the Court, Or render his body to Prison in Execution for the same Or on falure thereof that they shall do it for him, and the special Bail formerly taken herein is discharged from their undertaking

– **Joseph Casky** Plt
against In Case
**John January** Deft

This day came the Parties aforesaid by their attornies and on the motion of the [ ] It is ordered that a former Order of this Court, refering this cause to referrees be set a side, and the award made upon the same is Ordered to be Quashed, and the Cause is continued until the next Court

– **James Arbuckle** Plt

against In Case
**Samuel Kitchens** Deft

By Consent of Parties all matters in difference between them respecting this suit is refered to the arbitration and determination of **John James**, **Ralph Williams**, **John Drewry Lee** and **Reubin Stringer**, whose award Or the award of any three of them be the Judgment of the Court, and the [page 116] Cause is Continued until the next Court

– Ordered that the Court be adjourned until Tomorrow morning nine OClock

**J G Hunter**

At a Circuit Court Continued and held for the Pulaski Circuit at the Courthouse in the Town of Sommerset on Wednesday the 24th day of April 1805

Present the Honourable **James G Hunter**, **John Smith**, and **John Prather** Gent

– **John Hill** Complt
against On Motion for an Injunction
**John Smith** Deft

This day came the Parties aforesaid by their attornies, and after hearing the bill, and the Arguments of Counsil for both sides, the Court are of Opinion that the motion be Over ruled, and that the Defendant recover his Costs by him about this motion expended

– **Kizziah Chapple** by **Jesse Chapple**, her next friend Plts
against In Case
**William Burton** Deft

This day came the Parties aforesaid by their attornies, and thereupon came also a Jury to wit, **Fortunatus Dodson** Senr, **Thomas Harris**, **Shaderick Stogsdal**, **John Wilkerson**, **George W Saunders**, **William Hays**, **Samuel Dick**, **Aaron Sargent**, **James Blacklidge**, **John Evans**, **Jacob Blacklidge** and **Vardiman Anderson**, who being elected tried and sworn the truth to speak upon the Issue Joined upon [page 117] their Oaths do say that the said Defendant is guilty in manner and form as the Plaintiffs against them hath declared and they do assess the Plaintiffs Damages by Occasion thereof to One hundred and twenty Pounds besides her Costs. It is therefore Considered by the Court, that the Plaintiffs recover against the said Defendant the Damages aforesaid by the Jurors in their Verdict afsd assessed, and her costs by them about their suit in this behalf expended and the said Defendant may be taken &c.

– **James Eastham** Senr Complt
against On motion in Chancery
**John Blacklidge** Deft

This day came the Parties aforesaid by their attornies and on the motion of the said Defendant to Disolve the Complainants Injunction Continued "till Tomorrow Notice of this motion being Proved

– **Kizziah Chapple** by **Jesse Chapple** her next friend Plt
against In Case
**Jesse Burton** Deft

On the motion of the Defendant It is Ordered that the Judgment and writ of Inquiary awarded against him in the Clerks Office be set a side, and the said Deft by his attorney now comes and defends the wrong and Injury, when and where &c and says he is not guilty in manner and form as the Plaintiff against [page 118] him hath declared, and of this he puts himself upon the Country and the said Plaintiff likewise, thereupon let a Jury come here &c and the cause is continued until the next Court

– **John Weirs** admor Plt
against In Case
**Nathaniel Forbis** Deft

– The Same Plt
against In Case
The Same Deft

Ordered that these suits be continued until the next Term of this Court
– **George Taylor**, by Governor Plt
against In Debt
**Robert Smith** Constable &c Defts

This day came the Parties aforesaid by their attornies and on the motion of the said Defendant by their attorney to Obtain a new trial on the Verdict of the Jury, and Judgment Obtained here after hearing the arguments of Counsil On both sides, and mature deliberation being thereon had, It is Ordered that the said motion be Over ruled and that the Plaintiff recover his Costs by him about this motion expended
– Ordered that the Court be adjourned until Tomorrow morning nine OClock

**J G Hunter**

[page 119] At a Circuit Court continued and held for the Pulaski Circuit at the Courthouse in the Town of Sommerset On Thursday the 25th day of April 1805

Present the Honourable **James G Hunter**, **John Smith** and **John Prather**, Gent
– **Andrew Herrin** Assee Plt
against In Debt
**John Brooks** Deft

This day came as well the Plaintiff by his attorney, as the said Defendant in his Proper Person, And **Nicholas Jasper** of Pulaski County came into Court and undertook for the said Deft that if he shall be cast in the action aforesaid that he shall satisfy and pay the condemnation of the Court. Or render his body to prison in Execution for the same, Or on falure thereof that he the said **Nicholas Jasper** shall do it for him, And the said Defendant says he cannot gainsay the Plaintiffs action against him for ______ the Debt in the Declaration mentioned, Therefore with Assent of the Plaintiff It is considered by the Court that the Plaintiff recover against the said Defendant the sum acknowledged as aforesaid, and his costs by him about his suit in this behalf expended, and the said Deft in mercy Note this Judgment is to bare legal Interest thereon from the ___ day of ____ until paid & Costs, Note absent, in this Cause

**Will Fox**

[page 120] **John Mitchell** for the benifit of **Edward Cooper** Plt
against In Case
**Philip A Sublette** Deft

Ordered that this suit be Dismissed It being agreed
– **Nicholas Jasper, John Jasper** & **Andrew Jasper** Complts
against In Chancery
**Tunstall Quarles** Deft

This day came the Parties aforesaid by their attornies, and on hearing the Bill, answer, exhibits and Sundry Depositions filed in this Cause, and the arguments of Counsil On both sides, the Court took time to consider of their Decree
– **James Eastham** Complt
against On motion In Chancery
**John Blacklidge** Deft

This day came the Parties aforesaid by their attornies, and on the motion of the said Defendant by his attorney to disolved the Complainants Injunction filed herein Continued "till Tomorrow
– Ordered that the Court be adjourned until Tomorrow morning Seven OClock

**J G Hunter**

[page 121] At a Circuit Court Continued and held for the Pulaski Circuit at the Courthouse in Sommerset On Friday the 26th day of April 1805

Present the Honourable **James G Hunter, John Smith**, and **John Prather**, Gentlemen
– **Kizziah Chapple** by **Jesse Chapple** her next friend Plt

against In Case
**William Burton** Deft

This day came the Parties aforesaid by their attornies, and On the motion of the said Defendant by his attorney, a new trial is awarded him, On the Verdict of the Jury and Judgment Obtained herein at this Term, On the said Defendants paying Costs

– **William Buford** Plt
against In Case
**Charles Debrell** Shff of Wayne County Deft

Ordered that this suit be continued until the next Court

– **Harry Grindstaff** Plt
against
**Robert Gilliland** adm[or] Deft

– **Obediah Payne** Plt
against
The Same Deft

Ordered that these suits be continued until the next Court

[page 122] **James Eastham** Complt
against On motion in Chancery to Desolve Injunction
**John Blacklidge** Deft

This day came the Parties aforesaid by their attornies, And on the motion of the said Defendant by his Council on hearing the bill answer exhibits and Sundry Depositions filed herein, and the Arguments of Council on both sides, the Court are of Opinion that said motion be Over ruled, and that the said Complainant recover his costs by him about his motion expended

– **Hugh Donigy** Plt
against
**Joseph Casky** Deft

This day came the Parties aforesaid by their attornies, and It is Ordered that this Cause be remanded to the Rule Dockette and on the motion of the said Plaintiff by his attorney, leave is granted him to amend his Declaration herein, and that the said Defendant recover his Costs &[c].

– **James Kerr** Plt
against In Case
**Andrew Evans** Deft

On the motion of the said Defendant, It is Ordered that the Judgment and writ of Inquiry awarded against him in the Clerks Office be set a side, and the said Defendant by his attorney now comes and defends the wrong and Injury when and Where &[c] and says he is not guilty in manner and form as the Plaintiff against him hath declared, and of this he puts himself upon the Country and the said Plaintiff likewise therefore It is commanded [page 123] the Sheriff that he cause to come here Immediately twelve good and lawful men by whom &[c] and thereupon came also a Jury, **Robert Smith, John Wilkerson, Jonas Irvine, David Puckett, John Cowan, McWhorter, John West, Thomas Harris, Edward Cooper, Aaron Lawson, Temple Sargent** & **Aaron Sargent** who being elected tried and Sworn the truth to speak upon the Issue Joined, after One of the Jurors, to wit, **David Puckett**, was withdrawn and the Cause is Continued until the next Court

– **Charles** Plt
against In Covenant
**Vincent Garner** Deft

Ordered that this suit be dismissed at the Defendants Costs the Deft now in Court

– **Matthew Hickson** Complt
against In Chancery
**George Taylor** &[c] Defts

This day came the Parties aforesaid by their attornies and It is Ordered that this suit be dismissed

– **Thomas Montgomery** Plt

against In Case
**John Young** Deft

On the motion of the Defendant It is Ordered that the [page 124] Judgment and Writ of Inquiry, awarded against him in the Clerks Office be set a side, and the said Defendant by his attorney now comes and defends the wrong and Injury, when and where &c. and says he is not guilty in manner and form as the Plaintiff against him hath declared and of this he puts himself upon the Country and the said Plaintiff likewise therefore It is commanded the Sheriff that he cause to come here Immediately twelve good and lawful men by whom &c. and thereupon came also a Jury to wit, **Jesse Chapple, Alexander Crawford, Gilmore Cowen, Richard Westberry, Sam[l] Combest, James Spencer, Wyatt Adkins, Samuel S[ ]ds, Christopher Claunch, David McAlister**, and **James Cary** who being elected tried and sworn the truth to speak upon the Issue Joined, upon their Oaths do say that the said Defendant is not guilty in manner and form as the Plaintiff against him hath declared. It is therefore considered by the Court that the Plaintiff take nothing by his bill but for his false clamor be in mercy &c. and that the Defendant go thereof without day and recover of the said Plaintiff his Costs by him about his defence in this behalf expended

– **Barnabus Hughes** Plt
against In Debt
**John January** Deft

On the motion of the Plaintiffs attorney It is ordered that this suit be Dismissed

[page 125] Absent **James G Hunter** Gentleman

– **Bartlette Hilliard** Plt
against In Case
**William J Sallee** Deft

This day came the Plaintiff by his attorney and the said Defendant was Solomnly called but came not, Therefore It is Commanded the Sheriff that he cause to come here Immediately twelve good and lawful men by whom &c and thereupon came Also a Jury, to wit, **Andrew Whitley, William Hunt, William Churchwell** Junr, **William Cooper, Thomas Jarvis, James Cooper, James Simpson, George Dingins, John Price, John Segewick, Micajah Cooper** and **Airs Dors** who were sworn well and truly to Inquire what Damages the Plaintiff hath sustained in the Premises upon their Oaths do say that the Plaintiff hath sustained Damages by Occasion thereof to eleven Pounds eighteen Shillings besides his Costs, It is therefore considered by the Court that the Plaintiff recover against the said Defendant his Damages aforesaid by the Jurors in their Verdict aforesaid assessed and his Costs by him about his suit in this behalf expended and the said Defendant in mercy &c.

– **David Swope** Plt
against In Debt
**Roger Oatts & Debrell** Shff Deft

This day came the Plaintiff by his attorney, and the said Defendants being Solomnly called but Came not, Therefore It is commanded the Sheriff that he cause to come here Immediately twelve good and lawful men by whom &c and thereupon came Also a Jury to wit, **Andrew Whitley, William Hunt, William Churchwell** Junr, **William Cooper** [page 126] **Thomas Jarvis, James Cooper, James Simpson, George Dungins, John Price, John Segewick, Micajah Cooper** and **Airs Dors** who were Sworn well and truly to enquire what Damage the Plaintiff hath sustained in the Premises upon their Oaths do find for the Plaintiff the Debt in the Declaration mentioned and assess the Plaintiffs Damages by Occasion of the Detension thereof to one penny, inclusive of legal Interest &c It is therefore Considered by the Court that the Plaintiff recover against the said Defendant the said Debt in the Declaration mentioned, his Damages, Interest & Costs by the Jurors in their Verdict aforesaid assessed, Note this Judgment is to be Discharged by the payment of thirty pounds with Interest thereon from the fourteenth day of October One thousand eight hundred and three until paid & Costs

– **Frederick Williams** Plt
against In Debt

**Harland Hinds** &c Defts

This day came the Plaintiff by his attorney, and the said Defendants being solemnly Called but came not, And on the motion of the said Plaintiff by his attorney, It is Ordered that the Sheriff cause to come here Immediately twelve good and lawful men by whom &c and thereupon came also a Jury to wit, **Andrew Whitley**, **William Hunt**, **William Churchwell** Junr, **William Cooper**, **Thomas Jarvis**, **James Cooper**, **James Simpson**, **George Dungins**, **John Price**, **John Segewick**, **Micajah Cooper** & **Airs Dors** who were sworn well and truly to Inquire what Damage the Plaintiff hath sustained [page 127] in the premises do find for the Plaintiff the Debt in the Declaration mentioned, and do assess his Damages by Occasion of the Detention thereof to One Cents inclusive of legal Interest besides his Costs It is therefore considered by the Court that the Plaintiff recover against the said Defendant the said Debt in the Declaration mentioned his Damages inclusive of legal Interest aforesaid, and his costs by him about his suit in this behalf expended, and the said Defendant in mercy &c. Note this Judgment is to be discharged by the payment of two hundred and twenty Dollars, with legal Interest thereon from the first day of August One thousand eight hundred and four until paid and Costs

– **Isaac Haus** Plt
against In Debt
**Henry Francis**

This day came the Plaintiff by his attorney and the said Defendant being Solomnly Called but came not Therefore On the motion of the Plaintiff It is Commanded the Sheriff that he cause to come here Immediately twelve good and lawful men by whom &c and thereupon came also a Jury, to wit, **Andrew Whitely**, **William Hunt**, **William Churchwell** Junr, **William Cooper**, **Thomas Jarvis**, **James Cooper**, **James Simpson**, **George Dungins**, **John Price**, **John Sagewick**, **Micajah Cooper** and **Airs Dors** who were sworn well and truly to Inquire what Damage the Plaintiff hath sustained in the premises upon their Oaths do find for the Plaintiff the Debt in the Declaration mentioned and do assess the Plaintiffs Damages by Occasion thereof to One Cent inclusive of legal Interest besides his Costs. It is Therefore [page 128] Considered by the court that the Plaintiff recover against the said Defendant the said debt in the Declaration mentioned together with his Damages and Interest aforesaid by the Jurors in their Verdict aforesaid assessed, and his Costs by him about his suit in this behalf expended and the said Defendant in mercy &c. Note this Judgment is to be Discharged by the payment of fifty Dollars with legal Interest thereon from the eleventh day of August One thousand eight hundred and three until paid & Costs

– Elder Grant, ie, **Samuel McKee** Plt
against In Eject
Trouble Entry Deft

By Consent **Joseph Patterson** is made a Defendant in the room of the now defendant, Trouble entry, pleads the General Issue, Confesses lease entry and Ouster in the Declaration supposed and agrees to Insist upon the title Only, at trial, and the cause is continued until the next Term of this Court, and on the motion of [page 129] the said Plaintiff by his attorney It is Ordered that the Surveyor of Pulaski County do go on the Lands in controversy, between the Parties on the day if fair if not then on the next fair day and then another Survey and lay of the same as either party would have it having regard to all Deeds and Other evidence that may be produced Report all matters of fact specially, return four fair Platts & Certificates thereof to the Clerks Office of this Circuit thirty days before the day of hearing

– Ordered that the Court be adjourned until Tomorrow morning ten OClock

**John Smith**

At a Circuit Court continued and held for the Pulaski Circuit at the Courthouse of Pulaski County in Sommerset On the 27th day of April 1805

Present the Honourable **John Smith** and **John Prather** Gentlemen

– **James Kerr** Plt
against In Case

**Andrew Evans**

Ordered that this suit be Dismissed, and that each party pay an equal Proportion of the Costs expended herein Agreeable to the Order of said Parties

– **Andrew Cowen** Complt
against In Chancery
**Tunstall Quarles** Deft

– **William Evans** Plt
against In Covenant
**John Robertson** Deft

[page 130] **Andrew Roy** Plt
against In Case
**William & Diannah Burnham** Deft

– **Jesse Burton** Plt
against In Trespass assault & Battery
**Jonathan Stephens** Deft

– **Michael Stoner** Plt
against In Case
**Jonathan Stephens** Deft

– **Joseph Casky** Plt
against In Trespass Assault & Battery
**Robert Smith** Deft

– **George W Saunders** & wife Plts
against Same
**John Griffen** Deft

– **George W Saunders** Plt
against Same
The Same Deft

– The Same Plt
against In Trespass
The Same Deft

– **John Griffin** by Governor Plts
against In Debt
**George W Saunders** Deft

Ordered that these suits be continued until the next Court

– **Tunstall Quarles** Plt
against In Debt
**Robertson Burge** Deft

This day came the Plaintiff by his attorney and on his [page 131] motion It is ordered that the Judgment and writ of Inquiry awarded against the said Defendant in the Clerks Office be waved, and on the motion of the Plaintiff It is Ordered that Judgment be granted him against the said Defendant for four hundred Pounds, the Debt in the Declaration mentioned besides his Costs, Note this Judgment is to be discharged by the payment of two hundred pounds with legal Interest thereon from the first day of November One thousand eight hundred and two until paid & Costs, But to have credit for four hundred Dollars paid on the seventh day of January One thousand eight hundred and three, Also for One hundred and eighty Dollars paid on the twenty seventh day of September One thousand eight hundred and three

– **Frederick Williams** Plt
against On motion to sustain Errors in arrest of Judgment herein &c
**Harland Hinds** &c Defts

On hearing the arguments of Council on both sides, and mature deliberation being thereon had It is Ordered by the Court that the said errors be Over ruled, and that the Plaintiff recover his Costs by him about this motion expended

– Ordered that the Court be adjourned until Court in Course

**John Smith**

[page 132] At a Circuit Court held for the Pulaski Circuit at the Courthouse of Pulaski County in Sommerset On Monday the 22nd day of July 1805

Present the Honourable **James G Hunter, John Smith**, and **John Prather** Gentlemen

– A Grand jury were sworn for the Pulaski Circuit, **John Hardgrove** Senr foreman, **David Buster, John Evans, Henry James, Jonathan Smith, William Hays, John Singleton, William Fears, Aaron Lawson, Richard Price, Thomas Stogsdal, Willis Embry, Cornelius Dulin, William Buster, Isaac Ingram, Richard Churchwell** Senr & **Benjamin Thurman**, who having received their charge retired to consider of their presents. And afterward returned into Court and having no Presentments to make were discharged by the Court

– The Commonwealth Plt
against upon an Indictment
**John Griffen** Deft

This day came as well the Attorney for the Commonwealth as the Defendant by his attorney who moved the Court to quash the Indictment herein, after hearing the Arguments of the Council on both sides It is Ordered that the said motion be Over ruled and that the said Defendant pay the costs of this motion &c

– The Commonwealth Plt
against upon an Indictment for Perjury
**Michael Stoner**, labourer Deft

who stands bound by a recognizance to appear here, on this day [page 133] Appeared according to the conditions of his recognizance, and being arraigned pleaded not guilty to the Indictment, and for his trial puts himself upon god and his Country, and the attorney for the Commonwealth likewise, whereupon came a Jury, to wit, **Samuel Caughron, William Lynch, Thomas C Sinclear, Gilmore Cowen, Linsey Hardgrove, James Davis, Johnston Sargent, Richard Churchwell** Senr, **John Beard, John Saunders, Thomas Smiley** and **Richard Beason** who being elected tried and sworn the truth to speak upon the Issue Joined and having heard the evidence and the arguments of the Counsil on both sides, Continued "till Tomorrow morning

– **Wyatt Adkins** an affrayer being brought into Court, and being heard by himself It is Ordered by the Court that he be fined five pounds for the Contempt Offered to them, and that he pay the costs &c.

– **Thomas Owsley** Plt
against In Covenant
**William Lair** Deft

Ordered that this suit be Dismissed

– **Daniel Duncan** Complt
against upon Attachment
**Allin Burton** Deft

– **William Barrow** Complt
against The Same
The Same Deft

On the motion of the Complainants by their attorney It is Ordered [page 134] that these Attachments be Dismissed

– **Nancy Thompson** Plt
against In Case
**Temple Sargent** Deft

The Defendant came into Court, and confessed Judgment herein for the Costs, (except for attornies fee, and the case Dismissed

– The Commonwealth Plt
against upon an Indictment

**Michael Stoner** Deft

The Defendant being Indicted &c and the Venire not having returned their Verdict herein, On the motion of the Defendant by his Council he is permitted to give bail for his appearance before this Court on Tomorrow, whereupon the said **Michael Stoner**, together with **Thomas Montgomery, Tunstall Quarles** Junr & **Samuel McKee** Esquires, his Securities severally acknowledged themselves Indebted to his excellency **Christ° Greenup** Esqr Governor of the Commonwealth of Kentucky in the sum of one thousand Dollars, the said **Michael Stoner** in the sum of five hundred Dollars, and his Securities, **Montgomery, Quarles**, & **McKee** in the sum of five hundred Dollars also to Discharged on the following Conditions, to wit, that he make his personal appearance as aforesaid before this Court on Tomorrow morning at [ ] OClock and not depart from there without the leave of said Court

– Ordered that the Court be adjourned until tomorrow morning eight OClock

**J G Hunter**

[page 135] At a Circuit Continued and held for the Pulaski Circuit at the Courthouse of Pulaski County in Sommerset On Tuesday the 23rd day of July 1805

Present the Honourable **James G Hunter**, & **John Prather** Gentlemen

– **Charles Hutcherson** Complt
against In Chancery
**Mashack Hicks** Deft

The referees appointed in this Cause, returned into Court their award in the words and figures following, to wit, Agreeable to an order of the worshipful Court for the Pulaski Circuit appoint **William Jennings, James Thompson, & Benjamin Letcher** or any two of them to settle by way of Arbitration a certain matter of Controversy now depending and undetermined in said Court wherein **Laurence Hutcherson** is Complt and **Meshick Hicks** is Defendant, being first duly sworn, and then hearing the Parties, and their evidence, we do finally Order and determine in manner and form following (viz), that **Mashick Hicks** pay **Laurence Hutcherson** twenty Dollars and all legal Cost that has accrued in the prosecution of the said Suit Or that may accrue to the and of said Controversy in Testimony whereof we have hereunto set Our hands and seals the 22nd day of June 1805

**W Jinnings**
**Benj Letcher**

To three Arbitrators attendg One day at 9/ each pr day

The Parties aforesaid by their attornies being now in Court [page 136] & On the motion of the Complainant by his attorney, the said Award is made the Judgment of the Court, Note this Judgment is to have credit for nine shillings

– **Andrew Cowen** Complt
against In Chancery
**Tunstall Quarles** Deft

Ordered that this suit be Continued

– Present **John Smith** Esqr

– The Commonwealth Plt
against upon an Indictment
**John Griffin** Deft

This day came as well the attorney for the Commonwealth as the said Defendant by his attorney, The Deft by his attorney comes and defends the wrong and Injury when and where &c and crys Oyer of the Indictment exhibited against him which reads in the words and figures following, to wit, State of Kentucky &c and says the Pltf her prosecution aforesaid Ought not to have and maintain because he saith that the Indictment and the matter and things therein contained are insufficient in law to support the same and that he has no necessity to answer thereto neither is he bound by the law of the land to answer thereto and this he is ready to verify, and Demurs thereto, and agreeable to the Act of Assembly in such cases made and provided sets down the following causes of Demurer, to wit, 1st that it does not appear as it Ought in the Indictment that the Jurors were Housekeepers and residents in the Jurisdiction of the Circuit Court [page 137] of Pulaski and Wayne, or that they were of the body of the Circuit of Pulaski & Wayne 2 that it does not appear from the Indictment that there were a sufficient number of Grand jurors to present an Offense of the kind presented in the Indictment 3 that it does not appear upon what day and year the Indictment was Issued by the Grand Jury (4) that it does not appear when the Indictment was found (5) that it does not appear upon the face of the Indictment, that the person upon whom the assault is said to have been Committed, was in the pase [?] of the Commonwealth, 6, that the Indictment does not onclude against the peace and dignity of the Commonwealth of Kentucky 7 that the Indictment is altogether insufficient, informal and uncertain &c that it does not appear that the Indictment was taken before a Court of Competent Jurisdiction for the trial of Offences of the kind presented

**Davis Owsley** & Deft

and the Commonwealth by her Attorney says that for any thing set forth in the Defts Demurer, she Ought not to be bard or Precluded from supporting her Indictment aft him because she says that the matters and things set forth in the Indictment is sufficient in law to have and maintain her sd Indictment wherefore she prays Judgment

**Mills**

The matters of law arrising upon the Defendants Demurer and the Plaintiffs Indictment, being argued It is considered by the Court that the Demurer aforesaid and the matter therein Contained are not Sufficient in law to bar the [page 138] Commonwealth from having and maintaining her Action aforesaid against the said Defendant, It is therefore Ordered that the said Demurer be Over ruled with Costs &c and on the motion of the said Defendant by his attorney leave is given him put in a Plea herein, And the said Defendant by his attorney now comes and defends the wrong and Injury when and where &c and says he is not guilty in manner and form as the attorney for the Commonwealth in the Indictment against him hath declared and of this he puteth himself upon the Country, and the Attorney for the Commonwealth likewise, Therefore it is Commanded the Sheriff that he cause to come here Immediately twelve good and lawful men by whom &c and thereupon came also a Jury to wit, **George McWhorter**, **Robert Smith**, **Robert Smith** Cons, **John Debrell**, **Elisha Franklin**, **John Baker**, **Charles Debrell**, **Amos Hannon**, **John Bustle**, **Abner McWhorter**, **John Chesney** & **Lambert White** who being elected tried and sworn the truth to speak upon the Issue Joined upon their Oaths do say that the said Defendant is guilty in manner and form as the attorney for the Commonwealth in the Indictment against him hath declared. and they do assess the Commonwealths Damages by Occasion thereof to twelve Dollars and fifty cents besides Costs It is therefore Considered by the Court that the said Defendant make his fine to the Commonwealth by paying the Damages aforesaid by the Jurors in their Verdict aforesaid assessed and the Costs of this Prosecution and may be taken &c.

[page 139] **Hugh Caldwell** Plt
against In Chancery
**Franklin** & **Beard** Defts

This day came the Parties aforesaid by their attornies, and on the motion of the said Defendants, leave is granted them to file their answer, and the cause is remanded to the Rule Docket

– Commonwealth Plt
against upon an Indictment
**Isaac Mayfield** Deft

This day came as well the attorney for the Commonwealth as the said Defendant in his proper person, who acknowledges Judgment for the Costs in this Case, and for reasons appearing to the Court It is Ordered that this Indictment be Dismissed and the said Deft pay the Costs &c

– **John Weirs** admor Plt
against In Case 2nd Case
**Nathaniel Forbis** Deft

Ordered that this suit be Continued until the next Court

– **Elizabeth Sharp** Plt
against In Chancery
**Michael Stoner** Deft
– **Michael Stoner** Plt
against In Case
**William Sharp** Deft

Ordered that these suits be Dismissed It being agreed

[page 140] **William Buford** Plt
against In Case
**Charles Debrell** Shff of Wayne County Deft

On the motion of the Defendant it is Ordered that the Judgment and writ of Inquiry awarded against him in the clerks Office be set a side and the said Defendant by his attornies now comes and defends the wrong and Injury and where &c, and says he is not guilty in manner and form as the Plaintiff against him hath declared, and of this he puts himself upon the Country and the said Plaintiff likewise. Therefore it is commanded the Sheriff that he cause to come here Immediately twelve good and lawful men by whom &c and thereupon came also a Jury, to wit, **John Tumbleson, Charles Neal, Martin Barrier, Micajah Hogan, John Cowan, William Ussery, Nicholas Jasper** Junr, **Arch$^d$ Rainey, Richard Harris, Jonas Irvine, Thomas Simpson** & **Thomas Castelow**, who being elected tried and sworn the truth to speak upon the Issue Joined, the Plaintiff being Solomnly Called but came not, neither is his suit further prosecuted, Therefore on the motion of the Defendant, It is considered by the Court, that the Jury from rendering any Verdict herein be discharged, and that the Plaintiff be nonsuited together with his Pledges &c. and that the said Defendant go hence without day and recover of the said Plaintiff his Costs by him about his defence in this behalf expended

[page 141] The Commonwealth Plt
against upon an Indictment
**Michael Stoner** Deft

The Jurors Sworn herein & Continued yesterday, returned into Court and upon their Oaths do say that the said **Michael Stoner** is not guilty of the Perjury aforesaid as in pleading he hath alledged, and proclamation being made at the Door of the Courthouse, and nothing further appearing, Or being alledged against him, It is therefore Considered by the Court that he be Acquitted of the Perjury aforesaid and go thereof without day & recover his Costs &c against the Prosecutor

– Ordered that the Court be adjourned until tomorrow morning nine OClock

**J G Hunter**

At a Circuit Court Continued and held for the Pulaski Circuit, at the Courthouse of Pulaski County in Sommerset On Wednesday the 24th day of July 1805

Present the Honourable **James G Hunter**, **John Smith**, and **John Prather** Gentlemen

– On the motion of **Roger Oatts** for an Injunction to stay all further proceedings on a Judgment Obtained against him at Common Law by **David Swope**, in this Court, he having first filed his Bill and made Oath to the same as the law directs, It is Ordered that an Injunction Issue, to said **Oatts** staying all further proceedings On seventy Dollars of said Judgment whereupon the said **Oatts** acknowledges bond with **Nicholas Jasper** his Security conditioned as the law directs

[page 142] **John Rogers** Plt
against In Case
**John McWhorter** Deft

On the motion of the Defendant by his attorney It is Ordered that the appearance bail bond taken herein by the Sheriff is Ordered to be quashed, and leave given the said Defendant to enter a common appearance without entering Special Bail

– **John Green** Plt
against In Debt

**William Evans** Deft

Ordered that this suit be Dismissed at the Defendants Cost the Parties Present

– **John Evans** Plt
against In Covenant
**John Collier** &c Deft

Ordered that this suit be continued until the next Term at the Defendants Costs

– **James Eastham** Complt
against In Chancery
**John Blacklidge** Deft

This day came the Parties aforesaid by their attornies, and On the motion of the Complainant leave is given to amend his Bill herein, and by Consent the motion to Disolve the Injunction Obtained &c Continued "till the next Term of this Court

[page 143] **Obediah Paine** Plt
against In Case
**Robert Gillilands** admor & adminx Deft

Ordered that this suit be Continued until the next Court at the Plaintiffs Costs And on the motion of the Plaintiff by his attorney, an attachment is award him against **Jacob Grindstaff**, of Knox County to appear here on the second day of the next Term of this Court to show Cause if any he can why he shall not be find for a Contempt Offered them in failing to attend as a Witness in this Case at this Term, agreeable to a Summons Executed upon him &c

– **William Barnett** & **John Adair** Complt
against In Chancery
**William Crawford** & **William Fox** Defts

This day came the Parties aforesaid by their attornies, and on the motion of the complainants by their Council It is Ordered that the Office Dismission taken herein be set a side and the Cause is remanded to the rule Docket. And on the motion of the Defendants by their Counsil to discharge a former Order of this Court & Bond restraining the Defendant **Fox** from paying away the money effects &c of the property of the said Deft **Crawford**, which is now in his hands of the property of the said **Crawford**, Continued "till Tomorrow morning

– **Henry Grindstaff** Plt
against In Case
**Robert Gilliland** admor & adminx Deft

This day came the Parties aforesaid by their attornies, and thereupon [page 144] came also a Jury, to wit, **Thomas Casteloe, Joseph Rainey, John Loveless, Lewis Singleton, Christo Clonch, Joseph Porter, William Ussery, John Griffin, Thomas Burk, William Ussery** Senr, **John Jasper** and **Joseph Erwin**, who being elected tried and sworn the truth to speak upon the Issue Joined, The Plaintiff being Solemnly Call'd but came not, neither is his suit further prosecuted. Therefore on the motion of the said Defendants by their attornies It is Considered by the Court that the Jury from rendering any Verdict herein be discharged and that the Plaintiff be nonsuited together with his pledges &c and the said Defendants go hence without day and recover of the said Plaintiff their costs by them about their defence in this behalf expended

– **Joseph Caskey** Plt
against In Case
**John January** Deft

Ordered that this suit be Continued until the next Court at the Defendants Costs

– **Joseph Corler** Assee Plt
against In Debt
**Robertson Burge** Deft

– **John Hiatt** Assee Plt
against In Debt
The Same Deft

**John Newby**, came into Court and undertook for the said Defendant that if he shall be cast in the Actions aforesaid that he shall satisfy and pay the condemnation of the Court Or render his body to Prison in execution for the same Or on falure [page 145] thereof that he the said **John Newby** shall do it for him

– **Joseph McDonald** Plt
against In Covenant
**Hamlet Thomas** Deft

John Smith, came into Court and undertook for the said Defendant that if he shall be cast in the action aforesaid that he shall satisfy and pay the condemnation of the Court, Or render his body to Prison in Execution for the same, Or on falure thereof that he the said **John Smith** shall do it for him,

– **Kizziah Chapple** &c Plt
against In Case
**William Burton** Deft

By Consent of parties all matters in difference between them respecting this suit is refered to the arbitration and determination of **William Owens, John Jasper, William Lynch, Israel Hart, Robert Smith** & **William Hill** whose award or the award of any three of them shall be the Judgment of the Court, and the same is Ordered accordingly

– **Kizziah Chapple** &c Plt
against In Case
**Jesse Burton** Deft

This day came the Parties aforesaid by their attornies, and the said Defendant came into Court, and made Oath that he had never Spoken any thing Slanderous of the character of the said **Kizziah Chapple**, It is therefore agreed between the Parties that this suit be Dismissed

[page 146] **Holkum Robertson** Complt
against upon Attachment
**George Etherington** Deft

This day came the Plaintiff by his attorney, and the said Defendant being Solemnly Called but came not, On the motion of the Plaintiff by his attorney It is Considered by the Court that the Plaintiff recover against the said Defendant twenty Dollars and his costs by him about this attachment expended, and the said Defendant in mercy &c & Order of Sale as to the Attach'd effects in the hand of the Garnishee

– **John Weirs** admor Plt
against In Case
**Nathaniel Forbis** Deft

This day came the Plaintiff by his attorney, and the said Defendant being Solemnly Called but came not Therefore on the motion of the Plaintiff It is Commanded the Sheriff that he cause to come here Immediately twelve good and lawful men by whom &c and thereupon came also a Jury to wit, **Robert Smith, James P Burton, Reubin Bundy, Joseph Porter, Andrew Evans, William Price, Lewis Singleton, John Griffin, John Scrimiger, John Black, Thomas Banks** & **James Campbell**, who were sworn well and truly to enquire what Damage the Plaintiff hath sustained in the premises upon their Oaths do say that the Plaintiff hath sustained Damage by Occasion thereof to ten pounds, two Shillings, and six pence besides his Costs It is therefore Considered by the Court that the Plaintiff recover against the said Defendant his Damage [page 147] aforesaid by the Jurors in their Verdict aforesaid assessed and his Costs by him about his suit in this behalf expended, and the said Defendant in mercy &c.

– **Michael Stoner** Plt
against In Case
**Jonathan Stephens** Deft

This day came the Plaintiff by his attorney, and the Defendant being Solomnly Called, came into Court and acknowledged himself indebted to the Plaintiff for six pounds eighteen Shillings, Therefore with assent of the Plaintiff It is Considered by the Court that the Plaintiff recover against the said Defendant the sum acknowledged as aforesaid and his Costs by him about his suit in this behalf expended and the said Defendant in mercy &c. Note this Judgment is to bare legal Interest from the twenty third day of July One thousand eight hundred and three until paid & Costs

– **Francis Stephens** Plt
against In Case
**Burdin & Barns** Deft

By Consent of Parties all matters in difference between them respecting this suit is refered to the arbitration, and determination of **John Smith, Samuel Gilmore**, and **Drewry Elkins**, whose award, or the award of any two of them be the Judgment of the Court and the same is Ordered Accordingly

– **Samuel Cole** Plt
against In Case
**Cornelius Dabs** Deft

Ordered that this suit be Continued until the next Court

[page 148] **William Evans** Plt
against In Covenant
**John Robertson** Deft

Ordered that this suit be continued until the next Court at the Defendants Cost

– **Joseph Caskey** Plt
against In Trespass assault and Battery
**Robert Smith** Deft

On the motion of the Defendant. It is ordered that the Judgment and writ of Inquiry awarded against him in the Clerks Office be set a side and the said Defendant by his attorney now comes and defends the wrong and Injury when and where &c. and says if he did assault the Plaintiff it was Occasioned by the Plaintiff giving the first assault and this he prays may be enquired of by the Country and the said Plaintiff likewise, Therefore let a Jury come here &c. and the cause is Continued until the next Court

– **Jesse Burton** Plt
against In Trespass Assault & Battery
**Jonathan Stephens** Deft

On the motion of the Defendant. It is Ordered that the Judgment and Writ of Inquiry awarded against him in the Clerks Office be set a side, and the said Defendant by his attorney now Comes & defends the wrong and Injury when and where &c. and says he is not guilty in manner and form as the Plaintiff against him hath declared, and of this he puteth himself upon the Country and the said Plaintiff likewise, And the said Defendant for further plea herein says that if he did assault the [page 149] Plaintiff It was Occasioned by the Plaintiffs giving the first assault. and of this he also puts himself upon the Country and the said Plaintiff likewise, Therefore It is commanded the Sheriff that he cause to come here Immediately twelve good and lawful men by whom &c. and thereupon came also a Jury, to wit, **William Hail, George Dungins, John Hardgrove** Senr, **Aaron Sargent, Robert Smith, William McCoy, John Smith, Benjamin Long, David Pucket, Jonathan Smith, Andrew Evans** and **John Blacklidge** who being elected tried and sworn the truth to speak upon the Issue Joined upon their Oaths do say that the said Defendant is guilty in manner and form as the Plaintiff against him hath declared, and they do assess the Plaintiffs Damages by Occasion thereof to eighteen shillings besides his Costs It is therefore Considered by the Court that the Plaintiff recover against the said Defendant his Damages aforesaid by the Jurors in their Verdict aforesaid assessed, and his Costs by him about his suit in this behalf expended, and the said Defendant may be taken &c.

– Ordered that the Court be adjourned until Tomorrow morning ten OClock

**J G Hunter**

At a Circuit Court Continued and held for the Pulaski Circuit at the Courthouse of Pulaski County in Sommerset on Thursday the 25th day of July 1805

Present the Honourable **James G Hunter** & **John Smith** Gent

[page 150] **Hugh Donigy** Plt
against In Covenant
**Joseph Caskey** Deft
– **Andrew Roy** Plt
against In Case
**W^m & Dianah Burnham** Deft
Ordered that these suits be Continued until the next Court
– **Alexander Hambleton** Plt
against In Case
**Samuel Monday** Deft
Ordered that this suit be Discontinued
– **Nicholas Jasper** & Al^s Complt
against In Chancery
**Tunstall Quarles** Deft

This day came the Parties aforesaid, by their attornies, and this cause being argued at the last Term of this Court, and the Court having arrived of an Concerning the Premises, and being divided, and unable to give an Opinion, It is Considered by the Court, that questions of Law now and default do arise in this Cause do therefore Order, that the said Cause be adjourned to the General Court for trial &^c.

– Present the Honourable **John Prather** Gent
– Ordered that **Peter Fuller** be find five Dollars. and be imprisoned four hours, for a Contempt offered to this Court. on this day and that he pay Costs &^c.
[page 151] **James Skidmore** Complt
against In Chancery
**Francis Stephens** Deft
This day came the Complainant by his Counsil and files his amended Bill herein
– **George W Saunders** & wife Plts
against In Trespass Assault & Battery
**John Griffin** Deft

On the motion of the Defendants It is ordered that the Judgment and Writ of Inquiry awarded against them in the Clerks Office be set a side and the said Defendants by their attorney now comes and defends the wrong and Injury when and where &^c. and says he is not guilty in manner and form as the Plaintiff against him hath declared and of this he puteth himself upon the Country, and the said Plaintiff likewise, And the said Defendant for further plea herein says that if he did assault the Plaintiffs It was Occasioned by the Plaintiffs giving the first Assault. and the said Plaintiffs say that the assault was not Occasioned by them as in pleading the Defendant hath alledged, and this, they pray may be enquired of by the Country. and the said Defendant likewise, Therefore let a Jury Come here &^c. and the cause is Continued until the next Court.

– **George W Saunders** Plt
against In Trespass assault & Battery
**John Griffin** Deft

On the motion of the Defendant It is Ordered that [page 152] the Judgment and Writ of Inquiry awarded against him in the Clerks Office be set a side and the said Defendant by his Attorney now comes and defends the wrong and Injury when and where &^c. and says he is not guilty in manner and form as the Plaintiff against him hath declared, and of this he puts himself upon the Country. and the said Plaintiff likewise, And the said Defendant for further plea herein says that if he did assault the Plaintiff It was Occasioned by the Plaintiffs giving the first assault. and the said Plaintiff by his attorney says It was not by his the said Plaintiffs giving the first assault, and this he prays may be enquired of by the Country and the said Defendant likewise, Therefore let a Jury come here &^c and this Cause is Continued until the next Court.

– **George W Saunders** Plt
against In Trespass

**John Griffin** Deft

On the motion of the said Defendant. It is ordered that the Judgment and Writ of Inquiry awarded against him in the Clerks Office be set a side, and the said Defendant by his attorney now comes and defends the wrong and Injury when and where &c. and says he is not guilty in manner and form as the Plaintiff against him hath declared and of this he puts himself upon the Country and the said Plaintiff likewise. Therefore let a Jury come here &c. and the cause is Continued until the next Court

[page 153] **John Griffin** &c Plt
against In Debt
**George W Saunders** Deft

On the motion of the defendant. It is Ordered that the Judgment and Writ of Inquiry awarded against him in the clerks Office be set aside and the said Defendant by his attorney now comes and defends the wrong and Injury when and where &c. and says he Oweth nothing of the Debt in the declaration mentioned in manner and form as the Plaintiff against him hath declared. And of this he puteth himself upon the Country, and the said Plaintiff likewise, Therefore let a Jury come here &c. and the cause is Continued until the next Court at the Defendants Costs

– **Barnabus Hughes** Plt
against In Debt
**William J Sallee** Deft

This day came as well the Plaintiff by his attorney as the said Defendant in his proper person, who says he cannot gainsay the Plaintiffs Action against him for One hundred and seventeen Dollars and twenty five cents the Debt in the Declaration mentioned. Therefore with assent of the Plaintiff It is considered by the Court that the Plaintiff recover against the said Defendant the said one hundred Seventeen Dollars and twenty five cents the Debt in the Declaration aforesaid mentioned and his costs by him about his suit in this behalf expended and the said Defendant in mercy, Note this Judgment is to bare legal Interest from the nineteenth day of May One thousand eight hundred and five until paid & costs, But to have credit for sixty six Dollars paid on the thirty first day of August One thousand eight hundred and four

[page 154] **James Birney** Plt
against In Debt
**William J Sallee** Deft

This day came the Parties aforesaid by their attornies, and the said Defendant saith he cannot gainsay the Plaintiffs action against him for the Debt in the Declaration mentioned, therefore with assent of the Plaintiff It is considered by the Court that the Plaintiff recover against the said Defendant the Debt in the declaration mentioned, and his Costs. by him about his suit in this behalf expended. and the said Defendant in mercy &c.

Note this Judgment is to be discharged by the payment of twenty seven pounds, thirteen shillings, with legal Interest thereon from the first day of April one thousand eight hundred and four until paid & Costs

– **John Griffin** Plt
against In Trespass assault & Battery
**George W Saunders** & wife Defts

On the motion of the Defendants It is ordered that the Judgment and Writ of Inquiry awarded against them in the Clerks Office be set a side and the said Defendants by their attorney now come and defend the wrong and Injury when and where &c and say that they are not guilty in manner and form as the Plaintiff against them hath declared and this they pray may be Inquired of by the Country and the said Plaintiff likewise, And the said Defendants by their attornies for further plea herein say, that if they did make an assault upon the Plaintiff It was Occasioned by the Plaintiffs making the first assault. And the said Plaintiff by his attorney says that the Assault aforesaid was not first Occasioned by him [page 155] and of this he puteth himself upon the country and the said Defendants likewise, Therefore let a Jury Come here &c and the Cause is Continued until the next Court at the Defendants Costs

– **Nicholas Jasper, John Jasper** & **Andrew Jasper** Complts
against In Chancery
**Tunstall Quarles** Deft

Whereas from a disagreement amongst the Judges of the Court, no decree Could be pronounced, and the case being now respecting land & new & difficult & being about to be adjourned by the Court to the General Court, which in the Opinion of the Complainant & their Counsil would lend unnecessary to the accumulation of Costs & perhaps delay, do agree that their Bill may be by the Order of the Court be dismissed for the Purpose of bringing the Case directly before the Court of Appeals upon an appeal to be by the Complainant now taken, it being fully understood that no advantage is to be taken of their agreement to a dismission: therefore pursuant to the argument aforesaid, & for the purpose of record it is decreed & ordered, that the Injunction herein to Disolved and that the Defendant take the benefit of the Judgment at Common law and that the defendant herein recover his Costs expended in this suit
* [see below]

– **George W Saunders** Plt
against
**John Griffin** Deft

On the motion of the Plaintiff by his attorney an attachment is awarded him against **John French** returnable here on the third day of the next Term of this Court to show cause if any [page 156] he can why he shall not be fined for a contempt Offered to this Court by failing to attend as a Witness herein at this present Term

– **James Arbuckle** Plt
against In Case
**Samuel Kitchens** Deft

The referrees appointed in this cause returned into Court their award in the word and figures following, to wit, we the arbitrators appointed by the above Order are of opinion from the Testimony to us delivered that the plaintiff hath a Just Cause of Action, that the Deft pay the Plaintiff twenty Dollars and the legal Costs agreeable to law Given under our hands & Seals at Cap[n] **John Griffins** this 20[th] of May 1805

**John James**
**Ralph Williams**
**John Smith**
**Drewry Lee**
**Reubin Stringer**

And the same is Ordered to be the Judgment of the Court

– **John Burdit** Plt
against In Case
**Jesse Richardson** Deft

On the motion of the Defendant It is Ordered that the Judgment and writ of Inquiry awarded against him in the Clerks Office is Ordered to be set a side, and the said Defendant by his attorney now comes and defends the wrong and Injury when and where &[c]. and says he is not guilty in manner and form as the Plaintiff against him hath declared, and of this he [page 157] puts himself upon the Country and the said Plaintiff likewise, therefore let a Jury come here &[c]. and the Cause is continued until the next Court

– **Charles Inglish** & **Thomas Clark** Plts
against In Case
**Thomas McGuire** & **Thomas Jacobs** Defts

On the motion of the Defendants It is Ordered that the Judgment and writ of Inquiry awarded against him in the Clerks Office be set a side. and the said Defendants by their attornies now comes and defends the wrong and Injury when and where &[c]. and says they did not assume upon themselves in manner and form as the Plaintiff against them hath declared, and of this they puteth themselves upon the Country and the said Plaintiffs likewise, therefore It is Commanded the

Sheriff that he cause to come here immediately twelve good and lawful men by whom &c and thereupon came also a Jury, to wit, **Solomon Albert, James Johnson, Early Albertson, David Smith, John Fitzgerald, Ephraim Harris, Lambert White, Daniel Matthews, John Green, Thomas Banks, David McWhorter** and **Benjamin Long**, who being elected tried and sworn the truth to speak upon the Issue Joined upon their Oaths do say that the said Defendants did assume upon themselves in manner and form as the Plaintiffs against them hath declared and they do assess the Plaintiffs Damages Occasion thereof to six Pounds, one shilling and seven pence besides his Costs. It is Therefore Considered by the Court that the Plaintiffs recover against the said Defendants their Damages aforesaid by the Jurors in their Verdict aforesaid assessed and their Costs by them about their suit in this behalf [page 158] expended and the said Defendant in mercy &c.
* [see above] And on the prayer of the Complainant, and appeal is granted them to the Court of Appeals, on their entering into Bond in the Clerks Office within twenty Days with **John Hardgrove** Senr their Security in the Penalty of two hundred Dollars Conditioned as the law directs

– **Robertson Burge** Plt
against In Case
**David Clark** Deft

On the motion of the Defendant It is Ordered that the Judgment and Writ of Inquiry awarded against him in the Clerks Office be set a side and the said Defendant by his attorney now comes and defends the wrong and Injury when and where &c and saith that he is not guilty in manner and form as the Plaintiff against him hath declared, and of this he puteth himself upon the Country, and the said Plaintiff likewise, therefore let a Jury come here &c. and the cause is Continued until the next Court

– Ordered that **Arch[d] Rainey** be fined, ten Dollars, and be Imprisoned until Tomorrow morning nine OClock for a Contempt Offered to this Court. and that he pay the Costs. and may be taken &c

– **Edward Flowers** Plt
against In Covenant
**Henry Francis** Deft

Ordered that this suit be Discontinued at the Defendants costs excepting an attornies fee [page 159] Ordered that **Archabald Rainey** be fined ten Dollars and be Imprisoned until Tomorrow Evening Seven OClock, for a contempt offered to this Court, and that he pay the Costs and may be taken &c, for abusing **John Daniel** one of the Deputy Shffs of this County

– **Obediah Denham** Plt
against In Case
**John Cundiff** Deft

On the motion of the Defendant. It is Ordered that the Judgment and Writ of Inquiry awarded against him in the Clerks Office be set a side, and the said Defendant by his attorney now comes and defends the wrong and Injury when and where &c. and says he did not assume upon himself in manner and form as the Plaintiff against him hath declared, and of this he puteth himself upon the Country and the said Plaintiff likewise, Therefore let a Jury Come here &c. and the cause is Continued until the next Court

– Ordered that **Peter Fuller**, be fined ten Dollars and be Imprisoned until Tomorrow morning nine OClock, for a Contempt Offered to this Court, and that he pay the Costs and may be taken &c.

– **John Christian** Plt
against In Case
**Robertson Burge** Deft

This day came as well the Plaintiff by his attorney as the said Defendant in his proper person, who says he cannot gainsay the Plaintiffs action against him for twenty Dollars [page 160] It is therefore with Assent of the Plaintiffs Attorney considered by the Court that the Plaintiff recover against the said Defendant twenty Dollars, the sum acknowledged as aforesaid and his Costs by hm about his suit in this behalf expended, and the said Defendant in mercy &c.

– **Balzar Detrick** Plt
against In Covenant

**Andrew Russell** & **John Mills** Deft

This day came the Plaintiff by his attorney as the Defendant **Russell** in his proper person, who says he cannot gainsay the Plaintiffs action against him for thirty nine Pounds, therefore with assent of the Plaintiffs attorney It is Considered by the Court that the Plaintiff recover against the said Defendant the said thirty nine Pounds, the sum confessed as aforesaid. and his Costs by him about his suit in this behalf expended and the said Defendant in mercy &c

– Ordered that **Archabald Rainey**, now in Jail, be tied or confined by the Jailer, for his disorderly behaviour in said Jail towards **Peter Fuller**, who is also Imprisoned, in that way that will prevent him the said **Rainey** from abusing said **Fuller**

– **William Barnett** &c Complt
against In Chancery
**William Crawford** &c Deft

This day came the parties aforesaid by their attornies and the Defendants by their counsil moved the Court to discharge the Order restraining the [ ] in the hands of the [page 161] Defendant **Fox**, from paying away &c being argued the Court took time to consider thereof

– Ordered that the Court be adjourned until Tomorrow morning six OClock, The preciding Judge being not present the minutes of these proceedings were signed

**John Smith**

At a Circuit Court continued and held for the Pulaski Circuit in Sommerset On Friday the 26th day of July 1805

Present the Honourable **James G Hunter**, **John Smith** and **John Prather** Gentlemen

– **Charles Inglish**, & **Thomas Clark** Plt
against In Case
**Thomas McGuire** & **Thomas Jacobs** Defts

On the motion of the Defendants for to obtain a new trial on the Verdict of the Jury and Judgment Obtained herein yesterday after hearing the arguments of Counsil on both sides and mature deliberation being thereon had, It is Ordered that the said Motion be Over ruled. and that the said Defendants pay the costs of the motion &c.

– **Charles Warren** Plt
against In Debt
**William Ussery** Deft

This day came as well the Plaintiff by his attorney, as the said Defendant in his proper person, who says he cannot gainsay the Plaintiffs Action against him for thirty Dollars, the Debt in the declaration mentioned, Therefore with assent of the Plaintiff It is considered by the Court that the Plaintiff [page 162] recover against the said Defendant the said Debt in the Declaration mentioned, and his Costs by him about his suit in this behalf expended and the said Defendant in Mercy &c. Note this Judgment is to bare legal Interest thereon from the nineteenth day of September one thousand eight hundred and four until paid and Costs But to have credit for ten Shillings and six pence

– **Balzar Detrick** Plt
against In Covenant
**William Ussery** Deft

This day came as well the Plaintiff by his attorney as the said Defendant in his proper person who says he cannot gainsay the Plaintiffs action against him for six pounds, three shillings, and seven pence therefore with assent of the Plaintiff It is Considered by the Court that the Plaintiff recover against the said Defendant the sd Debt in the Declaration mentioned and his costs by him about his suit in this behalf expended and the said Defendant in Mercy &c.

– **William Fox** Plt
against In Covenant
**William Ussery** Deft

This day came as well the Plaintiff by his attorney as the Defendant in his proper person, who says he cannot gainsay the Plaintiffs action against him for twenty Dollars. Therefore with assent of the Plaintiff It is Considered by the Court that the Plaintiff recover against the said Defendant the sum Acknowledged as aforesaid and his Costs by him about his [page 162] Suit in this behalf expended, and the said Defendant in mercy &c. Note execution to be stayed three months

– **Frederick Troxell** Complt
against In Chancery
**William Burton** Deft

This day came the Parties aforesaid by their attornies, and the motion of the said Defendant by his attorney to Disolve the Complainants Injunction herein, Continued until the second day of the next Term of this Court.

– **William Williams** Plt
against In Case
**Henry Willis** Deft

On the motion of the Defendant It is ordered that the Judgment and Writ of Inquiry awarded against him in the Clerks Office be set a side, and the said Defendant by his attorney now comes and defends the Wrong and Injury when and where &c and says he is not guilty in manner and form as the Plaintiff against him hath declared and this he prays may be inquired of by the Country and the said Plaintiff likewise therefore let a Jury come here &c and the Cause is Continued until the next Court

– **David Waddle** Plt
against In Debt
**Frederick Troxell** Deft

This day come the Plaintiff by his attorney and the said Deft in his proper person who acknowledges the Plaintiffs action against him for twenty Dollars. Therefore with assent of the Plaintiff It is Considered by the Court that the Plaintiff recover against the said Defendant the said twenty Dollars, and his Costs by him about [page 164] his suit in this behalf expended and the said Defendant in mercy &c. Note this Judgment is to bare legal Interest from the fifteenth day of March one thousand eight hundred and five until paid & Costs

– **William Churchwell** Plt
against In Debt
**Micajah Hogan** Deft

This day came as well the Plaintiff by his attorney as the said Defendant in his proper person who says he cannot gainsay the Plaintiffs action against him for Seventy Dollars the Debt in the Declaration mentioned, Therefore with assent of the Plaintiff It is Considered by the Court that the Plaintiff recover against the said Defendant the said Debt in the Declaration mentioned and his Costs by him about his suit in this behalf expended and the said Defendant in mercy &c. Note this Judgment is to bare legal Interest thereon from the twenty fifth day of December One thousand eight hundred and three until paid & Costs

– **William Barnett & John Adair** Complts
against In Chancery
**William Crawford & William Fox** Defts

On the motion of the complainants leave is given them to amend their bill herein, and by consent of Parties by their attornies this cause is to be removed to the Garrard Circuit Court and said Garrard Circuit Court is by consent of parties to have and possess the same Jurisdiction as if the said suit had [page 165] Originated in the said Garrard Court

– **Reubin Smith** Plt
against In Debt
**Benjamin Cundiff** Deft

This day came the Plaintiff by his attorney, and the Defendant being Solomnly Called but came not, Therefore On the motion of the Plaintiff by his attorney It is Ordered that the Judgment and Writ of Inquiry awarded against the said Defendant in the Clerks Office be waved. And It is

Ordered that the Plaintiff recover against the said Defendant six pounds sixteen shillings and six pence the Debt in the Declaration - and his Costs by him about his suit in this behalf expended and the said Defendant in mercy &c. Note this Judgment is to bare legal Interest from the seventh day of August One thousand eight hundred and four until paid & costs

– **William Simpson** Ass^ee of **W^m Worley** Plt
against In Debt
**James Alderson** Deft

This day came the Plaintiff by his attorney, and the Defendant being Solemnly Called but Came not. Therefore on the motion of the said Plaintiff by his attorney It is Or^d that the Judgment and Writ of Inquiry awarded against the Defendant in the Clerks Office be waved, and on the motion of the Plaintiff Judgment is granted him against the said Defendant for thirty Dollars the Debt in the Declaration mentioned and his Costs by him about his suit in this behalf expended and the said Defendant [page 166] mercy &c. Note this Judgment is to bare legal interest from the twenty fifth day of December One thousand eight hundred and four until paid & Costs

– **William Simpson** Ass^ee of **Andrew Russell** Plt
against In Debt
**James Alderson** Deft

This day came the Plaintiff by his attorney, and the said Defendant being solemnly Called but came not, therefore It is Commanded the Sheriff that he cause to come here Immediately twelve good and lawful men by whom &c. and thereupon came also a Jury, to wit, **Fortunatus Dodson, Stephen English, William Hays, William Evans, John D Young, George W Saunders, Robert G Foster, Joseph Porter, Nathaniel Black, John Decker, Henry Hardister**, and **Andrew Cowen**, who were sworn well and truly to enquire what damage the Plaintiff hath sustained in the premises, upon their Oaths do say that the Plaintiff hath sustained Damages by Occasion thereof to two dollars and thirty nine cents and find for the plaintiff the Debt in the Declaration mentioned, besides his costs It is therefore Considered by the Court that the Plaintiff recover against the said Defendant twenty five Dollars, the s^d Debt in the Declaration mentioned his Damages aforesaid by the Jurors in their Verdict aforesaid assessed and his Costs by him about his suit in this behalf expended and the said Defendant in mercy &c.

[page 167] **Philip A Sublette** Ass^ee Plt
against In Covenant
**Campbell & Snelgrove** Defts

This day came the Plaintiff by his Attorney, and the said Defendants being Solemnly Called but came not. Therefore the sheriff is Commanded to cause to come here Immediately twelve good and lawful men by whom &c. and thereupon Came also a Jury to wit, **Fortunatus Dodson, Stephen English, William Hays, W^m Evans, John D Young, George W Saunders, Robert G Foster, Joseph Porter, Nathaniel Black, John Decker, Henry Hardister**, and **Andrew Cowen**, who were sworn well and truly to enquire what Damage the Plaintiff hath sustained in the premises upon their Oaths do say that the Plaintiff hath sustained Damage by Occasion thereof to twelve pounds, twelve shillings besides his Costs It is therefore Considered by the Court that the Plaintiff recover against the said Defendant his Damages aforesaid by the Jurors in their Verdict aforesaid assessed, and his Costs by him about his suit in this behalf expended, and the said Defendants in mercy &c.

– **Tunstall Quarles** Junr Ass^ee Plt
against In Covenant
**Julious Bunch** Deft

This day came the Plaintiff by his attorney, and the Defendant being solemnly Called but came not Therefore it is Commanded the Sheriff that he cause to come here Immediately twelve good and lawful men by whom &c. and thereupon came also a Jury to wit, **Fortunatus Dodson, Stephen English, William Hays, William Evans, John D Young, George W Saunders, Robert Foster, Joseph Porter** [page 168] **Nathaniel Black, John Decker, Henry Hardister** and **Andrew Cowen**, who were sworn well and truly to Inquire what Damages the Plaintiff hath sustained in the premises upon their Oaths do say that the Plaintiff hath sustained Damages by Occasion thereof to ten pounds thirteen shillings besides his Costs It is therefore Considered by the Court. that the Plaintiff recover against the said Defendant his Damages aforesaid by the Jurors in their Verdict aforesaid assessed and his costs by him about his suit in this behalf expended, and the said Defendant in mercy &c.

– **Ephraim Churchwell** Plt
against In Case
**Julious Bunch** Deft

This day came the Plaintiff by his attorney and the said Defendant being Solemnly called but came not. Therefore on the motion of the Plaintiff by his attorney It is commanded the Sheriff that he cause to come here Immediately twelve good & lawful men by whom &c and thereupon came also a Jury to wit, **Fortunatus Dodson, Stephen English, William Hays, William Evans, John D Young, George W Saunders, Robert G Foster, Joseph Porter, Nathaniel Black, John Decker, Henry Hardister** & **Andrew Cowen** who were sworn well and truly to inquire what damage the Plaintiff hath sustained in the premises upon their Oaths do say that the Plaintiff hath sustained Damage by Occasion thereof to twenty two dollars and forty cents besides his Costs. It is therefore Considered by the Court that the Plaintiff recover against the said Defendant his damages aforesaid by the Jurors in their Verdict aforesaid assessed and his Costs by him about his suit in this behalf [page 169] expended, and the said Defendant in mercy &c. Note this Judgment is for the benifit of **Balzer Detrick**, by Order of the Plts Attorney

– **Samuel McKee** Assee Plt
against In Debt
**James Alderson** Deft

This day came the Plaintiff by his attorney, and the Defendant being solemnly called but came not. Therefore on the motion of the Plaintiff by his attorney It is Commanded the Sheriff that he cause to come here Immediately twelve good and lawfull men by whom &c. and thereupon came also a Jury. **Fortunatus Dodson, Stephen English, William Hays, William Evans, John D Young, George W Saunders, Robert G Foster, Joseph Porter, Nathaniel Black, John Decker, Henry Hardister** and **Andrew Cowen** who were sworn well and truly to enquire what Damage the Plaintiff hath in the Premises upon their Oaths do find for the Plaintiff the Debt in the Declaration mentioned besides his Costs It is therefore Considered by the Court that the Plaintiff recover against the said Defendant the said Debt in the Declaration mentioned and his Costs by him about his suit in this behalf expended and the said Defendant in mercy &c. Note this Judgment is to be discharged by the payment of ninety Dollars with Interest thereon from the first day of August One thousand eight hundred and four until paid & Costs

– **Christopher Clonch** Assee Plt
against In Debt
**Robert Gillilands** admor & adminx Defts

[page 170] This day came the Plaintiff by his attorney, and thereupon came Also a Jury, to wit, **Fortunatus Dodson, Stephen English, William Hays, William Evans, John D Young, George W Saunders, Robert G Foster, Joseph Porter, Nathaniel Black, John Decker, Henry Hardister**, and **Andrew Cowen**, who were sworn well and truly to enquire what Damage the Plaintiff has sustained in the Premises upon their Oaths do find for the Plaintiff the Debt in the Declaration mentioned with Interest &c. besides his Costs. It is therefore Considered by the Court that the Plaintiff recover against the said Defendant eighty Dollars the said Debt in the Declaration mentioned, his Interest &c. by the Jurors in their Verdict aforesaid assessed and his Costs by him about his suit in this behalf expended and the said Defendant in mercy &c. Note this Judgment is to bare legal Interest from the first day of September One thousand eight hundred and three until paid and Costs

– **Absolem Brown** Plt
against In Debt
**George W Saunders** Deft

This day came as well the Plaintiff by his attorney as the said Defendant in his proper person, who says he cannot gainsay the Plaintiffs action against him for twenty Dollars, the Debt in the Declaration mentioned, Therefore with assent of the Plaintiff It is Considered by the Court that the Plaintiff recover against the said Defendant the said Debt in the Declaration mentioned and his Costs by him about his suit in this behalf expended and the said Defendant in mercy &c. with the reservation of Equity. Note this Judgment is to bare legal Interest thereon from the twenty fifth day of September [page 171] One thousand eight hundred and four until paid & Costs

– Ordered that **Wyatt Adkins**, **Peter Fuller**, and **Archabald Rainey**, who has been fined during this present Term of this Court for Contempt offered to the Judges thereof, It is ordered that they be released from the payment thereof

– **Isaac Eoff** Plt
against In Debt
**Henry Francis** Deft

This day came the Plaintiff by his attorney and thereupon came also a Jury, to wit, **William Hunt, Robert Hunt, Nathaniel Barber, Robert G Foster, James Lang, Joseph Porter, Solomon Turpin, Allin Fuller, Joseph N Dodson, David Johnson, John Eastham**, and **Henry Hardister**, who were sworn well and truly to enquire what Damages the Plaintiff hath sustained in the premises upon their Oaths do find for the Plaintiff the Debt in the Declaration mentioned with legal Interest thereon from the first day of May One thousand eight hundred and four until paid besides his Costs and they do assess the Plaintiffs Damages by Occasion of the Detention thereof to one Penny. It is therefore considered by the Court that the Plaintiff recover against the said Defendant twenty one pounds the said debt in the Declaration mentioned, his Interest and Damages aforesaid by the Jurors in their Verdict aforesaid assessed and his Costs by him about his suit in this behalf expended and the said Defendant in mercy &c. Note this Judgment is to have credit for ten Dollars paid on the twenty second day of August One thousand eight hundred and four

[page 172] **John** & **William Allin** Plts
against In Covenant
**William Hays** Deft

**Joseph Evans** of Pulaski County came into Court and Justified &c. and undertook for the said Defendant that if he shall be cast in the action aforesaid that he shall satisfy and pay the Condemnation of the Court or render his body to prison in Execution for the same or on falure thereof that he the said **Joseph Evans** shall do it for him

– The Same Plt
against In Covenant
**Joseph Evans** Deft

**William Hays** of Pulaski County came into Court and undertook for the said Defendant that if he shall be cast in the Action aforesaid that he shall satisfy and pay the condemnation of the Court or render his body to prison in Execution for the same Or on falure thereof that he the said **William Hays** shall do it for him

– Elder Grant (ie, **Samuel McKee** Plt
against In Ejectment
Trouble Entry (ie **Joseph Patterson** Deft

This day came the Plaintiff by his attorney The said Deft and his attorney were both called but came not, Therefore On the motion of the Plaintiff It is commanded the Sheriff that he cause to come here Immediately twelve good and lawful men by whom &c. and thereupon came also a Jury to wit, **William Hunt, Robert Hunt, Nathaniel Barber, Robert G Foster, James Lany, Joseph Porter, Solomon Turpin, Allin Fuller, Joseph N Dodson**, [page 173] **David Johnson, John Eastham** & **Samuel Caughron** who being elected tried and sworn the truth to speak upon the Issue Joined upon their Oaths do say that the said Defendant is guilty of the Trespass and Ejectment in the Declaration mentioned in manner and form as the Plaintiff against him hath declared and they do assess the Plaintiffs Damages by Occasion thereof to one penny besides his Costs. It is therefore considered by the Court that the Plaintiff recover of the said Defendant his Term yet to come and unexpired of and in the premises in the Declaration mentioned, together with his Damages aforesaid by the Jurors in their Verdict aforesaid and his Costs by him about his suit in this behalf expended and the said Defendant in mercy &c And on the motion of the Plaintiff by this attorney It is Ordered that the Commonwealth writ of Habere facias Possessionum be awarded him to cause him to have possession &c.

– **John McConnil** Plt
against In Trespass assault & Battery
**John Eastham** Deft

Ordered that this suit be Discontinued by Order of the Plaintiffs attorney

– **Robert Gillilands** admor & adminx Plt
against In Case
**Samuel Hobs** Deft

– **Jesse Wommack** Plt
against In Case
**Charles Rusk** Deft

– **Golfin Manor** Plt
against In Case
**Joseph Evans** Deft

[page 174] **Robertson Burge** Plt
against In Case
**Joseph Porter** Deft

Ordered that these suits be continued until the next Court

– **Ephraim Churchwell** Plt
against In Debt
**William J Sallee** Deft

Ordered that this suit be dismissed at the Defendants Cost (excepting an attornies fee

– **William J Sallee**
against In Case
**Ephraim Churchwell** Deft

Ordered that this suit be dismissed

– Absent **James G Hunter** Esquire

– Ordered that the Court be adjourned until Tomorrow morning ten OClock

**John Smith**

At a Circuit Court Continued and held for the Pulaski Circuit at the Courthouse of Pulaski County in Sommerset On Saturday the 27th day of July 1805

Present the Honourable **John Smith** and **John Prather** Esquires

– Ordered that it be certified to the Auditor of Public Accounts that **John January** has served this Court as Jailor eighteen days since the 24th day of September one thousand eight hundred and four up to the present date

**John Smith**

[page 175] Ordered that the Court be adjourned till Court in Course

On the fourth Monday in October 1805 being the 28th day of the said Inst and being the day fixed upon by law for holding Court for the Pulaski Circuit, at the Courthouse of Pulaski County in Sommerset.

Present the Honourable **John Prather** Esqr One of the assistant Judges of the Circuit aforesaid and he being the Only Judge appearing It is Ordered that the Court be adjourned until Court in Course

**John Prather**

At a Circuit Court holden for the Pulaski Circuit at the Courthouse in Sommerset on Monday the

28th day of April 1806

Present the Honbl **William Kelly, John Smith** & **John Prather** Gentlemen

– **Hugh Caldwell** Complt
against In Chancery
**Joseph Beard, Charles Cocks** & **Franklin** Defts

This day came the Parties aforesaid by their counsil, and on the motion of the Defendants by their Counsil It is Ordered that the rule taken here setting this cause for hearing is Ordered to be set a side, and the cause remanded to the Rule Docket, And on the motion of the Defendants Counsil It is ordered that **William Beard** be made a Defendant hereto, And it is further Ordered that the Judgment taken down herein in the Clerks Office as to the Judgment [ ] be set a side, and also remanded to the Rule Docket

– **John Logan** Esqr Produced a licence authorizing him to practice law &c who took the necessary Oaths &c.

[page 176] A Grand jury was sworn for the Pulaski Circuit, to wit, **Jonathan Smith** foreman, **William Williams, Stephen Coudry, John Evans, Ephraim Churchwell, Jesse Williams, Jesse Kizzar, William Mayfield, William Lynch, Isaac Mayfield, William Hail, Johnston Sargent, William White, Cornelious Doolin, Abner McWhorter, William Burton, Ambrose Mayfield** & **Edward Cooper**, who having received their charge retired to consider of their presentments

– **John Leach** Plt
against In Debt
**Wm Ussery** & **Thos Whites** Defts

– **Daniel Duncan** Plt
against In Debt
**James P Burton** & others Defts

Ordered that these suits be Dismissed by order of the Plaintiffs

– **Andrew Cowen** Complt
against In Chancery
**Tunstall Quarles** Deft

– **John Weirs** Admor Plt
against In Case
**Nathaniel Forbis** Deft

Ordered that these suits be Continued until the next Court

– **John Beard** Complt
against In Chancery
**George Saunders** & Als Defts

This day came the Parties aforesaid by their Counsil, and on motion It is ordered that this Cause be remanded to the Rule Docket

– The Grand jury returned into Court an Indictment The Commonwealth against **William Ussery** Junr a true Bill

[page 177] **Kizziah Chappel** by **Jesse Chappel** her next friend Plt
against In Case
**William Burton** Deft

Ordered that this suit be continued until the next Court for award

– **Obediah Paine** Plt
against In Covenant
**Robert Gillilands** admor Defts

Ordered that this suit be Continued until the next Court at the Plaintiffs Costs

– The Commonwealth of Kentucky
against upon an Indictment for Horse stealing
**William Ussery** Junr laborer

The said **William Ussery**, who stands Indicted for felony was led to the bar in Custody of the Jailer, and thereof arraigned and plead not guilty to the Indictment, and for his trial puts himself upon God and his Country and the attorney for the Commonwealth likewise, whereupon came a Jury, to wit, **George Allcorn, James Hays, Andrew Evans, Richard Muse, Andrew Davidson, Frederick Williams, Robert Whitesides, James Cowen, Andrew Cowen, Smith Williams, Simon Stacy** & **David Buster**, who being elected tried and sworn the truth to speak of and upon the premises, and having heard the evidence as well as the Arguments of counsil, upon their Oaths do say that the said **William Ussery** is Guilty of the felony aforesaid, in manner and form as the Indictment against him is alledged and In consequence of which do decide & ascertain that he shall [ ] a Confinement in the Jail & Penitenciary House for the Commonwealth of Kentucky for the period of two years, and the same is made the Judgment of the court And the said prisoner is remanded to Jail &c.

[page 178] **William Barrot** Plt
against In Debt
**James Gibson** Deft

This day came as well the Plaintiff by his attorney as the said Defendant in his proper person, who says he cannot gainsay the Plaintiffs Action against him for nine pounds 16/ the Debt in the Declaration mentioned Therefore with Assent of the Plaintiff It is considered by the Court that the Plaintiff recover of the said Defendant, the said Debt in the Declaration mentioned and his costs by him about his suit in this behalf expended and the said Defendant in mercy &c. Note this Judgment is to bare legal Interest from the sixteenth day of July one thousand eight hundred and two until paid & Costs

– The Grand jury Impanneled and sworn this day, are Ordered to be disch[d] by the Court;

– Ordered that the Court be adjourned "till Tomorrow morning ten OClock

– The Presiding Judge being absent the minutes of these proceedings are signed

**John Smith**

At a Circuit Court Continued and held for the Pulaski Circuit at the Courthouse in the Town of Sommerset on Tuesday the 29th day of April 1806

Present the Honourable **John Smith** & **John Prather** Gentlemen

– **James Johnson** Ass[ee] Plt
against In Covenant
**Joseph Evans** Deft

[page 179] **John Long** Ass[ee] Plt
against In Covenant
**Joseph Evans** Deft

– **Jarrot Harbin** Plt
against In Debt
**Joseph Evans** & **Forbis** Deft

**John Evans** & **William Hays** of Pulaski County came into Court and undertook for the Defendant **Evans** in the case is aforesaid that if he shall be cast in the Action aforesaid that they shall satisfy and pay the condemnation of the Court or render his body to prison in execution for the same or on falure thereof that they shall do it for him

– **Joseph Casky** Plt
against In Case
**John January** Deft

This day came the Parties aforesaid by their Attornies and thereupon came also a Jury (to wit) **Thomas McGuire, Stephen Coudry, Andrew Evans, Andrew Turner, Joseph Raincy, Abram Barrier, Benjamin Slone, William Owens, Richard Churchwell, Thomas Harris, Abner McWhorter** & **David Roper** who being elected tried and sworn the truth to speak upon the Issue Joined (Be it remembered that on the trial of this cause the Deft **January** by his attorney asked **Tho[s] Fox**, a Witness sworn in the cause if he was Acquainted with the hand writing of the Plaintiff, and then produced and shew paper to the said **Fox** is in the words and figures following to wit) Mr **Januarys** [ ] Mr **Januarys** account do 2 Galins of whisky Dito to six Gallins and one half of whisky Dito to one Gallon and pint Ditto to thirteen Gallons of whisky Ditto to five Gallons and half Ditto to Seventy four Gallons of whisky Ditto halling one lod from my Home to the Town Ditto to fourty six pounds of beef Ditto ___ enty Gallons of brandy Dito to One Do [ ] of salt Ditto to Seventy four and half Gallons of Cyder, and one Barrel eight shillings Dito to fifty three Gallons and one pint of brandy

* [see below]

[page 180] **Amos Harmon** Plt
against In Trespass assault & Battery
**Joseph Porter** Deft

– The Same Plt
against In Covenant
The Same Deft

Ordered that these suits be Dismissed by Order of the Parties, and the Defendant to pay half the Plaintiffs Costs herein

– **Joseph Porter** Plt
against In Case
**Amos Harmon** Deft

Ordered that this suit be Dismissed by Order of the Plaintiff

* Ditto to One hundred and Seventy pounds of beef Ditto 11 pounds of Tallow 1 Bushell Salt 21/ Beef 10 Dollars, and then Asked the Witness if the said paper was or was not in the hand writing of the Plt **Casky** which question asked by the Att[y] afs[d] was Objected to by the att[y] for the Pltff which Objection was Sustained by the Court, and the court determined and adjudged that the Deft should not ask said Question nor should said paper go to the Jury as evidence to which Jud[t] and Determination of the Court, the Deft excepts and prays that this his bill of exceptions may be Signed Sealed and recorded Agreeable to the Act of Assembly in such cases made and provided

**John Smith**
**John Prather**

* upon their Oaths do say that the said Defendant did not assume upon himself in manner and form as the Plaintiff against him hath declared Therefore It is Considered by the Court that the Plaintiff take nothing by his Bill but for his false clamour be in mercy &[c] and that the said Defendant go thereof without day [page 181] and recover of the said Plaintiff his Costs by him about his defence in this behalf expended &[c].

– **Joseph Bridges** Plt
against In Covenant
**Uriah Hand** Deft

This day came as well the Plaintiff by his attorney as the said Defendant in his proper person who says he cannot gainsay the Plaintiffs action against him for thirty Dollars. Therefore with the assent of the Plaintiff It is Considered by the Court that the Plaintiff recover against the said Defendant the said Thirty Dollars, and his Costs by him about his suit in this behalf expended and the said Defendant in mercy &[c]. Note this Judgment is to be discharged by the payment of said thirty Dollars with legal Interest thereon from the first day of May One thousand eight hundred and five until paid & Costs

– **Robertson Burge** Plt
against In Case
**David Clark** Deft

– **John Burdit** Plt
against In Case
**Jesse Richardson**

Ordered that these suits be continued until the next Court, and the Cause first named continued at the Plaintiffs Costs

– Ord that the Court be adjourned till Tomorrow morning eight OClock

**John Smith**

At a Circuit Court Continued and held for Pulaski Circuit at the Courthouse in Sommerset on Wednesday the 30th day of April 1806

Present the Honourable **John Smith** & **John Prather** Gentlemen

– **Frederick Reperdon** Complt
against In Chancery
**Joseph Casky** Deft

[page 182] This day this cause coming in to be heard & upon View of the bill answer exhibits in this cause filed & by consent of the parties & their attornies, It is therefore decreed and ordered that the complaintant recover of the Defendant the sum of twenty six pounds seventeen shillings with Interest thereon after the rate of six percentum per annum from the 27th day of April 1804 "till paid and that the Defendant do pay the same to the complainant on or before the 30th day of July next, and on failure thereof that **Andrew Cowen, Robert Modrell,** & **Jonathan Smith** any two of them who are hereby appointed Commissioners do proceed Immediately after & all and convey the tract of land in the bill and exhibits mentioned or so much thereof of either side or and that said Defendant shall order as will be sufficient to satisfy sd Complainants Debt Interest and Costs for ready money, so much as it will bring having previously advertised the time & place of said sale One month in the Informant Printed in Danville and that the Commissioners on application of the Complainant or his agent do pay over to him the said sum, or so much as shall be made from the Sale of said land & that they make report of their Proceedings to the next October Court, and that the Complainant recover of the said Defendant his Costs in this suit expended all of which is decreed & Ordered Accordingly

– The Commonwealth
against upon Indictment
**William Ussery** Junr

The said **William Ussery** was this day at the bar in custody of the Sheriff when it was demanded of him if he has any matter or cause to alledge why the Court should not now Proceed to Pronounce the Judgment of Law or the Verdict of the Jury herein found; whereupon the said **William Ussery** the Defendant moved the Court for a new trial upon which motion the arguments of Counsil were heard and after [ ] [page 183] due deliberation Over ruled. Therefore it is considered by the Court that the said **William Ussery** do sundrys in Confinement in the Jail and Penitentiary House of the Commonwealth of Kentucky for the period of two years agreeable to the Verdict aforesaid and it is Ordered that the said Defendant be remanded to the Jail of Pulaski County there to remain until removed therefrom by due Course of law

– **Obediah Denham** Plt
against In Case
**John Cundiff** Deft

This day came the Parties aforesaid by their attornies and It is Ordered that this suit be dismissed It being agreed

– **William Williams** Plt
against In Case
**Henry Willis** Deft

– **Henry Willis** Plt
against In Case
**William Williams** Deft

This day came the Parties aforesaid by their attornies, and by Consent of Parties all matters in difference between the Parties aforesd are refered to the Arbitration and determination of **Joseph Erwin, George Kerr, Andrew Evans, Robert Modrel, Robert Scott** & **Thos McGuire**, whose award shall be the Judgment of the Court, But in Case of their disagreement the said referrees are to chuse another person & the cause is Continued

– **James Doran & Co** Plt
against In Debt
**James Johnston** Deft

– **John** & **William Allin** Plt
against In Covenant
The Same Deft

**Holcomb Robertson**, of Pulaski County came into Court and Justified and undertook for the said Defendant that if he shall be Cast [page 183] In the actions aforesaid that he shall satisfy and pay the Condemnation of the Court or render his body to prison in execution for the same or on falure thereof that he shall do it for him

– **James S Davis** Plt
against In Covenant
**William Brooks** Deft

**John Brooks**, of Pulaski County came into Court. and Justified and undertook for the said Defendant that if he shall be Cast in the action aforesaid that he shall satisfy and pay the Condemnation of the Court or render his body to Prison in execution for the same or on falure thereof that he the said **John Brooks**, shall do it for him

– **Heu Pearce** Plt
against In Covenant
**Holcomb Roberson** Deft

**Nathaniel Forbis** of Pulaski County Came into court and Justified and undertook for the said Defendant that if he shall be cast in the Action aforesaid that he shall satisfy and pay the Condemnation of the Court or render his body to prison in execution for the same or on falure thereof that he the said **Nathaniel Forbis** shall do it for him

– **William Evans** Plt
against In Covenant
**John Robertson** Deft

Ordered that the suit be Continued until the next Court at the Defendants Costs

– **Hugh Donigy** Plt
against In Covenant
**Joseph Casky** Deft

Ordered that this suit be continued until the next Term of this court at the Defendants Costs, And on the motion of the said Deft by his attorney, an attachment is awarded him to Mercer County against **John McAnnellon** who has failed to attend herein as a witness at this Present T^m^

[page 185] **Joseph Casky** Plt
against In Trespass assault & Battery
**Robert Smith** Deft

Ordered that this suit be continued until the next Court at the Plaintiffs costs And on the motion of the Plaintiff by his attorney a Dedimus is awarded him to take the Depositions of **Robert** & **Anson Taylor** Debe ne esse to be read as witness herein, the said Dedimus to be directed to any two Justices of the Peace in the State of Kentucky

– **Andrew Roy** Plt
against In Case
**W^m^** & **Dianah Burnham** Deft

Ordered that this suit be Dismissed It appearing the Plaintiff in this case is not an Inhabitant of Kentucky, and having failed to enter Security for Costs as directed by the Act of the General Assembly Kentucky in that case made and provided

– **John Brown** Plt
against In Debt
**McKee** & **Montgomery** Defts

– The Same Plt
against In Debt
The Same Defts

**Thomas Montgomery** of Lincoln County & **William Fox** of Pulaski County came into Court and undertook for the said Defts that if they shall be cast in the Actions aforesaid that they shall satisfy and pay the Condemnation of the Court or render their bodies to Prison in execution for the same, or on falure thereof that they the said **Thomas & William** shall do it for them

– **John Cabell** Plt
against In Case
**John Hardgrove** Senr Deft

This day came as well the Plaintiff by his attorney as the said Defendant in his proper person who says he cannot gainsay the Plaintiffs Action against him for One hundred and Seven Pounds four shillings, [page 186] and nine pence as from Plffs [ ] herein therefore with the assent of the Plaintiff by his attorney It is considered by the Court that the Plaintiff recover against the said Defendant the said sum of One hundred and Seven pounds four shillings and nine pence, Confessed as aforesaid, and his Costs by him about his suit in this behalf expended, and the said Defendant in mercy &c. Note ninety eight pounds fourteen shillings and four pence part of the said Judgment is to bare Interest after the rate of six percentum per annum from the fifteenth day of May one thousand eight hundred and four and the residue of said Judgment which is twelve pounds ten shillings and five pence to bare Interest after the same rate from the fifteenth day of May One thousand eight hundred and three until paid & Costs And Execution to be staid till the first day of August next

– **Joseph Casky** Plt
against In Case
**John January** Deft

This day came the Parties aforesaid by their attornies, and the Plaintiff by his attorney moved the Court to Obtain a new trial herein on the Verdict, and Judgment Obtained against him yesterday by the said Defendant, after hearing the Arguments of Counsil on both sides, and mature deliberation being thereon had, It is Ordered that said motion be Over ruled, and that Defendant recover of the said Plaintiff his Costs by him about his defence relative to this motion expended

– **Conley Finly & Co** Plt
against In Debt
**John Harmon** Deft

**Henry Moore** of Pulaski County came into Court and undertook for the said Defendant that if he shall be Cast in the Action Aforesaid that he shall satisfy and pay the Condemnation of [page 187] the Court, or render his body to prison in execution for the same or on falure thereof that he the said **Henry Moore** shall do it for him

– **George W Saunders** & wife Plts
against In Trespass Assault & Battery
**John Griffin** Deft

This day came the parties aforesaid by their attornies, And the said Defendant for further plea herein says that if he did assault the Plaintiff **Dorcas Saunders**, wife of the said **George Saunders**, it was Occasioned by the said **Dorcas** give the first Assault, and of this he puteth himself upon the Country, and the said Plaintiff likewise Therefore is it commanded the Sheriff that he cause to come here immediately twelve good and lawful men by whom &c and thereupon came Also a Jury, to wit, **James Kerr, Jonas Erwin, Absolem Brown, William Southerland, Stephen Hail, William White, John Chesney, William Addison, Joel Evans, John Knox, William Hill** and **David Richardson** who being elected tried and sworn the truth to speak upon the Issue Joined, Afterwards one of the Jurors to wit **John Knox** was withdrawn by consent and the cause ordered to be Continued until the next Court

– **John & William Allin** Plts
against In Covenant
**John Newby** Deft

**Nicholas Jasper** of Pulaski County came into court and undertook for the said Defendant that if he shall be Cast in the Action aforesaid that he shall satisfy and pay the Condemnation of the Court, or render his body to prison in execution for the same, or on falure thereof that he the said **Nicholas Jasper**, shall do it for him

– **William Williams** Plt
against In Case
**Henry Willis** Deft
– **Henry Willis** Plt
against In Case
**William Williams**

[page 188] This day came the Parties aforesaid by their attornies and the referees appointed by Order of Court to settle and determine all in difference between the said Parties relative said suit, returned into Court their award in these words and figures, to wit, by Virtue of an Order of Court we the undernamed referees after mature deliberation on matter of difference between **Henry Willis** and **William Williams** do find a Verdict in favor of **Williams**, Seventeen pounds and cost on both suits Given under our hands this 30th of April 1806

**Joseph Erwin** **George Karr**
**Robert Scott** **Reubin Hill**
**Andrew Evans** **Jesse Richardson**
**Robert Modrel**

And the same is made the Judgment of the Court

– **Elijah Wray** Plt
against In Debt
**Benjamin Cundiff** Deft

**Richard Churchwell** Junr of Pulaski County came into Court and undertook for the said Defendant that if he should be cast in the Action aforesaid that he shall satisfy and pay the Condemnation of the Court or render his body to prison in execution for the same, or on falure thereof that he the said **Richard Churchwell** shall do it for him

– **Thomas McGuire & Thos Jacobs** Complts
against upon motion In Chancery
**Charles Inglish & Thos Clark** Defts

This day came the parties aforesaid by their Counsil And on the motion of the Complainants by their Counsil for an Injunction to stay all further proceedings &c on a Judgment Obtained against them at Common by the Defendants to this motion, after hearing the bill, and the arguments of Counsil on both sides the Court took time to consider of their Opinion, And the motion is Continued until Friday next

– **Robt Modrel** Late Shff
against upon Motion Continued "till Tomorrow morning
**Jas McAlister** his Deputy

[page 190] Ordered that the Court be adjourned till Tomorrow morning eight OClock

**John Smith**

At a Court Continued and held for the Pulaski Circuit at the Courthouse in Sommerset on Thursday the first day of May 1806

Present the Honbl **John Smith & John Prather** Gentlemen

– On the motion of the attorney for the Commonwealth in the Pulaski Circuit Court, Ordered that the Clerk of this Court do Issue a writ De Idista Inquirenda to enquire whether **John Barns** of Pulaski County be of sound mind or not it being Suggested that he is of unsound mind returnable to the first day of the next Term of this Court

– **James Skidmore** Complt
against In Chancery
**Francis Stephens** Deft

By Consent of the parties by their Counsil Ordered that this suit be set down for hearing at the next Term of the Court, notwithstanding, there is not five months between the filing of the Replication and the sitting for hearing, and it is further ordered that each party, have leave to file any exhibits or depositions between this Term and the day of hearing

– **John Rogers** Plt
against In Case
**John McWhorter** Deft

On the motion of the Defendant, It is Ordered that the Judgment and writ of Inquiry awarded against him in the Clerks Office be set a side and the said Defendant by his attorney now comes and defends the wrong and Injury when and where &c and says he is not guilty in manner and form as the Plaintiff against him hath declared and of this he puteth himself upon the Country and the said Plaintiff likewise, Therefore let a Jury Come here &c.

– **George W Saunders** Plt
against In Trespass Assault & Battery
**John Griffin** Deft

This day came the Parties aforesaid by their attornies, and the said Defendant for further Plea herein says if he did Assault the Plaintiff [page 190] it was Occasioned by the Plaintiff making the first assault therefore he puteth himself upon the Country and the said Plaintiff likewise Therefore it is commanded the Sheriff that the cause to come here immediately twelve good and lawful men by whom and thereupon came also a Jury, to wit, **Hansford Price, John Preston, John Guinn, Reubin Hill, Thomas Banks, William Williams** Junr, **John Evans, John Brooks, Zachariah Evans, Charles Collier, Samuel Cole** & **William Williams** who being elected tried and sworn the truth to speak upon the Issue Joined upon their Oaths do say that the said Defendant is not guilty in manner and form as the Plaintiff against him hath declared It is therefore Considered by the Court that the Plaintiff take nothing by his bill but for his false clamor be in mercy &c and that the said Defendant go thereof hence without day and recover of the said Plaintiff his Costs by him about his defence in this behalf expended

– **George Taylor** Complt
against upon Attachment
**Dennis Farnwell** Deft

This day came the Parties aforesaid by their attornies, and on the motion of the Deft by his attorney It is ordered that this Attachment be Dismissed for Irregularity and that the Defendant recover his Costs

– **Elijah Wray** Plt
against In Debt
**Benjamin Cundiff** Deft

This day came the Plaintiff by his attorney, and on his motion It is Ordered that the Judgment and Writ of Inquiry awarded against the said Defendant be waved, Therefore It is considered by the Court that the Plaintiff recover against the said Defendant the Debt in the Declaration mentioned and his Costs by him about his suit in this behalf expended, and the said Defendant in mercy &c. Note this Judgment is to be discharged by the payment of seven pounds eight shillings and six pence with legal Interest thereon from the twenty second day of August [page 191] One thousand eight hundred and five until paid & Costs But to have Credit for nine Shillings paid up credit given in the note filed herein

– **George W Saunders** Plt
against In Trespass Vict Armis &c
**John Griffin** Deft

This day came the parties aforesaid by their attornies and thereupon came Also a Jury, to wit, **Jonathan Smith, William Bustard, Samuel Coupenheifer, John Hardgrove** Senr, **Joseph Evans, Henry Willis, William Southerland, John Baker, John Thompson, Jesse Thompson, Willis Tucker** & **Thomas Murphey**, who being elected tried and sworn the truth to speak upon the Issue Joined upon their Oaths do say the said Defendant is guilty in manner and form as the Plaintiff against him hath declared, and do assess the Plaintiffs Damages by Occasion thereof to twelve and a half Cents besides his costs It is therefore Considered by the Court that the Plaintiff recover against the said Defendant his Damages aforesaid by the Jurors in their Verdict aforesaid and his costs by him about his suit in this behalf expended and the said Defendant may be taken &c.

– **Robert Modrel** late Shff of Pulaski County Plt
against upon motion Cont[d] "till this day
**James McAllister** his Deputy Deft

This day came the Plaintiff by his attorney and the Defendant herein being Solemnly Called but came not, Therefore on the motion of the Plaintiff by his attorney It is considered by the Court that the Plaintiff recover against the said Defendant his Deputy as afs[d] the sum of ninety pounds, with a leave for said Defendant to come forward and exhibit any legal vouchers of payment to his principal the Plaintiff in this motion accreditted within six months from this day, and that the Plaintiff recover against the said Defendant his Costs by him about this motion expended and the said Defendant in mercy &[c].

[page 192] **John Green** Plt
against In Case
**Philip A Sublette** Deft

This day came the Parties aforesaid by their attornies, and on motion this suit is ordered to be continued until the next Court, and It is further Ordered that Commission be awarded to take the Depositions before any magistrate without the state of Kentucky

– **Philip A Sublette** Plt
against In Case
**Joel Jackson** Deft

Ordered that this suit be Continued until the next Court

– **Simon Engleman** Plt
against In Debt
**Benjamin Cundiff** Deft

**James Cundiff** of Pulaski County came into Court and Justified and undertook for the Defendant that if he shall be Cast in the action aforesaid that he shall satisfy and pay the condemnation of the Court or render his body to prison in execution for the same or on falure thereof that he the said **James Cundiff** shall do it for him

– **Philip A Sublette** Plt
against In Case
**Joel Jackson** Deft

This day came the parties aforesaid by their attornies, and by their agreement **Frederick Williams** of Pulaski County came into Court and undertook for the said Defendant that if he shall be Cast in the Action aforesaid that he shall satisfy and pay the Condemnation of the Court or render his body to prison in execution for the same or on fallure thereof that he the said **Frederick Williams** shall do it for him

– **Samuel Cole** Plt
against In Case
**Cornelius Dulin** Deft

On the motion of the said Defendant It is Ordered that the Judgment [page 193] and Writ of Inquiry awarded against him in the Clerks Office be set a side and the said Defendant by his attorney now Comes and defends the wrong and Injury when and where &[c]. and says he is not guilty in manner and form as the plaintiff against him hath declared, and of this he puteth himself upon the Country and the said Plaintiff likewise Therefore let a Jury Come here & and the Cause is Continued until the next Court

– Samuel Mathews Plt
against In Case
**Benjamin Guin** Deft

The Plaintiff having made the necessary Oath &[c] as directed by the Act of the General Assembly of Kentucky in this case made and provided, The clerk is therefore Ordered by the Court to endorse on the Writ Issued herein directing the Sheriff to take bail of the said Defendant in the sum of fifty Dollars

– **Robertson Burge** Plt

against In Case
**Joseph Porter** Deft

On the motion of the Defendant It is Ordered that the Judgment and writ of Inquiry awarded against him in the Clerks Office be set a side and the said Defendant by his attorney now comes and defends the wrong and Injury when and where &c and says that he is not guilty in manner and form as the Plaintiff against him hath declared, and of this he puteth himself upon the Country and the said Plaintiff likewise & Therefore let a Jury come here &c and the cause is Continued until the next Court

– **John Griffin** who sues as well for himself as the County of Pulaski Plt
against In Debt
**George W Saunders** Deft

Ordered that this suit be Continued until the next Court at the Defendants [page 194] cost

– Ordered that it be certified to the County Court of Pulaski County that this Court allows to **Arch^d E Mills** Esq^r their attorney the sum of eighty dollars for his services as Commonwealth Attorney for the Circuit of the County aforesaid for the last year preceding the last October Term of this court

– **John Griffin** Plt
against In Trespass Assault & Battery
**George W Saunders** Deft

This day came the Parties aforesaid by their Attornies and thereupon came also a Jury, to wit, **John Brooks, Charles Collier, Francis Taylor, W^m Collier, Zachariah Evans, Daniel Matthews, Nicholas Jasper, Philip A Sublette, Andrew Jasper, Martin Barrier, John Funk** & **Robert Smith** who being elected tried and sworn the truth to speak upon the Issue Joined, afterwards one of the Jurors to wit, **Philip A Sublette**, withdrawn, by Consent, and the cause continued until the next Court

– **Jesse Wommack** Plt
against In Case
**Charles Rusk** Deft

Ordered that this suit be continued until the next Court

[page 195] **Robert Smith** Complt
against upon motion for an Injunction
**George Taylor** Deft

to stay all further proceedings on a Judgment obtained against him at Common law in the Pulaski Circuit court by said Defendant after hearing the Bill exhibited herein and the Observations made by the Complainants Counsil, the motion Continued until Tomorrow

– **George W Saunders** Complt
against upon Attachment
**Samuel Saunders** Deft

This day came the Complaintant by his Counsil, and the said Defendant being solemnly called but came not, Therefore it is commanded the Sheriff that he cause to come here Immediatly twelve good and lawful men by whom and &c and thereupon came Also a Jury, to wit, **James Doran, Benjamin Long, Cornelius Dodson, John Preston, John Evans, William McCoy, John Stuck, James Smith, Anderson Smith, William Southerland, Samuel Cole** & **Jesse Richardson** who being well and truly to enquire what Damages the Plaintiff hath sustained in the premises, upon their Oaths do say that the Plaintiff hath sustained Damages by Occasion thereof to seventeen pounds fourteen shillings, besides his Costs It is therefore Considered by the Court that the Plaintiff recover against the said Defendant his Damages aforesaid by the Jurors in their Verdict aforesaid assessed and his Costs by him about his suit in this behalf expended and the said Defendant in mercy

[page 196] **George W Saunders** Plt
against on motion In Trespass assault & Battery
**John Griffin** Deft

This day came the parties aforesaid by their attornies, and the Plaintiff by his attorney moved the Court for a new Trial on the Verdict of the Jury and Judgment herein, which is granted him on his paying Costs &c.

– Ordered that the Court be adjourned until tomorrow morning eight OClock

**John Smith**

At a Circuit Court Continued and held for the Pulaski Circuit at the Courthouse in Sommerset on Friday the 2nd day of May 1806

Present the Same Judges as yesterday

– **Joseph Casky** Plt
against In Case
**John January** Deft

On the motion of the Plaintiff by his attorney for a new trial on the Judgment Obtained against him by the Defendant at this term, after hearing the arguments of Counsil on both sides, the Assistant Judges being divided the said motion is Over ruled with Costs

– **William Eastham** Assee Plt
against In Covenant
**William Ussery** Deft

**William Hays** of Pulaski County came into Court and Justified, and undertook for the said Defendant that if he shall be Cast in the Action aforesaid that he shall satisfy and pay the Condemnation of the Court or render his body to prison in execution for the same, or on falure thereof that he the said **William Hays** shall do it for him

– **Simon Engleman** Plt
against In Debt
**Benjamin Cundiff** Deft

[page 197] This day came the Plaintiff by his attorney, and upon motion It is Ordered that the Judgment and writ of Inquiry awarded against the said Defendant in the Clerks Office be waved, And on the motion of the said Plaintiff by his attorney, Judgment is granted him against the said Defendant for the Debt in the Declaration mentioned besides his cost by him about this suit in his behalf expended and the said in mercy &c. Note this Judgment is to be discharged by the payment of thirty one pounds, one shilling with legal interest thereon from the thirteenth day of June One thousand eight hundred and four until paid & Costs

– **Frederick Williams** Plt
against In Debt
**Olliver Sallee** Deft

This day came the Plaintiff by his attorney, and on motion It is Ordered that the Judgment and writ of Inquiry awarded against the said Defendant in the Clerks Office be waved. And upon the motion of the said Plaintiff by his attorney Judgment is granted him against the said Defendant for eighty Dollars the Debt in the Declaration mentioned, and his Costs by him about this suit in this behalf expended and the said Defendant in mercy &c. This Judgment is to bare legal Interest thereon from the ____ day of ____ until paid and Costs

– **Joseph Casky** Plt
against In Case
**Martin Barrier** Deft

On the motion of the Plaintiff by his attorney a Dedimus is awarded him herein to take the Deposition of **Robert** and **Anson Taylor** before any two Justices of the peace without the state of Kentucky

– **Golfin Minor** Plt
against In Case
**Joel Evans** Deft

This day came the Plaintiff by his attorney and the said Defendant [page 198] says he cannot gainsay the Plaintiffs Action against him for twenty Dollars, therefore with the assent of the Plaintiff It is Considered by the Court that the Plaintiff recover against the said Defendant the said sum of twenty Dollars, with legal Interest thereon from the nineteenth day of November One thousand eight hundred and four and his Costs by him about his suit in this behalf expended and the said Defendant in Mercy &c.

– **John Evans** Plt
against In Covenant
**Collier** & **Preston** Defts

On the Defendants **Robert Modrel**, of Pulaski County came into Court and undertook for the said Defendants that if they shall be Cast in the Action aforesaid that he shall satisfy and pay the condemnation of the Court or render their bodies to Prison in execution for the same or on falure thereof that he the said **Robert Modrel** shall do it for them, Therefore it is Ordered that the Jgment and Writ of Inquiry awarded against the said Defendants in the Clerks Office be set a side and the said Defendant by their attorney now comes and defends the wrong and Injury when and where &c and says the Plaintiff his Action aforesaid Ought not to have and maintain his action aforesaid because they say the Plaintiff did not before the Commencement of the Action aforesaid demand of the Defendants to keep and perform their Covenant in the Declaration mentioned, and demand perform the work therein mentioned and this they are ready to verify wherefore they pray Judgment &c And this Defendant for further plea herein this behalf pray that the Plaintiff by his actions aforesaid ought not to have and maintain because they say they did before the commencement of the Action aforesaid, to wit, on the ___ day of ____ 180_ in the Circuit aforesaid then and there tender a true performance of the Covenant aforesaid and at all times since have been ready and still are ready [page 199] to keep and perform their covenant aforesaid and this they are ready to Verify wherefore they pray Judgment &c And the said Plaintiff **John Evans** by his attorney says that he Ought not to be bared from having and maintaining his Action aforesaid against the said Defendants by any thing in their first plea above pleaded because he says he did demand a performance of the Covenant in the Declaration mention in manner and form as in the Declaration is alledged to wit, on the day and year & at the place therein mentioned, and this he prays may be enquired of by the Country, and the Defendants doth so likewise, and the said Plaintiff for replication to the 2nd plea of the Defendant above pleaded, says that he Ought not to be bared from having & maintaining his Action aforesaid against them by any thing in their said second plea alleged because he says, they did not before the commencement of the said Action tender a performance of their said Covenant, and this he prays may be enquired of by the Country.

And the Defendant likewise, therefore it is commanded the Sheriff cause to come here Immediately twelve good and lawful men by whom &c and thereupon came also a Jury, to wit, **James Matthews, James Doran, Thomas Green, Thomas Jacob, Frederick Williams, John McCullough, Joel Evans, Lambert White, Jesse Richardson, John Chesney, John James** & **Joseph Evans**, who being elected tried and sworn the truth to speak upon the Issue Joined upon their Oaths do say that the Defendants hath not kept and performed their Covenant in the Writing mentioned as in Pleading he hath alledged, but hath broken the same in manner and form as the Plaintiff against them hath declared, and they do assess the Plaintiffs Damages by Occasion thereof to thirty three pounds besides his Costs It is therefore considered by the Court that the Plaintiffs recover against the said Defendants his Damages aforesaid by the Jurors in their Verdict afores[d] assessed and his Costs by him about his suit in this behalf expended and the said Defendants in mercy &c.

[page 200] **Thomas Jacobs** & **Thomas McGuire** Complts
against In Chancery
**Charles Inglish** & **Thomas Clark** Defts

On the motion of the Complainants by their Counsil, an Injunction is granted him to stay all further proceeding, on a Judgment Obtained against them at Common by the said Defendant in this Court, they having filed their Bill herein, and that they enter into Bond in the clerks Office of the Pulaski Circuit with **George W Saunders** their Security in the penalty of seventy Dollars, within twenty days from the rising of the Court at the present Term

– **Benjamin Upton** Plt

against In Covenant
**Bird & Julious Bunch** Defts

This day came the Plaintiff by his attorney and thereupon came Also a Jury, to wit, **William Hays, Vincent Garner, Zachariah Evans, John Evans, Thomas Burk, William Collier, George Humphreys, John Decker, William J Sallee, George W Saunders, Samuel Caughron, & William Ussery**, who were sworn well and truly to enquire what damage the Plaintiff hath sustained in the premises upon their Oaths do say that the Plaintiff hath sustained Damage by Occasion thereof to six pounds eight shillings and six pence besides his Costs It is therefore Considered by the Court that the Plaintiff recover against the said Defendant his Damages aforesaid by the Jurors in their Verdict aforesaid assessed and his Costs by him about his suit in this behalf expended and the said Defendant in mercy &c.

– **Balzar Detrick** Plt
against In Covenant
**Alderson & Russell** Defts

This day came the Plaintiff by his attorney and thereupon came Also a Jury to wit, **William Hays, Vincent Green, Zachariah** [page 201] **Evans, John Evans, Thomas Burk, William Collier, George Humphreys, John Decker, William J Sallee, George W Saunders, Samuel Coughran & William Ussery**, who being sworn well and truly to enquire what damages the Plaintiff hath sustained in the premises upon their Oaths do say that the Plaintiff hath sustained Damages by Occasion thereof to eight pounds fourteen Shillings besides his Costs It is therefore Considered by the Court that the Plaintiff recover of the said Defendant his damages aforesaid by the Jurors in their Verdict Aforesaid assessed and his costs by him about his suit in this behalf expended and the said Defendant in mercy &c.

– **Jacob Lishey** Assee Plt
against In Covenant
**James Alderson** Deft

This day came the Plaintiff by his attorney and thereupon came also a Jury, to wit, **William Hays, Vincent Garner, Zachariah Evans, John Evans, Thomas Burk, William Collier, George Humphreys, John Decker, William J Sallee, George W Saunders, Samuel Coughron, & William Ussery**, who were sworn well and truly to enquire what damage the Plaintiff hath sustained in the premises upon their Oaths do say the Plaintiff hath sustained damage by Occasion thereof to seven Pounds fourteen shillings and nine pence besides his Costs. It is therefore considered by the Court that the Plaintiff recover against the said Defendant his Damages aforesaid by the Jurors in their Verdict aforesaid assessed and his Costs by him about his suit in this behalf expended and the said Defendant in mercy &c.

– **William Bryan** Plt
against In Debt
**Ezekiel Harlin & Philip A Sublette** Defts

This day came the Plaintiff by his attorney, and thereupon came also a Jury, to wit, **William Hays, Vincent Garner, Zachariah** [page 202] **Evans, John Evans, Thomas Burk, William Collier, George Humphreys, John Decker, William J Sallee, George W Saunders, Samuel Coughron & William Ussery** who were sworn well and truly to enquire what Damage the Plaintiff hath sustained in the premises upon their Oaths do find for the Plaintiff thirty four Dollars the Debt in the declaration mentioned and for the detention thereof do assess his Damages by Occasion thereof to one Penny besides his Costs. It is therefore Considered by the Court that the Plaintiff recover against the said Defendant the said Debt in the Declaration mentioned, his Damages afores^d by the Jurors in their Verdict aforesaid assessed and his Costs by him about his suit in this behalf expended and the said Defendant in mercy &c. Note this Judgment is to be discharged by the paym^t of the said thirty four Dollars with legal Interest thereon from the 16th day of August One thousand eight hundred and four until paid & Costs

– **Thomas Jacobs** Plt
against In Case

**Joel Evans** Deft

By Consent all matters in difference between the Parties aforesaid relative to this Cause is refered to the arbitration and determination of **Robert Modrel, John James, Joseph Erwin, Henry James & Adonijah Morgan** whose award to be made the Judgment of the Court and the same is Ordered Accordingly

– **John Evans** Plt
against In Case
**John Collier** Deft

This day came the Plt by his attorney, and made Oath as required by the Act of Assembly in that case made and provided, and moved the Court to direct the clerk to under and upon the writ this day Issued herein, directing the Sheriff to take Bail of s[d] Defendant, which motion was Objected by the Defendant Counsil, and on hearing the Arguments of Counsil adjudged good & that he recover his [page 203] Costs by him about his defense relative to this motion expended

– **Detrick & Lishey** Plts
against In Covenant
**James Alderson** Deft

This day came the Plaintiffs by their attornies and thereupon came Also a Jury, to wit, **James Matthews, Thomas Green, Temple Sargent, Joseph Evans, Thomas Jacob, Abraham Barrier, Joel Evans, Philip A Sublette, Amos Evans, Charles Rusk, James Doran, & Lambert White** who were sworn well and truly to enquire what Damage the Plaintiff hath sustained herein upon their Oaths do say that the Plaintiff hath Sustained Damage by Occasion thereof to thirteen pounds seven Shillings, besides his Costs. It is therefore Considered by the Court that the Plaintiff recover against the said Defendant the Damages aforesaid by the Jurors in their Verdict aforesaid assessed and their Costs by them about their suit in this behalf expended and the said Defendant in mercy &[c].

– **Spencer McDaniel** Plt
against In Debt
**William J Sallee** Deft

This day came the Plaintiff by his attorney and thereupon came also a Jury, to wit, **James Matthews, Thomas Green, Temple Sargent, Joseph Evans, Thomas Jacob, Abraham Barrier, Joel Evans, Philip A Sublette, Amos Evans, Charles Rusk, James Doran & Lambert White,** who were sworn well and truly to enquire what Damage the Plaintiff hath sustained in the premises upon their Oaths do find for the Plaintiff the sum of ten pounds one shilling and nine pence the Debt in the Declaration mentioned with legal Interest thereon from the fourth Monday in March One thousand eight hundred and four until paid & Costs and the same is made the Judgment of the Court and the said Defendant in mercy &[c].

[page 204] **Vincent Goldsmith** Plt
against In Trespass Assault & Battery
**John Bradford** Deft

This day came the Plaintiff by his attorney, and thereupon came also a Jury, to wit, **James Matthews, Thomas Green, Temple Sargent, Joseph Evans, Thomas Jacob, Abraham Barrier, Joel Evans, Philip A Sublette, Amos Evans, Charles Rusk, James Doran, & Lambert White** who were sworn well and truly to enquire what Damage the Plaintiff hath sustained in the Premises upon their Oaths do say the Plaintiff hath sustained Damage by Occasion thereof to one penny besides his Costs It is therefore Considered by the Court that the Plaintiff recover against the said Defendant his Damages aforesaid by the Jurors in their Verdict afores[d] assessed and his costs by him about his suit in this behalf expended and the said Defendant may be taken &[c].

– **Robertson Burge** Plt
against In Debt
**William Ussery** Deft

This day came the Plaintiff by his attorney and thereupon came also a Jury to wit, **James Matthews, Thomas Green, Temple Sargent, Joseph Evans, Thomas Jacob, Abraham Barrier,**

**Joel Evans, Philip A Sublette, Amos Evans, Charles Rusk, James Doran & Lambert White** who were sworn well and truly to enquire what Damage the Plaintiff hath sustained in the Premises, upon their Oaths do find for the Plaintiff the Debt in the Declaration mentioned with legal Interest Therefore It is Considered by the Court that the Plaintiff recover against the said Defendant the sum of twenty two Dollars and eighteen cents the said Debt in the Declaration mentioned with Legal Interest thereon from the twelfth day of February One thousand eight hundred and five until paid & Costs and the said Defendant in mercy &c.

[page 205] **William Lair** Plt
against In Covenant
**William Evans & Christ^o Simpson**

**William Hays** of Pulaski county came into Court and undertook for the said Defendant **Evans** that if he shall be cast in the Action Aforesaid that he shall satisfy and pay the condemnation of the Court or render his body to prison in execution for the same or on falure thereof that he the said **William Hays** shall do it for him

– Ordered that the Court be adjourned until Tommorrow morning nine OClock

**John Smith**

At a Circuit Court Continued and held for the Pulaski Circuit at the Courthouse in Sommerset on Saturday the 3rd day of May 1806 Present the Honourable **John Smith & John Prather** Gent

– **John D Young** Plt
against In Trespass Assault & Battery
**Britton Bailey** Deft

This day came the Defendant by his attorney & moved the Court that this suit be Dismissed for this, to wit, that the said Plaintiff has removed himself without this state, and has failed to enter Security for Costs as directed by the Act of the General Assembly Kentucky in that case made and provided

– **John & James Warren** Complt
against In Chancery
**Olliver & William J Sallee** Defts

This day came the Parties aforesaid by their attornies and by consent the following Decree is pronounced and made the Judgment of the Court as follows, to wit, State of Kentucky Pulaski Circuit April Term 1806

**John & James Warren** Complt against **Olliver & William J Sallee** Deft [ ] [page 206] this day this cause was brought on by the mutual consent of the parties to be heard the parties waving all and in the proceedings herein and in bringing this cause to hearing at this Term, and the bill answer and other exhibits being examined by the Court and by the Consent of the parties and their attornies it is moved and Ordered that the Complainants recover of the Deft the Sum of £186-4-4 with Interest thereon after the rate of 6 pr centum pr annum from the 23d day of January 1805 until paid and that the Dfts do pay the same to the Complainants on or before the first day of July next. and on falure thereof that **John McWhorter, John Nasby Philip A Sublette**, or any two of them are hereby Appointed Commissioners to proceed immediately after and all and Convey the premises in the bill and exhibits mentioned or so much thereof as will be Sufficient to satisfy the Complts Debt Interest & costs for ready money they having previously advertise the same three weeks at an public place in Pulaski County or in the informant printed in Danville [ ] the Commissioners on Application of the complainants or his attorney do pay over to them or [ ] the sum of £186-4-4 with Interest thereon as afsd and Costs or so much as shall be made by the sale of said Premises and that they make report of their proceedings to the next July Term of this Court and that the Complainants recover of the Defendant their Costs in this behalf expended all of which is decreed and Ordered &c.

– **Tunstal Quarles** Plt
against In Debt
**Frederick Williams** Deft

This day came the Plaintiff by his attorney as well as the said Defendant in his proper person, And upon the motion of the said Plts Attorney It is Ordered that the Judgment and writ of Inquiry awarded against the said Defendant in the Clerks Office be Waved And Judgment is granted him against the said Defendant for One hundred pounds the Debt in the declaration mentioned therefore with the assent of the Plaintiff It is considered by the court that the Plaintiff recover against the said Defendant the said Debt in the Declaration mentioned, and his Costs by him about his suit in this behalf expended, and the said Defendant in mercy &c. Note this Judgment is to bare legal Interest from the second day of June One thousand eight hundred and four until paid & costs But to have Credit for One hundred and fifteen Dollars and fifty Cents paid the twenty seventh day of May One thousand eight hundred and four

[page 207] **Mark Evans** Ass[ee] Plt
against In Debt
**John Brooks** & Al[s] Defts

**Charles Richardson** of Pulaski County came into Court and Justified and undertook for the said Defendant **Brooks** that if he shall be cast in the Action aforesaid that he shall satisfy and pay the Condemnation of the Court or render his body to prison in execution for the same or on falure thereof that he the said **Charles Richardson** shall do it for him

– **John** & **William Allin** Plts
against
**William J Sallee** Deft

Ordered that this suit be Dismissed at the Defts Costs by Consent

– **Robert Smith** Complt
against upon a motion for an Injunction to stay all further Proceedings
**George Taylor** Deft

on a Judgment Obtained against him at Common law in the Pulaski Circuit by the said Defendant after hearing the Bill and Arguments of counsil on both sides the Court are of Opinion that the Complainants Bill doth not contain a sufficient equity to authorize the Granting of an Injunction Therefore it is Ordered that said motion be Over ruled with Costs &c.

– **John Evans** Plt
against In Covenant
**Collier** & **Preston** Defts

This day came the Parties aforesaid by their attornies And on the motion of the said Defendant by his attorney for to Obtain a new trial on the Verdict and Judgment of the Jury Obtained herein yesterday after hearing the arguments of Counsil on both sides and mature deliberation being thereon had It is Considered by the Court that said motion be Over ruled and that the Plaintiff recover his Costs by him about this motion expended

[page 208] **Allin** v **Ben[j] Cundiff** Dism[d] and the Costs to be equally divided between the Parties

– **Ebenezar Best** Plt
against In Debt
**Ephraim Churchwell** Deft

This day came the Plaintiff by his attorney and It is ordered that the Judgment and Writ of Inquiary awarded against the said Defendant in the Clerks Office be Waved, and on the motion of the Plaintiff by his Attorney Judgment is granted him against the said Defendant for twenty Dollars the Debt in the Declaration mentioned, with legal Interest thereon from the twenty fifth day of December One thousand eight hundred and three until paid & Costs

– **John** & **William Allin** Plts
against In Covenant
**William Ussery** Deft

This day came the Plaintiff by his attorney and upon their motion It is Order[d] that the Judgment and Writ of Inquiry awarded against the said Defendant in the Clerks Office be waved, and the said Deft now herein in Court Acknowledged the Plaintiffs action against him for twenty four pounds fourteen shillings and eight pence, therefore with the assent of the Plaintiff It is

Considered by the Court that the Plaintiffs recover against the said Defendant the said twenty four Pounds fourteen Shillings and eight pence therein Acknowledged aforesaid with legal Interest thereon from the twentieth day of July One thousand eight hundred and four until paid & Costs. and the said Defendant in mercy Note Execution to be staid two months

[page 209] On the motion of **Joseph Casky** by his Attorney for a new Trial in the Verdict & Judgment obtained against him by **John January** the Defendant herein after hearing the Arguments of Counsil on both sides It is the Opinion of the Court that said motion be Over ruled with Costs &c

– **John** & **William Allin** Plts
against In Covenant
**Joseph Evans** Deft

the Defendant having entered special bail herein Therefore on his motion It is Ordered that the Judgment and writ of Inquiry awarded against him in the clerks Office be set a side, and the Defendant by his attorney comes and defends the wrong and Injury &c and whatsoever else he Ought to defend &c and craves Oyer of the Original Writ, Declaration and Writing Obligatory in the declaration which being read & heard says the Plaintiff his action aforesaid against him ought not to have and maintain because he saith that the matters and things therein Contained are not and sufficient in law, neither is he bound by the law of the land to answer thereto but demurs in law, and here sets down the following cause of Demurer first that he writing Obligatory in the Declaration mentioned was not payable nor due untill the 25th day of July in the year 1805, and the Original writ was [ ] on the 24th day of July in the year 1805 which was one day before the sd writing Obligatory was due and that the said Original writ and Declaration is wholly insufficient & informal, wherefore for want of Sufficient Writ & declaration in this behalf he prays Judgment &c And the Plaintiff by their attorney says they Ought not to be bared from having and mainting their action aforesaid against the said Defendant because they say the Original Writ, Declaration and the Writing Obligatory herein are good and sufficient in law wherefore they pray Judgment &c and the cause is Continued until the next Court. Afterward on the motion of the Plaintiffs attorney It is Ordered that this suit be dismissed, and that the said Defendant recover his Costs by him about his defence in this behalf expended and One hundred [page 210] and fifty pounds of Tobacco as directed by the Act of the General Assembly in this case made and provided &c.

– **William Eastham** Assee Plt
against In Covenant
**William Ussery** Deft

This day came as well the Plaintiff by his attorney and on hi motion It is Ordered that the Judgment and writ of Inquiry awarded against the said Defendant be waved, and the said Defendant now here in Court says he cannot gainsay the Plaintiffs action against him for nine pounds Therefore with the Assent of the Plaintiff It is considered by the Court that the Plaintiff recover against the said Defendant the said nine pounds with legal Interest thereon from the fifteenth day of April One thousand eight hundred and five until paid & Costs But to have credit for Sixteen shillings & /6 paid the ninth day of February One thousand eight hundred and five and for fourteen shillings and three pence paid on the fifteenth day of July One thousand eight hundred and five, Execution to be staid two months

– **Dick Patridge** Plt
against In Trespass Assault & Battery
**Richard Tutt** Deft

– **Robert Gillilands** Admor Plt
against In Case
**Samuel Hobbs** Deft

– **Thomas Whites** Plt
against upon Attachment
**William Ussery** Deft

– **William G Bowen**

against The Same
**Joseph Taylor** Deft
– **Jesse Womack** Ass^ee Plt
against In Chancery
**Isom Gibson** Deft
[page 211] **Spencer McDaniel** Plt
against In Debt
**James Alderson** Deft
**Zachariah & Robert Bakker** Plt
against In Covenant
**Alexander Crawford** Deft
– **Israel Hart** Plt
against In Debt
**Scrimiger & Benton** Defts
– **Joseph McDonald** Ass^ee Plt
against In Covenant
**Hamlet Thomas** Deft
– **George Denny** Ass^ee Plt
against In Debt
**William Ussery** Deft
– **Henry Willis** Plt
against In Trespass Assault & Battery
**Ephraim Churchwell** Deft
**Thomas Owsley** Plt
against In Covenant
**Willaim Lair** Deft
– **Henry Grindstaff** Plt
against In Case
**Robert Gillilands** adm^or Deft
– **John Guin** Plt
against In Case
**James Skidmore** Deft
– **Thomas McGuire** Plt
against In Debt
**Inglish & Jacobs** Deft
[page 212] **William Hiatt** Plt
against In Case
**Charles Rusk** Deft
– **John Hiatt** Ass^ee Plt
against In Debt
**Robertson Burge** Deft
– **Joseph Coiler** Ass^ee Plt
against In Debt
**Robertson Burge** Deft
– **Solomon Turpin** Plt
against In Trespass Assault & Battery
**Moses Martin** & ux Defts
– **Thomas Mease** Plt
against In Debt
**George Lankford** Deft
– **James Kitchens** Plt
against In Case

**Christ° Myers** Deft
– **John Cocke** Plt
against In Case
**Nathaniel Forbis** Deft
– John Doe (ie **Samuel McKee** Plt
against upon Ejectment
Richard Roe (ie **John Puckett** Deft
Ordered that these suits be continued until the next Court
– **John & William Allin** Plt
against In Covenant
**William Hays** Deft
This day came the Parties aforesaid by their attornies, and the said Defendant having given of Special Bail herein, On his motion It is Ordered that the Judgment and Writ of Inquiry awarded against him in the Clerks Office be set a side, and the said Defendant by his Attorney comes and defends the wrong and Injury &c. and whatsoever [page 213] else he Ought to defend &c and craves Oyer of the declaration and Writing Obligatory in Declaration mentioned which being read and heard says the Plaintiffs their aforesaid Action against him Ought not to have and maintain because he says the matters and things therein contained are not good and Sufficient in law, neither is he bound by the law of the land to answer thereto, but demurs in law and here sets down the following causes to wit first that the declaration does not [ ] that the Plts appointed any particular place in the Town of Sommerset for the Defts to deliver said Bear and Deer Skins, or that they give the said Deft any notice thereof 2nd that the Plt does not [ ] in their said declaration that the said Deft did not deliver said Bear & Deer skins in the town of Somerset on the 20th day of July 1805 nor any day before or since that time, 3rd that the said Declaration does not state that the Plaintiff made any demand of the Deft for said Bear and Deer skins which by law they Ought to have done & Previous to the commencement of said suit 4thly that the Writing Obligatory call for the sum of £10-17-3 which may be discharged by good merchantable Bear and Deer skins &c and the Declaration states that the writing Obligatory calls for £10-17-3 to be discharged in good merchantable Bear and Deer skins &c which said words in said Declaration is materially variant from the writing Obligatory and that the said Declaration is wholly insufficient & informal wherefore for want of a sufficient Declaration &c the said Deft prays [ ] &c and the said Plaintiff by their attorney says they Ought not to be bared from having and supporting their said action against the said Defendant for any thing or his Plea above precluded &c And the Court after hearing the arguments of Counsil on both sides and the matter of law arrising upon the Defendants Demurrer to the Plaintiffs declaration, and mature deliberation being thereon had, It is considered by the Court that the Defts Demurer and the matter therein Contained are not sufficient in law to bar and preclude the Plaintiff from having and supporting their action against the said Defendant Therefore It is Ordered that Demurer be Over ruled with Costs & the cause Continued until the next Court
[page 214] **Benjamin Slone** Plt
against In Covenant
**John Gwin** Deft
**Ralph Williams** of Pulaski County came into Court and Justified And undertook for the said Defendant that if he shall be cast in this Action aforesaid that he shall satisfy and pay the Condemnation of the Court or render his body to prison in execution for the same or on falure thereof that he the said **Ralph Williams** shall do it for him
– Pulaski County Court Plt
against In Debt
**Robertson & January** Defts
The day came the Plaintiff by his attorney, and thereupon came also a Jury, to wit, **John Chesney, Robert Smith, Temple Sargent, Nathaniel Thacker, George Decker, John Woods, Henry Bird, Martin Barrier, Daniel Duncan, Joel Jackson, Stephen Sargent & John Hardgrove** who were sworn well and truly to enquire what Damage the Plaintiff hath sustained in

the premises upon their Oaths do find for the Plaintiff twenty Dollars and sixty two Cents the Debt in the declaration mentioned besides his Costs. It is therefore considered by the Court that the Plaintiff recover against the said Defendants the said Debt in the Declaration mentioned with legal Interest thereon from the twenty second day of September One thousand eight hundred and four until paid & Costs and the said Defts in mercy &c.

**John** & **William Allin** Plts
against In Covenant
**John Newby** Deft

This day came the Plaintiffs by their attorney and thereupon came also a Jury, to wit, **John Chesney, Robert Smith, Temple Sargent, Nathaniel Thacker, George Decker, John Woods, Henry Bird, Martin Barrier, Daniel Duncan, Joel Jackson, Stephen Sargent** & **John Hardgrove**, who were sworn well and truly to enquire what damage the Plaintiff hath sustained in the Premises upon their Oaths do say the Plaintiff hath sustained Damage by Occasion thereof [page 215] to five pounds four shilling three pence with legal Interest thereon from the 23rd day of July 1805 besides their Costs. It is therefore considered by the Court that the Plaintiffs recover against the said Defendant his Damages & Interest by the Jurors in their Verdict aforesd assessed and their Costs by them about their suit in this behalf expended and the said Defendant in mercy &c.

– **Thomas Ball** Assee Plt
against In Debt
**Jesse Chappel**

This day came the Plaintiff by his attorney and thereupon came also a Jury, to wit, **John Chesney, Robert Smith, Temple Sargent, Nathaniel Thacker, George Decker, John Woods, Henry Bird, Martin Barrier, Daniel Duncan, Joel Jackson, Stephen Sargent** & **John Hardgrove** who were sworn well and truly to enquire what Damage the Plaintiff hath sustained in the premises upon their Oaths do find for the Plaintiff the Debt in the Declaration mentioned and do assess the Damages by Occasion of the Detention thereof to one penny besides his Costs. It is therefore Considered by the Court that the Plaintiff recover against the said Defendant the said Debt in the Declaration mentioned his Damages and Costs, aforesaid, and the said Defendant in mercy &c. Note this Judgment is to be discharged by the payment of twenty Dollars with legal Interest thereon from the twenty seventh day of March One thousand eight hundred and four until paid & Costs &c.

– **Alexander Hambleton** Plt
against In Covenant
**Davison** & Deft

This day came the Plaintiff by his attorney, and thereupon came also a Jury, to wit, **John Chesney, Robert Smith, Temple Sargent, Nathaniel Thacker, George Decker, John Woods, Henry Bird, Martin Barrier, Daniel Duncan, Joel Jackson, Stephen Sargent** & **John Hardgrove** who were sworn well and trully to enquire what Damage the Plaintiff hath Sustained in the premises upon their Oaths do say the Plaintiff hath Sustained Damage by Occasion thereof to sixty seven dollars besides his Costs [page 216] It is therefore considered by the Court that the Plaintiff recover against the said Defendant and Bail his Damages aforesaid by the Jurors in their Verdict aforesaid assessed and his Costs by him about his suit in this behalf expended and the said Defendant in mercy &c.

– **Thomas Owsley** Assee Plt
against In Debt
**Ayres Dors** Deft

This day came the Plaintiff by his attorney and thereupon came also a Jury, to wit, **John Chesney, Robert Smith, Temple Sargent, Nathaniel Thacker, George Decker, John Woods, Henry Bird, Martin Barrier, Daniel Duncan, Joel Jackson, Stephen Sargent,** & **John Hardgrove** who were sworn well and truly to enquire what Damage the Plaintiff hath sustained in the premises upon their Oaths do find for the Plaintiff the Debt in the Declaration mentioned with legal Interest besides his Costs It is therefore considered by the Court that the Plaintiff recover against the said Defendant Seventeen dollars the Debt in the Declaration mentioned with legal Interest thereon from the first day of July One thousand eight hundred and five until paid & Costs and the said Defendant in mercy &c.

– **Jahu Baker** Plt
against In Debt
**James Alderson** Deft

This day came the Plaintiff by his attorney and thereupon came also a Jury, to wit, **John Chesney, Robert Smith, Temple Sargent, Nathaniel Thacker, George Decker, John Woods, Henry Bird, Martin Barrier, Daniel Duncan, Joel Jackson, Stephen Sargent** & **John Hardgrove** who were sworn well and truly to enquire what Damage the Plaintiff hath sustained in the premises upon their Oaths do find for the Plaintiff the Debt in the Declaration mentioned, and do assess his Damage by Occasion of the Detention thereof to One Cent, besides his costs It is therefore considered by the Court that the Plaintiff recover against the said Defendant forty Dollars the Debt in the Declaration [page 217] mentioned with legal Interest thereon from the twenty fifth day of December One thousand eight hundred and three until paid & Damages & Costs and the said Defendant in mercy &c

– **Jahu Baker** Plt
against In Debt
**James Alderson** Deft

This day came the Plaintiff by his attorney and thereupon came also a Jury, to wit, **John Chesney, Robert Smith, Temple Sargent, Nathaniel Thacker, George Decker, John Woods, Henry Bird, Martin Barrier, Daniel Duncan, Joel Jackson, Stephen Sargent** & **John Hardgrove** who were sworn well and truly to enquire what Damage the Plaintiff hath sustained in the premises upon their Oaths do find for the Plt the Debt in the Declaration mentioned, and do assess his Damage by Occasion of the Detention thereof to One Cent, besides his costs It is therefore considered by the Court that the Plaintiff recover against the said Defendant thirty Dollars the Debt in the Declaration mentioned his Damages aforesaid by the Jurors in their Verdict aforesaid assessed and his Costs by him about his suit in this behalf expended and the said Defendant in mercy &c Note this Judgment is to bare legal Interest from the first day of May One thousand eight hundred and four until paid & Costs But to have Credit for twenty Dollars paid the eleventh day of February one thousand eight hundred and five

– The Court allows to **William Fox** as their clerk the sum of thirty Dollars for public Service performed by him in the execution of his Office for the last year Preceeding the last October Term of this Court which is Ordered to be Certified to the Auditor of Public Accounts

– The Clerk of this Court exhibited herein in Court and Account for paper furnished for the use of his Office which was Ordered to be Certified to the Auditor of Public Accounts

[page 218] **William Ussery** Plt
against upon Attachment
**William Evans** Deft

– **James Johnson** Plt
against Same
**Joseph Evans** Deft

– **John Bradford** Plt
against Same
**William Ussery** Deft

– **William Evans** Plt
against Same
**William Ussery** Deft

Ordered that these attachments be dismissed

– Ordered that the Court be adjourned "till Court in Course

**John Smith**

At a Circuit Court held for the Pulaski Circuit at the Courthouse of Pulaski County in Sommerset on Monday the 28th day of July 1806

Present the Honbl **William L Kelly, John Smith & John Prather**

– A Grand jury was sworn for the Pulaski Circuit to wit, **Henry James, James Harril, Daniel Duncan, Robt Modrel** Junr, **Stephen Wilkerson, Spencer McDaniel, Jonathan Smith, William Southerland, Alexander Ramsey, David Buster, William Hail, Richard Brown, George Allen, Drewry Clark** [page 219] **William Buster, Thomas Murphey, George W Saunders, Johnson Sargent, Ambrose Mayfield, John Cundiff, Thomas McGuire, & Charles Carter**, who having received their charge retired to consider of their Presentments

– Ordered that **Lewis Fitzgerald, John Duncan, James Wilkerson, James Cowen, William Lynch, Richard Muse & Thomas Clear** be summoned to appear here at the next Term of this Court to shew Cause if any they can why they may not be find for failing to attend as Grand jury at this present Term, agreeably to the Act of the General Assembly Kentucky in that case made and provided

– **Jesse Wommack** Plt
against In Case
**Charles Rusk** Deft

Ordered that this suit be Dismissed by Order of the Plaintiff

– **William G Cowen** Plt
against upon Attachment
**Joseph Taylor** Deft

Ordered that this attachment be Dismissed for want of prosecution

– **John Rogers** Plt
against In Case
**John McWhorter** Deft

This day came the parties aforesaid by their attornies, and by their consent all matters in difference between them relative to this cause is refered to the arbitration and final determination of **Robert Modrel** Senr **John Smith & Nicholas Jasper**, whose award be made the Judgment of the Court and the same is Ordered Accordingly

[page 220] **Andrew Cowen** Complt
against In Chancery
**Tunstal Quarles** Deft

– **John Weirs** Admor Plt
against In Case
**Nathaniel Forbis** Deft

Ordered that this suit be continued until the next Term of the Court

– **Jesse Wommack** Assee Plt
against In Chancery
**Isom Gibson** Deft

Ordered that this suit be Dismissed, and that the Deft recover his Costs herein expended

– **William Evans** Plt
against In Covenant
**John Roberson** Deft

This day came the Deft by his attorney, and upon his motion It is Ordered that the Judgment and writ of Inquiry awarded against him in the Clerks Office be set a side and the said Defendant by his attorney now comes and defends the wrong and Injury when and where &c and says he hath well and truly kept and performed the Bond Covenants in the writing herein mentioned upon his part and of this he puteth himself upon the Country and the Plaintiff doth the same likewise, and the said Defendant for further plea herein says [page 221] Therefore it is commanded the Sheriff that he cause to come here Immediately twelve good and lawful men by whom &c and thereupon came also a Jury, to wit, **A[ ] Ross, Samuel Hand, Edward White, Brice Mayfield, Thomas Sargent, Henry Sage, Willis Embry, William Denham, James Mattheson, John**

**Wolverton, John Brooks** & **Samuel Crow**, who being elected tried and sworn the truth to speak upon the Issue Joined, upon their Oaths do say that the said Defendant hath not kept and performed the several Covenants in the Writing mentioned on his part as in pleading he hath alledged, but hath broken the same in manner and form as the Plaintiff in his Declaration against him hath declared, and they do assess the Plaintiffs Damages by Occasion thereof to fifty Pounds besides his Costs. It is therefore Considered by the Court that the Plaintiff recover against the said Deft his Damages aforesaid by the Jurors in their Verdict afs[d] assessed, and his Costs by him about his suit in this behalf expended and the said Deft in mercy &[c].

– **James S Davis** Plt
against In Covenant
**William Brooks** Deft

This day came as well the Plaintiff by his attorney, as the said Defendant in his proper person, and It is Ordered that this suit be dismissed at the said Defendants Costs

– **Moses Preston** Complt
against Upon Recognizance
**Daniel McClure** & others Deft

The Plaintiff being solemnly called but came not therefore on the motion of the Defendant who appeared in discharge of said recognizance, It is ordered that said recognizance be Dismissed for want of prosecution, and the said Defendants recover their Costs &[c].

[page 222] **Joseph Casky** Plt
against In Trespass Assault & Battery
**Robert Smith** Deft

Ordered that this suit be Continued until the next Court at the Plaintiffs Costs

– On the motion of **George W Gibbs** esquire who produced licence authorizing him to practice law & whereupon the said **Gibbs** esquire took the necessary Oaths &[c].

– The Grandjury returned into Court, the following presentments to wit, Pulaski Circuit Term July 1806, The Jurors of the Grand jury for the body of the said County and Circuit aforesaid upon our Oaths present **William Griffin** Senior Surveyor of the Road leaving the Town of Sommerset Pulaski County aforesaid to the Crab Orchard Beginning at Buck Creek from thence to the County line of said County for not keeping the same in good repair on the twenty eighth day of this present July 1806 against the form of the Statute in such cases made and provided, as well as against the Law and dignity of this Commonwealth by the information given by **William Southerland**, and **Thomas Murphey**, both of the Grand jury and residenters of the County aforesaid

**Henry James** foreman of the Grand Jury

State of Kentucky the Circuit Composed of the County of Pulaski at the July Circuit Term 1806 The Jurors of the Grand jury for the body of the County and Circuit aforesaid upon our Oaths present **Zachariah Evans** farmer of the County aforesaid for committing perjury on the second day of May last past in the Courthouse in Sommerset, and County of Pulaski aforesaid in the trial of the cause **John Evans**, against **John Collier**, and **John Preston**, said Oath administered by the clerk of the Circuit Court of Pulaski aforesaid against the form of the Statute in such cases made and provided as well as against the Law & [page 223] dignity of this Commonwealth by the information of **John Preston** farmer not of the Grand jury & a residenter of Pulaski County

**Henry James** foreman of the Grand Jury

Pulaski Circuit Term July 1806, The Jurors of the Grand jury for the body of said County & Circuit aforesaid upon our Oaths present **John Hughes**, Surveyor of the road leaving from the Town of Sommerset Pulaski County aforesaid to the flat Lick in said County, for not keeping the same in repair on the 28[th] day of the present July 1806 against the form of the Statute in such cases made and provided as well as against the peace and dignity of this Commonwealth by the information of **Thomas McGuire** & **Thomas Murphey** both of the Grand jury & residenters of Pulaski County

**Henry James** foreman of the Grand jury

Pulaski Circuit Term July 1806, the Jurors of the Grand jury for the body of said County and Circuit aforesaid upon Our Oaths present **Adonijah Morgan**, Surveyor of the road leading from the Town of Sommerset Pulaski County to the Crab Orchard beginning at Pitmans Creek, thence to Buck Creek in said County for not keeping the same in repair on the 28th day of the present July 1806 against the form of the Statute in such cases made and provided, as well as against the peace and dignity of the Commonwealth, by the information of **George W Saunders & Wm Southerland** both of the Grand jury and residenters of the County of Pulaski

**Henry James** foreman

And the Grand jury having nothing further to present were dischd by the Court and Delinquents Ordered to be Summoned &c.

[page 224] **John Cocke** Plt
against In Case
**Nathaniel Forbis** Deft

This day came the Plaintiff by his attorney, and on his motion It is Orderd that the Judgment and Writ of Inquiry awarded against the said Defendant in the Clerks Office be waved. And the said Defendant now here in Court says he cannot gainsay the Plaintiffs Action against him for sixty Dollars Therefore with the Assent of the Plaintiff It is considered by the Court that the Plaintiff recover against the said Defendant the said Sixty Dollars the sum acknowledged as aforesaid and his Costs by him about his suit in this behalf expended and the said Defendant in mercy &c Note Execution is to be staid two months

– **Condley Findley & Co** Plts
against In Debt
**John Harmon** Deft

This day came the Plaintiffs by their attorney, and It is Ordered that the Judgment and Writ of Inquiry awarded against the said defendant in the Clerks Office be waved, and on the motion of the Plaintiff by his attorney Judgment is awarded him against the said Defendant for the Debt in the Declaration mentioned and his Costs by him about his suit in this behalf expended, and the said Defendant in mercy &c. Note this Judgment is to be discharged by the payment of five pounds thirteen shillings and seven pence with legal Interest thereupon from the 1st day of October 1803 until paid & Costs, With stay of Execution three months

– **Thomas McGuire** Plt
against In Debt
**John Bradford** Deft

[page 225] This day came the Plaintiff by his attorney, and on his motion It is Ordered that the Judgment and Writ of Inquiry awarded against the said Defendant in the Clerks Office be waved, and that the Plaintiff recover against the said Defendant the Debt in the Declaration mentioned, and his costs by him about his suit in this behalf expended and the said Defendant in mercy &c. Note this Judgment is to be discharged by the payment of twelve pounds with legal Interest thereon from the ____ day of ____ until paid & Costs

– **Hugh Donigy** Plt
against In Covenant
**Joseph Casky** Deft

On the motion of the said Defendant, he having entered Special Bail herein, It is Orderd that the Judgment and writ of Inquiry awarded against him in the Clerks Office be set a side, and the said Deft by his Attorney comes and defends the wrong and Injury when and where &c. and craves Oyer of the bond in the Declaration mentioned which is read to him in the words and figures, to wit, and saith the Plaintiff his action aforesaid ought not to have and maintain because he saith that the Plaintiffs Declaration and the matters and things therein contained are insufficient in law to maintain the action aforesaid, to which said Declaration and to matters and things therein contained the Defendant has no necessity to answer neither is he bound by the law of the land to answer thereto, and this he is ready to verify, wherefore he Demurs agreeable to an Act of the General Assembly made for the Commonwealth of Kentucky in such case made and provided, The Defendant sets down the following Causes of Demurrer, to wit, 1st that the Plt has not said in his declaration a special Demand 2d that he has not alledged that he previous to the [page 226]

Commencement of the said Action demanded of the Deft at his usual place of residence to keep his Covenant, and pay the Plaintiff one hundred and sixteen Gallons of proof whisky 3rd that there is in the Declaration an averment which is addition to and repayment to the Deed of Covenant 4th that the Declaration is altogether informal insufficient &c.

**McKee** & **Owsley**

and the said Plaintiff by his attorney saith that by any thing in the Defts Demurer he Ought not to be bared or precluded from having and supporting his Action afsd and this he is ready to verify wherefore he prays Judgment &.

**Bridges** for Plt

Whereupon the matters of law arrising upon the Defendants Demurrer to the Plaintiffs Declaration being argued, It is Considered by the Court that the said Demurrer be sustained &c And on the motion of the Plaintiff by his attorney leave is given him to amend his Declaration herein and the Cause to be remanded to the Rule Docket on the payment of Costs

– **George W Saunders** & ux Plt
against In Trespass Assault & Battery
**John Griffin** Deft

– **John Griffin** & County Plt
against In Debt
**George W Saunders** & ux Deft

– **John Griffin** Plt
against In Trespass assault & Battery
**George W Saunders** & ux Defts

– **George W Saunders** Plt
against Same
**John Griffin** Deft

[page 227] This day came the parties aforesaid by their attornies, and by their consent all matters in difference between them relative to the above suits are refered to the Arbitration and determination of **Jesse Richardson, John Funk, Thomas McGuire, Philip A Sublette** & **Edward Prather** whose award or the award of any three of them be the Judgment of the Court and the same is Ordered accordingly

– Ordered that the Court be adjourned until Tommorow morning nine OClock

**William L Kelly**

At a Circuit Court Continued and held for the Pulaski Circuit at the Courthouse in Sommerset on Tuesday the 29th day of July 1806

Present the Honbl **William L Kelly** & **John Smith** Gent

– **Robertson Burge** Plt
against In Case
**David Clark** Deft

Ordered that this suit be continued until the next Court

– **Jarrot Harbin** Plt
against In Debt
**Joseph Evans** &c Defts

This day came as well the Plaintiff by his attorney and the said Defendant **Evans** in his proper person, wh acknowledged the Plaintiffs action against him for thirty five Dollars and eighty five and ¾ cents the Debt in the Declaration mentioned Therefore with the assent of the Plaintiff It is Considered by the Court that the Plaintiff recover against the said Defendant the sum aforesaid with legal Interest thereupon the twenty fifth day of May One thousand eight hundred and five until paid & [page 228] Costs with stay of Execution three months, and the said Defendant in mercy &c.

– Present **John Prather** Esqr

– **Robertson Burge** Plt
against In Case

**Joseph Porter** Deft

This day came the Parties aforesaid by their attornies and thereupon came also a Jury, to wit, **James Matthews, Henry Sage, Fortunatus Dodson, William Burton, Ayres Dors, Willis Embry, Henry Willis, George Modrel, Alexander Montgomery, Samuel Gilmore, Jonathan McConnel & Joseph Evans,** who being elected tried and sworn the truth to speak upon the Issue Joined upon their Oaths do say that the Defendant is Guilty in manner and form as the Plaintiff against him hath declared, and they do assess the Plaintiffs damages by Occasion thereof to twenty Dollars, besides his Costs It is therefore Considered by the Court that the Plaintiff recover against the said Defendant his Damages aforesaid by the Jurors in their Verdict aforesaid assessed and his Costs by him about his suit in this behalf expended, and the said Defendant in mercy &c.

– **John Burdit** Plt
against In Case
**Jesse Richardson** Deft

This day came the parties aforesaid by their attornies and thereupon came also a Jury, to wit, **Jacob Baker, Hamlet Thomas, John Smith, John Wolverton, James Ingram, Temple Sargent, Andrew Jasper, Cornelius Dollehide, Stephen Fields, Robertson Burge, William Richardson & William Southerland** who being elected tried and sworn the truth to speak upon the Issue Joined upon their [page 229] Oaths do say that the said Defendant is not guilty in manner and form as the Plaintiff against him hath declared. Therefore It is Considered by the Court that the Plaintiff take nothing by his bill but for his false clamour be in mercy &c and that the said Defendant go thereof hence without day and recover against the said Plaintiff his Costs by him about his defence in this behalf expended and the said Plaintiff my be taken

– **Robert Gillilands** admor Plt
against In Case
**James L Hobbs** Deft

This day came the Plaintiffs by their attorney and thereupon came also a Jury, to wit, **Jacob Blacklidge, John Evans, Smith Williams, Samuel Coupenheifer, Samuel Allin, James Kerr, William Eastham, John Chesney, Edward White, William Williams, Jeremiah Clonch, & Jonas Erwin,** who were Sworn well and truly to enquire what damage the Plaintiffs hath sustained in the premises upon their Oaths do say that the Plaintiffs hath sustained Damage by Occasion thereof to sixteen pounds seven shillings besides his Costs It is therefore considered by the Court that the Plaintiff recover of the said Defendant their Damages afsd by the Jurors in their Verdict aforesd assessed & their Costs by them about their suit in this behalf expended and the said Defendant in mercy &c.

– **Thomas Owsley** Plt
against In Covenant
**William Lair** Deft

Ordered that this suit be Discontinued, agreeable to the Order of the Plaintiffs attorney and that the Plaintiff recover his Costs agreeable to an agreement between the parties

[page 230] **Joel Evans** Plt
against In Case
**Philip A Sublette** Deft

This day came the Parties aforesaid and It is Ordered that this suit be dismissed at the Plaintiffs costs (excepting the Defendants attorneys fee

– **Samuel Cole** Plt
against In Case
**Cornelius Doolan** Deft

This day came the Parties aforesaid by their attornies, and thereupon came Also a Jury, to wit, **Jacob Blacklidge, John Evans, Smith Williams, Samuel Coupenheifer, Samuel Allin, James Kerr, William Eastham, John Chesney, Edward White, John Wolverton, Jeremiah Clonch, & Jonas Erwin,** who being elected tried and sworn the truth to speak upon the Issue Joined upon their Oaths do say that the said Defendant is guilty in manner and form as the Plaintiff against him hath declared and they do assess the Plaintiffs Damages by Occasion thereof to forty five Dollars besides his Costs. It is therefore Considered by the Court that the Plaintiff recover against the said Defendant his Damages aforesaid by the Jurors in their Verdict afores[d] assessed and his Costs by him about his suit in this behalf expended and the said Defendant may be taken &[c]

– **James Johnson** Ass[ee] Plt
against In Covenant
**Joseph Evans** Deft

This day came as well the Plaintiff by his attorney as the said Deft in his proper person who says he cannot gainsay the Plaintiffs action against him for thirty Dollars the sum in the Declaration [page 231] mentioned Therefore with the assent of the Plaintiff It is Considered by the Court that the Plaintiff recover against the said Defendant the sum acknowledged as afores[d] with legal Interest thereon from the tenth day of April One thousand eight hundred and five until paid and costs and the said Defendant in mercy &[c]. Execution to be staid three months

– **Dick Patridge** Plt
against In Trespass Assault and Battery & false Imprisonment
**Richard Tutt** Deft

This day came the Defendant by his attorney and on his motion It is Ordered that the Judgment and Writ of Inquiry awarded against him in the Clerks Office be set a side, and the said Defendant now comes and defends the wrong and Injury when and where &[c] and says that he is not guilty in manner and form as the Plaintiff against him hath declar[d] and of this he puteth himself upon the Country and the said Plaintiff likewise Therefore It is commanded the sheriff that he cause to come here Immediately twelve good and lawful men by whom &[c] and thereupon came also a Jury, to wit, **David Richardson, John Puckett, Henry Bird, Stephen Hail, Charles Richardson, Andrew Turner, Henry Willis, Hamlet Thomas, William Owens, John Smith, John Westerman** & **Richard Lewis** who being elected tried and sworn the truth to speak upon the Issue Joined upon their Oaths do find the Plaintiff to be entitled to his freedom and the Defendant guilty of the Trespass Assault and Battery and false Imprisonment in the Declaration Mentioned and do assess the Plaintiffs Damages In consequence thereof to One penny besides his Costs. It is therefore Considered by the Court that the Plaintiff recover of the said Defendant his freedom aforesaid together with his Damages aforesaid by the [page 232] Jurors in their Verdict aforesaid assessed and his Costs by him about his suit in this behalf expended and the said Deft may be taken &[c]

– **William Guthrie** Ass[ee] Plt
against In Debt
**John Smith** Deft

**David Richardson** of Pulaski County who came into Court and Justified, and undertook for the said Defendant that if he shall be Cast in the action aforesaid that he shall satisfy and pay the condemnation of the Court or render his body to prison in Execution for the same or on falure thereof that he the said **David Richardson** shall do it for him

– **Spencer McDaniel** Plt
against In Debt
**James Alderson** Deft

**John Fitzgerald** of Pulaski County came into Court and Justified, and undertook for the said Defendant that if he shall be cast in the Action aforesaid that he shall satisfy and pay the Condemnation of the Court or render his body to prison in execution for the same or on falure thereof that he the said **John Fitzgerald** shall do it for him

[page 233] Ordered that the Court be adjourned until Tomorrow morning nine OClock

**William L Kelly**

At a Circuit Court continued and held for the Pulaski Circuit at the Courthouse in Sommerset on Wednesday the 30[th] day of July 1806

Present the Honourable **William L Kelly, John Smith**, and **John Prather** Gentlemen

– **John Collier** & **John Preston** Complt
against In Chancery upon motion to Desolve Injunction
**John Evans** Deft

This day came the parties aforesaid by their attornies and on the motion of the said Defendant to Desolve the complainants Injunction on the face of the bill, after hearing the Bill &c and the arguments of Counsil on both sides, the Court took time to Consider & afterwards It was Ordered that the Injunction be Sustained & said motion be Overruled with Costs

– **William Evans** Plt
against In Covenant
**John Robertson** Deft

This day came the parties aforesaid by their attornies, and on the motion of the Defendant by his attorney for a new trial on the Verdict of the Jury and Judgment Obtained herein, after hearing the arguments of Counsil on both sides, It is considered by the Court that a new trial be awarded herein, on the paym<sup>t</sup> of Costs. Therefore on the m° of the Plaintiff by his attorney, an Order of Survey is awarded him directed to the Surveyor of Lincoln County commanding him to go on the lands in Controversy between the parties on the ___ day of ____ next if fair if not then on the next fair day and then and there Survey and lay off the same as either party would [page 233] have it having regard to all Deeds and other evidence that may be produced report all matters of fact specially, return four fair platts and certificates to the Clerks Office before the day of hearing and the cause is cont[d] till the next Court

– **John Burdit** Plt
against In Case
**Jesse Richardson** Deft

This day came the parties aforesaid by their attornies and upon the motion of the Plaintiff by his attorney for to Obtain a new trial on the Verdict of the Jury and Judgment herein, after hearing the arguments of Counsil on both sides and mature deliberation being thereon had, It is Considered by the Court that said motion be Over ruled, and that the Defendant recover his Costs by him about his defence relative to said Motion

– **Obediah Paine** Plt
against In Case
**Robert Gillilands** adm[or] Deft

This day came the parties aforesaid by their attornies and the Plaintiff being solemnly called but came not neither is his suit further prosecuted, Therefore on the motion of the Deft It is Ordered that the Plaintiff take nothing by his bill but for his false Clamour be in mercy &c. and that the Defendant go hence without day, and recover of the said Plaintiff their Costs by them about their defense in this behalf expended

– **Spencer McDaniel** Plt
against In Debt
**James Alderson** Deft

This day came the parties aforesaid by their attornies, and it is Ordered that this suit be continued until the next Court

[page 235] **Philip A Sublette** Plt
against In Case
**Joel Jackson** Deft

On the motion of the Defendant It is Ordered that the Judgment and Writ of Inquiry awarded against him in the Clerks Office be set a side and the said Defendant by his attorney now comes and defends the Wrong and Injury when and where &c and says he did not assume upon himself in manner and form as the Plaintiff against him hath declared and of this he puteth himself upon the Country and the said Plaintiff likewise Therefore it is Commanded the Sheriff that he cause to come here Immediately twelve good and lawful men by whom &c and thereupon came also a Jury, to wit, **John Westerman, John Griffin, John Decker, John Evans, John Funk, James Kerr, David McKeeton** [?] **Edward Cooper, Joseph Erwin, David Clark, Jonathan McConnel**

& **Absolem Sargent**, who being elected, tried and sworn the truth to speak upon the Issue Joined upon their Oaths do say that the said Defendant did assume upon himself in manner and form as the Plaintiff against him hath declared and they do assess the Plaintiffs Damages by Occasion thereof to twenty five Pounds besides his Costs It is therefore Considered by the Court that the Plaintiff recover against the said Defendant his Damages aforesaid by the Jurors in their Verdict aforesaid assessed and his Costs by him about his suit in this behalf expended and the said Defendant in mercy &c

– **Joel Jackson** Plt
against In Covenant
**William Addison** Deft

**Philip A Sublette**, of Pulaski County, came into Court and Justified &c and undertook for the said Defendant that if [page 236] shall be cast in the action aforesaid that he shall satisfy and pay the condemnation of the Court or render his body to prison in Execution for the same or on falure thereof that he the said **Philip A Sublette** shall do it for him

– Ordered that **John McCullough** be Summoned to appear here on the first day of our next Term of this Court to shew cause if any he can why he shall not be fined agreeable to an Act of the General Assembly Kentucky in this case made and provided, for failing to attend as a Juror when Summoned to attend by the Sheriff at this Term when Summoned today

– **Jesse Richardson** & **Thomas Owsley** Complts
against In Chancery
The Heirs and legal Representative of **James Christy** Decd Defts

This day came the complainants by their Counsil, and the many and places of residence of said Defendants being unknown On the motion of the Complainants by their Counsel It is ordered that the said Defendants do enter their appearance herein on the third day of the next October Term of this Court and answer the Complainants bill, or upon their failure, the same shall be taken as confessed against them, and further that this Order be Published for eight weeks successively in the Informant printed in Danville, according to the act of the General Assembly Kentucky in such cases made and provided

– **Zachariah** & **Robt Belsha** Plts
against In Covenant
**Alexander Crawford** Deft

This day came the Plaintiffs by their attorney and thereupon came also a Jury, to wit, **William Ussery, John s** [page 237] **Samuel Cowpenheifer, William Thompson, John Gwin, Jacob Baker, William Addison, Smith Williams, Andrew Turner, James Cox, William Williams**, and **George S Burton**, who were sworn well and truly to enquire what damages the Plaintiffs hath sustained in the premises upon their Oaths do say that the Plaintiffs hath sustained Damages by Occasion thereof to thirty seven Dollars fifty two and a half Cents besides his Costs It is therefore Considered by the Court that the Plaintiff recover against the said Defendant his Damages aforesaid by the Jurors in their Verdict aforesaid assessed and his Costs by him about his suit in this behalf expended and the said Defendant in mercy &c.

– **William Griffin** Plt
against In Case
**William Evans** Deft

This day came the Defendant by his attorney, and on his motion It is ordered that the Judgment and writ of Inquiry awarded against the said Defendant in the Clerks Office be set a side and the said Defendant by his attorney now comes and defends the wrong and Injury when and where &c and says he did not assume upon himself in manner and form as the Plaintiff against hath declared and of this he puteth himself upon the Country and the said Plaintiff likewise therefore let a Jury come here &c.

– **George Denny** Assee Plt
against In Debt
**William Ussery** Deft

This day came as well the Plaintiff by his attorney, as the said Defendant in his proper person who says he cannot gainsay the Plaintiffs Action against hm for twenty five Dollars the Debt [page 238] in the Declaration mentioned, Therefore with the assent of the Plaintiff It is Considered by the Court that the Plaintiff recover against the said Defendant the sum of twenty five Dollars acknowledged as aforesaid, and his Costs by him about his suit in this behalf expended and the said Defendant in mercy &c. Note this Judgment is to bare legal Interest on the sum therein mentioned from the Seventeenth day of December one thousand eight hundred and four until paid & Costs

– **Joseph McDonald** Ass[ee] Plt
against In Covenant
**Hamlet Thomas** Deft

This day came the Plaintiff by his attorney and thereupon came also a Jury, to wit, **William Ussery, John McFall, Samuel Cowpenheifer, William Thompson, John Gwin, Jacob Baker, William Addison, Smith Williams, Andrew Turner, James Cox, William Williams**, and **George S Benton**, who were sworn well and truly to enquire what Damage the Plaintiff hath sustained in the premises upon their Oaths do say the Plaintiff hath sustained Damage by Occasion thereof to twenty six Dollars and ninety eight Cents besides his Costs It is therefore Considered by the Court that the Plaintiff recover against the said Defendant his Damages aforesaid by the Jurors in their Verdict aforesaid assessed and his Costs by him about his suit in this behalf expended and the said Defendant in mercy &c.

– **Israel Hart** Plt
against In Debt
**Scrimiger** & **Benton** Defts

This day came the Plaintiff by his attorney and It is Ordered that [page 239] that this suit be dismissed

– **John Hiatt** Ass[ee] Plt
against In Debt
**Robertson Burge** Deft

This day came the parties aforesaid by their attornies, and on the motion of the said Defendant by his attorney leave is given him to withdraw his Demurrer and plea filed herein, And says he cannot gainsay the Plaintiffs Action against him for one hundred dollars the Debt in the Declaration mentioned, Therefore with the assent of the Plaintiff It is considered by the Court that the Plaintiff recover against the said Defendant the said sum of one hundred Dollars acknowledged as aforesaid, with legal Interest thereon from the third day of January One thousand eight hundred and five until paid & Costs and the said Defendant in mercy &c

– **Joseph Coiler** Ass[ee] Plt
against In Debt
**Robertson Burge** Deft

This day came the parties aforesaid by their attornies, and on the motion of the said Defendant by his attorney leave is given him to withdraw his Demurrer and plea filed herein, And says he cannot gainsay the Plaintiffs Action against him for sixty nine dollars the Debt in the Declaration mentioned, Therefore with the assent of the Plaintiff It is considered by the Court that the Plaintiff recover against the said Defendant the said sum acknowledged as aforesaid, with legal Interest thereon from the first day of March One thousand eight hundred and five until paid & Costs and the said Defendant in mercy &c

[page 240] **Henry Willis** Plt
against In Trespass Assault & Battery
**Ephraim Churchwell** Deft

Ordered that this suit be Dism[d] at the Plaintiffs Costs (except an attornies fee for which not to be taxed in the bill of Cost

– **Henry Grindstaff** Plt
against In Case
**Robert Gillilands** adm[or] Defts

On the motion of the Defendant It is Ordered that the Judgment and writ of Inquiry awarded against him in the Clerks Office be set a side and the said Defendant by their attorneys now comes and defends the wrong and Injury when and where &c and say they did not assume upon themselves in manner and form as the Plaintiff against them hath declared and of this they puteth themselves upon the Country and the said Plaintiff likewise, Therefore let a Jury Come here &c and the cause is Continued until the next Court

– **John Gwin** Plt
against In Case
**James Skidmore** Deft

Ordered that this suit be continued until the next Court

– **Abraham Bear** Plt
against In Debt
**Isaac Beason** & **Rich[d] Beason** Defts

**John Hardgrove** Junr of Pulaski County came into Court and undertook for the said Defendant **Rich[d] Beason** that if he shall be cast in the action aforesaid that he shall satisfy and pay the condemnation of the Court or render his body to prison in execution for the same or on falure [page 241] thereof that he the said **John Hardgrove** shall do it for him

– **Jn[o] & William Allin** Plt
against In Covenant
**William Hays**

This day came the parties aforesaid by their attornies and the said Deft acknowledged the Plaintiffs action against him for ten pounds seventeen Shillings and three pence together with legal Interest thereon from the twentieth day of July One thousand eight hundred and five until paid, Therefore with assent of the Plaintiffs It is Considered by the Court that the Plaintiff recover against the said Deft the sum with Interest acknowledged aforesaid and his Costs by him about his suit in this behalf expended and the said Deft in mercy &c.

– **John Green** Plt
against In Case
**Philip A Sublette** Deft

– **Thomas McGuire** Plt
against In Debt
**Charles Inglish** &c Defts

– **James Kitchens** Plt
against In Case
**Christ[o] Myers** Deft

– **William Evans** Plt
against In Covenant
**Lambert White** Deft

– **William Evans** Plt
against In Case
**William Ussery** Deft

[page 242] **Thomas Jacobs** Plt
against In Case
**Evans & Rusk** Deft

– **Philip A Sublette** Plt
against In Covenant
**William Evans** Deft

– **James Davis** Plt
against In Case
**John Fitzgerald** Deft

This day came the parties aforesaid by their Attornies, and It is Ordered that these suits be continued until the next Court

– **Joseph Casky** Plt
against In Case
**Martin Barrier** Deft

This day came the Plt aforesaid by his attorney, and on motion leave is given the Plaintiff to take the Depositions of **Rob**[t] and **Anson Taylor** of Tenessee Debeneesse, by a Dedimus which is awarded him before any two Justices of the peace of s[d] State & the Cause is continued until the next Court

– **William Hiatt** Plt
against In Case
**Charles Rusk** Deft

Ordered that this suit be continued until the next Court and on the motion of the Plaintiff by his attorney a Dedimus is awarded him to take the Deposition of **William Floyd**, of Lincoln County in chief to be read as evidence herein, the Deposition to be taken before a Single Justice of the Peace

[page 243] **Solomon Turpin** Plt
against In Trespass Assault & Battery
**Moses Martin** & wife Deft

Ordered that this cause be continued until the next Court

– **Thomas Mease** Plt
against In Debt
**George Lankford** Deft

This day came the Plaintiff by this attorney, and on his motion It is Ordered that the Writ of Inquiry awarded against the Deft in the Clerks Office be waved therefore It is Considered by the Court that the Plaintiff recover against the said Deft the sum of forty five Dollars it being the Debt in the Declaration mentioned, with legal Interest thereon from the first day of August One thousand eight hundred and five until paid & Costs and the said Defendant in mercy &[c]

– **John Prather** Plt
against In Debt
**James Alderson** & others Deft

This day came the Plaintiff by his attorney and upon his motion It is Ordered that the writ of Inquiry awarded against the said Deft in the Clerks Office be waved, Therefore on the motion of the Plaintiff by his attorney It is Ordered that the Plaintiff recover against the said Defts eighty five pounds the Debt in the Declaration mentioned and his Costs by him about his suit in this behalf expended and the said Defendant in mercy &[c] Note this Judgment is to be dischd by the payment of eighty five pounds with legal Interest thereon from the fifteenth day of May One thousand eight hundred and five until paid & Costs

[page 244] **Joseph & Tho**[s] **Welsh** Plt
against In Debt
**Adonijah Morgan** Deft

This day came the Plaintiffs by their attorney, and on his motion It is Ordered that the Writ of Inquiry awarded against the said Defendant in the Clerks Office be waved, therefore It is Ordered that the Plaintiffs recover against the said Defendant the Debt in the Declaration mentioned and their Costs by them about their suit in this behalf expended and the said Defendant in mercy &[c]. Note this Judgment is to be discharged by the payment of nineteen pounds three shillings and seven pence with legal Interest thereon from the eleventh day of January one thousand eight hundred and six until paid & Costs

– **Richard Davenport** Plt
against In Debt
**William J Sallee** Deft

This day came the Plaintiff by his attorney and thereupon came also a Jury, to wit, **Ambrose Mayfield, Francis Stephens, Thomas Stephens, Stephen Hail, Jesse Kizie, James Burton, John Turley, Edward White, John Jarvis, Thomas Paskel, James Elder** & **James Cox**, who were sworn well and truly to enquire what Damage the Plaintiff hath sustained in the premises upon their Oaths do find for the plaintiff the Debt in the Declaration mentioned which is 4 Dollars [ ] half cents and do assess the Plaintiffs Damages by Occasion of the detention thereof to One penny besides his Costs. It is therefore Considered by this Court that the Plaintiff recover against Defendant his Debt & Damages aforesaid by the Jurors in their Verdict afores[d] assessed and his Costs by him about his suit in this behalf expended and the said Deft in mercy &[c]. Note this Judgment [page 245] is to bare legal Interest thereon from the twenty first day of August One thousand eight hundred and four until paid & Costs But to have Credit for fifteen Dollars paid the twenty first day of February One thousand eight hundred and five

– **Joseph Casky** Plt
against upon a Scirafaciase to revise a Judgment for Costs
**John January** Deft

This day came the parties aforesaid by their attornies, and on the motion of the Defendant by his attorney puts in his plea of ahoff [?] herein, and after hearing the arguments of Counsel on both sides and the matter of law arrising upon said plea, It is Ordered by the Court that said plea be Overruled with costs, The Sheriff having returned a Writ of Scifacias herein executed, Therefore on the motion of the Plaintiff by his attorney the writ of Inquiry taken herein in the Clerks Office is Or[d] to be [ ] It is Considered by the Court that the Plaintiff may have his Execution against the said Deft for the sum of four Dollars forty eight and a half cents as specified in said Writ &[c] and his Costs by him about this suit expended and the said Defendant in mercy &[c]

– **John Colyer** & **John Preston** Complts
against In Chancery
**John Evans** Deft

This day came the said Defendant and made oath to his answer in Court to the Complainants Bill filed herein &[c].

– **George Dooley** Ass[ee] Plt
against In Debt
**Micajah Hogan** Deft

This day came the Plaintiff by his attorney, and on his motion It is Ordered that the writ of Inquiry awarded against the Defendant in the clerks Office herein be waved Therefore on the motion of the Plaintiff [page 246] by his attorney It is Considered by the Court that the Plaintiff recover against the said Defendant the Debt in the Declaration mentioned and his Costs by him about his suit in this behalf expended and the said Defendant in mercy &[c]

Note this Judgment is to be disch[d] by the payment of fifty six Dollars with legal Interest thereupon from the twentyfifth day of December One thousand eight hundred and three until paid & Costs

– **William Lair** Plt
against In Covenant
**William Evans** Deft

Ordered that this suit be Continued until the next Court

– **George Wilson** Plt
against In Covenant
**Anderson** & **Bobbit** Deft

This day came the Plaintiff by his attorney, and thereupon came also a Jury, to wit, **Ambrose Mayfield, Francis Stephens, Thomas Stephens, Stephen Hail, Jesse Kizzer, James Burton, John Turley, Edward White, John Jarvis, Thomas Paschel, James Elder**, and **James Cox** who were sworn well and truly to enquire what damage the Plaintiff hath sustained in the premises upon their Oaths do say the Plaintiff hath sustained Damages by Occasion thereof to fourteen pounds one shilling and four pence besides his Costs It is therefore Considered by the Court that the Plaintiff recover against the said Defendant his Damages aforesaid by the Jurors in their Verdict aforesaid assessed and his Costs by him about his Suit in this behalf expended and the said Defendant in mercy &[c].

- **William Hays** Ass[ee] Plt
against In Covenant
**Philip A Sublette** Deft

**George W Saunders** and **Stephen Hail** of Pulaski County came into Court [page 247] and undertook for the said Defendant that if he shall be cast in the Action aforesaid that they shall satisfy and pay the condemnation of the Court or render his body to prison in execution for the same or on falure thereof that they the said **Saunders** and **Hail** shall do it for him and on motion It is Ordered that the Judgment and writ of Inquiry awarded against the said Defendant in the Clerks Office be set a side and the said Defendant by his attorney now comes and defends the wrong and Injury when and where &c.

and after hearing the arguments of Counsel on both sides and the matters of law arrising on said Demurer, and mature deliberation being thereon had It is considered by the Court that the said Demurrer be Sustained and adjudged good, and that the Defendant recover of the said Plt his Costs relative thereto expended &c. Therefore on the motion of the Plt leave is given him to amend his Declaration herein, and the cause is remanded to the Rule Docket &c

- **Daniel McIlvey** Plt
against In Debt
**George W Saunders** Deft

**Elihu Saunders** of Pulaski County came into Court and Justified &c and [page 247a] undertook for the said Defendant that if he shall be cast in the Action aforesaid that he shall satisfy and pay the condemnation of the Court or render his body to prison in execution for the same or on falure thereof that he the said **Elihu Saunders** shall do it for him

- **John Simpson** Plt
against In Covenant
**John Jarvis** Deft

By consent of Parties all matters and difference between them relative to this suit is refered to the arbitration and determination of **William Owens, Richard Musse, Andrew Davidson, James Benton** Senr, **John McWhorter**, and **Edward Prather**, whose award or the award of any four of them be the Judgment of the Court and the same is Ordered accordingly

- **John** & **William Allin** Plt
against In Covenant
**James Johnson** Deft

This day came the Plaintiffs by their attorney, and on his motion It is Ordered that the writ of Inquiry awarded against the said Defendant in the clerks Office be waved, and that the Plaintiff recover against the said Defendant the Debt in the declaration mentioned and his costs by him about his suit in this behalf expended and the said Defendant in mercy &c

Note this Judgment is to be discharged by the payment of ten pounds nineteen shillings and two pence with legal Interest thereon from the twentieth day of June One thousand eight hundred and five until paid & Costs, but to have credit for seventeen Dollars paid on the 30th of July 1805

[page 248] **Balzar Detrick** & **Valentine Fehe** Plts
against In Case
**Ephraim Churchwell** Deft

This day came the Plaintiffs by their attorney and on his motion It is Ordered that the Writ of Inquiry awarded against the said Defendants in the Clerks Office be waved, and on the motion of the Plaintiffs by their attorney It is Ordered that the Plaintiffs recover against the said Defendant the sum in the Declaration mentioned, and their Costs by them about their suit in this behalf expended and the said Defendant in mercy &c. Note this Judgment is to be discharged by the payment of six pounds, and execution to be staid three months

- **James Doran & Co** Plts
against In Debt
**James Johnson** Deft

This day came the Plaintiffs by their attorney and It is Ordered that the Writ of Inquiry awarded against the said Defendant in the Clerks Office be waved, Therefore upon the motion of the Plaintiffs by their attorney It is Considered by the Court that the Plaintiff recover against the said Defendant twenty one Dollars and twenty five cents the Debt in the Declaration mentioned and his Costs by him about his suit in this behalf expended and the said Defendant in mercy &c Note this Judgment is to be discharged by the payment of the said twenty one Dollars and twenty five cents with legal Interest thereon from the thirtieth day of November One thousand eight hundred and five until paid & Costs

– **Thomas McGuire** Plt
against In Debt
**John Bradford** Deft

[page 249] This day came the Plaintiff by his attorney, and It is Ordered that the Writ of Inquiry awarded against the said Defendant in the Clerks Office be waved. Therefore on the motion of the Plt by his attorney It is Considered by the Court that the Plaintiff recover against the said Defendant twelve pounds besides his Costs, and the said Defendant in mercy &c. Note this Judgment is to bare legal Interest thereon from the twenty fifth day of December One thousand eight hundred and five until paid & Costs

– **Philip A Sublette** Assce Plt
against In Debt
**Joseph Evans** Deft

This day came the Plaintiff by his attorney, and It is Ordered that the writ of Inquiry awarded against the said Defendant in the clerks Office be waved, and on the motion of the Plaintiff by his attorney Judgment is granted him against the said Deft for the Debt in the Declaration mentioned, and his Costs by him about his suit in this behalf expended and the said Defendant in mercy &c. Note this Judgment is to be dischd by the payment of thirty two pounds ten shillings and ten pence with legal Interest thereon from the tenth day of April One thousand eight hundred and six until paid & Costs

– **Jno & William Allin** Plts
against In Covenant
**Joseph Porter** Deft

This day came the Plaintiffs by their attorney, and It is Ordered that the writ of Inquiry awarded against the said Defendant in the Clerks Office be waved. Therefore on the motion of the said Plaintiffs by their attorney It is Ordered that the Plts recover against the said Deft twenty six pounds twelve shillings and four pence the Debt in the Declaration mentioned, and their Costs by them about their suit [page 250] in this behalf expended and the said Defendant in mercy &c.

Note this Judgment is to bare legal Interest thereon from the third day of August One thousand eight hundred and four until paid and Costs, with stay of Execution three months

– **Thomas Jacob** Plt
against In Case
**Amos Evans** Senr Deft

Ordered that this suit be Continued until the next Court

– Ordered that the Court be adjourned "till Tomorrow morning ten OClock

– The Presiding Judge being absent the Record of these proceedings are signed

**John Smith**

At a Circuit Court Continued and held for the Pulaski Circuit at the Courthouse of Pulaski County in Sommerset on Thursday the 31st day of July 1806

Present **John Smith & John Prather** Gent

– **John Green** Plt
against In Covenant
**Philip A Sublette** Deft

This day came the parties aforesaid by their attornies, and by consent It is Ordered that this suit be dismissed it being agreed

– **Philip A Sublette** Plt
against In Case
**Joel Jackson** Deft

This day came the parties aforesaid by their attornies, and on the motion of the Defendant by his attorney for to Obtain a new trial herein on the Verdict of the Jury and Judgment Obtained herein at this present Term of the Court after hearing the arguments of the Counsil on both sides, and mature deliberation being thereon had It is Ord[d] [page 251] that said motion be Overruled and that the Plaintiff recover his Costs by him about said motion expended

– **James Eastham** Complt
against In Chancery
**John Blacklidge** Deft

This day came the Deft and filed his amended answer herein and made Oath to the same in Court

– **George Givens** Plt
against In Debt
**William Ussery** Deft

**Philip A Sublette** of Pulaski County came into Court and undertook for the said Defendant that if he shall be cast in the action aforesaid that he shall satisfy and pay the Condemnation of the Court or render his body to prison in execution for the same or on falure thereof that he the said **Philip A Sublette** shall do it for him

– **James Doran & Co** Plt
against In Debt
**William Evans** Deft

This day came the Plaintiff by his attorney, and It is Ordered that the writ of Inquiry awarded against the said Defendant in the Clerks Office be waved, Therefore it is Considered by the Court that the Plaintiff recover against the said Defendant the Debt in the Declaration mentioned and his Costs by him about his suit in this behalf expended and the said Defendant in mercy &[c]. Note this Judgment is to be discharged by the payment of five pounds fourteen shillings and ten pence with legal Interest thereon from the first day of December One thousand eight hundred and four until paid & Costs

[page 252] **John Long** Plt
against In Covenant
**Joseph Evans** Deft

– **Thomas Whites** Plt
against In Case
**William Ussery** Senr Deft

– **Benjamin Slone** Plt
against In Covenant
**John Gwin** Deft

– **Edward White** & ux Plt
against In Case
**Ch[s] Collier** Deft

– **Jn[o] & William Allin** Plt
against In Covenant
**William Churchwell** Deft

– **William Griffin** Plt
against In Case
**William Evans** Deft

Ordered that these suits be Continued until the next Court

– **James Doran & Co** Plt
against In Covenant
**William Evans** Deft

This day came the Plaintiff by his attorney and thereupon came also a Jury, to wit, **John Westerman, Charles Westerman, Joseph Thompson, Martin Barrier, John Evans, Elijah Barns, Thomas Thompson, Lambert White, Henry Willis, William Boyd, Thos Warren & James Campbell** who were sworn well and truly to enquire what Damages the plaintiff hath sustained in the premises upon [page 253] their Oaths do say that the Plaintiff hath sustained Damage by Occasion thereof to six pounds four shillings and six pence, besides their Costs. It is therefore Considered by the Court that the Plaintiff recover against the said Defendant their Damages aforesaid by the Jurors in their Verdict aforesaid assessed and their Costs by them about their suit in this behalf expended and the said Defendant in mercy &c.

– **Daniel McIlvey** Plt
against In Debt
**George W Saunders** Deft

This day came the Plaintiff by his attorney, and the Deft tho solomnly called came not, and thereupon came Also a Jury, to wit, **John Westerman, Charles Westerman, Joseph Thompson, Martin Barrier, John Evans, Elijah Barns, Thomas Thompson, Lambert White, Henry Willis, William Boyd, Thomas Warren & James Campbell,** who were sworn well and truly to enquire what Damage the Plaintiff hath sustained in the premises upon their Oaths do find for the Plaintiff the Debt in the Declaration mentioned, and do assess the Plaintiffs Damages by Occasion of the Detention thereof to three pounds eight shillings besides his Costs. It is therefore considered by the Court that the Plaintiff recover against the said Defendant forty two pounds ten shillings the said Debt in the Declaration mentioned & the Damages aforesaid by the Jurors in their Verdict aforesaid assessed and his Costs by him about his suit in this behalf expended and the said Defendant in mercy &c.

[page 254] **John Evans** Plt
against In Case
**John Collior** Deft

On the motion of the Defendant It is Ordered that the Judgment and Writ of Inquiry awarded against him in the Clerks Office be set a side and the said Defendant by his attorney now comes and defends the Wrong and Injury when and where &c. (Plea of set off. Plead but not filed) and of this he puteth himself upon the Country and the said Plaintiff doth the same likewise therefore it is Commanded the Sheriff that he cause to come here Immediately twelve good and lawful persons by whom &c and thereupon came also a Jury, to wit, **John Westerman, Charles Westerman, Joseph Thompson, Martin Barrier, William Griffin, Elijah Barns, Thos Thompson, Lambert White, Henry Willis, William Boyd, James Campbell & Thomas Warren**, who being elected tried and sworn the truth to speak upon the Issue Joined upon their Oaths do say that the Defendant is not entitled to a set off or [ ] as in pleading he hath alledged, and they do assess the plaintiffs Damages by Occasion thereof to thirty five Dollars besides his Costs It is therefore Considered by the Court that the Plaintiff recover against the said Deft his Damages aforesaid by the Jurors in their Verdict aforesaid assessed and his costs by him about his suit in this behalf expended and the said Defendant in mercy &c.

Note the thirty five Dollars Damages, named in this Judgment is to bare legal Interest thereon from the 28th day of February 1803 until paid & Costs

[page 255] **John & William Allin** Plts
against In Covenant
**Joseph Evans** Deft

This day came the Plaintiff by his attorney, and It is Ordered that the writ of Inquiry awarded against the said Defendant in the Clerks Office be waved And the Plaintiff by his attorney upon motion Judgment is granted him against the said Defendant for five pounds four shillings and six pence the sum in the declaration mentioned, and his Costs by him about his suit in this behalf expended and the said Defendant in mercy &c. Note this Judgment is to bare legal Interest on the sum therein mentioned from the twenty fifth day of July One thousand eight hundred and five until paid & Costs

– **White** & wife Plt
against In Case
**Charles Collier** Deft

This day came the parties aforesaid and by their consent all matters in difference between them respecting this suit is refered to the arbitration and determination of **John McCullough**, **William Worson**, **John Thompson**, **Christ^o^ Clonch** & **David McKinsey** whose award or the award of any three of them be the Judgment of the Court and the same is Ordered Accordingly
– Ordered that the Court be adjourned until Tomorrow morning ten OClock

**John Smith**

At a Circuit Court continued and held for the Pulaski Circuit at the Courthouse of Pulaski County in Sommerset on Friday the first day of August 1806

Present **John Smith** & **John Prather** Gentlemen

[page 256] **John Turley** Complt
against upon Attachment
**Isaac Avery** Deft

Ordered that this attachment be continued until the next Court
– Ordered that the Court be adjourned until Court in Course

**John Smith**

At a Circuit Court held for Pulaski County on Monday the 27th day of October 1806, at the Courthouse in Sommerset

Present the Honourable **William L Kelly** esquire
– Ordered that **Nicholas Jasper**, Sheriff of Pulaski County be fined ten dollars for failing to attend to the duties of his Office, in not attending on the Court, for the Pulaski Circuit before twelve OClock on this present day, and that he pay the Costs &c
– Present **John Smith** & **John Prather** esquires
– A Grand jury was sworn for the Pulaski Circuit, to wit, **John Singleton**, foreman, **John Hudson**, **Ambrose Mayfield**, **James Mayfield**, **Richard Beason**, **Jonathan Smith**, **James P Benton**, **James Wilkerson**, **Fortunatus Dodson**, **William Gun**, **George Dougherty**, **Simon Macy**, **Thomas Murphy**, **William Southerland**, **Martin Barrier**, **James Smith**, **George Lankford** and **Samuel Cornbest** who having received their charges retired to consider of their Presentment
– The Commonwealth
against for failing to attend as Grand jurors at the last Term of this Court
**John Duncan**, **Rich^d^ Muse** & **James Wilkerson** Defts

This day came the Defendants, and made their excuses to the Court which being heard was adjudged good &c and further proceeding Dismissed
[page 257] The Commonwealth
against upon Presentment for failing to keep the road in repair as Surveyor
**William Griffin** Senr

This day came as well the attorney for the Commonwealth as the said Defendant in his proper person, Therefore upon the motion of the said Attorney Judgment is granted against the said Defendant for fifteen shillings as per fine, and that he pay the costs of this Prosecution and may be taken &c
– The Commonwealth
against upon Presentment
**John Hughes**
– The Same
against Same
**Adonijah Morgan**
– The Same by **John Preston**

against upon Presentment for Perjury
**Zachariah Evans**
– **Thomas Whites** Complt
against upon Attachment
**William Ussery** Deft
– **Edward White** & wife Plt
against In Case
**David Garland** & wife Defts
– The Same Plts
against In Case
**Richard Collier** & wife Defts
– The Same Plts
against In Case
**Charles Collier** & wife Defts
Ordered that the above cases be Dismissed by Order of the Plaintiffs
[page 258] The Commonwealth
against for failing to attend as a Grand juror at the last Term of this Court
**William Lynch**
This day came the Defendant, and after hearing his excuse It is Ordered by the Court that he be fined One Dollar, for the failure afores[d] and that he pay the Costs &[c].
– **Andrew Cowen** Complt
against In Chancery
**Tunstall Quarles** Deft
– **John Weirs** adm[or] Plt
against In Case
**Nathaniel Forbis** Deft
Ordered that these suits be Continued until the next Court
– **William Evans** Plt
against In Covenant
**John Roberson** Deft
– **Joseph Casky** Plt
against In Trespass Assault & Battery
**Robert Smith** Deft
Ordered that these suits be Continued until the next Court at the Plaintiffs Costs, and that the said Defendants recover their Costs by them about their defence as to said Continuance expended
– **Robertson Burge** Plt
against In Case
**David Clark** Deft
Ordered that this suit be Continued until the next Court
– The Grand jury returned into Court an Indictment, the Commonwealth against **Zachariah Evans** a true Bill
**John Singleton** foreman of the Grand jury
[page 259] The Grandjury Also returned into Court the following Presentments to wit, State of Kentucky the Circuit Composed of the County of Pulaski, to wit at their October Circuit Term eighteen hundred and six, the Jurors of the Grand jury for the State and Circuit aforesaid upon their Oaths do present **William Wilson** yeoman of the County of Pulaski and Circuit aforesaid for Selling Spiritous Liquors without Ordinary License, to wit, Whisky by the half pint on the fourth Monday in August last past in the County of Pulaski aforesaid contrary to the form of the Statute in such cases made and provided as well as against the peace and dignity of this Commonwealth of Kentucky, and information given by **William Green**, and **Jonathan Smith**, both of the Grand jury, State of Kentucky the Circuit composed of the County of Pulaski, to wit, At their October Circuit Term

eighteen hundred and six the Jurors of the Grand jury for the State and Circuit aforesaid upon their oaths do present **Philip A Sublette** innkeeper of the County Pulaski and Circuit aforesaid for selling Spiritous Liquors without Ordinary License, to wit, whisky by the half pint on the fourth Monday in July last past and the ninth of October 1806 in the County of Pulaski aforesaid contrary to the form of the Statute in such cases made and provided as well against the peace and dignity of this Commonwealth of Kentucky and information given by **James P Burton** and **Jonathan Smith**, both of the Grand jury. State of Kentucky the Circuit Composed of the County of Pulaski, to wit, at their October Circuit Term eighteen hundred and six the Jurors of the Grand jury for the State and Circuit aforesaid upon their Oaths present **John January** Innkeeper, of the County of Pulaski and Circuit aforesaid for selling Spiritous liquors without Ordinary Licence, to wit, whisky by the half pint on the 4th Monday of September last past in the County of Pulaski aforesaid in the Town of Sommerset Contrary to the form of the Statute in such case made and provided as well as against the peace and dignity of the Commonwealth of Kentucky and [page 260] Information given by **Martin Barrier** and **George Lankford**, both of the Grand jury, State of Kentucky the Circuit Composed of the County of Pulaski, to wit, at their October Circuit Term eighteen hundred and six the Jurors of the Grand jury for the State and Circuit aforesaid upon their Oaths present **John McWhorter**, Innkeeper of the County of Pulaski and Circuit aforesaid for selling Spiritous liquors without Ordinary licence, to wit, whisky by the half pint on the ___ day of July and August last past in the County of Pulaski and County aforesaid in Sommerset Contrary to the form of the Statute in such cases made and provided as well as against the peace and dignity of the Commonwealth of Kentucky and Information given by **James P Burton** and **James Wilkerson** both of the Granjury, State of Kentucky the Circuit composed of the County of Pulaski to wit, at their October Circuit Term eighteen hundred and six the Jurors of the Grand jury for the state and Circuit aforesaid upon their Oaths present **Vinson Garner** Innkeeper of the County of Pulaski and Circuit aforesaid for selling Spiritous liquor without Ordinary licence, to wit, whisky by the half pint on the ___ day of September last past in the County of Pulaski aforesaid and Town of Sommerset Contrary to the form of the Statute in such Cases made and provided as well as against the peace and dignity of the Commonwealth of Kentucky; and information given by **Fortunatus Dodson** and **Samuel Cornbest** both of the Grand jury, The Grandjury having nothing further to present was discharged by the Court and Delinquents ordered to be Summoned

– **John Thomas** Plt
against In Covent
**George W Saunders** Deft

Ordered that this suit be Dismissed, agreeable to the Order of the Plt

– Ordered that the Court be adjourned until Tomorrow morning nine OClock

**William L Kelly**

[page 261] At a Circuit Court Continued and held for the Pulaski Circuit at the Courthouse of Pulaski County in Sommerset on the 28th day of October 1806

Present the Honourable **William L Kelly**, & **John Prather** Gent

– **John Beard** Complt
against In Chancery
**George W Saunders** & Als Deft

This day came the Parties aforesaid by their attornies and on the motion of the said Defendants by his attorney It is Ordered that this suit be Continued until the next Term of this Court at the said Defendants costs, and that the Complainant recover his Costs by him about said continuance expended, And on the motion of said Defendant by his attorney leave is given him to take Depositions

– **Samuel McKee** Complt
against In Chancery
**John Brown**

This day came the parties aforesaid by their attornies and upon the motion of the said

Defendant by his attorney to set a side the Rules taken in the Clerks Office herein. after hearing the Arguments of counsil on both sides It is Ordered by the Court that said motion be Over ruled Therefore upon the motion of the Complt by his Counsil this cause came on for trial, and after hearing the Bill herein, and the Arguments of counsil on both sides the Court took time to Consider of their Decree &c.

[page 262] **John Long** Plt
against In Covenant
**Joseph Evans** Deft

This day came the parties aforesaid by their attornies, and the said Defendant says he cannot gainsay the Plaintiffs action against him for fifty Dollars, therefore with the assent of the Plaintiff It is Considered by the Court that the Plaintiff recover against the said Defendant the fifty Dollars aforesaid, and his Costs by him about his suit in this behalf expended and the said Defendant in mercy &c. Memo execution to be staid three months

– **Spencer McDaniel** Plt
against In Debt
**James Alderson** Deft

This day came the Plaintiff by his attorney, and upon his motion It is Ordered that the Writ of Inquiry awarded against the said Defendant in the Clerks Office be waved, and that the Plaintiff recover against the said Defendant the Debt in the Declaration mentioned and his Costs by him about his suit in this behalf expended and the said Defendant in mercy &c. Note this Judgment is to be discharged by the payment of fifty Dollars with legal Interest thereon from the twenty fifth day of December, One thousand eight hundred and three until paid & Costs

– **John Rogers** Plt
against In Case
**John McWhorter**

– **Solomon Turpin** Plt
against In Trespass Assault & Battery
**Moses Martin** & wife Defts

Ordered that this suit be Dismissed it being agreed

[page 263] **James Kitchens** Plt
against In Case
**Christo Myers** Deft

The Plaintiff herein being called but came not, Therefore it is Ordered by the Court that his suit be Dismissed for want of Prosecution

– John Doe (ie, **James Tompkins** Plt
against upon Ejectment
Richard Roe (ie **John Puckett**

This day came the parties aforesaid by their attornies, and it is Ordered that the suit be Continued until the next Court, And it is agreed that the Survey returned may be filed in the same manner as though an Order had been made, and it is further agreed by the Attornies that the Plaintiff may make any legal addition to his Survey afsd

– **Robertson Burge** Assee Plt
against In Debt
**Joseph Porter** Deft

**John McWhorter** of Pulaski County came into Court and Justified and undertook for the said Defendant that if he shall be cast in the Action aforesaid that he shall satisfy and pay the condemnation of the Court or render his body to prison in execution for the same or on falure thereof that he the said **John McWhorter** shall do it for him, and on the motion of the Defendant It is Ordered that the Judgment and writ of Inquiry awarded against him in the Clerks Office be set a side and the Defendant by his attorney now comes and defends the wrong and Injury when and where &c and says the plaintiff his action afsd against him ought not to have and maintain because he says he hath well and truly paid the Debt in the Declaration mentioned and this he is ready to verify wherefore he prays Judgment &c And the plaintiff by his attorney says his action aforesaid [page 264] against the said Defendant he Ought to have and maintain because he says the said Defendant hath not well and truly paid the Debt in the Declaration mentioned as in pleading he hath alledged, and of this he puteth himself upon the Country and the said Defendant likewise therefore let a Jury Come here &c

– **Shadrick Felphs** Plt
against In Debt
**Vincent Garner** Deft

**George Humphreys** of Pulaski County came into Court & Justified and undertook for the said Defendant that if he shall be cast in the action aforesaid that he shall satisfy and pay the condemnation of the Court or render his body to prison in execution for the same or on falure thereof that he the said **George Humphreys** shall do it for him, And on the motion of the said Defendant It is Ordered that the judgment and Writ of Inquiry awarded against him in the clerks Office be set a side, and the said Defendant by his attorney now comes and defends the wrong and Injury when and where &c and says the Plaintiff his action aforesaid against him ought not to have and maintain because he says he hath well and truly paid the Debt in the Declaration mentioned, and this he is ready to verify, whereupon he prays Judgment &c And the plaintiff by his attorney says his action aforesaid against the said Defendant he ought to have and maintain because he says the said Defendant hath not well and truly paid the Debt in the Declaration mentioned as in pleading he hath alledged, and of this he puteth himself upon the Country, and the said Defendant likewise, Therefore let a Jury come here &c.

– **Henry Grindstaff** Plt
against In Case
**Robert Gillilands** adm[or] Deft

This day came the parties aforesaid by their attornies, and the Defendant acknowledges the Plaintiffs action against them for forty nine dollars and sixty cents, Therefore with the assent of the plaintiff [page 265] It is considered by the Court that the Plaintiff recover of the said Defendant the forty nine Dollars and sixty cents acknowledged as aforesaid to be levied of the Goods and chattles of the said Decedent in the hands of the adm[or]s to be administered. And his costs by him about his suit in this behalf expended, and the said Defendants in mercy &c Note this Judgment is to be credited with the Costs of the said Defts of a former suit between the said Parties

– **John S Moore & Co** Plt
against In Debt
**John Breedan** Deft

**Alexander Crawford** of Pulaski County came into Court and Justified and undertook for the said Defendant that if he shall be cast in the action aforesaid that he shall satisfy and pay the condemnation of the Court or render his body to prison in execution for the same, or on falure thereof that he the said **Alexander Crawford**, shall do it for him, and on the motion of the said Defendant It is Ordered that the Judgment and writ of Inquiry awarded against him in the clerks Office be set a side, and the said Defendant by his attorney now comes and defends the wrong and Injury when and where &c and says the Plaintiff his action aforesaid against him Ought not to have and maintain because he saith he hath well and truly paid the Debt in the Declaration mentioned and this he is ready to verify wherefore he prays Judgment &c And the plaintiff by his attorney says his action aforesaid against the said Defendant he Ought to have and maintain because he says the Defendant has not well and truly paid the Debt in the Declaration mentioned as in pleading he hath alledged, and of this he puteth himself upon the Country, and the said Defendant likewise therefore let a Jury come here &c.

[page 266] **James Eastham** Complt
against upon motion in Chancery notic proven
**John Blacklidge** Deft

This day came the parties aforesaid by their attornies, and on the motion of the said Defendant by his attorney to disolve the Complainants Injunction, after hearing the bill, answer and affidavits filed in the cause, and the arguments of Counsil on both sides the Court took time to advise &c.

– The Commonwealth
against for failing to attend as a Grand juror
**Lewis Fitzgerald**

when Summoned by the Sheriff to attend at the last Term of this Court, after hearing the excuse of said **Fitzjerald** It is Ordered by the Court that he be discharged &c.

– **James Doran & Co** Plts
against In Debt
**Philip A Sublette** Deft

**William Wilson**, of Pulaski County, came into Court and Justified &c and undertook for the said Defendant that if he shall be cast in the action aforesaid that he shall satisfy and pay the condemnation of the Court or render his body to prison in execution for the same or on falure thereof that he the said **William Wilson**, shall do it for him, and on the motion of the Defendant It is Ordered that the Judgment and writ of Inquiry awarded against him in the Clerks Office be set a side and the said Defendant by his attorney now comes and defends the wrong and Injury when and where &c and says the Plaintiff his action aforesaid against him Ought not to have and maintain because he says he has well and truly paid the Debt in the Declaration mentioned and this he is ready to verify wherefore he prays Judgment &c and the Plaintiff by his attorney says his action aforesaid against the said Defendant [page 267] he Ought to have and maintain because he says the said Deft has not paid the Debt in the declaration mentioned, as in pleading he hath alledged, and of this he puteth himself upon the Country and the said Defendant likewise, Therefore let a Jury come here &c.

– Ordered that the Court be adjourned until tomorrow morning nine OClock

**William L Kelly**

At a Circuit Court continued and held for the Pulaski Circuit at the Courthouse of Pulaski County in Sommerset on the 29th day of October 1806

Present the Honourable **William L Kelly, John Smith** and **John Prather** Gent

– **William Guthrie** Assee Plt
against In Debt
**John Smith** Deft

This day came the parties aforesaid by their attornies, and the Defendant having given Special bail herein It is ordered that the Judgment and writ of Inquiry awarded against the said Defendant in the Clerks Office be set a side and the said Defendant by his attorney now comes and defends the Wrong and Injury when and where &c and says the Plaintiff his action aforesaid against him Ought not to have and maintain because he says he has well and truly paid the Debt in the Declaration mentioned and this he is ready to verify wherefore he prays Judgment &c And the plaintiff by his attorney says his action aforesaid against the said Defendant he Ought to have and maintain because he says the said Defendant has not well and truly paid the Debt in the Declaration mentioned as in pleading he hath alledged, and of this he puteth himself upon the Country, and the said Defendant likewise, Therefore let a Jury come here &c.

[page 268] Ordered that it be certified to the County Court of Pulaski County that this Court allows to **Archabald E Mills** Esqr as Commonwealth Attorney for the Pulaski Circuit, One hundred Dollars for his services, in the execution of his Office for the last year preceeding this date

– **John Collier** & **John Preston** Complts
against on motion in Chancery
**John Evans** Deft

This day came the parties aforesaid by their attornies, and the said Defendant by his attorney move the Court to Desolve the Complainants Injunction Obtained herein, notice of said motion being proven, the said motion is Ordered to be continued until the third day of the next Term of this Court, And on the motion of the Complainants by their Counsil a Commission is awarded them

to take Depositions before a single Justice of the Peace in or out of this State
– **Philip A Sublette** Plt
against In Covenant
**William Evans** Deft
– **William Evans** Plt
against In Case
**William Ussery** Deft
– The Same Plt
against In Covenant
**Lambert White** Deft
– **Edmond Williams** Plt
against In Case
**Robert McAlister** & Al[s] Defts
– **Thomas Whites** Plt
against In Case
**William Ussery** Deft
[page 269] **William Griffin** Plt
against In Case
**William Evans**
– **Thomas McGuire** Plt
against In Debt
**Charles Inglish** &[c] Deft
Ordered that these suits be Continued until the next Court
– **James Davis** Plt
against In Case
**John Fitzjerald** Deft
This day came the Plaintiff by his attorney, and thereupon came also a Jury, to wit, **Isaiah Baker, Christ[o] Clonch, Samuel Crow, John Rogers, Simon Alderson, Edward White, John Gwin, Joseph Evans, Henry Willis, John Preston, William Zachary,** & **John Condry** who were sworn well and truly to Inquire what Damages the plaintiff hath sustained in the premises upon their Oaths do say the Plaintiff hath sustained Damage by Occasion thereof to twelve pounds four shillings and six pence besides his Costs, It is therefore Considered by the Court that the Plaintiff recover against the said Defendant his Damages aforesaid by the Jurors in their Verdict afores[d] assessed and his Costs by him about his suit in this behalf expended and the said Defendant in mercy &[c].
– **Samuel McKee** Complt
against In Chancery
**John Brown** Deft
This day came the parties afs[d] by their attornies, and this cause being argued before the Court yesterday, and the Court not being sufficiently advised of and concerning the premises took time until the next Term of this Court to Deliver in their Decree herein, Therefore upon the [page 270] motion of the Complainant by his attorney, a Commission is awarded him to take the Deposition of **John Tully** of Tennissee before a Single Justice of the Peace of said State, and the cause is continued until the next Court
– **Edward White** & wife Plts
against In Case
**Charles Collier** Deft
This day came the parties aforesaid by their attornies and by Consent It is Ordered that the Order of reference Obtained here at the last Term of this Court be set a side, and on the motion of the said Defendant by his attorney, It is ordered that the Judgment and writ of Inquiry awarded against him in the clerks Office be set a side and the said Defendant by his attorney now comes and defends the wrong and Injury when and where &[c] and says he is not guilty in manner and form as

the Plaintiff against him hath declared and this he prays may be enquired of by the Country and the said Plaintiff likewise Therefore let a Jury Come here &c and the cause is continued until the next Court

– **Benjamin Sloane** Plt
against In Covenant
**John Gwin** Deft

This day came the parties aforesaid by their attornies, and the Defendant having given special bail herein It is Ordered that the Judgment and writ of Inquiry awarded against the said Defendant in the Clerks Office be set a side and the said Defendant by his attorney now comes and defends the wrong and Injury when and where &c and says he has well and truly kept and performed the several covenants in the writing mentioned on his part, and hath [page 271] not broken the same in manner and form as the plaintiff against him hath declared, and of this he puts himself upon the Country, and the said Plaintiff likewise, thereupon let a Jury come here &c and the cause is continued until the next Court

– **William Lair** Plt
against In Covenant
**William Evans** Deft

On the motion of the Defendant It is Ordered that the Judgment and writ of Inquiry awarded against him in the Clerks Office be set a side and the said Defendant by his attorney now comes and defends the wrong and Injury when and where &c and says he has well and truly kept and performed the several Covenants in the writing mentioned on his part, and has not broken the same in manner and form as the Plaintiff against him hath declared and leave is given to plead any special matter in said cause and of this he puteth himself upon the Country and the said Plaintiff likewise therefore let a Jury come here &c and the cause is continued until the next Court

– **John & William Allin** Plts
against In Covenant
**William Churchwell** Deft

Ordered that this suit be dismissed it being agreed

– **James Eastham** Complt
against In Chancery
**John Blacklidge** Deft

This day came the parties aforesaid by their attornies and the Court being now sufficiently advised herein, two of them, to wit, the two assistant Judges are of Opinion that the Injunction Obtained by the Complainant herein Ought to be sustained until the final [page 272] hearing whereupon It is decreed and ordered that the motion of the Defendant for the Desolution of the Injunction be Over ruled and further that the Complainant recover against the said Defendant his Costs incured by Occasion of said motion, from which Opinion the Circuit Judge **William L Kelly** Esq[r] directed his dissent to be entered of Record, and the said Defendant from the Decree aforesaid overruling his motion aforesaid prays an appeal which is granted him, upon his executing and Appeal Bond in the Clerks Office within twenty days with **Arch[d] E Mills** his security in the penalty of two hundred Dollars, which bond was executed Immediately in Court Conditioned as the law directs

– **Joseph Casky** Plt
against In Case
**Martin Barrier** Deft

This day came the parties aforesaid by their attornies, and on the motion of the said Defendant by his attorney, It is Ordered that the Judgment and writ of Inquiry awarded against him in the Clerks Office be set a side, and the said Defendant by his attorney now comes and defends the Wrong and Injury where and where &c and says he did not assume upon himself in manner and form as the plaintiff against him hath declared and of this he puteth himself upon the Country and the said Plt likewise Therefore it is commanded the Sheriff that he Cause to come here immediately twelve good and lawful men by whom &c and thereupon came a Jury, to wit, **John Preston, Isaiah**

**Baker, Christ° Clonch, Sam' Crow, John Rogers, Simon Alderson, James Kizzick, John Gwin, Joseph B Evans, Henry Willis, Hugh Logan** and **John Condry** who being elected tried and sworn the truth to speak upon the Issue Joined upon [page 273] their Oaths do say that the said Defendant did not assume upon himself in manner and form as the Plaintiff against him hath declared, Therefore It is Considered by the Court that the Plaintiff take nothing by his bill but for his false clamour be in mercy &c and that the said Plaintiff go thereof hence without day and recover against the said Plt his Costs by him about his defence in this Behalf expended

– **Benjamin Ranard** Plt
against In Case
**Thomas Green** Deft

By consent of parties all matters and difference between them relative to this suit is refered to the arbitration and determination of **Ralph Williams, Thomas Burk, Daniel McKinsey, John McWhorter, George McWhorter, Samuel Allin** & **John Prather**, whose award or the award of any four of them be the Judgment of the Court and the same is Ordered Accordingly

– **Edmond Williams** Plt
against In Case
**Robert McAlister** & Al^s Defts

By consent of parties all matters and difference between them relative to this suit is refered to the arbitration and final determination of **Henry James** & **William Stogsdal**, whose award or the award of either of them together with an umpire by them chosen in Case of their disagreement be made the Judgment of the Court and the same is Ordered accordingly

[page 274] The Commonwealth against **John Barns**, upon a writ of De Idiost Inquirendo

The Inquisition returned herein rec^vd in these word and figures, to wit, Pulaski County July 22^nd 1806 Agreeable to a writ from the Circuit Court of the County aforesaid to the Sheriff aforesaid we being duly summoned and sworn met at the home of **John James** Esq^r in Order to inquire into the standing of **John Barnes**, whether he is a man of a sound mind or not but agreeable to the evidence to us delivered we do all agree that the said **Barns** is not a man of a sound mind nor hath been for twelve months and upwards &c and has contracted some of his personal estate to the Injury of his family in the course of seven months past, and Also one Horse that he rode away in the space of one month from this date and said that he had given up said Horse unto **James Doran** for some goods that he had got of said **Doran**, An Inventory of his estate now remains in his hands, 200 acres head right land 14 acres cleared and rents for one third is made, one Horse worth twenty six pounds, three Cows and Calves, one two year old Heiffer one yearling and some Hogs, the said **John Barns** has a wife and five children and the oldest is a Girl and is about thirteen or fourteen years of age and the next is twins female about seven years old, also another about four years old and one boy about two years of age Given under Our hands and seals year and date above written Signed,

| | | |
|---|---|---|
| **Henry James** | **David Roper** | **William Richardson** |
| **Sam^l Gilmore** | **John Evans** | **William Herries** |
| **Shadrick Herries** | **Thomas Crow** | **Peter Lee** |
| **Stephen Condra** | **James Bobbett** | **John Gill** |

[page 275] Whereupon It is decreed and ordered that **Henry James** & **David Roper** be appointed a Committee for the restraint and safekeeping of the said **John Barns**, and further that they have full power and authority to appropriate so much of the estate of said **Barns** in the Inquisition aforesaid as will be sufficient to support him &c.

– **Moses Justis** & **James Galy** Plt
against In Debt
**James Anderson**

**John McCullough**, of Pulaski County came into Court and Justified, and undertook for the said Defendant that if he shall be cast in the action aforesaid that he shall satisfy and pay the condemnation of the Court or render his body to prison in execution for the same or on falure thereof that he the said **John McCullough** shall do it for him

– **Thomas Jacob** Plt

against In Case
**Amos Evans** Senr Deft

This day came the Plaintiff by his attorney and thereupon came also a Jury, to wit, **Josiah Evans, Aquila Evans, Hamlet Thomas, Thomas Green, Thomas Murphey, Robert Graves, Edward White, John Cundiff, Richard Beason, Benjamin Rannard, Martin Barrier**, and **James Elder** who were sworn well and truly to enquire what Damage the Plaintiff hath sustained in the premises upon their Oaths do say that the Plaintiff hath sustained Damages by Occasion thereof to fifty Dollars besides his Costs. It is therefore considered by the Court that the Plaintiff recover against the said Defendant his Damages aforesaid by the Jurors in their Verdict aforesaid assessed and his Costs by him about his suit in this behalf expended and the said Deft may be taken &c

[page 276] **Thomas Jacob** Plt
against In Case
**Amos Evans** & **Rusk** Defts

This day came the plaintiff by his attorney and thereupon came also a Jury, to wit, **Isaiah Baker, John Puckett, John Kelly, William White, Lambert White, William Westerman, Thomas Burks, Samuel Evans, Walter Macy, Burgis Matthews, Martin True**, & **William Williams**, who were sworn well and truly to enquire what Damage the Plaintiff hath sustained in the premises upon their Oaths do say that the Plaintiff hath sustained Damage by Occasion thereof to One penny besides his Costs. It is therefore Considered by the Court that the Plaintiff recover against the said Defendant his Damages afores[d] by the Jurors in their Verdict aforesaid assessed and his Costs by him about his suit in this behalf expended and the said Defts may be taken &c.

– **William Hiatt** Plt
against In Case
**Charles Rusk** Deft

This day came the Defendant by his attorney, and upon his motion It is Ordered that the Judgment and writ of Inquiry awarded against him in the Clerks Office be set a side and the said Deft by his attorney now comes and defends the wrong and Injury when and where &c and says he is not guilty in manner and form as the Plaintiff against him hath declared, and this he prays may be enquired of by the Country, and the said Plaintiff likewise, therefore let a Jury come here &c and the cause is continued until the next Court

– **Mark Evans** Ass[ee] Plt
against In Debt
**John Brooks** Deft

This day came the parties aforesaid by their attornies, and the Deft [page 277] having entered Special Bail herein, on his motion It is Ordered that the Judgment and writ of Inquiry awarded against him in the Clerks Office be set a side, and the said Defendant by his attorney now comes and defends the Wrong and Injury when and where &c and says the Plaintiff his action aforesaid against him ought not to have and maintain because he says he has well and truly paid the Debt in the Declaration mentioned and this he is ready to verify wherefore he prays Judgment &c And the Plaintiff by his attorney says his actions aforesaid against the said Defendant he Ought to have and maintain because he says the said Defendant has not well and truly paid the Debt in the Declaration mentioned as in pleading he has alledged, and of this he puteth himself upon the Country and the said Defendant likewise therefore let a Jury come here &c.

– **Thomas Hutchings** Ex[ors] Plt
against In Covenant
**Charles Collier** Deft

**Elijah Barns** Junr & **John Collier** of Pulaski County came into Court & Justified and undertook for the said Defendant that if shall be cast in the action aforesaid that he shall satisfy and pay the condemnation of the Court or render his body to prison in execution for the same or on failure thereof that they the said **Elijah** and **John** shall do it for him

– **John Gwin** Plt
against In Case

**James Skidmore** Deft

This day came the Plaintiff by his attorney and thereupon came also a Jury, to wit, **Robert Ping, Jesse Bullock, Robert Graves, Thomas Jacob,** [page 278] **Hamlet Thomas, Abijah Kelly, John Westerman, Elijah Barns** Junr, **Richard Beason, Thomas Simpson, Edward White** & **George Golliday** who were sworn well and truly to enquire what Damage the Plaintiff hath sustained in the premises upon their Oaths do say that the Plaintiff hath sustained Damage by Occasion thereof to forty five Pounds besides his Costs It is therefore Considered by the Court that the Plaintiff recover against the said Defendant his Damages aforesaid by the Jurors in their Verdict aforesaid assessed and his Costs by him about his suit in this behalf expended and the said Defendant in mercy &c.

– **William Owens**, a Constable of Pulaski County, exhibited in Court an Act for public services rendered to the Commonwealth in the execution of his Office, which account being examined by the Court was Ordered to be Certified to the Auditor of Public Accounts

– Ordered that the Court be adjourned until Tomorrow morning nine OClock

**John Smith**

At a Circuit Court Continued and held for the Pulaski Circuit at the Courthouse of Pulaski County in Sommerset on Thursday the 30th day of October 1806

Present the Honourable **William L Kelly, John Smith** and **John Prather** Gentlemen

– **Richard Singleton** Plt
against In Case
**John Knox** Deft

– **Ransom Thacker** &c Plts
against In Case
**Lewis Whitesides** Deft

– **Joel Jackson** Plt
against In Covenant
**William Addison** Deft

[page 279] **John Brown** Plt
against In Debt
**Samuel McKee** Deft

– The Same Plt
against In Debt
The Same Deft

– **John Scrimiger** Plt
against In Trespass Assault & Battery
**John & William Burton** Deft

Ordered that these suits be continued until the next Court

– **Frederick Reperdan** Complt
against In Chancery
**Joseph Casky** Deft

In pursuance to a Decree of the Honorable Pulaski Circuit Court pronounced at their April Term 1806 wherein the above **Frederick Reperdan** is Complainant and **Joseph Casky** is Defendant we the Commissioners appointed in the aforesaid decree having first advertised agreeable to said Decree pronounced on the 17th day of September 1806 to make sale of the tract of land alluded to in said Decree, and did sell the whole of the same to **Frederick Reperdon**, for the sum of twenty four Dollars, he being the highest bidder, on the day of Sale, But by reason of the aforesaid tract of land not being surveyed we could not make any conveyance, witness our hands and seals Signed,

**Andrew Cowan**
**Jonathan Smith**
**Robt Modrel**

This day the Commissioners appointed to make sale of the mortgaged property in the Decree of the last April Term of this court pronounced between the above named parties returned their report by which it appears [page 280] that the property described in the said Mortgage was sold for the sum of twenty four Dollars and three Dollars of which is allowed to the said Commissioners for their services, It is therefore Considered by the Court that the Defendant have a credit for the sum of twenty three dollars out of the Judgment aforesaid pronounced, and that the Complainant proceed to have execution for the ballance of the said Judgment which is yet unsatisfied, and all his Costs which was not Included in the former Decree But it appears from said report that the Commissioners have not yet conveyed the aforesaid tract of land to the purchaser. It is further ordered that the said Commissioners have until the end of the next Term of this Court to make said Conveyance all of which is Decreed and Ordered accordingly

– **Hue Pearce** Plt
against In Covenant
**Holcomb Roberson** Deft

This day came the Plaintiff by his attorney and thereupon came also a Jury, to wit, **Shaderick Stogsdal, John Vardeman, Thomas Owsley, Charles Neal, Andrew Cowen, Alexander Crawford, Benjamin Sloane, Thomas Jacob, John Rogers, John Decker, David Cowen, & Michael Miller**, who were sworn well and truly to enquire what Damage the Plaintiff hath sustained in the premises upon their Oaths do say the Plaintiff hath sustained Damages by Occasion thereof to sixty three Dollars besides his Costs It is therefore Considered by the Court that the Plaintiff recover against the said Defendant his Damages aforesaid by the Jurors in their Verdict aforesaid assessed and his Costs by him about his suit in this behalf expended and the said Defendant in mercy &c.

[page 281] **Speed & Richardson** Plts
against In Case
**George McWhorter** Deft

Ordered that this suit be continued until the next Court

– **Samuel Matthews** Plt
against In Case
**Benjamin Gwin** Deft

The Defendant by his attorney now comes and defends the wrong and Injury when and where &c and says the Plaintiff his action aforesaid against him ought not to have and maintain because he says he did not Assume upon himself in manner and form as the Plaintiff in his declaration against him hath declared, and this he is ready to verify wherefore he prays Judgment &c and the said Plaintiff by his attorney says his Action aforesaid against the said Defendant he Ought to have and maintain because he says the Defendant did assume upon himself in manner & form as he the Plaintiff against him in his said Declaration hath declared and of this he puts himself upon the Country and the said Defendant likewise therefore let a Jury come here &c and the cause is continued until the next Court

– **John January** Plt
against upon a Scirafacias
**Joseph Casky** Deft

This day came the Plaintiff by his attorney, and upon his motion It is ordered that the writ of Inquiry awarded against the said Defendant in the clerks Office be waved, Therefore upon the motion of the said Plaintiff by his attorney Judgment is granted him against the said Defendant for four pounds ten shillings as per mention and his Costs by him about his suit in this behalf expended and the said Defendant in mercy &c.

[page 282] **Hugh Donigy** Plt
against In Covenant
**Joseph Casky** Deft

This day came the parties aforesaid by their attornies, and on the motion of the Defendant by his attorney It is Ordered that the Judgment and writ of Inquiry awarded against the said

Defendant in the Clerks Office be set a side and the said Defendant by his attorney now Comes and defends the wrong and Injury when and where &c (Plea Denying Demand Replication & Joinder plead on the minutes but not filed) Also the plea of accordance Satisfaction Replication & Joinder, plead on the minutes but not filed as aforesaid )

and this he puteth himself upon the Country and the said Plaintiff likewise Therefore It is commanded the Sheriff that he cause to come here Immediately twelve good and lawful men by whom &c and thereupon came also a Jury, to wit, **Shaderick Stogsdal, John Vardiman, Thomas Owsley, Charles Neal, Andrew Cowen, Alexander Crawford, Benjamin Sloane, Thomas Jacob, John Rogers, John Decker, David Cowen & Michael Miller**, who being elected tried and sworn upon their Oaths do say that the Plaintiff did make a Demand of the said Defendant as in his Declaration herein Declared, and that the said Defendant has not made Satisfaction to the Plaintiff as in pleading he hath alledged and they are [page 283] assess the Plaintiffs Damages by Occasion thereof to thirteen pounds fourteen shillings besides his Costs It is therefore considered by the Court that the Plaintiff recover against the said Defendant his Damages aforesaid by the Jurors in their Verdict aforesaid assessed and his Costs by him about his suit in this behalf expended and the said Defendant in mercy &c

– The Commonwealth
against upon a writ of De Iuita Inquirindo
**John Barns**

On the motion of **David Roper**, who was appointed by this Court as one of the Committee for the restraint and safe keeping of said **Barns**, It is Ordered that he be discharged from the undertaking aforesaid and that **Thomas McGuire**, be appointed in his stead for the purpose aforesaid, and that the clerk in making Out the Order for said Committee Insert said **McGuire** & make out the Order agreeable to the Act of the General Kentucky in such case made and provided

– **William Hays** Assee Plt
against In Covenant
**Philip A Sublette** Deft

The Defendant having given Special Bail herein, on his motion It is Ordered that the Judgment and writ of Inquiry awarded against the said Defendant in the Clerks Office be set a side and the said Defendant for further plea herein says the Plaintiff his action aforesaid against him Ought not to have and maintain because he says the said plaintiff did not at the time and place in his Declaration mentioned, nor at any Other time demand a Conveyance of the Land in the writing Obligatory mentioned. And of this he puteth himself upon the Country and the plaintiff likewise, and the said Defendant for further plea says the plaintiff his action aforesaid against him Ought not to have and maintain because he says the plaintiff did not prior to the [page 284] commencement of the action aforesaid direct him the Defendant in what manner he would have the said 200 acres of land laid off and of this he puteth himself upon the Country, and the Plaintiff likewise, and the said Defendant for further plea herein says that the Plaintiff his action aforesaid against him Ought not to have and maintain because he says he did not prior to the Commencement of the action aforesaid Convey the said two hundred acres of land to any person whatever, and of this he puteth himself upon the Country, And the said Defendant for further plea herein says the Plaintiff his action aforesaid ought not to have and maintain because he says he could not have laid off the said two hundred acres of land by parallel lines so as to exclude the said Improvement & include a good spring and of this he puteth himself upon the County, And on the motion of the Plaintiff and Order of Survey is granted him directed to the Surveyor of Pulaski County Commanding him to go on the land in Controversy between the said parties on the ___ day of ____ next if fair if not then on the next fair day and then and there survey and lay off the same as either party would have it having regard to all Deeds and Other evidence that may be produced report all matters of fact specially return four fair Platts & Certificates thereof to the Clerks Office before the day of hearing, And the cause if continued until the next Court

– **Nicholas Gwin** Plt
against In Case

**George McWhorter** Deft
– **George McWhorter** Plt
against In Case
**Nicholas Gwin** Deft

By consent of Parties all matters and difference between them relative to these suits are refered to the arbitration and determination of [page 285] **John Gwin** and **John McWhorter**, whose award, or in case of their disagreement, leave by consent given to said referrees to make choice of two other persons to act with them &c and their award shall be the Judgment of the Court, and the same is Ordered Accordingly, and the cause continued until next Court

– **Mordicai Gregory** Assee Plt
against In Covenant
**Nicholas Gwin** & **Henry Willis** Defts

This day came as well the Plaintiff by his attorney, as the said Defendants in their proper person, and on the motion of the said Plaintiff by his attorney It is ordered the writ of Inquiry awarded against the said Defendants in the Clerks Office be waved, and the said Defts here now in Court Acknowledged the Plaintiffs action against them for fifty Dollars with legal Interest thereon from the first day of April Last past. Therefore with the assent of the plaintiff It is considered by the Court that the Plaintiff recover against the said Defendants the Sum acknowledged as aforesaid together with legal Interest as aforesd until paid & Costs. and the said Defendants in mercy &c.

– **William Beard** Plt
against upon a Scirafacias
**Martin Turpin** Deft

This day came the Plaintiff by his attorney, and upon his motion t is Ordered that the writ of Inquiry awarded against the said Defendant in the Clerks Office be waved, Therefore on the motion of the plaintiff by his attorney Judgment is granted him against the said Defendant for nine Dollars eleven and a half cents [ ] Costs of a former Judgment and his Costs by him about his suit in this behalf expended and the said Defendant in mercy &c.

[page 286] **Anthoney Owsley** &c Plts
against In Detinue
**Jesse Richardson** Deft
– **Edward Wirley** Plt
against In Trespass Assault & Battery
**John Hughes** Deft
– **John S Moore & Co** Plt
against In Debt
**John Breedon** Deft
– **William Guthrie** Assee Plt
against In Debt
**John Smith** Deft

This day came the parties aforesaid by their attornies, and on the motion of the said Defendants by their attornies, these suits are Ordered to be continued until the next Term of this court, at the said Defts costs. And that the plaintiffs recover their Costs by them relative to said Continuances expended

– **William Fox** Plt
against In Covenant
**John Decker** Deft

**Jesse Richardson** of Pulaski County came into Court and undertook for the said Defendant that if he shall be cast in the action aforesaid that he shall pay the condemnation of the Court or render his body to prison in execution for the same or on falure thereof that he the said **Jesse** shall do it for him, and the said Defendant now comes and defends the wrong and Injury when and where &c and says he has well and truly kept and performed the several Covenants in the writing mentioned in his part and of this he puteth himself upon the Country and the said Plaintiff likewise therefore It is [page 287] Commanded the Sheriff that he cause to come here Immediately twelve good and lawful men by whom &c and thereupon came also a Jury, to wit, **George McWhorter, Richard Beason, Hamlet Thomas, Samuel Matthews, William White, Lambert White, William Hunt, Martin Barrier, John Ashly, John Hughes, David Roper**, and **John Condra** who being elected tried and sworn the truth to speak upon the Issue Joined upon their Oaths do say that the said Defendant has not broken his Covenant in manner and form as the Plaintiff against him hath declared, It is therefore Considered by the Court that the Deft recover his Costs &c.

– **Nicholas Gwin** Plt
against In Covenant
**John Turley** &c Deft

This day came the Plaintiff by his attorney and thereupon came also a Jury, to wit, **Thomas Owsley, Thomas Jacob, Abijah Kelly, John Burton, Robert Smith, Abram Smith, Isaac Smith, Alexander Matthews, William Burton, John Decker, Walter Maxy** and **John Jarvis** who were sworn well and truly to inquire what Damage the Plaintiff hath sustained in the premises upon their Oaths do say that the Plaintiff hath sustained Damage by Occasion thereof to fifty three Dollars besides his Costs, It is therefore Considered by the Court that the Plaintiff recover against the said Defendant his damages aforesaid by the Jurors in their Verdict aforesaid assessed and his Costs by him about his suit in this behalf expended and the said Defendant in mercy &c.

– **Robertson Burge** Assee Plt
against In Debt
**Joseph Porter** Deft

This day came the parties aforesaid by their attornies, and on motion [page 288] the said Defendant by his attorney says he cannot gainsay the Plaintiffs action against him for One hundred Dollars the Debt in the Declaration mentioned, Therefore with assent of the plaintiff It is Considered by the Court that the Plaintiff recover against the said Defendant the One hundred Dollars aforesd Confessed together with legal Interest thereon from the twenty seventh day of June One thousand eight hundred and four until paid & Costs and the said Deft in mercy &c. Note this Judgment is Confessed with the reservation of Equity

– **Shaderick Felphs** Plt
against In Debt
**Vincent Garner** Deft

This day came the parties aforesaid by their attornies, and the said Defendant by his attorney says he cannot gainsay the plaintiffs Action against him for thirty six pounds, the Debt in the Declaration mentioned, therefore with the assent of the Plaintiff It is considered by the Court that the Plaintiff recover against the said defendant the sum of thirty six pounds confessed aforesd and his Costs by him about his suit in this behalf expended and the said in mercy &c. Note this Judgment is to bare legal Interest from the fifth day of March One thousand eight hundred and six until paid & Costs. But to have credit for fifteen and a half dollars paid on the 18th day of April 1806 and execution to be staid three months

– **Mark Evans** Assee Plt
against In Debt
**John Brooks** Deft

[page 289] This day came the Parties aforesaid by their attornies, and the said Defendant by his attorney says he cannot gainsay the Plaintiffs Action against him for forty seven pounds fifteen shillings and four pence, the Debt in the Decn mentioned Therefore with the assent of the Plaintiff It is considered by the Court that the Plaintiff recover against the said Defendant the sum acknowledged as aforesaid with Interest thereon from the ___ day of ___ until paid & Costs Note this Judgment was Confessed with the reservation of equity, and It is agreed that the said Defendant may make the same defence in equity which he could have made at law

– **James Doran & Co** Plt
against In Debt

**Philip A Sublette** Deft

This day came the parties aforesaid by their attornies, and the said Defendant by his attorney says he cannot gainsay the plaintiffs Action against him for thirty two Pounds ten shillings and ten pence the Debt in the Declaration mentioned Therefore with the assent of the Plaintiff It is considered by the Court that the Plaintiff recover against the said Defendant the sum acknowledged as afores[d] and his Costs by him about his suit in this behalf expended and the said Defendant in mercy &[c]. Note this Judgment is to bare legal Interest from the thirtieth day of April 1806 until paid & costs

– **George W Saunders** & wife Plt
against In Trespass Assault & Battery
**John Griffin** Deft

– **John Griffin** & County Plt
against In Debt
**George W Saunders** Deft

[page 290] **John Griffin** Plt
against In Trespass Assault & Battery
**George W Saunders** & wife Deft

– **George W Saunders** Plt
against In Trespass
**John Griffin** Deft

Ordered that these suits be Continued until the next Term of this Court for awards

– It is Ordered that an Order made on the first day of this term fining the Sheriff of Pulaski County ten Dollars for failing to attend to the Duties of his Office be set a side and the said fine remitted

– On the motion of **John Gwin**, a Dedimus is awarded him to take the Deposition of **William Dodson** of Tennessee before a single magistrate, to be read as evidence on the trial between **Benjamin Sloane** & said **Gwin**

– **Nicholas Gwin** Plt
against In Covenant
**John Turley** Deft

On the motion of the Defendant by his attorney to obtain a new trial herein on the Verdict of the Jury and Judgment Obtained on this present day after hearing the arguments of Counsil on both sides and mature deliberation thereon had It is Or[d] that said motion be Over ruled with Costs

– Ordered that the Court be adjourned until Tomorrow morning twelve OClock

**John Smith**

[page 291] At a Circuit Court continued and held for the Pulaski Circuit at the Courthouse in Sommerset on Friday the 31[st] day of October 1806

Present **John Smith** and **John Prather** esquires

– The Commonwealth
against upon an Indictment
**Zachariah Evans**

On the motion of the Commonwealths attorney for the Pulaski Circuit It is ordered that the Clerk of said Circuit Issue a Capias against said **Evans** agreeable to an Act of the General Assembly Kentucky in such case made and provided and direct Bail to be taken

– **John Tinley** Complt
against upon attachment
**Isaac Avery** Deft

This day came the complainant by his attorney an the Defendant being Called but came and the attachment herein being returned executed, on a Horse of the value of fifty dollars in good trade one hundred weight of salt petre, in the hands of **William Hays** who being summoned by the Complainant declared upon Oath that the above effects was in his hands of said Defendant, also the attachment is returned executed on two hundred acres of land the property of said Defendant. And the Complainant declares he has in his possession one cow beast and the one half of a twenty gallon Kettle the property of said Defendant upon which said att[a] is also returned execution Therefore on the motion Complainant [page 292] by his Counsil Judgment is granted him against the said Defendant for forty eight pounds and his costs by him about said attachment expended and the said Deft in mercy &[c] And on the motion of the Complainant by his Counsil It is Ordered that the Sheriff make sale of the attached effects according to law and apply the money arrising from said sales toward satisfying this Judgment and return the overplus if any to the Defendant

– The Clerk exhibited an account for paper, Books &[c] furnished by him for the use of his Office for the last year preceding this date which account being examined by the Court was Ordered to be Certified to the Auditor of Public Accounts

– The Sheriff of Pulaski County exhibited two Accounts for services rendered to the commonwealth which being examined was Ord[d] to be Certified to the Auditor of Public Accounts

– Or[d] that it be Certified that this Court allows to **John January** as their Jailer the sum of sixteen dollars for his services for the last year preceding this date.

– Ordered that it be certified that this Court allows to **William Fox**, as their Clerk the sum of thirty Dollars for public service performed by him in the execution of his Office for the last year preceding this date

– Ordered that the Court be adjourned until Court in Course

**John Smith**

[page 293] At a Circuit Court holden for the Pulaski Circuit at the Courthouse of Pulaski County in Sommerset on Monday the 27[th] day of April 1807

Present the Honourable **William L Kelly** Esq[r]

– A Grand jury was sworn for the Pulaski Circuit, to wit, **Henry James** foreman, **James Going, Isaac Muse, David Richardson, David Dodson, Isaac Mayfield, Jesse Williams, Seaton Lee, Daniel Duncan, Abner McWhorter, Thomas C St Clear, James Cowen, William Lynch, John Burton, Robert Modrel, John Roberts, James Langdon, William Denham, Samuel Hand, David Roper, George Dougherty, Zachariah Jones** & **Stephen Hail**, who having received their charge retired to consider of their Presentments

– Present **John Smith** & **John Prather** Gentlemen

– The Commonwealth
against upon an Indictment for Perjury
**Zachariah Evans**

The said **Zachariah Evans** was led to the bar in custody of the Jailer, and thereof arraigned and pleaded not guilty to the said Indictment, and for this trial puts himself upon God and his Country and the attorney on behalf of the Commonwealth likewise, whereupon came a Jury, to wit, **Andrew Evans, Spencer Tinsley, Samuel Kelly, John Ping, James P Benton, Devalt Kellar, Jonathan L Gill, Martin True, Thomas Benton, Samuel Dick, George S Benton** & **William Mayfield** who being elected tried and sworn the truth of and upon the premises to speak and having heard the evidence upon their Oaths do say that the said **Zachariah Evans** is not Guilty of the Perjury aforesaid in manner and form as the Indictment against him hath alledged, and Proclamation being made as the manner is and nothing further appearing [page 294] alledged against him, It is therefore considered by the Court that he be discharged from his Indictment

– The Grandjury returned into Court the following Presentment, to wit, Commonwealth of Kentucky Circuit Court April Term 1807 we the Grand jury for the body of the County and Circuit aforesaid upon our Oaths do present **William Davis**, for profanely cursing Once Ill be God Damd to Hell, on Tuesday the 7[th] day of April 1807 at the Dwelling House of **Willis Embry** in the County and Circuit aforesaid Contrary to the form of the Statute in such cases made and provided, greatly against the Dignity of the Commonwealth &[c]

**Robert Modrell**
**Abner McWhorter**

both of the Grand jury & residentors of the County of Pulaski and Circuit aforesaid, And the Grand

jury having nothing further to present were discharged by the Court, And Delinquent Ordered to be summoned
– The Commonwealth
against upon Presentment
**William Wilson**
– The Same
against Same
**Philip A Sublette**
– The Same
against Same
**William J Salle**
– The Same
against Same
**John January**
[page 295] The Commonwealth
against upon Presentment
**John McWhorter**
– The Same
against Same
**Vincent Garner**

Ordered that these presentments be quashed

– **James Matthews** Plt
against In Covenant
**Archabald Moore** Deft

This day came the Plaintiff, and on his motion It is Ordered that this suit be dismissed

– **William Hiatt** Plt
against In Case
**Charles Rusk** Deft

This day came as well the Plaintiff by his attorney as the said Defendant in his proper person and on their motion It is Ordered that this suit be dismissed it being agreed

– **Frederick Troxwell** Complt
against In Chancery
**William Burton** Deft

This day came the parties aforesaid by their attornies, and this cause came on to be heard, and upon hearing the Bill, answer, and Sundry depositions filed herein, and the arguments of counsil on both sides, and mature deliberation thereon had it seems to the Court that there is not sufficient equity on the part of the Complainant to preclude the Defendant from proceding against him with his Judgment at Common law. It is Therefore Ordered that the Complainants Injunction [page 296] herein be disolved, and that the Defendant may proceed with his Judgment against the said Complainant at common law

And It is further Ordered that the Complainants bill be dismissed for want of sufficient equity therein, And that the said Deft recover against the Complt ten percentum, on the Judgment at law Agreeably to an Act of the General Assembly Kentucky on the Disolution of Injunctions, in this case made and provided, and his Costs by him about his defence in this behalf expended

– **John Weirs** Adm^or^ Plt
against In Case
**Nathaniel Forbis** Deft

Ordered that this suit be Continued until the next Court at the Defendants Costs, and that the plaintiff recover his Costs relative to the continuance expended

– **William Evans** Plt
against In Covenant
**John Roberson** Deft

– **William Evans** Plt
against In Case
**William Ussery** Deft
– The Same Plt
against In Covenant
**Lambert White** Deft
– **Robertson Burge** Plt
against In Case
**David Clark** Deft

Ordered that these suits be Continued until the next Court

[page 297] **Drewry Lee** Ass[ee] Plt
against In Debt
**Spencer Griffin** Deft

**Philip A Sublette**, & **James Griffin** of the County of Pulaski came into Court and undertook for the said Defendant that if he shall be Cast in the Action aforesaid that they shall satisfy and pay the Condemnation of the Court or render his body to prison in Execution for the same or on falure thereof that they the said **Sublette & James Griffin** shall do it for him

– **Joseph Casky** Plt
against In Trespass Assault & Battery
**Robert Smith**

Ordered that this suit be Continued until the next Term of this Court at the Cost of the Plaintiff and that the said Defendant recover against the said Plaintiff his Costs relative to said Continuance expended

– Ordered that **Moses Hanks, William Addison, John Hardgrove, John McFall, John Vardiman, Hansford Price** & **Asa Dodson** be sommoned to appear here on the first day of the next July Term of this Court, to shew cause if any they can why they shall not be fined, for failing to attend a petty Jurors in this Court, when Summoned agreeable to an Act of the General Assembly in such cases made and provided

– **Philip A Sublette** Plt
against In Covenant
**William Evans** Deft

This day came the Plaintiff by his attorney and thereupon came also a Jury, to wit, **James Anderson, James Modrel, John McCullough, David Johnson, Thomas Vanhook, John Cundiff, John Cowen, Benjamin Harris, Martin Gibson, Hugh Logan, Lovell H Dogan**, & [page 298] **Thomas Haines**, who were sworn well and truly to enquire what Damage the Plaintiff hath sustained in the premises upon their Oaths do say that the Plaintif hath sustained Damage by Occasion thereof to two hundred and eighteen Dollars and eighty five cents besides his Costs It is Therefore considered by the Court that the Plaintiff recover against the said Defendant his Damages aforesaid by the Jurors in their Verdict aforesaid assessed, and the said Defendant in mercy &[c].

– Doe (ie, **James Thompson** Plt
against upon Ejectment
Roe (ie, **John Puckett** Deft

This day came the parties aforesaid by their attornies, and It is Ordered that this suit be Continued until the next Court. And leave is given to amend Survey as either Party would have it &[c]

– Ordered that the Court be adjourned until Tomorrow morning nine OClock

**William L Kelly**

At a Circuit Court continued and held for the Pulaski Circuit at the Courthouse of Pulaski County in Sommerset on Tuesday the 28[th] day of April 1807

Present the Honorable **William L Kelly & John Prather** Gentlemen

– Present **John Smith** Esq[r]

– **John Griffin** & County Plt

against In Debt
**George W Saunders** Deft
[page 299] **John Griffin** Plt
against In Trespass Assault & Battery
**George W Saunders** & wife Defts
– **George W Saunders** & wife Plt
against Same
**John Griffin** Deft
– **George W Saunders** Plt
against In Trespass
**John Griffin** Deft

This day came the parties aforesaid by their attornies, and the persons chosen herein to settle all matters in difference between the above named parties, returned their awards in said Cases which awards being Objected to by the party herein **John Griffin** by his attorney for Irregularity in the same, therefore on the motion of said **Griffin**, by his attorney to quash said award, and after hearing the arguments by Counsil upon both sides and mature deliberation thereon had It is Ordered that said Award herein be quashed, and held at naught, and that said **Griffin** recover his Costs relative to the said motion expended

– **John Beard** Complt
against In Chancery
**George W Saunders** & **Benjamin Burch** Defts

this day came the parties aforesaid by their Counsil, and after hearing the Bill, answer, exhibits, and Sundry Depositions filed herein, and the arguments of Counsil on both sides, the Court took time to consider their Decree

– **William Griffin** Plt
against In Case
**William Evan** Deft

This day came the parties aforesaid by their attornies and thereupon came also a Jury, to wit, **Thomas McGuire**, **Stephen Hail**, **Benjamin** [page 300] **Harris**, **Aaron Dors**, **William Hunt**, **John Hail**, **William Woods**, **John Stanton**, **James Johnson**, **William Benton**, **Samuel Matthews** & **Martin Barrier** who being elected tried and sworn the truth to speak upon the Issue Joined upon their Oaths do say that the said Defendant did assume upon himself in manner and form as the Plaintiff against him hath declared, and they do assess the Plaintiffs Damages by Occasion thereof to One hundred Dollars besides his costs It is Therefore Considered by the Court that the Plaintiff recover against the said Defendant his Damages aforesaid by the Jurors in their Verdict aforesaid assessed and his Costs by him about his suit in this behalf expended and the said Defendant in mercy &c.

– **Moses Justis** & **James Galy** Plt
against In Debt
**James Anderson** Deft

**John McCullough** & **Andrew Evans** of Pulaski County came into Court and undertook for the said Defendant that if he shall be cast in the Action aforesaid that they shall satisfy and pay the Condemnation of the Court or render his body to prison in execution for the same or on falure thereof that they the said **John** & **Andrew** shall do it for him & the Cause is continued until the next Term of this Court

– **Edward White** & wife Plts
against In Case
**Charles Collier** Deft

This day came the Parties aforesaid by their attornies, and the Plaintiff herein being solemnly called but came not, neither is their suit further prosecuted, Therefore on the motion of the Defendant by his attorney It is Ordered that this suit be dismissed for want of prosecution, and that the said Defendant recover against the Plaintiff One hundred & fifty weight of Tob° agreeable to an

Act of the General Assembly Kentucky [page 301] in such cases made and provided, and that he recover his costs by him about his defense in this behalf expended

– **Benjamin Sloan** Plt
against In Covenant
**John Gwin** Deft

This day came the parties aforesaid by their attornies and on the motion of the Plaintiff by his attorney It is Ordered that this suit be Continued until the next Term of this Court, and that the said Defendant recover against the Plaintiff his Costs by him about his defence relative to this continuance expended

– **Benjamin Ranard** Plt
against In Case
**Thomas Green** Deft

This day came the parties aforesaid by their attornies and the referrees chosen herein to settle all matters and difference between said parties relative to this cause, returned their award in the words and figures following, to wit, we **Ralph Williams, Thomas Burk, Daniel McKinsey, John McWhorter, George McWhorter, Samuel Allin** & **John Prather** having met at **Charles Neals** in Pulaski County on a controversy between **Benjamin Rannard** Complainant and **Thomas Green** Defendant after being sworn & hearing the witnesses of both parties, are unanimously of Opinion that the Defendant shall pay the Complainant a good beast as the one contended for provided it was a sound beast & to pay all lawful Costs as witness Our hands and seals this 31[st] day of April 1806

Signed **George McWhorter** **R Williams**
**Sam[l] Allin** **Thomas Burk**
**John Prather** **Daniel McKinsey**
**John McWhorter**

[page 302] And the same is made the Judgment of the Court

– **Thomas Whites** Plt
against In Case
**William Ussery** Deft

This day came the Plaintiff by his attorney and thereupon came also a Jury, to wit, **Thomas McGuire, Stephen Hail, Benjamin Harris, Aaron Dors, William Hunt, John Hail, William Woods, John Stanton, James Johnson, William Benton, Samuel Matthews,** & **Martin Barrier** who were sworn well and truly to enquire what Damage the Plaintiff hath sustained in the premises upon their Oaths do say that the Plaintiff hath sustained Damage by Occasion thereof to nineteen Dollars and forty two cents besides his Costs It is therefore Considered by the Court that the Plaintiff recover against the said Defendant his Damages aforesaid by the Jurors in their Verdict afores[d] assessed and his costs by him about his suit in this behalf expended and the said Defendant in mercy &[c]

– **William Lair** Plt
against In Covenant
**William Evans** Deft

Ordered that this suit be Dismissed, it being by the direction of the Plaintiffs attorney, and the Deft recover his Costs

– **John Scrimiger** Plt
against In Trespass Assault & Battery
**John & William Benton** Defts

On the Motion of the Defendants It is Ordered that the Judgment and writ of Inquiry awarded against them in the Clerks Office be set a side and the said Defendants by their attorney now comes and defends the wrong and Injury when and where &[c] and say they are not guilty in manner and form as the Plaintiff against them hath declared and of this they put themselves upon the Country and the Plaintiff doth [page 303] the same likewise. Therefore let a Jury come here &[c] and the cause is continued until the next Court

– **Richard Singleton** Plt
against In Case
**John Knox** Deft

On the motion of the Defendant, It is Ordered that the Judgment and Writ of Inquiry awarded against him in the Clerks Office be set a side and the said Defendant by his attorney now comes and defends the wrong and Injury when and where &c and says he is not guilty in manner and form as the Plaintiff in his Declaration against him hath alledged and this he prays may be enquired of by the Country, and the said Plaintiff likewise, Therefore It is commanded the sheriff that he cause to come here Immediately twelve good and lawful men by whom &c and thereupon came also a Jury, to wit, **Benjamin Harris, John Hail, Stephen Hail, William Hunt, Aaron Dors, Samuel Matthews, Wm Woods, Martin Barrier, James Johnson, Thomas McGuire, John Stanton** & **Thomas Stanton**, who being elected tried and sworn the truth to speak upon the Issue Joined upon their Oaths do say that the Defendant is guilty in manner and form as the plaintiff against him hath declared, and they do assess the Plaintiffs Damages by Occasion thereof to fifteen Dollars besides Costs, It is therefore Considered by the Court that the Plaintiff recover against the said Defendant his Damages aforesaid by the Jurors in their Verdict aforesaid assessed and his costs by him about his suit in this behalf expended and the said Defendant may be taken &c.

[page 304] **Speed & Richardson** Plt
against In Case
**George McWhorter** Deft

– **William Hays** Assee Plt
against In Covenant
**Philip A Sublette** Deft

– **Ransom Thacker** & Plt
against In Case
**Lewis Whitesides** Deft

Ordered that these suits be Continued until the next Term of this Court

– **Nicholas Gwin** Plt
against In Case
**George McWhorter** Deft

– **George McWhorter** Plt
against In Case
**Nicholas Gwin** Deft

This day came the parties aforesaid by their attornies and It is Ordered that these suits be Continued for award

– **Samuel Matthews** Plt
against In Case
**Benjamin Gwin** Deft

Ordered that this suit be continued until the next Court at the Defendants costs, and that the Plaintiff recover against the said Defendant his costs by him about his suit relative to this continuance expended

– A Writing exhibited into Court, relative to **Robert Gilliland** Decd in his lifetime having obtained a Certificate for land &c and the widow of said **Gilliland** having resided on said land, agreeable to an Act of the General Assembly Kentucky in such case made and provided, the said writing being sworn to in Court by **John Smith & Henry James** [page 305] is ordered to be Certified &c

– **Edward Wirley** Plt
against In Trespass Assault & Battery
**John Hughes** Deft

This day came the Parties aforesaid by their attornies, and upon the motion of the said Defendant by his attorney It is ordered that this suit be Dismissed, It appearing to the satisfaction of this Court that the Plaintiff has removed himself out of the Commonwealth of Kentucky. and has not given security for Costs as required by law in such cases made and provided, and that the said

Defendant recover his costs by him about his defense in this behalf expended
– **Joel Jackson** Plt
against In Covenant
**William Addison** Deft

This day came the parties aforesaid by their attornies, and the Defendant having given special Bail herein, Therefore on his motion It is Ordered that the Judgment and writ of Inquiry awarded against him in the Clerks Office be set a side and the said Defendant by his attorney now comes and defends the wrong and Injury when & where &c and says the Plaintiff his action aforesaid against him Ought not to have and maintain because he says he has well and truly kept and performed the several covenants in the writing mentioned on his part and this he is ready to verify wherefore he prays Judgment &c And the said Plaintiff says his action aforesaid against the said Defendant he ought to have and maintain because he says, the said Defendant hath not well and truly kept and performed the several covenants in the writing mentioned on his part as in pleading he has alledged But has broken the same in manner and form as the plaintiff against him in the Declaration hath declared, and this he prays may be enquired of by the Country & the said Deft likewise, and leave is given the said Defendant [page 306] to file a special plea herein, Wherefore let a Jury come here &c and the cause is continued until the next Court
– **Anthoney Owsley** & Plts
against In Detinue
**Jesse Richardson**

This day came the parties aforesaid by their attornies, and upon their motion It is Ordered that this suit be dismissed it being agreed
– **John S Moore & Co** Plts
against In Debt
**John Breeden** Deft

This day came the parties aforesaid by their attornies, and thereupon came also a Jury, to wit, **Robert Smith, John Wolverton, John Lash, Spencer Tinsley, Jonathan Smith, Joseph Erwin, John Knox, Moses Nash, John Jasper, James Cumming, P A Sublette**, & **William Williams** who being elected tried and sworn the truth to speak upon the Issue Joined upon their Oaths do say that the said Defendant hath not well and truly paid the Debt in the Declaration mentioned as in pleading he hath alledged, and do find for the Plaintiff the Debt in the Declaration mentioned and do assess his Damages by Occasion of the Detention thereof to penny besides his Costs. It is therefore Considered by the Court that the Plaintiff recover against the said Defendant the Debt and Damages aforesaid by the Jurors in their Verdict aforesaid assessed and his Costs by him about his suit in this behalf expended and the said Defendant in mercy &c Note this Judgment is to be discharged by the payment eighteen Dollars and twenty five cents with legal Interest thereon from the ninth day of December one thousand eight hundred and five until paid & Costs But to have credit for five shillings and ten pence as pr credit on the writ herein paid the 3rd of April 1806
[page 307] **William Guthrie** Assce Plt
against In Debt
**John Smith** Deft

This day came the Parties aforesaid by their attornies, and the said Defendant for further plea herein says the plaintiff his action aforesd against him Ought not to have and maintain because he says the writing professed in the Declaration was executed & Delivered to the Obligee therein named, **Abraham Smith**, as a free gift without any commination and that it was agreed by the said **Abraham Smith** the Obligee at the time of executing the said writing that a suit should not be brought on the said Writing to Compell him the said defendant to pay the amount of the said writing Obligatory and that it should carry no Interest and that an endorsement to that effect was endorsed on the writing aforesaid of which endorsement the Defendant craves Oyer, and the Defendant avers that upon having oyer of the endorsement aforesaid he will verify the matters of his plea wherefore &c. and the plaintiff says he Ought not to be bound by any thing in the plea last pleaded from having and maintaining his action aforesaid against said Defendant neither is he bound by the law of the land to answer thereto wherefore he prays Judgment &c. whereupon the matters of law arrising upon the Plaintiffs Demurrer to the Defendants plea being argued, It is Considered by the Court that the said Demurrer be Over ruled with Costs. and leave is given the plaintiff to withdraw his Demurrer, the Plaintiff by his attorney saith that for any thing by the Defendant in pleading above alledged to Ought not to be bared or precluded from having his action aforesaid against him said Defendant because he saith the Defendant did not deliver the writing professed in the Declaration to **Abraham Smith** his Assigner as a free gift without any Consideration nor was it [ ] by said **Smith** that suit should not [page 308] be brought on said note against said Defendant and this he prays may be enquired of by the Country, and the Defendant likewise Therefore it is Commanded the Sheriff that he cause to come here Immediately twelve good and lawful men by whom &c and thereupon came also a Jury, to wit **Jacob Blacklidge, John Westerman, John Wolverton, Spencer Tinsley, John Knox, Samuel Owens, William Williams, Martin Vanhook, John Jasper, James Cumming, Martin Gibson & Marvel Nash**, who being elected tried and sworn the truth to speak upon the Issue Joined upon their Oaths do say that the said Defendant hath not well and truly paid the Debt in the Declaration mentioned as in pleading he has alledged, and they do find for the Plaintiff the Debt in the Declaration mentioned without Interest, and do assess his Damages by Occasion of the Detention thereof to One Cent, besides his Costs. It is therefore considered by the Court that the Plaintiff recover against the said Defendant, one hundred dollars, the said Debt in the Declaration without Interest, and his Damages afores[d] by the Jurors in their Verdict aforesaid assessed and his Costs by him about his suit in this behalf expended and the said Defendant in mercy &c.

– Ordered that the Court be adjourned until tomorrow morning nine OClock

**William L Kelly**

At a Circuit Court continued and held for the Pulaski Circuit at the Courthouse of said County in Sommerset on Wednesday the 29th day of April 1807. Present the Honourable **William L Kelly** & **John Smith** Gentlemen

– **John Griffin** & County Plt
against In Debt
**George W Saunders** Deft
[page 309] **John Griffin** Plt
against In Trespass Assault & Battery
**George W Saunders** & wife Deft
– **George W Saunders** & wife Plt
against Same
**John Griffin** Deft
– **George W Saunders** Plt
against In Trespass
**John Griffin** Deft

This day came the parties aforesaid by their attornies, and upon the motion of the party **John Griffin** herein, by his attorney, It is Ordered that the Order of reference awarded herein by this Court be set a side. and the cause continued until the next Court

– Present **John Prather** Esq[r]

– Trustees of Sommerset Plts
against upon Petition & Summons
**Jim & John Cundiff** Defts

This day came as well the Plaintiffs by their attorney as the said Defendants in their proper person, who acknowledged the Plaintiffs Action against them for twenty five Dollars, with stay of Execution three months without the benefit of a replevy Therefore It is considered by the Court that the Plaintiffs recover against the said Defendants the sum acknowledged as afores[d] in manner and form aforesaid, and their Costs by them in this behalf expended, and the said Defendant in mercy &c. Note this Judgment is to bare legal Interest on the said sum of twenty five Dollars from

the 28th day of April 1806 until paid & Costs But to have credit for five dollars
– **John Beard** Complt
against In Chancery
**George W Saunders & Benjamin Bunch** Deft
[page 310] The Court having Sufficiently advised of and [ ] the premises herein delivered in the following written Opinion in these words. This cause now came on & was heard on the Bill answer depositions, Plat & other Exhibits filed, and the arguments of the Counsel on both sides, were heard, and due consideration had by the Court. Whereupon it is decreed and Ordered that the Defendants do in or before the first day of the next July Term of this court, Convey unto the said Complainant by Deed with a clause of a General Warranty all the land within the Patent of the Defendant **George W Saunders**, and within the [ ] lines Black line **A,B** & part of the black line as represented on the Plat containing by the estimation of the Surveyor, One hundred & seventy one acres three quarters & eight poles and further that the Complainant recover against the said Defendants the value of the ballance of 400 acres of land, to wit, 228 acres and 12 poles to be laid off out of the land of **John Saunders** from the line **A,B** on the Plat and with the Lines of his survey, for the quantity; but because it is unknown to the Court, what is the value of the said land, It is further decreed and Ordered that a Jury be empanneled and sworn on the 3rd day of the next July term of this Court to ascertain the value of the said 228 acres & 12 poles of land, the decree as to Costs is reserved until the execution of the enquiry afores$^{d}$ Signed

**William L Kelly**
**John Smith**
**John Prather**

[page 311] On the motion of **John Preston** by his attorney, It is ordered that an Execution Issue from the Clerks Office of the Pulaski Circuit Court against the Estate of the said **John Preston**, as prosecutor for the Commonwealth, in favor of **Zachariah Evans**, the prosecuted, be quashed
– **John Collier & John Preston** Complts
against on motion In Chancery
**John Evans** Deft

This day came the parties aforesaid by their attornies, and the said Defendant moved the Court to Desolve the Complainants Injunction herein, and previous notice of this motion being proven, Whereupon on hearing the Bill, answer, exhibits and Sundry Depositions, and mature deliberation thereon had, It seems to the Court that there is not sufficient equity on the part of the Complainant to preclude the Defendant from proceding against them at Common law It is therefore ordered that the Complainants Injunction be Desolved and that the Defendant may proceed with his Judgment against the said Complainants at Common law and on the motion of the said Defendant by his attorny Judgment is granted him against the said Complt for the ten percentum on the Judgment at law agreeable to an act of the General Assembly Kentucky in this case made and provided, and that the Defendant recover against the said Complainants his Cost by him about his defence in this behalf relative to said motion expended
– **Samuel Smith** Plt
against In Trespass Assault & Battery
**Thomas Owsley**

On the motion of the Defendant is Ordered that the Judgment and writ of Inquiry awarded against him in the Clerks Office be set a side and the said Defendant by his attorney now comes and defends the wrong and Injury when and where &c and says he is not guilty in manner and form as the Plaintiff against him hath declared, and of this he puts himself upon the Country & [page 312] the said Plaintiff likewise, therefore let a Jury come here &c and the Cause is Continued until the next Term of this Court
– **Duncan Gullion** Plt
against In Debt
**James Irvin** Deft

This day came the Plaintiff by his attorney, and thereupon came also a Jury, to wit, **Ichabud Blacklidge, Thomas Whites, Jeremiah Jackson, John Preston, James Kerr, Abijah Kelly, Frederick Williams, John Blacklidge, Richard Barns, Temple Sargent, John Cundiff** & **James White** who were sworn well and truly to enquire what Damage the Plaintiff hath sustained in the premises upon their Oaths do find for the Plaintiff the Debt in the Declaration mentioned, and do assess his Damages by Occasion of the Detention thereof to ten Dollars and fifty cents besides his Costs. It is therefore Considered by the Court that the Plaintiff recover against the said Defendant ninety five Dollars and thirty seven cents the said Debt in the Declaration mentioned and his Damages aforesaid by the Jurors in their Verdict aforesaid assessed and his Costs by him about his suit in this behalf expended, and the said Defendant in mercy &c.

– **George W Saunders** Plt
against upon a Scifa
**Samuel Stewart** & **Samuel Gilmore** Defts

This day came the Plaintiff by his attorney, and the Defendant **Samuel Stewart** on whom the process herein has been served, being solemnly called but came not, therefore on the motion of the Plaintiff by his attorney It is Ordered by the Court that the Plaintiff have Execution against the said Defendant **Stewart** for five Dollars sixty six & one half cents as pr Judgment, and recover against the said Defendant his costs by him in this behalf expended and the said Defendant in mercy

[page 313] **Drewry Lee** Assee Plt
against In Debt
**Spencer Griffin** Deft

On the motion of the Defendant It is Ordered that the Judgment and writ of Inquiry awarded against him in the clerks Office be set a side and the said Defendant by his attorney now comes & defends the wrong and Injury when and where &c and says he has well and truly paid the Debt in the Declaration mentioned & of this he puteth himself upon the Country and the said Plaintiff likewise Therefore it is commanded the sheriff that he cause to come here Immediately twelve good and lawful men by whom &c and thereupon came also a Jury, to wit, **Abijah Kelly, Temple Sargent, John McWhorter, John Fitzgerald, Nathaniel Black, John Cundiff, Samuel Gilmore, Moses Francis, Andrew Turner, William Wood, David Walker** & **Thomas Haines**, who being elected tried and sworn the truth to speak upon the Issue Joined upon their Oaths do say that the Defendant hath not well and truly paid the Debt in the Declaration mentioned as in pleading he hath alleged, and they do find for the plaintiff the Debt in the Declaration mentioned, and do assess his Damages by Occasion of the Detention thereof to one penny besides his Costs. It is therefore Considered by the Court that the Plaintiff recover against the said Defendant the said Debt in the Declaration mentioned his Damages aforesaid by the Jurors in their Verdict aforesaid assessed and his Costs by him about his suit in this behalf expended and the said Defendant in mercy &c. Note this Judgment is to be discharged by the payment of twenty one Pounds, with legal Interest thereon from the 28th day of August 1805 until paid & Costs

[page 314] **William Kavanaugh** Plt
against In Case
**William Griffin** Deft
– **Philip A Sublette** by Gov Plt
against In Debt
**Nicholas Jasper** Shff & Securities Defts

Ordered that these suits be Continued until the next Court

– **Hugh Caldwell** Complt
against In Chancery
**Joseph Beard** & Als Defts

This day came the Parties aforesaid by their attornies, and on the motion of the said Defendants by their attorney leave is given them to amend their answers filed herein, and It is agreed between said Parties that this cause shall brout for hearing at the next Term of this Court

– **William Griffin** Plt

against In Case
**George W Saunders** Deft
Ordered that this suit be Dismissed
– **Reubin Warren** Ass[ee] Plt
against In Covenant
**William Hays** Deft
This day came the Plaintiff by his attorney, and thereupon came also a Jury, to wit, **Thomas Scott, James L Davis, Samuel Evans, Josiah Evans, Walter Evans, John Williams, Elijah Barns, John Cundiff** Senr, **Edward White, Jeremiah Jackson,** & **Mashack Cundiff** & **Martin Gibson**, who were sworn well and truly to enquire what Damage the Plaintiff hath sustained in the Premises upon their Oaths do say that the Plaintiff hath sustained Damages by Occasion thereof to sixty Dollars & ninety two Cents besides his costs. It is therefore Considered by the Court that the plaintiff recover against the said Defendant [page 314a] his Damages aforesaid by the Jurors in their Verdict aforesaid assessed and his Costs by him about his suit in this behalf expended and the said Defendant in mercy &[c].
– **Thomas Hutchings** Ex[ors] Plt
against In Covenant
**Charles Collier** Deft
– The Same Plt
against Same
The Same Deft
**Richard Barns** of Pulaski County came into Court and Justified and undertook for the said Defendant in each Case that if he shall be cast in the actions aforesaid that he shall satisfy and pay the Condemnation of the Court or render his body to prison in Execution for the same, or on falure thereof that he the said **Richard Barns** shall do it for him
– **Thomas Smiley** Plt
against In Debt
**Benjamin Sloane** Deft
**Thomas Simpson** of Wayne County came into Court and undertook for the said Defendant that if he shall be cast in the action aforesaid that he shall satisfy and pay the condemnation of the Court or render his body to prison in Execution for the same or on falure that he the said **Thomas Simpson**, shall do it for him, Therefore on the motion of the Defendant It is Ordered that the Judgment and writ of Inquiry awarded against him in the Clerks Office be set a side and the said Defendant by his attorney now comes and defends the wrong and Injury when and where &[c] and says he has well and truly paid the Debt in the Declaration mentioned and of this he puteth himself upon the Country and the said Plaintiff [page 315] likewise, therefore let a Jury Come here &[c]
– **Zachariah Belsha** Plt
against In Case
**Samuel Gilmore** Deft
Ordered that this suit be Continued until the next Term of this Court and that the plaintiff recover against the said Defendant his Costs by him about this Continuance expended
– **Samuel Laurence** Plt
against upon Petition & Summons
**Philip A Sublette** Deft
This day came as well the Plaintiff by his attorney, as the said Defendant in his proper person who says he cannot gainsay the demand of the Plaintiff as specified in the Petition herein, Therefore It is considered by the Court that the Plaintiff recover against the said Defendant the sum of eighteen Dollars, as per note, with legal Interest thereon from the fifteenth day of October in the year One thousand eight hundred and six until paid & Costs and the said Defendant in mercy &[c].
– **Frederick Williams** Plt
against In Covenant

**Robertson Burge** Deft

**William Hays** of Pulaski County, and **William Lair** of Lincoln County came into Court and undertook for the said Defendant that if he shall be cast in the action aforesaid that they shall satisfy and pay the Condemnation of the Court or render his body ot prison in execution for the same, or on falure thereof that they the said **William Hays** & **William Lair** shall do it for him, And on the motion of the said Defendant It is Ordered that the Judgment and writ of Inquiry awarded against him in the Clerks Office be set a side, and the said Defendant by his attorney now comes and defends the wrong and Injury [page 316] when and where &c and says the Plaintiff his action aforesaid against him Ought not to have and maintain because he says he has well and truly kept and performed the several Covenants in the writing mentioned on his part and of this he is ready to verify wherefore he prays Judgment &c. And the Plaintiff by his attorney says that for any thing above pleaded by the Defendant in his plea he Ought now be bared and Precluded from having and maintaining his Action aforesaid against the said Defendant and of this he puteth himself upon the Country and the said Defendant doth the same likewise Therefore on the motion of the Defendant by his attorney leave is given him to withdraw his plea herein. and the said Defendant by his attorney comes and defends the wrong and Injury when & where &c and craves Oyer of the writing Obligatory in the Declaration mentioned which is read to him in these words, to wit &c and the Defendant says the Declaration of the Plaintiff and the matter therein Contained are not sufficient in law for the Plaintiff his Action aforesaid to have and maintain neither is the Defendant in any manner bound by the law to answer thereto and this he is ready to verify, whereupon he prays Judgment &c. and the said Defendant According to the Act of Assembly, now here shows the following Causes of Demurer, to wit, 1st that the said Decn does not aver or uttereth that a demand was [ ] made of the Negroe Girl, which the Defendant was by his Covenant, in writing bound to pay to the plaintiff, as by law he was bound to do 2nd there is a variance between the writ Declaration and writing Obligatory filed in the cause 3rd the said Declaracion is wholy insufficient wanting form and substance and proper averment, whereupon the matter of law arrising upon the Defendants Demurer to plaintiffs Declaration being argued It seems to the Court [page 317] that the law is for the Plaintiff It is therefore Ordered that the Defendants Demurer be Over ruled, with Costs, and that the Cause be enquired into by a Jury &c. Therefore It is Commanded the Sheriff that he cause to come here Immediately twelve good and lawful men by whom &c and thereupon came also a Jury, to wit, **Thomas Scott, Samuel Evans, Josiah Evans, Walter Evans, John Williams, Elijah Barns, John Cundiff, Edward White, Jeremiah Jackson, James Williams, Mashack Cundiff** & **John Preston,** who were sworn well and truly to enquire what Damage the Plaintiff hath sustained in the premises upon their Oaths do say the Plaintiff hath sustained Damage by Occasion thereof to four hundred and twenty seven Dollars and twenty five cents besides his Costs. It is therefore considered by the Court that the Plaintiff recover against the said Defendant his Damages aforesaid by the Jurors in their Verdict aforesaid assessed and his Costs by him about his suit in this behalf expended and the said Defendant in mercy &c.

– **Thomas Eastis** Plt

against upon Petition & Summons

**John McWhorter** Deft

This day came the Plaintiff by his attorney, and It appearing to the Satisfaction of the Court that the Defendant has been duly served with a copy of the Plaintiffs Petition and Summons herein, and the said Defendant being solomnly called but came not, On the Plaintiff by his attorney a writ of Inquiry is awarded him herein. Therefore It is Commanded the Sheriff that he cause to come here Immediately twelve good and lawful men by whom &c. and thereupon came also a Jury, to wit, **Thomas Scott, James S Davis, Samuel Evans, Josiah Evans, Walter Evans, John Williams, Elijah Barns, John Cundiff** Senr, **Edward White, Jeremiah Jackson, Mashack Cundiff,** and **Martin Gibson,** who were sworn well and truly to enquire what Damage the plaintiff hath sustained in the premises upon their Oaths do find for the Debt in the Petition [page 318] mentioned and do assess the Damages by Occasion of the Detention thereof to One Cent besides his Costs It is therefore Considered by the Court that the Plaintiff recover against the said Defendant thirty two

Dollars it being the Debt in the Petition mentioned & his Damage aforesaid by the Jurors in their Verdict aforesaid assessed and his Costs by him about his suit in this behalf expended and the said Defendant in mercy &c. Note the said Debt in the Petition specified is to bare legal Interest from the twenty seventh day of November 1806 until paid & Costs

– **Thomas Smiley** Plt
against In Debt
**Benjamin Sloan** Deft

This day came the Plaintiff by his attorney and thereupon came also a Jury, to wit, **Thomas Scott, James S Davis, Samuel Evans, Josiah Evans, Walter Evans, John Williams, Elijah Barns, John Cundiff** senr, **Edward White, Jeremiah Jackson, Mashack Cundiff & Martin Gibson**, who were sworn well and truly to enquire what Damage the Plaintiff hath sustained in the premises upon their Oaths do find for the Plaintiff the Debt in the Declaration mentioned, and do assess his Damages by Occasion of the Detention thereof to one cent, besides his Costs, It is therefore Considered by the Court that the plaintiff recover against the said Defendant the said Debt in the Declaration mentioned & his Damages aforesaid by the Jurors in their Verdict aforesaid assessed and his Costs by him about his suit in this behalf expended and the said Defendant in mercy &c. Note this Judgment is to be disch[d] by the payment of forty two Dollars with Interest thereon from the twenty sixth day of October 1806 until paid Damages & Costs

[page 319] **John Arnold** Plt
against upon Petition & Summons
**Henry Francis, George Alcorn & Philip A Sublette** Defts

This day came the Plaintiff by his attorney and It appearing that a copy of the Petition and Summons herein has been duly served upon each Defendant as required by the Act of the General Assembly and the said Defendants being solemnly Called but came not, Therefore on the motion of the Plaintiff by his attorney a writ of Inquiry is awarded him herein &c. It is therefore commanded the Sheriff that he cause to come here Immediately twelve good and lawful men by whom &c and thereupon came also a Jury, to wit, **Thomas Scott, James S Davis, Samuel Evans, Josiah Evans, Walter Evans, John Williams, Elijah Barns, John Cundiff** Senr, **Edward White, Jeremiah Jackson, Mashack Cundiff & Martin Gibson**, who were sworn well and truly to enquire what Damage the Plaintiff hath sustained in the Premises upon their Oaths do find for the Plaintiff the Debt in the Petition mentioned, and legal Interest & Damages In consequence of the Detension thereof, besides his Costs. It is therefore Considered by the Court that the plaintiff recover against the said Defendants the said Debt in the Petition mentioned his Interest Damages by the Jurors in their Verdict aforesaid assessed and his Costs by him about his suit in this behalf expended and the said Defendants in mercy &c. Note this Judgment is to be Discharged by the payment of eighty Dollars with legal Interest thereon from the first day of May 1806 until paid & Costs.

[page 320] **Samuel McKee** Complt
against In Chancery
**John Brown** Deft

The Bill in this cause has been taken as confessed, and the arguments of the Counsil on both sides was heard at the last term of this Court, when the Court took time to consider of their decree, and now the Court being fully advised of and concerning the premises do give and declare it is their Opinion that the bonds or Writing Obligatory executed by the Complainant to the Defendant & now unpaid Ought to be cancelled that the Complainant Ought to recover from the Defendant all the money which he has paid the Defendant Over eight shillings per acre for the land in the Bill mentioned with the deduction of $33.33 the money agreed to be Allowed for the Surplus land together with a reasonable for the Agency and expences of the said Defendant **Brown** in purchasing the said land, the ballance of the money over paid by the Complainant as above mentioned over the said $33.33 appears to be $361 and now it is decreed and Ordered that the Complainant recover against the said defendant the said sum of $361 with Interest thereon at the rate of six per centum per annum from the 2nd day of June 1806 until paid, but to be credited by the amount of the Value of the Defendants Services in agency as aforesaid with his expence, with Interest on the same after the above rate from the first day of May 1804 until ascertained and because it is uncertain to what the Defendants services in the agency aforesaid, and for the expences aforesaid amount, it is further decreed and ordered that a Jury be impannelled & sworn on the 3rd day of the next Term of this Court, to ascertain what sum the said defendant is entitled to for the agency & expences aforesaid. And It is further decreed and Ordered that all bonds concerning with the Defendant and executed under the Contract in the Bill mentioned be cancelled [page 321] Obliterated & put a side, the decree as to Cost is reserved until after the execution of the enquiry above mentioned

Signed, **William L Kelly**
**John Smith**

In this case the Defendant **Brown** by his attorney moved the Court on the first day of this Term to set a side the Office Judgment, and for leave to file his answer which was then ready to be filed & which was sworn to on the 18th day of October 1806 in the County of Franklin & which motion the Counsil of the Complainant Objected, and a majority of the Court sustained the Objection & overruled the motion of the Defendant to file his answer & to set aside the Judgment taken in the Office – To which Opinion of the Court the Defendant by his Counsel excepts and prays that this his bill of exceptions may be Signed and Sealed by the Court

Signed **William L Kelly**
**John Smith**

– **Jesse Richardson** & **Thomas Owsley** Complt
against In Chancery
**James Christy** & Heirs

This day came the Complainants by their Counsil, and It appearing to the satisfaction of the Court that the Defendants are not Inhabitants of the Commonwealth of Kentucky, Therefore upon the motion of the said Complainants It is Ordered that unless the said Defendants enter their appearance herein agreeable to law and the Rules of this Court [page 322] on the third day of the next July term of this Court, answer the Complainants Bill, Otherwise the same will be taken as Confessed against them, and further that this Order be published for two months successively in the Informant Printed in Danville, agreeably to an Act of the General Assembly Kentucky in such case made and provided

– **Samuel Dennis** Complt
against In Chancery
**William Evans** Deft

This day came the Complainant by his Counsil, and the Defendant not having entered his appearance herein, agreeably to law and the rules of this Court, and It appearing by satisfactory proof to the Court that the said Defendant is not an Inhabitant of the Commonwealth of Kentucky Therefore on the motion of the Complainant by his counsil It is Ordered that unless the said Defendant do enter his appearance herein, on the third day of the next July Term of this Court, and answer the Complainants bill the same will be taken for Confessed, and that a copy of this Order be published in the Informant Printed at Danville for two months Successively agreeably to an Act of the General Assembly of the State aforesaid, in such cases made and provided

[page 323] **Samuel Newill** Plt
against In Covenant
**Francis Lynch**

**James S Davis** of Pulaski County came into Court and undertook for the said Defendant that if he shall be cast in the action afores[d] that he shall satisfy and pay the condemnation of the Court or render his body to prison in Execution for the same or on falure that he the said **James S Davis** shall do it for him

– On the motion of **John Brooks**, to Obtain an Injunction to stay all further proceedings on a Judgment obtained against him in the Pulaski Circuit Court by **Mark Evans** Ass[ee] of **Daniel Mains** at common law after hearing the bill exhibited and filed in this Case and the arguments of Counsil, It is Ordered that an Injunction be granted agreeable to the prayer of the Complainants Bill, and that he enter into Bond in the Clerks Office of this Court within fifteen Days from the present day with

**John Warren** & **William Brooks** his security in the penalty of £40

– **John Brown** Plt
against In Debt
**Samuel McKee** &c Defts

This day came the parties aforesaid by their attornies, and the said Defendant having given special Bail herein, The said Defendant comes and defends the wrong and Injury when & where &c and prays Oyer of the bond in the declaration mentioned which read in the following Words and figures &c and says the Plaintiff his action aforesaid Ought not to have and maintain because he says the bond upon which the suit was brought is by a Decree of the Circuit Court of Pulaski Circuit since the last continuance of this cause canceled and set a side and this he is ready to verify where he prays Judgment &c. **Montgomery** & **Owsley**

[page 324] And the Plaintiff says he Ought not by any thing in the Defendants Plea pleaded, be bared or procluded from having & maintaining his Actions aforesaid because he says the bond upon which the suit was brought is not be a Decree of the Circuit Court of Pulaski Circuit since the last Continuance of this Cause Cancelled and set a side of which he prays may be inquired of by the County **Quarles** for Pltff

And the Defendant likewise **Montgomery** & **Owsley** for Deft

Therefore It is Commanded the Sheriff that he cause to come here Immediately twelve good and lawful men by whom &c and thereupon came also a Jury to wit, **Thomas Scott**, **Samuel Evans**, **Josiah Evans**, **Walter Evans**, **John Williams**, **Elijah Barns**, **John Cundiff**, **Edward White**, **Jeremiah Jackson**, **James Williams Mashack Cundiff**, & **John Preston** who being elected tried and sworn the truth to speak upon the Issue Joined upon their Oaths do say that the bond upon which this suit was brought is by a Decree of the Pulaski Circuit Court Canceled, as in pleading the said Defendant hath alledged, Therefore It is considered by the Court that the Plaintiff take nothing by his bill but for his false clamour be in mercy &c and that the Defendants go thereof hence without day and recover against the said Plaintiff their Costs by them about their defence in this behalf expended

– **John Brown** Plt
against In Debt
**Samuel McKee** Deft

This day came the parties aforesaid by their attornies, and the said Defendant having given special bail herein, the said Defendant comes and defends the wrong and Injury when and where &c and prays Oyer of the writing Obligatory in the declaration mentioned which read in the following words &c. and says the Pltf his action aforesaid Ought not [page 325] to have and maintain because he says the bond upon which this suit was brought is by a decree of the Circuit Court of Pulaski Circuit since the last continuance of this cause canceled and set a side and this the Defendant is ready to verify where he prays Judgment &c **Montgomery** & **Owlsey** for Deft

And the Plaintiff by his attorney says he Ought not by any thing in the Defendants Plea pleaded to be barred or precluded from having and maintaining his action aforesaid because he says the bond upon which this suit was brought is not by a decree of the Circuit Court of Pulaski Circuit since the last Continuance of the cause canceled and set a side of which he prays may be enquired of by the Country **Quarles** for Plft

And the Deft likewise **Montgomery** & **Owsley** for Deft

Therefore it is Commanded the Sheriff that he cause to come here Immediately twelve good and lawful men by whom &c and thereupon came also a Jury, to wit, **Thomas Scott**, **Samuel Evans**, **Josiah Evans**, **Walter Evans**, **John Williams**, **Elijah Barns**, **John Cundiff**, **Edward White**, **Jeremiah Jackson**, **James Williams**, **Mashack Cundiff** and **John Preston**, who being elected tried and sworn the truth to speak upon the Issue Joined upon their Oaths do say that the bond upon which this suit was brought, is by a Decree of the Pulaski Circuit Court Canceled, as in Pleading the said Defendant hath alledged, Therefore It is considered by the Court that the Plaintiff take nothing by his bill, but for his false clamour be in mercy, and that the Defendant go thereof hence without day and recover against the said Plaintiff their Costs by them about their defence in

this behalf expended
[page 326] **William Fox** Plt
against In Debt
**Hays & Evans** Defts

**David Walker** of Pulaski County came into Court, and Justified, and undertook for the said Defendants that if they shall be cast in the action aforesaid that he shall satisfy and pay the condemnation of the Court or render their bodies to prison in execution for the same or on falure thereof that he the said **David Walker** shall do it for them

– **James Hardgrove** Plt
against upon motion, notices proven
**Sam[l] Gilmore** Shff Deft

This day came as well the Plaintiff by his attorney, as the said Defendant in his proper person, who he cannot gainsay the Plaintiffs motion against him. Therefore acknowledges himself Indebted to the Plaintiff in the sum of seventeen pounds, eleven shillings and three pence half penny, And with the assent of the Plaintiff It is considered by the Court that the Plaintiff recover against the said Defendant the sum acknowledged as aforesaid and his Costs by him about said motion expended, and the said Defendant in mercy &[c]. (Included in two notices)

– **John McWhorter** Plt
against upon Petition & summons
**John Cundiff** Deft

This day came as well the Plaintiff by his attorney, as the said Defendant in his proper person who says he cannot gainsay the Plaintiffs Action against him for the Debt in the Petition mentioned, Therefore with the assent of the Plaintiff It is considered by the Court that the Plaintiff recover against the said Defendant the Debt in the [page 327] Petition mentioned as aforesaid, and his Costs by him about his suit in this behalf expended, and the said Defendant in mercy &[c].

Note this Judgment is to be discharged by the payment of forty pounds, with Interest thereon after the rate of six per centum per annum from the twenty fifth day of December one thousand eight hundred and six, until paid & Costs

– On the motion of **James Williams** Ass[ee] of **Norris Williams**, who Obtained a Certificate No 130 from the County Court of Pulaski County for two hundred acres of land, and it appearing from the Testimony of **Joseph Erwin** Esq[r] introduced as a witness herein, that the said Certificate was Obtained as aforesaid through Ignorance of the said assignor on Military land. Therefore leave is granted the said **James Williams** Assignee as aforesaid, to remove his said Certificate, and locate the same on any Vacant and unappropriated land as directed by an Act of the General Assembly Kentucky in such cases made and provided and the same is Ordered to be Certified

– Ordered that the Court be adjourned until Tomorrow morning eight OClock

**John Smith**

At a Circuit Court continued and held for the Pulaski Circuit at the Courthouse of Pulaski County in Sommerset on Thursday the 30[th] day of April 1807

Present the Honourable **John Smith** & **John Prather** Gentlemen

[page 328] **Philip A Sublette**, came into Court, and acknowledged himself Indebted to **William Bryant** in the sum of fifty Dollars, with Interest thereon from the 22[nd] day of February 1806 with the reservation of Equity, and Execution to be staid "till the next Term of this Court. Therefore It is considered by the Court that the said **William Bryant** recover against the said **Philip A Sublette** the sum acknowledged as aforesaid with Interest as afores[d] and his Costs by him in this behalf expended and the said **Sublette** in mercy &[c].

– **Richard Churchwell** Ass[ee]
against In Debt
**William Brooks** & **Lambert White** Defts

This day came as well the Plaintiff by his attorney, as the said Defendants in their proper persons, who say they cannot gainsay the Plaintiffs action against them for forty Dollars the Debt in

the Declaration mentioned, Therefore with the assent of the Plaintiff It is Considered by the Court that the Plaintiff recover against the said Defendants the said Debt in the Declaration mentioned and his Costs by hm about his suit in this behalf expended, and the said Defendants in mercy &c. Note this Judgment is to be discharged by the payment of ten Dollars, thirty Dollars of said Judgment being heretofore paid, to wit, before suit brought
– On the motion of **William Lynch**, It is Ordered that the fine imposed on him by this Court, for failing to attend as a Grandjuror when summoned and Execution Issued [page 329] therein be quashed & of none effect
– Ordered that the Court be adjourned until Court in Course

**John Smith**

A Sufficient number of Judges, not appearing in the first and Second days of the Present July Term 1807, of the Pulaski Circuit Court, to constitute a Court, But the Court standing adjourned from day to day as directed by law, Therefore on Wednesday the 29th day of July in the year afores^d it being the third day of said Term a Sufficient number of Judges attended to Constitute a Court, at the Courthouse of Pulaski County in Sommerset, and a Court was held for the said Circuit

Present the Honourable **William L Kelly** & **John Prather** Gent

– **Thomas Williams** Plt
against
**Whitaker Cox** Deft
– **Israel Hart** Plt
against
**Devalt Killer** Deft

Ordered that the above suits be Dismissed, and that the Plaintiffs recover their Costs by them about said suit expended

– **Andrew Cowen** Complt
against
**Tunstall Quarles** Deft
– **John Beard** Complt
against
**George W Saunders** &c Deft
– C Wealth Plt
against
**William Davis** Deft
[page 330] The Commonwealth Plt
against
**Moses Hanks** & others Deft
– **Samuel McKee** Complt
against
**John Brown** Deft
– **Hugh Caldwell** Complt
against
**Joseph Beard** & others Deft
– **Thos McGuire** Plt
against
**Inglish** & **Clark** Defts
– **James Skidmore** Complt
against
**Francis Stephens** Deft
– **Collyer** & **Preston** Complt
against
**John Evans** Deft

– **Kizziah Chappel** &c Plt
against
**William Benton** Deft
– **John Weirs** admor Plt
against
**Nicholas Forbis** Deft
– **William Evans** Plt
against
**John Robins** Deft
– **Joseph Casky** Plt
against
**Robert Smith** Deft
[page 331] **George W Saunders** & ux Plt
against
**John Griffin** Deft
– **John Griffin** & County Plt
against
**George W Saunders** Deft
– The Same Plt
against
**George W Saunders** & ux Deft
– **George W Saunders** Plt
against
**John Griffin** Deft
– **James Thompson** Plt
against
**John Puckett** Deft
– **William Evans** Plt
against
**William Ussery** Deft
– The Same Plt
against
**Lambert White** Deft
– **Robertson Burge** Plt
against
**David Clark** Deft
– **Edward Williams** Plt
against
**Robert McAlister** & Defts
[page 332] **Benjamin Sloane** Plt
against
**John Gwin** Deft
– **Thomas McGuire** Plt
against
**English** & **Clark** Deft
– **John Scrimiger** Plt
against
**John** & **William Benton** Defts
– **Speed** & **Richardson** Plts
against
**George McWhorter** Deft
– **Nicholas Gwin** Plt

against
**George McWhorter** Deft
– **Samuel Matthews** Plt
against
**Benjamin Gwin** Deft
– **William Hays** Ass[ee] Plt
against
**P A Sublette** Deft
– **Ransom Thacker** &[c] Plt
against
**Lewis Whitesides** Deft
– **George McWhorter** Plt
against
**Nicholas Gwin** Deft
– **Samuel Smith** Plt
against
**Thomas Owsley** Deft
[page 333] **Justis & Galy** Plt
against
**James Anderson** Deft
– **P A Sublette** &[c]
against
**Nicholas Jasper** Shff Deft
– **Thomas Hutchings** Ex[ors] Plt
against
**Charles Collyer** Deft
– The Same Plt
against
The Same Deft
– The Same Plt
against
The Same Deft
– **Zachariah Belsha** Plt
against
**Samuel Gilmore** Deft
– **George Smith** Plt
against
**Thomas Hansford** Deft
– **Absolem Taylor** Plt
against
**Shaderick Price** Deft
– **Samuel Clark** Plt
against
**Martin Barrier** Deft
[page 334] **Daniel Hill** Plt
against
**John Cundiff** & others Defts
– **George Lankford** Plt
against
**John Daniel** Deft
– **William Tinny** Plt
against

**Alexander McGuire** Deft
- **Moses Smith** Plt
against
**David Cowen** & wife Deft
- The Same Plt
against
**Richard Beason** Deft
- **William Wood** Plt
against
**James Chappel** Deft
- **George Humphrey** Plt
against
**P A Sublette** Deft
- **Benjamin Burton** Plt
against
**John Simpson** Deft
- **Nath[l] Forbis** Plt
against
The Same Deft
- **John Simpson** Plt
against
**P A Sublette** Deft
[page 335] **William Tring** Plt
against
**Tunstall Quarles** Deft
- **Prather & Sublette** Plt
against
**John Daniel** Deft
- **Allin Cocks** Plt
against
**Thomas Fox** Deft
- **John Simpson** Plt
against
**John Wood** Deft
- **Lovell H Dogan** Plt
against
**Martin Gibson** Deft
- **Samuel Newill** Junr Plt
against
**Francis Lynch** Deft

Ordered that these suits be continued until the next Court

- **Samuel Cole** Plt
against upon a Scirafacias to revise Judgment
**William Hill** Deft

This day came the Plaintiff by his attorney, and on his motion It is Ordered that the Judgment and writ of Inquiry awarded him against the said Defendant in the Clerks Office herein be waved. Therefore upon the motion of the said Plaintiff It is Ordered by the Court that the Plaintiff have execution against the said Deft for three Dollars and eighty cents as p[r] Judgment and recover against the said Defendant his Costs by him about his suit in this behalf expended and the said Defendant in mercy &[c].

[page 336] **William Kavanaugh** & Al[s] Plt
against In Case

**William Griffin** Deft

This day came the Plaintiff by his attorney and thereupon came also a Jury, to wit, **James Cumming, Aminisiah Morgain, Francis Clear, Stephen Harmon, John Burton, John Adair, Thomas Banks, James Hambleton, Stephen Hail, John Cundiff, Sabourn Hail & Jonathan Smith**, who were sworn well and truly to enquire what Damages the Plaintiff hath sustained in the Premises upon their Oaths do say that the Plaintiff hath sustained Damage by Occasion thereof to twenty four Dollars and forty Cents, besides his Costs. It is therefore considered by the Court that the Plaintiff recover against the said Defendant his Damages aforesaid by the Jurors in their Verdict aforesaid assessed, and his Costs by him about his suit in this behalf expended, and the said Defendant in mercy &c.

– **Jacob Blacklidge** Ass[ee] Plt
against upon Petition
**Alexander Crawford & Aaron Lawson** Defts

This day came the Plaintiff, by his attorney (and the Process herein not being served on the Defendant **Crawford**, It is therefore ordered that the suit abates as to the said Defendant **Crawford**) And thereupon came also a Jury, to wit, **Aminisiah Morgan, James Cumming, Francis Clear, Stephen Harmon, John Burton, John Adair, Tho[s] Banks, James Hambleton, Stephen Hail, John Cundiff, Sabrown Hail, & Jonathan Smith** who were sworn well and truly to Inquire what Damage the Plaintiff hath sustained in the Premises upon their Oaths do find for the Plaintiff the Debt the Petition [page 337] mentioned and one cent in Damages In consequence of the Detension thereof besides his Costs. It is therefore Considered by the Court that the Plaintiff recover against the said Defendant **Lawson**, one hundred Dollars the said Debt in the Petition mentioned, his Damages aforesaid by the Jurors in their Verdict aforesaid assessed and his Costs by him about his suit in this behalf expended and the said Defendant in Mercy &c. Note this Judgment is to bare legal Interest from the twenty fifth day of October One thousand eight hundred and six until paid Damages & Costs

– **Morgan Williams** Plt
against In Debt
**Benjamin Sloane** Deft

**John Daniel** of Pulaski County came into Court and Justified and undertook for the said Defendant that if he shall be cast in the action aforesaid that he shall satisfy and pay the Condemnation of the Court, or render his body to prison in execution for the same or on falure thereof that he the said **John Daniel** shall do it for him, Therefore It is Ordered that the Judgment and writ of Inquiry awarded in the Clerks Office herein be set a side, and the said Defendant comes and defends the wrong and Injury when and where &c and says he has well and truly paid the Debt in the Declaration mentioned and this he prays may be enquired of by the Country, and the said Plaintiff likewise, therefore It is commanded the Sheriff that he cause to come here Immediately twelve good and lawful men by whom &c and thereupon came also a Jury to wit, **Amasiah Morgan, James Cumming, Francis Clear, Stephen Harmon, John Burton, Tho[s] Adair, Tho[s] Brooks, James** [page 338] **Hambleton, Stephen Hail, John Cundiff, Sabourn Hail, & Jonathan Smith** who being elected tried and sworn the truth to speak upon the Issue Joined upon their Oaths do say that the said Defendant hath not well and truly paid the Debt in the Declaration mentioned as in pleading he hath alledged, and they do find for the plaintiff the Debt in the Declaration mentioned and do assess his Damages by Occasion of the Detention thereof to one cent besides his Costs. It is therefore Considered by the Court that the Plaintiff recover against the said Defendant the said Debt in the Declaration mentioned his Damages aforesaid by the Jurors in their Verdict afs[d] assessed, and his Costs by him about his suit in this behalf expended and the said Defendant in mercy &c.

Note this Judgment is to be disch[d] by the payment of One hundred and eighty Dollars, with legal Interest thereon from the twelfth day of June one thousand eight hundred and six, until paid Damages & Costs

– **James Doran & Co** Plt

against In Covenant
**James Davis** & **W^m Wood** Defts

**Nathaniel Black**, of Pulaski County came into Court and Justified and undertook for the said Defendants that if they shall be cast in the action afores[d] they shall satisfy and pay the Condemnation of the Court or render their bodies to Prison in execution for the same or on falure that he the said **Nathaniel** shall do it for them, Therefore It is Ordered that the Judgment and writ of Inquiry awarded against them in the [page 339] Clerks Office be set a side, and the said Defendants now comes and defends the wrong and Injury when and where &[c] and says they have well and truly kept and performed the several Covenants in the writing mentioned on their part, and of this they pray may be enquired of by the Country, and the said Plaintiff doth the same likewise therefore it is commanded the Sherif that he cause to come here Immediately twelve good and lawful men by whom &[c] and thereupon came also a Jury, to wit, **Adonijah Morgan, James Cumming, Francis Clear, Stephen Harmon, John Burton, John Adair, Tho[s] Banks, James Hambleton, Stephen Hail, John Cundiff, Sabourn Hail** & **Jonathan Smith**, who being elected tried and sworn the truth to speak upon the Issue Joined upon their Oaths do say that the said Defendants hath not well and truly kept and performed the several Covenants in the writing mentioned on their part as in pleading they have alledged, but have broken the same in manner and form as the Plaintiff against them hath declared, and they do find for the Plaintiff the Debt in the Declaration mentioned and do assess the plaintiffs Damages by Occasion thereof to one cent besides his Costs

Therefore It is Considered by the Court that the Plaintiff recover against the said Defendants the said Debt in the Declaration mentioned, together with his Damages aforesaid by the Jurors in their Verdict aforesaid assessed and his Costs by him about his suit in this behalf expended and the said Defendants in mercy &[c].

[page 340] **Vincent Garner** Plt
against upon Petition
**Charles Carter** Deft

This day came the Plaintiff by his attorney and thereupon came also a Jury, to wit, **Amasiah Morgan, James Cumming, Francis Clear, Stephen Harmon, John Burton, John Adair, Tho[s] Banks, James Hambleton, Stephen Hail, John Cundiff, Saborn Hail,** & **Jonathan Smith** who were sworn well and truly to enquire what Damages the Plaintiff hath sustained in the premises upon their Oaths do find for the Plaintiff the Debt in the Petition mentioned, and do assess his Damages by Occasion of the Detension thereof to one Cent besides his Costs. It is therefore Considered by the Court that the Plaintiff recover against the said Defendant the said Debt in the Petition mentioned, his Damages afores[d] by the Jurors in their Verdict afores[d] assessed and his Costs by him about his suit in this behalf expended and the said Defendant in mercy &[c]. Note this Judgment is to be discharged by the payment of fifty one Dollars, with legal Interest thereon from the second day of July 1807, until paid Damages & Costs

– **Joseph Stephens** Plt
against In Debt
**Benjamin Sloane** Deft

**John Daniel** of Pulaski County came into Court and Justified and undertook for the said Defendant that if he shall be cast in the action aforesaid that he shall satisfy and pay the condemnation of the Court or render his body to prison in execution for the same or on falure thereof that he the said **John** shall do it for him, Therefore It is Ordered that [page 341] the Judgment and writ of Inquiry awarded against him in the Clerks Office be set a side, and the said Defendant now comes, and defends the wrong and Injury when and where &[c] and says he hath well and truly paid the Debt in the Declaration mentioned, and of this he puteth himself upon the Country, and the said Plaintiff doth the same, likewise Therefore It is commanded the Sheriff that he cause to come here Immediately twelve good and lawful men by whom &[c] and thereupon came also a Jury, to wit, **Amasiah Morgan, James Cumming, Francis Clear, Stephen Harmon, John Burton, John Adair, Thomas Banks, James Hambleton, Stephen Hail, John Cundiff, Saborn**

**Hail** & **Jonathan Smith** who being elected tried and sworn the truth to speak upon the Issue Joined upon their Oaths do say that the said Defendant has not well and truly paid the Debt in the Declaration mentioned as in pleading he hath alledged, and do find for the Plaintiff the Debt in the Declaration mentioned and do assess his Damages by Occasion of the Detension thereof to one Cent besides his Costs. It is therefore Considered by the Court that the Plaintiff recover against the said Defendant the said Debt in the Declaration mentioned his Damages afs[d] by the Jurors in their Verdict aforesaid assessed and his costs by him about his suit in this behalf expended and the said Defendant in mercy &[c] Note this Judgment is to be disch[d] by the payment of thirty three Dollars and one third with legal Interest thereon from the twenty fifth day of December One thousand eight hundred and five until paid Damages & Costs

[page 342] **William Fox** Plt
against In Debt
**William Hays** & **John Evans** Defts

This day came the Plaintiff by his Attorney and thereupon came also a Jury, to wit, **Amarisiah Morgan, James Cumming, Francis Clear, Stephen Harmon, John Burton, John Adair, Thomas Banks, James Hambleton, Stephen Hail, John Cundiff, Saborn Hail**, & **Jonathan Smith** who were sworn well and truly to enquire what Damages the Plaintiff hath sustained in the premises upon their Oaths do find for the Plaintiff the Debt in the Declaration mentioned, – and do assess the Plaintiffs damages by Occasion thereof to one Cent – besides his Costs It is therefore Considered by the Court that the Plaintiff recover against the said Defendant the said Debt in the Declaration mentioned together with his Damages aforesaid by the Jurors in their Verdict aforesaid assessed and his costs by him about his suit in this behalf expended and the said Defendants in Mercy &[c]. Note this Judgment is to be discharged by the payment of seventy five Dollars and thirty four Cents with legal Interest thereon from the 27[th] day of January 1807 until paid Damages & Costs

– **Joel Jackson** Plt
against In Covenant
**William Addison** Deft

This day came the parties afores[d] by their attornies, and It is agreed that this suit be Dismissed, and that [page 343] the Plaintiff recover against the said Defendant the half of the Costs by him about his suit in this behalf expended

– **William Horner** Senr Plt
against In Debt
**Spencer Griffin** Deft

– **Joseph Reed** Plt
against In Debt
The Same Deft

**John McWhorter**, of Pulaski County came into Court and undertook for the said Defendant in the above cases (but being first sworn &[c]) and undertook for the said Defendant that if he shall be cast in the actions aforesaid that he shall satisfy and pay the condemnation of the Court or render his body to prison in execution for the same or on falure thereof that he the said **John McWhorter** shall do it for him It is therefore Ordered that the Judgment and writ of Inquiry awarded against the said Defendant in said Cases in the Clerks Office be set a side, and the said Defendant now comes and defends the wrong and Injury when and where &[c] and says he has well and truly paid the Debts in the Declaration mentioned and this he prays may be enquired of by the Country, and the Plaintiffs doth the same likewise, Therefore let a Jury come here &[c] and the causes are continued until the next Court

– Ordered that the Office Judgments of this Term, such as are not set a side & be Continued

[page 344] **William Fox** Plt
against upon Petition
**William Brooks** Deft

On the motion of the Plaintiff, It is ordered that this suit be discontinued

– **William Denham** Ass$^{ee}$ Plt
against upon Petition
**Robertson Burge & Jacob Blacklidge** Defts

This day came the Plaintiff by his Attorney (and the process herein not being served on the **Defendant Burge**, It is Ordered that the same abates as to him), and thereupon came also a Jury, to wit, **Adonijah Morgan, Washington Redmon, Frederick Williams, Tho$^{s}$ McGuire, Nath$^{l}$ Black, Moses Hanks, Samuel Gilmore, And$^{w}$ Turner, John Simpson, Joseph Porter, Amasiah Morgan & Jesse Richardson,** who were sworn well and truly to enquire what Damages the Plaintiff hath sustained in the premises upon their Oaths do find for the Plaintiff the Debt in the Petition mentioned, and do assess the Plaintiffs Damages by Occasion of the Detension thereof to one Cent besides his Costs It is therefore considered by the Court that the Plaintiff recover against the said Defendant the said Debt in the Petition mentioned together with his Damages aforesaid by the Jurors in their Verdict aforesaid assessed and his Costs by him about his suit in this behalf expended and the said Defendant in mercy &$^{c}$. Note this Judgment is to be discharged by the payment of four hundred Dollars with legal Interest thereon from the first day of February 1806 until paid Damages & Costs

[page 345] **John Simpson** Plt
against In Detinue
**P A Sublette** Deft

This day came the parties aforesaid by their attornies and on the motion of the Plaintiff a Commission is awarded him to take Depositions without the state before a single Justice of the Peace

– On the motion of **John Daniel,** is Commission is awarded him to take Depositions without the state before a single Justice of the Peace to be had as evidence in the case the said **Daniel** at the suit of **Sublette & Prather,** It being by consent &$^{c}$.

– The Commonwealth
against for failing to attend as a Juror when summoned by the Sheriff
**John McFall**

The said **McFall** appeared before this Court, on this present day and made his excuse which was adjudged good by the Court and he is discharged &$^{c}$.

– Ordered that the Court be adjourned until Court in Course

**William L Kelly**

At a Circuit Court held for the Pulaski circuit at the Courthouse of the County of Pulaski in Sommerset on Monday the 26$^{th}$ day of October 1807

Present the Honourable **John Smith & John Prather** Gentlemen

– A Grand jury was sworn for the Pulaski Circuit with **George Dougherty** foreman, **James Gyore, Alexander McGinnis, James Cowen, James McMan, Aaron Vanhook, Joseph Roy, Abraham Rusk, Isaac Mayfield** Junr, **Charles Richardson, Adonijah Morgan, Joseph Rainey, W$^{m}$ Cooper, Samuel Neal, Samuel Hand, Ben$^{j}$ Balogan** [?], John [ ], **Thomas** [page 346] **Jacob,** and **Samuel Matthews** who having received their charge retired to consider of their Presentments

– **Samuel Smith** Plt
against In Trespass Assault & Battery
**Thomas Owsley** Deft

This day came the parties aforesaid by their attornies, and upon the motion of the said Defendant by his attorney, It is Ordered that this suit be Dismissed, the Plaintiff having removed himself without the state of Kentucky, and not given Security for Costs as directed by an Act of the General Assembly Kentucky in such cases made and provided, and that the said Defendant recover of the Plaintiff his costs by him about his defence in this behalf expended

– **William Evans** Plt
against In Covenant
**Lambert White** Deft

This day came the parties aforesaid by their attornies, and upon the motion of the said Defendant by his attorney, It is ordered that this suit be Dismissed, the Plaintiff having removed himself without the State of Kentucky, and not given security for Costs as directed by an Act of the General Assembly Kentucky in such cases made and provided, and that the said Defendant recover against the Plaintiff his Costs by him about this defence in this behalf expended

– **Joseph Dillard** Plt
against In Trespass Assault & Battery
**Benjamin Barns** Deft

This day came the Plaintiff by his attorney, and on his motion a Dedimus is awarded him herein to take the Depositions of **Thomas Henderson** & **Jinny Henderson** Debenesse

– **John Collier** & **John Preston** Complt
against In Chancery
**John Evans** Deft

This day came the parties aforesaid by their Counsil, and Commission is awarded them to take Depositions without the [page 347] state of Kentucky before a single Justice of the peace, & the cause is continued until the next Term of this Court

– The Commonwealth
against upon Presentment
**William Davis**

Ordered that this presentment be Continued until the next Court

– John Doe (ie **James Thompkins** Plt
against In Ejectment
Richard Roe (ie **John Puckett** Deft

This day came the parties aforesaid by their attornies, and It is Ordered that this suit be Continued until the next Court, and that the said Defendant recover against the Plaintiff his Costs by him about his defence, relative to said Continuance expended

– **John Beard** Complt
against In Chancery
**George W Saunders** & **Benjamin Burch** Deft

This day came the parties aforesaid by their attornies, And it is Ordered that a Jury be immediately impanneled and sworn on tomorrow to enquire what is the Value of the 228 acres and twelve poles of land mentioned in the Interlocutary decree Pronounced herein at the last April Term of this Court

– **Samuel McKee** Complt
against In Chancery
**John Brown** Deft

On the motion of the complainant by his Counsil, It is Ordered that a Jury be impanneled and sworn on the third day of the Next Term of this Court to ascertain such fact or facts as were directed to be enquired into by the Interlocutary decree Pronounced in this cause at the last April Term

– On the motion of **Jesse Richardson** Ass[ee] of **John McFall**, who made satisfactory proof to this Court that the said **McFall** was an [page 348] actual and bonafide settler, and Obtained a Certificate from the County Court of Pulaski County No 282 for four hundred acres of land which is lost by a Military Claim. Therefore leave is granted the said **Jesse Richardson** Ass[ee] as aforesaid to remove and locate the same on Vacant lands, Agreeably to an Act of the General Assembly Kentucky in such cases made and provided

– On the motion of **Jesse Richardson**, Ass[ee] of **Richard Barrier** who made satisfactory proof to this Court that the said **Richard Barrier**, settled himself and obtained a Certificate from the County Court of Pulaski County for one hundred and fifty acres of land No 422 which is lost by a Military claim, Therefore leave is granted the said **Jesse Richardson** Ass[ee] as aforesaid to remove and locate the same on Vacant lands agreeably to an Act of the General Assembly of the state aforesaid in such case made and provided

– On the motion of **Jesse Richardson** Ass[ce] of **Tho[s] Banks**, who made satisfactory proof to this Court that the said **Thomas Banks** settled himself and Obtained a Certificate from the County Court of Pulaski County for two hundred acres of land No 168, which is lost by a Military Claim, Therefore leave is granted the said **Jesse Richardson** Ass[ce] as aforesaid, to remove and locate the same of Vacant lands, agreeably to an Act of the General Assembly of the State aforesaid, in such cases made and provided

– **Anderson Nunnaly** & **Thomas Owsley**, affrayers, being brought into Court, and after hearing their excuse, and the Testimony of sundry Witnesses, It is Ordered by the Court that the said **Nunnaly** be fined in the sum of ten Dollars, and the said **Owsley** in the sum of five Dollars for a contempt Offered to the Court herein, that they pay the Costs and may be taken &[c].

[page 349] **James Feland** Plt
against In Debt
**George W Saunders** Deft

This day came as well the Plaintiff by his attorney, as the said Defendant in his proper person who says he cannot gainsay the Plaintiffs action against him for the Debt in the Declaration mentioned, Therefore with the assent of the plaintiff It is considered by the Court that the Plaintiff recover against the said Defendant &[c] the said Debt in the Declaration mentioned, and hi Costs by him about his suit in this behalf expended and the said Defendant in mercy &[c].

Note this Judgment is to be disch[d] by the payment of eleven Pounds seven shillings and six pence with Interest thereon after the rate of six percentum per annum from the twentieth day of March, One thousand eight hundred and six until paid & Costs

– **Samuel Dennis** Complt
against In Chancery
**William Evans** Deft

This day came the complainant by his Counsil, and the said Defendant not having entered his appearance herein agreeably to law and the Rules of this Court, and It appearing to the Court that he is not an Inhabitant of this State, Therefore on the motion of the Complainant by his Counsil It is Ordered that unless the said Defendant appear here on the third day of the next Term of this Court, and answer the said Complainants Bill the same will be taken for Confessed, and that a copy of this Order be published in the Informant at Danville, for two months, agreeably to an Act of the General Assembly Kentucky in such cases made and provided

– **Speed** & **Richardson** Plt
against In Case
**George McWhorter** Deft

This day came the parties aforesaid by their attornies, and It is Ordered that this suit be Continued until the next Term of this Court And that the Plaintiff recover against the said Defendant his Costs by him about said Continuance expended

[page 350] **Moses Justis** & **James Galy** Plt
against In Debt
**James Anderson**

This day came the parties aforesaid by their attornies, and It is ordered that this suit be Continued until the next Term of this Court.

–The Commonwealth
against for failing to attend as Juror when summoned by the Sheriff
**Moses Hanks** & Others Deft

This day came as well the attorney for the Commonwealth as the said **Moses Hanks** & others, who made their excuse to the Court for failing to attend as aforesaid as Jurors, which be adjudged good by the Court it is ordered that said Defendants be discharged & without Costs

– **Hugh Caldwell** Complt
against In Chancery
**Joseph Beard** & Others Defts

Ordered that this suit abate, the Complainant being Dead

– **James Skidmore** Complt
against In Chancery
**Francis Stephens** Deft
– **Kizziah Chappel** by **Jesse Chappel** Plt
against In Case
**William Burton** Deft

This day came the parties aforesaid by their attornies and It is Ordered that these suits be Dismissed It being agreed

– **John Weirs** adm[or] Plt
against In Case
**Nathaniel Forbis** Deft

This day came the parties aforesaid by their attornies, and the said Defendant acknowledges the plaintiffs Action against him for twenty four pounds, eight shilling and two pence, with the reservation of equity, therefore It is considered by the Court that the Plaintiff Recover against the said [page 351] Defendant the said sum of twenty four pounds eight shillings and two pence acknowledged as aforesaid, and his Costs by him about his suit in this behalf expended and the said Defendant in mercy &[c].

– **Joseph Dillard** Plt
against In Trespass Assault & Battery
**Benjamin Barns** Deft

This day came the parties aforesaid by their attornies, and by Consent It is Ordered that this suit be Dismissed, and that the Costs relative thereto be equally divided between said parties

– The Grand jury returned into Court and made the following presentments, to wit, State of Kentucky the Circuit composed of the County of Pulaski to wit, the Jurors of the Grand jury for the body of the County and Circuit aforesaid in the name of the Commonwealth of Kentucky upon their Oaths present **Vinson Garner** Tavern keeper in the Town of Sommerset & County aforesaid for retailing spiritous liquors, to wit, whisky by the half pint without Ordinary license in the Town and County aforesaid on the 26[th] day of October 1807 Contrary to the form of the Statute in such cases made and provided as well as against the peace and dignity of the Commonwealth aforesaid by the Information of **James Cowen** & **James Goins** both of the grand jury & residenters of the county & Circuit aforesaid

**George Dougherty** foreman of the Grand Jury

State of Kentucky the Circuit composed of the County of Pulaski, to wit, the Jurors of the Grand Jury for the County and Circuit aforesaid in the name of the Commonwealth of Kentucky, upon their present **John Gibson** Surveyor of the road leading from his shop in the County of Pulaski afores[d] to where it Intersect the road leading to **Montgomerys** ferry near **Isaac Hays's** for not keeping the same in repair within three months last past, to wit, within the last three months previous to their present October Circuit Term 1807, by the Information of **James Cowen** & **James Goin's** both of the Grandjury and residenters of the County of Pulaski afores[d]

**George Dougherty** foreman of the Grand Jury

[page 352] State of Kentucky the Circuit composed of the County of Pulaski, to wit, at their October Term 1807, the Jurors of the Grand jury for the County and Circuit aforesaid in the name of the Commonwealth of Kentucky upon their Oaths present **John Dick** surveyor of the road leading from **Andrew Evans** Branch in the county and Circuit aforesaid to the Cliff of Fishing creek near **William Denhams** in the County and Circuit aforesaid with three months last past by the information of **Samuel Hand** & **Hugh Logan** both of the Grand jury and residentors of Pulaski County aforesaid

**George Dougherty** foreman of the Grand Jury

State of Kentucky the Circuit composed of the County of Pulaski, to wit, the Jurors of the Grand jury for the State and Circuit afores[d] in the name of the Commonwealth of Kentucky aforesaid upon our Oaths present the Surveyor of the road leading from the Town of Sommerset in the Circuit aforesaid to **Matthew Hicksons** in the Circuit of Pulaski for not keeping the same in repair on the

26th day of the present October, one thousand eight hundred and seven by the information of **Samuel Hand** and **William Cooper**, both of the Grandjury and residenters of Pulaski County aforesaid

**George Dougherty** foreman of the Grand jury

State of Kentucky the Circuit composed of the County of Pulaski the Jurors of the Grand jury for the state and circuit aforesaid in the name of the Commonwealth of Kentucky upon their Oaths present the Surveyor of the road leading from the foot of the Clift of Cumberland River to the Horse ford below **Montgomerys** Ferry in the circuit aforesaid, for not keeping the same in repair about the twentyninth day of September and twenty fifth day of October One thousand eight hundred and seven by the Information of **Thomas Jacob** and **James Goins** both of the Grandjury and residentors of Pulaski County aforesaid

**George Doughtery** foreman of the Grand jury

[page 353] The Grandjury having nothing further to present was discharged and Delinquents Ordered to be Summoned

– Ordered that the Court be adjourned until tomorrow morning ten OClock

**John Smith**

At a Circuit Court continued and held for the Pulaski Circuit at the Courthouse of Pulaski County in Sommerset on Tuesday the 27th day of October 1807.

Present the Honourable **John Smith**, & **John Prather** Gent

– **John Rogers** Complt
against In Chancery
**Thomas McLaughlin** Deft

This day came the parties aforesaid by their Counsil, and upon the motion of the said Defendant by his attorney to Disolve the Complainants Injunction Obtained herein, It is Ordered that the said motion be continued until the second day of the next Term of this Court, And leave is given to take Depositions before a Single Justice of the Peace without the State of Kentucky

– **William Evans** Plt
against In Covenant
**John Roberson** Deft

This day came the parties aforesaid by their attornies, and upon the calling of this suit the Defendant by his counsil offered the following pleas to be filed & admitted of Record the Defendant by his attorney comes and defends the wrong and Injury when and where &c and craves Oyer of the writing Obligatory in the Declaration mentioned which being read, and to him read, he saith that the plaintiff Ought not to have or maintain his action aforesaid against him because he saith that he hath not broken his covenant as the Plaintiff in pleading hath alledged and this he prays may be enquired of by the County &c **Davis & Owens** atto for Deft

And the Defendant for further plea in this behalf says the plaintiff his action aforesaid against him ought not to have and maintain because [page 354] he says the Plaintiff did receive from the Deft a Horse of the Value of £20 in full discharge and Satisfaction of the writing Obligatory in the Declaration mentioned, to wit, on the ___ day of ____ in the year ___ and this he is ready to verify wherefore he prays Judgment &c **Davis & Owens** atto for Deft

to which plea the Plaintiff by his Counsil Objected to the Defendants filing and the Court sustained said Objection, to which Opinion of the Court in rejecting said plea the Defendant by his Counsil excepts and prays that the same may be made a part of the Record

**John Smith**
**John Prather**

And thereupon came a Jury, to wit, **John Cundiff, John Buster, Thomas Alexander, John West, Amaziah Morgan, Henry Willis, John McCullough, Robert Modrel, Jonathan Hill, Charles Richardson, George Dungins & Frederick Williams**, who being elected tryed and sworn the truth to speak upon the Issue Joined, & Be it remembered the said Defendant by his attorney professed to the Court the following bills of exception which being signed & [ ] by the Court was ordered to be entered of Record, to wit, the Defendant by his counsil Objected to the plaintiffs introducing evidence to prove the Value of two hundred acres of land for which the Improvement was sold by the Defendant to the plt in as much as the plaintiff had never Obtained any Certificate from the Court of the Commissioners nor made any attempt for that purpose, but the Court Overruled the Defendants Objection and permitted the evidence to go to the Jury to which Opinion of the Court the Defendant by his Counsil excepts and files this his exception & prays that the same may be signed & enroled **John Smith**

**John Prather**

The Defendant by his Counsil Objected to the Plaintiffs using the Platt of Survey returned in this cause upon the Ground that the notice given by the Plaintiff to the Defendant of making said Survey was defective on the face but the Court Overruled their Objection and permitted said Platt to be read to which Opinion of the Court the Defendant by his counsil excepts and prays that this his Bill of exceptions may be signed & [page 355] enrolled

**John Smith**

**John Prather**

The Jurors upon their retirement upon their Oaths do say that the said Defendant hath not kept and performed the Several Covenants in the writing mentioned on his part as in pleading he hath alledged, but hath broken the same in manner and form as the Plaintiff against him in his Declaration herein has complained, and they do assess the Plaintiffs Damages by Occasion thereof to forty five pounds besides his Costs It is Therefore Considered by the Court that the Plaintiff recover against the said Defendant his Damages aforesaid by the Jurors in their Verdict aforesaid assessed and his Costs by him about his suit in this behalf expended, and the said Defendant in mercy &c.

– **Joel Jackson** & **Frederick Williams** Complt
against In Chancery
**Philip A Sublette** Defendant

This day came the parties aforesaid by their Counsils, and by Consent all matters in difference between them relative to this suit is refered to the Arbitration and final determination of **Robert Modrel**, **Jacob Blacklidge**, **Robert Scott**, **Andrew Cowen**, **James Montgomery** Senr & **John Evans**, whose award or the award of any five of them be the Judgment of the Court and the same is Ordered Accordingly

– **Robertson Burge** & **John Newby** Plts
against In Debt
**Charles Richardson** Deft

This day came as well the Plaintiffs by their attorney as the said Defendant in his proper person, and by consent It is Ordered that this suit be Discontinued, and that the Plaintiffs recover against the said Defendant his Costs by him about his suit in this behalf expended, and the note by agreement herein is Ordered to be delivered to the said Deft

[page 356] **John Beard** Complt
against In Chancery
**George W Saunders** & **Benjamin Burch** Defts

This day Came the parties aforesaid by their Counsil, and It is Ordered that the Interlocutary Order herein be continued until tomorrow

– Ordered that the Court be adjourned until Tomorrow morning ten OClock

**John Smith**

At a Circuit Court continued and held for the Pulaski Circuit at the Courthouse of Pulaski County in Sommerset on Wednesday the 28th day of October 1807

Present the Honourable **John Smith** & **John Prather** Gentlemen

– **John Beard** Complt
against In Chancery
**George W Saunders** & **Benjamin Burch** Defts

This day came the parties aforesaid by their Counsil, And agreeably to the Interlocutary Decree of this Court filed herein, It is Ordered that a Jury be Impanneled and sworn to ascertain the Value of 228 Acres & 12 Poles of land &c whereupon came a Jury, to wit, **Stephen Hail**, **Abraham Barrier**, **David Cowen**, **Aaron Doss**, **John Baker**, **Benjamin Gwin**, **Andrew Evans**, **Moses Hanks** Senr, **James Taylor**, **Joseph Evans**, **John Scrimiger** and **Robert Modrel** Junr who were sworn well and truly to enquire as to the Value of the said 228 acres and 12 poles of land to be laid off out of the land of **John Saunders** from the line **A,B** on the plat and with the lines of his Survey for the quantity. And upon their Oaths returned their Verdict in these words we of the Jury find that the two hundred twenty eight acres and twelve poles of land in the Interlocutory decree herein mentioned is of the value of five hundred and thirteen Dollars

[page 357] **Joseph Casky** Plt
against In Trespass Assault & Battery
**Robert Smith** Deft

This day came the parties aforesaid by their Attornies, and the said Defendant by his attorney comes and defends the wrong and Injury when and where &c and in addition to his former plea herein he says he is not guilty in manner and form as the Plaintiff against him hath Declared, and of this he puteth himself upon the Country and the Plaintiff doth the same likewise, Therefore it is commanded the Sheriff that he cause to come here Immediately twelve good and lawful men by whom &c and thereupon came also a Jury, to wit, **Thomas Whites**, **Henry Willis**, **Johnson Sargent**, **David Walker**, **Andrew Turner**, **Benjamin** [ ] **George Modrel**, **Samuel Gilmore**, **Thomas Jacob**, **William Denham**, **Aaron Lawson** & **Robert Modrel**, who being elected tryed and sworn the truth to speak upon the Issue Joined upon their Oaths do say that the said Defendant did make the first assault on the plaintiff, and that he is guilty in manner and form as the Plaintiff in his Declaration against him hath complained, and they do assess the plaintiffs Damages by Occasion thereof to one penny besides his Costs. It is therefore Considered by the Court that the Plaintiff recover against the said Deft his Damages aforesaid by the Jurors in their Verdict aforesaid assessed and his costs by him about his suit in this behalf expended, and the said Deft in mercy &c.

– **William Evans** Plt
against
**William Ussery** Deft

This day came the parties aforesaid by their attornies, and It appearing to the satisfaction of the Court that the said Plaintiff has removed himself without the State of Kentucky, and has failed to enter security for Costs as directed by Law, It is therefore Ordered that this suit be Dismissed In consequence thereof, and that the said Defendant recover his costs &c.

[page 358] **Robertson Burge** Plt
against In Case
**David Clark** Deft

Ordered that this suit be continued until the next Term of this Court and that the Plaintiff recover against the said Defendant his Costs by him relative to said Continuance expended

– **Edmond Williams** Plt
against In Case
**Robert McAlister** & Als Defts

– **Thomas McGuire** Plt
against In Debt
**Charles English** Deft

– **Thomas Hutchings** Exors Plt
against In Covenant
**Charles Collier** Deft

– The Same Plt
against In Covenant
The Same Deft

– The Same Plt
against In Covenant
The Same Deft
Ordered that these suits be Continued until the next Term of this Court
– **Nicholas Gwin** Plt
against In Case
**George McWhorter** Deft
– **George McWhorter** Plt
against In Case
**Nicholas Gwin** Deft
Ordered that these suits be continued until the next Term of this Court, for award
– **William Hays** Ass[ee] Plt
against In Covenant
**Philip A Sublette** Deft
This day came the parties aforesaid by their attornies and It is Ordered [page 359] that this suit be continued until the next Court and that the Plaintiff recover against the said Defendant his Costs by him about said continuance expended, and upon motion leave is given, to amend Declaration and It is Ordered that this Cause be remanded to the Rules
– **Ransom Thacker** &[c] Plt
against In Case
**Lewis Whitesides** Deft
– **George Smith** Plt
against In Trespass Assault & Battery
**Thomas Hansford** Deft
– **Absolem Taylor** Plt
against In Case
**Shaderick Price** Deft
Ordered that this suits be Continued until the next Term of this Court
– **Zachariah Belsha** Plt
against In Case
**Samuel Gilmore** Deft
On the motion of the Defendant It is Ordered that the Judgment and writ of Inquiry awarded against him in the Clerks Office be set a side and the said Deft by his attorney now Comes and defends the wrong and Injury when and where &[c] and says he did not assume upon himself in manner and form as the Plaintiff against him hath declared, and of this he puts himself upon the Country and the said Defendant doth the same likewise, And the said Defendant by his attorney comes and defends the wrong and Injury when and where &[c] and said the Plaintiff aforesaid his action aforesaid Ought not be have and maintain because he says that previous to the commencement of the action aforesaid the plaintiff aforesaid was Indebted to the defendant aforesaid the sum of £3..12.. By open account for work before that time done which he prays may be to [ ] in discount & [ ] of against so much of the demand of the Plaintiff aforesaid as set forth in his Declaration wherefor he prays Judgment &[c] **Quarles** P D
[page 360] And the Plaintiff for Replication to the plea of set off above says he Ought not to be bared or precluded from having & maintaining his actions aforesaid the sum of £3..12 mentioned in said plea because he says that he doth not Owe to the Defendant this said sum of £3..12 and this he prays may be enquired of by the Country and the Defendant likewise, therefore it is commanded the Sheriff that he cause to come here Immediately twelve good and true men by whom &[c] and thereupon came also a Jury, to wit, **Charles Collier, John Hudson, Henry Willis, David Matthews, Christ[o] Clonch, John McCullough, Walter Maxy, Alexander McGinnis, Samuel Matthews, Joseph Evans, John Scrimiger**, & **Robert Modrel** who being elected tryed and sworn the truth to speak upon the Issue Joined upon their Oaths do say that the Defendant did assume upon himself in manner and form as the plaintiff against him hath declared and after [ ] to the said

Defendant the amount of his Account as set forth in his said plea of set off, do assess the plaintiffs Damages by Occasion thereof to sixteen pounds twelve shillings, and eleven pence half penny besides his Costs. It is therefore considered by the Court that the Plaintiff recover against the said Defendant his Damages aforesaid by the Jurors in their Verdict aforesaid assessed and his Costs by him about his suit in this behalf expended and the said Defendant in mercy &c.

– **Samuel Clark** Plt
against In Case
**Martin Barrier** Deft

This day came the parties aforesaid by their attornies, And It is Ordered that this suit be Continued until the next Term of this court and that the plaintiff recover against the said Defendant his costs by him about his suit relative to said Continuance expended, And on the motion of the said Defendant, a Commission is awarded him to take the Deposition of **Alexander Matthews** before a Single Justice of the peace without the State of Kentucky

[page 361] **Samuel Matthews** Plt
against In Case
**Benjamin Gwin** Deft

Ordered that this suit be continued until the next Court and that the Plaintiff recover against the said Defendant his Costs by him about his suit relative to said Continuance expended

– **George Allcorn** Plt
against In Covenant
**James Taylor** &c Deft

**John Harmon**, of Pulaski County came into Court and Justified, and undertook for the said Defendant that if he shall be cast in the action aforesaid that he shall satisfy and pay the condemnation of the Court or render his body to prison in execution for the same or on falure thereof that he the said **John Harmon**, shall do it for him

– **Benjamin Sloane** Plt
against In Covenant
**John Gwin** Deft

This day came the parties aforesaid by their attornies, and It is ordered that this suit be continued until the next Term of this Court, and a Commission is awarded to take Depositions before a single Justice of the peace without the state of Kentucky

– **George Lankford** Plt
against In Case
**John Daniel** Deft

This day came the parties aforesaid by their attornies, and It is ordered that the Judgment and writ of Inquiry awd against sd Deft in the Clerks Office be set a side and the said Defendant by his attorney now comes and defends the wrong and Injury when and where &c and says he did not assume upon himself in manner and form as the Plaintiff against him hath declared, and of this he prays may be enquired of by the Country, and the said Plaintiff likewise therefore It is Commanded the Sheriff that he cause to come here Immediately twelve good and lawful men by whom &c and thereupon came also a Jury, to wit, **John Cundiff, John Fitzgerald, John Hardgrove** [page 362] **Ansen Stroud, Jesse Chappel, Jonathan Stephens, John McGinnis, Jacob Blacklidge, Moses Hanks** Senr, **Aaron Lawson, Martin Barrier** & **Thomas Owsley** who being elected tryed and sworn the truth to speak upon the Issue Joined, Afterwards one of the Jurors by consent, to wit, **John Cundiff** was withdrawn by the Court and the cause is continued until the next Court

– **Aaron Lawson** Plt
against upon motion as security for said **Crawford**
**Alexander Crawford** Deft

Ordered that this motion be continued until tomorrow

– **John Collyer** & **John Preston** Complt
against In Chancery
**John Evans** Deft

This day came the parties aforesaid by their attornies, and the Defendant by his attorney agrees to wave all exception to the manner of taking the Deposition of **Jesse Bryant**, and **William Collyer** and the complainants by their attornies, agree that **William Collyer** above mentioned was sworn and examined as a Witness in the Action at Common law

– **William Tinney** Plt
against In Case
**Alexander McGinnis** Deft

On the motion of the Defendant It is Ordered that the Judgment and Writ of Inquiry awarded against him in the Clerks Office be set a side, and the said Defendant by his attorney now comes and defends the Wrong and Injury when and where &c and saith he is not guilty in manner and form as the Plaintiff against him hath declared and this he prays may be enquired of by the Country and the said Plaintiff likewise, and leave to give evidence any legal matter upon any special plea, therefore It is commanded the Sheriff that he Cause to come here Immediately twelve good and lawful men by whom &c and thereupon came also a Jury, to wit, **Andrew Evans, John Hudson, Peleg Baker, Jesse Burton** [page 363] **Ivy Lankford, William Barns, Robert Smith, John Baker, Joseph Erwin, Henry James, James Benton** & **Thomas Stanton** who being elected tryed and sworn the truth to speak upon the Issue Joined upon their Oaths do say, that the said Defendant is guilty in manner and form as the Plaintiff against him hath declared, and they do assess the Plaintiffs Damages by Occasion thereof to two pounds and one penny besides his Costs. It is therefore considered by the Court that the Plaintiff recover against the said Defendant his Damages aforesaid by the Jurors in their Verdict aforesaid assessed and his Costs by him about his suit in this behalf expended, and the said Defendant may be taken &c.

– **John Scrimiger** Plt
against In Trespass Assault & Battery
**John** & **William Benton** Deft

By Consent all matters in difference between said Parties are refered to the arbitration and final determination of **John Fitzgerald, Bragly Hart, Bazil Meek** & **Micajah Hogan**, whose award or the award of any three of them be the Judgment of the Court, and the same is Ordered Accordingly

– **Benjamin Burton** Plt
against In Case
**John Simpson** Deft

This day came the parties aforesaid personally, and it is ordered by the Plaintiffs that this suit be dismissed

– Ordered that the Court be adjourned until tomorrow morning Nine OClock

**John Smith**

At a Circuit Court continued and held for the Pulaski Circuit at the Courthouse of Pulaski County in Sommerset on Thursday the 29th day of October 1807

Present the Honourable **John Smith** & **John Prather** Gentlemen

[page 364] **John Fitzgerald** Complt
against upon motion In Chancery
**James S Davis** &c Defendants

This day came the parties aforesaid by their Counsil, and the said Defendant by his Counsil moved the Court to desolve the Complainants Injunction Obtained herein, and on hearing the Bill and answer filed in this Cause, and the arguments of counsil on both sides, the Complaintant by his Counsil Objected to the said Disolution, which Objection was sustained by the Court. Therefore the motion for said disolution is Ordered to be Continued until the second day of the next Term of this Court

– **Aaron Lawson** Plt
against upon motion, notice proven
**Alexander Crawford** Deft

This day came the Plaintiff by his attorney & Judgment is granted him against the said Defendant for nineteen pounds sixteen Shillings, It being the amount of a Judgment and Costs which the Plaintiff has paid **Jacob Blacklidge** for a Judgment, which was Obtained at the last July term of this Court against the Plaintiff as Security for the said Defendant and that the plaintiff recover against the said Defendant his costs by him about this motion expended, and the said Defendant in mercy &c.

– **John Beard** Complt
against In Chancery
**George W Saunders & Benjamin Burch** Defts

This day came the parties aforesaid by their Counsil, and on the motion of the said Defendant by his counsil for to Obtain a new Inquiry on the Verdict of the Jury and Judgment obtained herein, after hearing the arguments of Counsil on both sides and mature deliberation being thereon had on the grounds of excessive Damages It is considered by the Court that said motion be sustained to which Opinion of the Court the Complainant by his counsil files [page 365] his exception in the words following to wit, On executing the Inquiry of the Value of the land in this suit One witness swore the land was worth two Dollars & a half, or three Dollars per acre, another that it was worth two Dollars and a quarter per acre, another that it was worth two dollars per acre, one of the Court stated it was worth two Dollars per acre without Oath the Oath not being required and a Witness for the Defense stated it was worth only one Dollar per acre, the Jury Valued the land at less than two & a quarter Dollars per acre, and the Defendant moved the Court to set a side the Verdict upon the Ground that the Damages or Valuation was excessive, and award a new Inquiry which motion was sustained by the Court, the Complainant by his Attorney excepts & prays this his Bill of exception may be signed, Sealed and entered of Record

Signed, **John Smith**
**John Prather**

which was Ordered to be entered of Record, and Inquiry continued until Tomorrow

– **Moses Smith** Plt
against In Case
**David Corven** & ux Defts

On the motion of the Defendants It is Ordered that the Judgment and Writ of Inquiry awarded against them in the Clerks Office be set a side and the said Defendant by his Attorney now comes and defends the Wrong and Injury when and where &c and says they are not guilty in manner and form as the Plaintiff against them hath declared, and this he prays may be enquired of by the Country, and the said Plaintiff likewise, therefore let a Jury come here & and the cause is Continued until the next Court

– **Moses Smith** Plt
against In Trespass Victarmis
**Richard Beason** Deft

On the motion of the Defendant is Ordered that the Judgment and writ of Inquiry awarded against him herein in the Clerks Office, be set a side and the said Defendant by his attorney now comes and defends the wrong and Injury when [page 366] and where &c and saith he is not guilty in manner and form as the Plaintiff against him hath declared, and of this he prays may be enquired of by the Country, and the said Plaintiff doth the same likewise, therefore let a Jury come here &c and the cause is continued until the next Court

– **George Humphreys** Plt
against In Covenant
**Philip A Sublette** Deft

This day came the parties aforesaid by their Attornies, and the said Defendant acknowledges the Plaintiffs action against him for thirteen pounds nine shillings and nine pence, with the reservation of equity, therefore With the assent of the Plaintiff It is considered by the Court that the Plaintiff recover against the said Defendant the said thirteen pounds nine shillings and nine pence, Acknowledged as aforesd and his Costs by him about his suit in this behalf expended and the said

Defendant in mercy &c.
– **James Newill** Junr Plt
against In Covenant
**Francis Lynch** Defendant

This day came the plaintiff by his attorney and thereupon came also a Jury, to wit, **Aaron Lawson, John Westerman, John Chesney, Henry Willis, Ichabod Blacklidge, John Westerman, Peleg Baker, Samuel Cornbest, Jacob Ard, Thomas Banks, John Ping** and **John Cundiff** who were sworn well and truly to enquire what Damage the Plaintiff hath sustained in the premises upon their Oaths do say the Plaintiff hath sustained Damages by Occasion thereof to sixty six Dollars and sixty six Cents besides his Costs It is therefore Considered by the Court that the Plaintiff recover against the said Defendant his Damages aforesaid by the Jurors in form aforesaid assessed and his Costs by him about his suit in this behalf expended and the said Defendant in mercy &c.

[page 367] **William Wood** Plt
against In Case
**James Chappell** Deft

Ordered that this suit be Continued until the next court And the [ ] of Writ Inquiry herein waved by the Plaintiffs Counsil, at the next Term of this Court, and to [ ] as tho the said Defendant had put in his plea at this Court

– **Prather & Sublette** Plts
against In Detinue
**John Daniel**

**Nicholas Jasper** of Pulaski County came into Court and undertook for the said Defendant, that if he shall be cast in the action aforesaid that he shall satisfy and pay the condemnation of the Court or render his body to prison in execution for the same, Otherwise return to the Plaintiff the Negroe Girl named **Matilda** in the Declaration mentioned, or on falure thereof that he the said **Nicholas Jasper** shall do it for him

– **John Fitzgerald** Complt
against In Chancery
**James L Davis** &c Deft

This day came the parties aforesaid their attornies, and It is Ordered that a Commission be awarded them to take Depositions without the State of Kentucky before a Single Justice of the Peace to be read as ev[d] herein

– **Nathaniel Forbis** Plt
against In Case
**John Simpson** Deft
– **Philip A Sublette** by Gov Plt
against In Debt
**Nicholas Jasper** Shff Deft

Ordered that these suits be continued until the next Term of this Court

[page 368] **William Trigg** Ass[ee] Plt
against In Covenant
**Tunstall Quarles**

This day came as well the Plaintiff by his attorney as the said Defendant in his proper person who says he cannot gainsay the Plaintiffs action against him for one hundred seven Dollars and fifty cents It is therefore with the assent of the Plaintiff considered by the Court that the Plaintiff recover against the said Defendant the sum of One hundred seven Dollars and fifty cents acknowledged as aforesaid, and his costs by him about his suit in this behalf expended and the said Defendant in mercy &c.

– A Writing exhibited into Court stating that **James Hutson** Dec[d] in his lifetime Obtained a Certificate from the Court of Commissioners four hundred acres of land, the said **Hutson** having resided on said land agreeably to an Act of the General Assembly Kentucky in such cases made and provided, the said Writing being sworn to in Court by **John Hutson** & **Peleg Baker** the Subscribers thereto, is Ordered to be Certified &c.

– On the motion of **Jesse Richardson** Assee of **John Cowpenheffer** satisfactory proof was made to this Court that the said **Cowpenheffer** settled himself and Obtained a Certificate No 391 for one hundred and forty acres of land which is covered by a Military Claim, therefore leave is granted the said **Jesse Richardson** Assee as aforesaid to remove and locate the same agreeably to an Act of the General Assembly Kentucky in such cases made and provided and the same is Ordered to be Certified

– On the motion of **Jesse Richardson** Assee of **John Ping** who made satisfactory proof to this Court that the said **John Ping** settled himself and Obtained a Certificate from the Lincoln County Court No 202 for two hundred acres of land which is covered by a military claim, therefore leave is granted the said **Jesse Richardson** Assee as aforesd to remove & locate [page 369] the same, on vacant land, as directed by an Act of the General Assembly Kentucky in such cases made and provided and the same is Ordered to be Certified &c.

– A Writing exhibited to the Court stating that **John Penter** Dd Obtained a Certificate for land from _____ in his lifetime the said **Penter** having resided on said land agreeably to an Act of the General Assembly Kentucky in such cases made and provided the said Writing being sworn to in Court by **Charles Westerman** & **John Ping** the Subscribers thereto is Ordered to be Certified &c.

– **Allin Cocks** Plt
against In Case
**Thomas Fox** Deft

On the motion of the Defendant it is Ordered that the Judgment and writ of Inquiry awarded against him in the clerks Office be set a side and the said Defendant by his attorney now comes and defends the wrong and Injury when and where &c and saith he is not guilty in manner and form as the Plaintiff against him hath declared and of this he prays may be enquired by the Country, and the Plaintiff likewise, therefore let a Jury come here &c and the cause is continued until the next Term of this Court

– **William Fox** Plt
against In Debt
**William Brooks** & Defts

Ordered that the Judgment taken in the Clerks Office herein be confirmed and that execution be stayed three months on the said Judgment

– **John Simpson** Plt
against In Trespass Assault & Battery
**John Wood** Deft

– **Vincent Garner** Plt
against upon Petition 1st Case
**Freeman** & **Williams** Defts

Ordered that these suits be Discontinued

[page 370] **Jack** _____ Plt
against In Trespass Assault & Battery
**George Allcorn** Deft

On the motion of the Defendant It is Ordered that the Judgment and Writ of Inquiry awarded against him in the Clerks Office be set a side and the said Defendant by his attorney now comes and defends the wrong and Injury when and where &c and says he is not guilty in manner and form as the Plaintiff against him hath declared and this he prays may be enquired of by the Country and the Plaintiff likewise, Therefore It is commanded the Sheriff that he cause to come here Immediately twelve good and lawful men by whom &c and thereupon came also a Jury, to wit, **Charles Westerman, Alexander McKinsey, Edward White, James Chappel, David Walker, John West, John Jasper, Robert Scott, Aaron Lawson, Andrew Evans, Samuel Devore** & **John Baker** who being elected tryed and sworn the truth to speak upon the Issue Joined upon their Oaths do say that the said ~~Negroe Jack~~ Defendant is guilty in manner and form as the Plaintiff against him hath declared and the find the said Negro **Jack** named in the Declaration free, and do give him one Cent in Damages, therefore It is considered by the Court that the Plaintiffs recover his freedom of the said Defendant together with his Damages aforesaid by the Jurors in their Verdict aforesaid assessed and his Costs by him about his suit in this behalf expended and the said Defendant may be taken &c.

– On the motion of **John Westerman**, who made satisfactory proof to this Court that he Obtained a Certificate No 551 from the Pulaski County Court for One hundred acres of land which appears to be on a military claim, therefore leave is granted the said **John Westerman** to remove and locate the same agreeably [page 371] to an Act of the General Assembly Kentucky in such cases made and provided, and the same is Ordered to be Certified

– Ordered that the Court be adjourned until tomorrow morning ten OClock

**John Smith**

At a Circuit Court Continued and held for the Pulaski Circuit at the Courthouse of the County aforesaid in Sommerset on Friday the 30th day of October 1807

Present the Honourable **John Smith** & **John Prather** Gentlemen

– **Joseph Red** Plt
against In Debt
**Spencer Griffin** Deft

This day came the parties aforesaid by their attornies, And on the motion of the said Defendant by his attorney leave is given him to wave his plea filed herein. Therefore upon the motion of the Plaintiff by his attorney Judgment is granted him against the said Defendant for the Debt in the Declaration mentioned and his Costs by him about his suit in this behalf expended and the said defendant in mercy &c. Note this Judgment is to be discharged by the payment of fifty four Dollars, with legal Interest thereon from the tenth day of April 1806 until paid & Costs

– **William Horner** Senr Plt
against In Debt
**Spencer Griffin** Deft

This day came the parties aforesaid by their attornies, and on the motion of the Defendant, leave is given him to withdraw his plea filed in this cause, Therefore upon the motion of the Plaintiff by his attorney It is Ordered by the Court that the Plaintiff recover against the said Defendant Seventy four Dollars & two thirds of [page 372] a Dollar with Interest thereon after the rate of six per centum pr annum from the first day of April One thousand eight hundred and three until paid & Costs and the said Defendant in mercy &c

– **Haratha Burns** &c Plts
against In Trespass Assault & Battery
**Samuel Cloyd** Deft

On the motion of the Defendant It is Ordered that the Judgment and Writ of Inquiry awarded against him in the Clerks Office be set a side and the said Defendant by his Attorney now comes and defends the Wrong and Injury when and where &c and says he is not Guilty in manner and form as the Plaintiff against him hath declared and of this he prays may be enquired of by the Country and the said Defendant with the same likewise, therefore let a Jury come here &c and the cause is Continued until the next Term of this Court

– **John Femister** Plt
against In Case
**Daniel Adams** Deft

– **Micajah Cooper** Plt
against In Case
**Johnson Sargent** Deft

– **Francis Lynch** Plt
against In Trespass Assault & Battery
**Sargent & Taylor** Defts

Ordered that these suits be Continued until the next Court

– **Joseph Campbell** Plt
against In Trespass Vict armis
**Ansen Stroud** Deft

On the motion of the Defendant, It is Ordered that the Judgment and writ of Inquiry awarded against him in the Clerks Office be set aside and the said Defendant by his attorney now comes and defends the wrong and Injury when and where &c and saith he is not guilty in manner and form as the Plaintiff against [page 373] him hath declared, and of this he prays may be enquired of by the Country, and the Plaintiff doth the same likewise, Therefore let a Jury come here &c and the cause is continued until the next Term of this court

– Ordered that it be Certified to the County Court of Pulaski County that this Court Allows to **Archabald E Mills** Esqr as their attorny the sum of One hundred Dollars, for his Services for the last year preceding this date

– Negroe **Jack** Plt
against In Trespass Assault & Battery &c
**George Allcorn** Deft

This day came the parties aforesaid by their attornies, and on the motion of the said Defendant by his attorney, to Obtain a new trial on the Verdict of the Jury and Judgment Obtained herein yesterday, after hearing the arguments of Counsil on both sides and mature deliberation being thereon had, It is Ordered that the Defendants motion be sustained, on the payment of Costs, and the cause Contd

– **John Simpson** Plt
against In Detinue
**Philip A Sublette** Deft

On the motion of the Defendant, It is Ordered that the Judgment and Writ of Inquiry awarded against him in the Clerks Office be set a side, and the said Defendant by his attorney now comes and defends the wrong and Injury when and where &c and saith that he doth not detain the Negroe boy **Willis** in the Declaration mentioned in manner and form as the Plaintiff in his declaration herein against him hath declared, and of this he puts himself upon the Country, and the Plaintiff doth the same likewise, Wherefore It is commanded the Sheriff that he cause to come here [page 374] Immediately twelve good and lawful men by whom &c and thereupon came also a Jury, to wit, **Henry Willis, William Hall, Aaron Lawson, John Jasper, Isaac Ingram, David Faine, William Hainey, John Cundiff, Henry James, Lovell H Dogan, William Brooks** & **Owen Sumner** who being elected tryed and sworn the truth to speak upon the Issue Joined upon their Oaths do say that the said Defendant doth not detain the said negroe **Willis** in manner and form as the Plaintiff against him hath declared, It is therefore considered by the Court that the Plaintiff take nothing by his bill but for his false clamour be in mercy &c and that the Defendant go thereof hence without day and recover of the Plaintiff his Costs by him about his defence in this behalf expended

– **Daniel Hill** Plt
against In Covenant
**John Cundiff** & others Defts

**Nicholas Jasper** of Pulaski County came into Court, and undertook for the said Defendants that if they shall be cast in the action aforesaid that he shall satisfy and pay the Condemnation of the Court, or render his body to prison in execution for the same or on falure thereof that he the said **Nicholas Jasper** shall do it for them Therefore on the motion of the said Defendants, by their attornies It is Ordered that the Judgment and Writ of Inquiry awarded against them in the Clerks Office be set a side, and the Defts by their attorney come and defend the wrong and Injury when and where &c and crave Oyer of the Deed of Covenant in the Declaration mentioned, and it is read to them in these words to wit, one or either of us do promise to pay or cause to be paid unto **Daniel Hill** on Order three hundred Dollars, to be discharged in three mares or Gelding at their Value in Cash to be paid on the tenth day of October 1806 as witness our hands and seals this 25th day of [page 375] Novr 1805

Test **William Hill** **John Cundiff**
**Drewry Lee** **Thomas McGuire**
**B Cundiff**

which being read and heard the Defts say that the Pltff his action aforesaid against them Ought not to have and maintain because they say the said Deed was executed by them in consideration of two tracts of land lying in Pulaski County sold by the pltff to the Defend[t] **John Cundiff** on which was due the Commonwealth of Kentucky from the said **Daniel Hill** the [ ] of fourteen Cents six mills on the one and four cents six mills on the other tract, and the Defendants Aver that the said tracts of land for the arrearages of Taxes aforesaid were sold by the Sheriff of Pulaski county aforesaid on the ___ day of September 1807 and this they are ready to verify [ ] they pray Judgment &[c]

**Quarles & Montgomery** att[o] for the Pltff

And the said Defendants for further plea herein say the pltff his action aforesaid ag[st] them Ought not to have and maintain because they say the said deed of Covenant was executed by them In consequence of two tracts of land lying in the County of Pulaski sold by the Pltff to the Deft **John Cundiff** one of which tracts containing 117 acres the other 37 acres the title papers for which the Pltff was to transfer to the said **John**, and the Defts aver that at the said Pltff was requested on the 4[th] Monday of December 1805 at Somerset in the County of Pulaski afs[d] to transfer to him the said **John** the title papers of the said tract of 37 acres yet he refused to make such transfer and this they are ready to verify wherefor they pray Judgment &[c]

**Quarles & Montgomery** for Defts

And the Plaintiff by his attorney says he Ought not to be bared or precluded from having and maintaining his action aforesaid by reason of any thing in the plea of the Deft first above pleaded which said plea and the matters and things therein contained are altogether Insufficient in law to bar or preclude the Plaintiffs action, to which s[d] plea the plaintiff has no necessity nor is he bound by the law of the land to answer thereto, and this the pltff is ready to verify But the Pltff demures thereto, and for causes of Demurer according to the act of General Assembly for the Commonwealth of Kentucky in such cases made and provided the plt sets down the following, to wit,

And the said Defts say the matters in his first plea contained is sufficient in law to bar the Pltff from having and maintaining his action aforesaid, whereupon & because the pltff hath wholy refused to receive the verification of the said plea, the Defts pray Judgment &[c]

**Quarles & Montgomery** for the Defts

And the said Defts say the matters contained in his second plea are sufficient in law to bar the pltff from having and maintaining his Action afores[d] agst them wherefore and because the Pltff hath refused to receive the Verification of the said plea, they pray Judgment &[c]

**Quarles & Montgomery** for the Defts

Whereupon the matters of law arrising upon the Pltffs Demurer to the Defts pleas being argued, and mature deliberation thereon being had, It is Ordered by the Court that the said Demurer be Overruled, and the motion of the Plaintiff to withdraw demurer & file pleas continued till the next Term of this Court

[page 376] On the motion of **Henry James**, one of the Committee appointed by this Court for the safe keeping of **John Barns**, a man of unsound mind, It is Ordered to be Certifyed to the Auditor of Public Accounts Kentucky, that this Court allows to the said **James** for keeping the said **Barns**, the sum of one hundred Dollars for the last year preceding this date

– **Edward Prather** & **Philip A Sublette** Plts
against In Detinue
**John Daniel** Deft

The Defendant having entered special bail herein, Therefore on his motion it is Ordered that the Judgment and writ of Inquiry awarded against him in the Clerks Office be set a side, and the said Defendant by his Attorney now comes and defends the Wrong and Injury when and where &[c] and saith he doth not detain the Negroe Girl **Matilda** in the declaration mentioned in manner and form as the Plaintiff against him hath Declared in his Declaration herein, and this he prays may be enquired off by the Country and the Plaintiff doth the same likewise, therefore it is Commanded the Sheriff that he cause to come here Immediately twelve good and lawful men by whom &c and thereupon came also a Jury, to wit, **John Evans, John Gibson, Thomas Crow, David Richardson, Martin Gibson, William Hainey, David Faine, James Taylor, Benjamin Harris, James Hardgrove, Aaron Lawson, & John Ping,** who being elected tried and sworn the truth to speak upon the Issue Joined upon their Oaths do say that the said Defendant doth detain the Negroe Girl **Matilda** in the declaration mentioned in manner and form as the Plaintiff therein against him hath [page 377] declared, and do find for the Plaintiffs the said Negroe Girl **Matilda** if she may be had and if she may not be had, two hundred Dollars her Value in Damages in lue thereof, besides their Costs. It is therefore considered by the Court, that the Plaintiff recover against the said Defendant the said Negroe Girl **Matilda** if she may be had, and if she may not be had, the said two hundred Dollars her Value in Damages in lue thereof by the Jurors in their Verdict aforesaid assessed and his Costs by him about their suit in this behalf expended, and the said Defendant in mercy &c.

– On the motion of **George Dungings** a Constable of Pulaski County, who exhibited to the Court an account of Public Service performed by him in the execution of his Office, which being examined and allowed by the Court was Ordered to be Certified to the Auditor of Public Accounts Kentucky

– An Instrument of Writing was exhibited to the Court stating as req[d] by an Act of the General Assembly Kentucky, in such cases made and provided, that **Matthew Carr** Dec[d] Obtained a Certificate for land, upon which he had settled and remained thereon til his death, which was proven by the Oaths of the subscribers and Ordered to be Certified &c.

– Same as to Same in another Instrument of Writing, proven as in the above Order, and ordered to be Certified &c.

– **Robert Chesney** Plt
against
**David Walker** Deft

This day came the parties aforesaid by their attornies and It is Ordered that this suit be dismissed it being agreed

[page 378] **John Beard** Complt
against In Chancery
**Saunders & Burch** Defts

This day came the parties aforesaid by their Counsil, and It is ordered that the Inquiry awarded the Complainant herein be Continued until Tomorrow

– Negroe **Jack** Plt
against In Trespass Assault & Battery &c
**George Allcorn** Deft

This day came the parties aforesaid by their attornies, and on the motion of the Plaintiff by his attorney, a commission is awarded him, to take depositions be to read as evidence herein, before a single Justice of the Peace without this state

– **Lovell H Dogan** Plt
against In Ejectment
**Martin Gibson** Deft

This day came the parties aforesaid by their attornies and by their mutual Consent, this Cause came on for trial at this Term on this present day, and the said Defendant by his attorney comes and defends the wrong and Injury when and where &c and for plea herein says that he is not guilty of the Trespass and Ejectment in the Declaration mentioned and this he prays may be enquired of by the County and the Plaintiff doth the same likewise, Therefore it is Commanded the Sheriff that he cause to come here Immediately twelve good and lawful men by whom &c and thereupon came also a Jury, to wit, **John Emmerson, Jesse Chapple, Reubin Gossit, John Chesney, William Hays, Alexander Crawford, Solomon Turpin, Philip A Sublette, Thomas Banks** [page 379] **James Montgomery, William Hall, & Robert Modrel** who being elected tried

and sworn the truth to speak upon the Issue Joined upon their Oaths do say that the said Defendant is guilty of the Trespass and Ejectment, in the Declaration mentioned in manner and form as the Plaintiff therein against him hath Declared, and do find for the Plaintiff the land in said Declaration mentioned, and assess his Damages by Occasion thereof to one cent besides his Costs, It is therefore Considered by the Court that the Plaintiff recover of the said Defendant the land aforesaid together with his Damages aforesaid by the Jurors in their Verdict aforesaid assessed and his Costs by him about his suit in this behalf expended and the said Defendant in mercy &c. And on the motion of the said Plaintiff by his attorney the Commonwealth Writ of Haberfacias Possessonium is awarded him to cause him to have possession &c.
– Ordered that the Court be adjourned until Tomorrow morning ten OClock

**John Smith**

At a Circuit Court continued and held for the Pulaski Circuit at the Courthouse of Pulaski County, in Sommerset on Saturday the 31st day of October 1807

Present the Honbl **John Smith** & **John Prather** Gentlemen

– The Clerk of this Court exhibited an account for a Book, paper &c furnished by him for the use of his Office for the last year preceding this date, which being examined and allowed by the Court was Ordered to be Certified to the Auditor of Public Accounts Kentucky
– Ordered that it be Certified to the Auditor of Public Accounts that this Court allows to **William Fox** as their Clerk the sum of thirty Dollars, for public services performed by him in the execution of his Office, for the last year preceding this date
[page 380] The Commonwealth
against upon Presentment
**Vincent Garner** Deft

This day came as well the Attorney for the Commonwealth as the said Defendant by his attorney, who moved the Court to quash the presentment found against him by the Grand jury at this present Term. And after hearing the Arguments of Counsil on both sides and mature deliberation being thereon had, It is Ordered by the Court that the said motion be overruled with Costs

– **James Feland** Plt
against In Debt
**George W Saunders** Deft

This day came the Plaintiff by his Attorney, and on his motion It is Ordered that the Confession of Judgment taken herein in this Case at the present Term be set a side, Therefore on the motion of the Plaintiff by his attorney a writ of Inquiry is awarded him herein &c. And it is Ordered that the Sheriff cause to come here Immediately twelve good and lawful men by whom &c to enquire what Damages the Plaintiff hath Sustained &c and thereupon came a Jury, to wit, **Benjamin Thurman, Solomon Turpin, William Hays, Samuel Devoor, Benjamin Harris, Thomas Banks, John Buster, John Cowen, David Puckett, William Brooks, Willis Embry** & **David Richardson**, who were sworn well and truly to enquire what Damage the Plaintiff hath Sustained in the Premises upon their Oaths do find for the Plaintiff the Debt in the Declaration mentioned herein and do assess his Damages by Occasion of the detension of the same to one penny besides his Costs It [page 381] is therefore Considered by the Court that the Plaintiff recover of the said Defendant the said Debt in the declaration mentioned together with his Damages aforesaid by the Jurors in their Verdict aforesaid in form assessed and his costs by him about his suit in this behalf expended and the said Defendant in mercy &c.

Note this Judgment is to be discharged by the payment of eleven pounds, seven shillings and six pence with Interest thereon to be computed after the rate of six per centum per annum from the twentieth day of March One thousand eight hundred and six until paid Damages & Costs

– **Abraham Hunt** Plt
against In Case
**William Churchwell** Deft

This day came the Plaintiff by his Attorney and thereupon came also a Jury, to wit, **Benjamin Thurman, Solomon Turpin, William Hays, Samuel Devore, Benjamin Harris, Thomas Banks, John Buster, John Cowen, David Puckett, William Brooks, Willis Embry** & **David Richardson**, who were sworn well and truly to enquire what Damage the Plaintiff hath sustained in the premises upon their Oaths do say that the Plaintiff hath sustained Damages by Occasion thereof to fifty five Dollars besides his Costs It is therefore Considered by the Court that the Plaintiff recover against the said Defendant his Damages aforesaid by the Jurors in their Verdict aforesaid assessed and his Costs by him about his suit in this behalf expended and the said Defendant in mercy

– **Vincent Garner** Plt
against upon Petition
**Freeman** & **Williams** Defts

This day came the Plaintiff by his attorney, and thereupon came also a Jury, to wit, **Benjamin Thurman, Solomon Turpin,** [page 382] **William Hays, Samuel Devore, Benjamin Harris, Thomas Banks, John Buster, John Cowen, David Puckett, William Brooks, Willis Embry** & **David Richardson** who were sworn well and truly to enquire what Damages the Plaintiff hath sustained in the premises upon their Oaths do find for the Plaintiff the Debt in the Petition herein, and assess his Damages by Occasion of the detension of the same to one cent besides his Costs It is therefore considered by the Court that the Plaintiff recover against the said Defendant the said Debt in the Petition mentioned together with his Damages aforesaid by the Jurors in their Verdict aforesaid assessed and his Costs by him about his suit in this behalf expended and the said Defendant in mercy &c.

Note this Judgment is to be discharged by the payment of two hundred Dollars with Interest thereon after the rate of six per centum per annum, from March One thousand eight hundred and seven until Paid Damages & Costs

– **David Walker** Plt
against In Trespass Assault & Battery
**Samuel Devore** Deft

Ordered that this suit be continued until the next Term of this Court

– On the motion of **Jesse Richardson** Ass[ee] of **Benjamin Hansford**, who obtained a Certificate from the Court of Commissioners at Standford for ___ acres of land ___ of which being covered b a Military claim, leave is granted the said **Jesse Richardson** Ass[ee] as aforesaid to remove and locate the covered part &c agreeably to an Act of the General Assembly Kentucky in such cases made & provided

[page 383] **John Beard** Complt
against In Chancery
**Saunders** & **Burch** Defts

This day came the parties aforesaid by their Counsil And It is ordered that the Inquiry awarded herein be continued until the third day of the next Term of this Court

– **John Daniel** Deft
ads In Detinue
**Prather** & **Sublette** Pltff

This day came the parties aforesaid by their counsils motion for new trial Covenanted [?] and the said Defendant by his attorney excepts to the Opinion of the Court &c which exceptions being signed sealed &c by the Court was ordered to be entered of Record, And on the motion of the said Defendant by his attorney an appeal is granted him to the Honourable the high Court of Appeals Kentucky, on his entering into bond in the Clerks Office of this Court within twenty days, in the penalty of five hundred Dollars Conditioned as the law directs, with **Nicholas Jasper John Simpson** & **Henry Francis** his securities or any two them on the payment of Costs

– **Joseph Erwin** Complt
against upon Attachment
**Duncan Gullion** Deft

This day came the Complainant by his attorney and the Sheriff having returned the attachment herein executed on one Execution in favor of **Duncan Gullion**, against **James Erwin**, the said Deft being solemnly called and faling to appear, Therefore on the motion of the complainant by his attorney It is Considered by the Court that the Complainant recover against the said Defendant the [page 385] sum of seven pounds eighteen shillings and four pence and his Costs by him about this attachment expended and the said Defendant in mercy &c And It is Ordered that the Sheriff make sale of the attached effects according to law and apply the money arrising from the sale towards satisfying the Complainants Judgment

– **George Allcorn** Plt
against In Covenant
**James Taylor** Deft

This day came the Plaintiff by his attorney, and thereupon came also a Jury, to wit, **John Cowen, Benjamin Thurman, James Montgomery, Benjamin Harris, William Hays, John Jasper, Thomas Banks, William Hunt, David Puckett, David Walker, Willis Embry** & **David Richardson** who were sworn well and truly to enquire what Damage the Plaintiff hath sustained in the premises upon their Oaths do say that the Plaintiff hath sustained Damage by Occasion thereof to forty seven pounds fourteen shillings besides his costs It is therefore Considered by the Court that the Plaintiff recover against the said Defendant his Damages aforesaid by the Jurors in their Verdict aforesaid assessed and his Cost by him About his suit in this behalf expended and the said Defendant in mercy &c

– The Office Judgments of this Term such as have not been set a side agreeable to law is ordered to be confirmed by the Court

– **John Daniel**, Deputy Sheriff for **Bazil Meek** Sheriff of Pulaski County exhibited to the Court an account of public Services performed by him in the execution of his Office for the last year preceding this date, which was ordered to be Certified to the [page 385] Auditor of Public Accounts Kentucky

– **Samuel Erwin** a Constable of Pulaski County exhibited an account for public services performed by him in the Execution of his Office which being examined was ordered to be Certified to the Auditor of public accounts Kentucky

– Ordered that it be Certified to the auditor of Public accounts that this Court allows to **John January** as their Jailor the sum of eleven Dollars, for his services performed in the Execution of his Office for the last year preceding this date

– Ordered that it be Entered of Record that this Court makes choice of **Tunstall Quarles** Esqr as their Commonwealths attorney in the stead of **Archd E Mills** esqr the said **Mills** having removed himself without this Circuit, and Inconsequence thereof great Inconvenience frequently arrises on the part of the Commonwealth

– Ordered that the Court be adjourned until Court in Course

**John Smith**

At a Circuit Court held for Pulaski County at the Courthouse of Pulaski County in Sommerset on Monday the 24th day of April 1807

Present the Honorable **John Prather** & **John James** Gentlemen

– **Robert P Letcher** and **Rodes Grith**, esquires having Obtained a licence authorizing them to practice law in this Commonwealth, took the several Oaths required by law & they are authorized to practice law in the Pulaski Circuit Court

[page 386] **John McWhorter** Plt
against In Covenant
**Robertson Burge** Deft

**Robert Modrel** of Pulaski county came into Court and undertook for the said Defendant that if he shall be cast in the Action aforesaid that he shall satisfy and pay the condemnation of the Court or render his body to prison in execution for the same, or on falure thereof that he the said **Robert Modrel** shall do it for him, And on the motion of the said Defendant It is ordered that the

Judgment and Writ of Inquiry awarded against him in the Clerks Office be set a side and the said Defendant by his attorney now comes and defends the wrong and Injury when and where &c and says he hath well and truly kept and performed the several covenants in the writing mentioned on his part, and this he prays may be enquired of by the Country, and the Plaintiff doth the same likewise, Therefore let a Jury Come here &c.
– A Grandjury was sworn for Pulaski County, to wit, **Andrew Cowen** foreman, **William Buster**, **George Dougherty**, **Isaac Mayfield**, **John Roberts**, **David Dutton**, **Willis Embry**, **Seaton Lee**, **William Addison**, **Hansford Price**, **William G Cowen**, **Robert Whitesides**, **John Stottz**, **Andrew Davidson**, **Isaac Muse**, **Thomas Hail**, **Aaron Sargent**, **Adam Morris**, **George Evans** & **Edward Cooper**, who having received their charge retired to consider of their presentments
– The Commonwealth
against upon a Presentment
**John Wilkerson**
– The Same
against Same
**Vincent Garner**
– The Same
against Same
**John Gibson**
[page 387] The Commonwealth
against upon Presentment
**John Dick**
– The Same
against Same
**John Jasper**
– The Same
against Same
**Frederick Williams**

Ordered that these Presentments be quashed for a defect in the same &c
– The Commonwealth
against upon Presentment
**William Davis**

This day came the attorney for the Commonwealth, and the said **William Davis** being solemnly called, but came not, Therefore on the motion of the said Attorney Judgment is granted against the Defendant for five shillings as per fine that he pay the Costs of this Presentment, and may be taken &c
– **Joseph Erwin**, esquire returned a Certificate of the Hon[ble] **John James** One of the assistant Judges of the Pulaski Circuit Court having taken the necessary Oaths &c in the words and figures following, to wit, Pulaski to wit, March the 22nd 1809 this day **John James** Esquire came before me **Joseph Erwin**, one of the Justices of this County and produced a Commission for his appointment as assistant Judge for said County, and was qualified as the law directs Given under my hand and seal

Signed **Joseph Erwin**

and the same was Ordered to be entered of Record
[page 388] **P A Sublette** Ass[ee] of **James Doran & Co** Plt
against upon Petition
**William Coughron** Deft

This day came as well the Plaintiff by his attorney as the said Defendant in is proper person who says he cannot gainsay the Plaintiffs action against him for nine pounds sixteen shillings and five pence the Debt in the Petition herein mentioned, therefore with the assent of the Plaintiff It is considered by the Court that the Plaintiff recover against the said Defendant, the said Debt in the Declaration mentioned with legal Interest thereon from the second of June one thousand eight hundred and seven untill paid & Costs, and the said Defendant in mercy &c

– **Charles Carter** Complt
against upon Attachment
**Robert Williams** Deft

– **William Griffin** Assee Plt
against The Same
**Joshua Baker** Deft

Ordered that these Attachments be dismissed for want of Prosecution

– John Doe (ie **James Thompkins** Plt
against In Ejectment
Richard Roe (ie **John Puckett** Deft

This day came the parties aforesaid by their attornies, and It is Ordered that this suit be continued until the next Term of this Court at the Plaintiffs Costs. And on the motion of the Plaintiff by his Attorney an Attachment is awarded him to Adair County against **Robert Todd**, of said County for failing to attend as a Witness for the Plaintiff herein, at this present Term, when summoned &c.

[page 389] **Joseph Campbell** Plt
against In Trespass Vict armis
**Ansen Stroud** Deft

This day came the parties aforesaid by their attornies, and It is Ordered that this suit be dismissed at the Defendants costs the said Defendants Attorney now here present in Court and assented to the same

– The Grandjury returned into Court and made the following presentments, to wit, we of the Grand in the name of the Commonwealth Present **William Denham**, Overseer of the road leading from Fishing Creek to **John Loveless's** for not keeping the same in repair, by leaving dead trees lying a cross the same, and not keeping the clift in repair near **Aaron Vanhook** on the twenty fourth of April one thousand eight hundred and nine, against the peace and dignity of the Commonwealth and the Statute in that case made and provided and upon the Information of **Aaron Sargent** and **Adam Morris**, both of the Grand jury, and residenters of Pulaski County

**Andrew** foreman of the Grand jury

We of the Grandjury in the name of the Commonwealth present **John Cowen** Overseer of the road leading from Sommerset to **Henry Francis's** for not keeping the same in repair, by leaving dead trees lying a cross the same on the twentyfourth of April one thousand eight hundred and nine near the plantation of **Henry Francis** against the peace and dignity of the Commonwealth & of the Statute in that case made and provided, and upon the Information of **Andrew Davidson** and **John Stottz**, both of the Grand jury and residentors of Pulaski County

**Andrew Cowen** foreman of the Grand jury

We of the Grand jury in the name of the Commonwealth present **John Ingram**, labourer, for profane swearing by uttering the following words I will be god Damned and God Damn to the amount of twenty Oaths on the fourteenth of April one thousand eight hundred and nine [page 390] in the fields of **Aaron Lawson**, in the county of Pulaski against the Peace and dignity of the Commonwealth and the statute in that case made and provided, upon the information of **Charles Richardson** of Pulaski County

**Andrew Cowen** foreman of the Grand jury

The Commonwealth
against upon an Indictment, the Grandjury returned as follows a true Bill
**John Daniel**

**Andrew Cowen** foreman of the Grandjury

The Grandjury having nothing further to present were discharged by the Court and the delinquents Ordered to be Summoned

– The Commonwealth
against

**John Daniel**

The said **John Daniel** being bound by a Recognizance, to appear here before this Court on this Present day, to answer to an Indictment which was to be prefered by the Grand jury against him for forgery, the said **John Daniel**, though solemnly called came not but made default, the said Indictment was prefered to the Grand jury as aforesaid, upon which they returned a true Bill

– **John Scrimiger**
against In Trespass Assault & Battery
**John & William Burton** Defts

This day came the parties aforesaid by their attornies, and the following award being exhibited to the Court herein, was ordered to be entered of Record, to wit, we the arbitrators chosen by the parties to determine an action of Trespass Assault and Battery wherein **John Scrimiger** is Plaintiff and **William Burton & John Burton** Defts having According to an Order of the Honorable Circuit Court holden for the Pulaski Circuit Court met at [page 391] the House of **Peter Tarter** in the County of Pulaski, on the sixth day of April 1808 and being first duly sworn and after hearing the evidence and all parties being present do award and determine that the plaintiff recover nothing from the Defendants Inconsequence of said assault and Battery, and we also finally award and determine that the plaintiff pay all legal costs of the aforesaid suit Given under our hands and seals the day and date above mentioned

**John Fitzgerrell**
**Spencer McDaniel**
**Joseph Thomas**
**Bagley Hart**

And the same is made the Judgment of the Court

– Ordered that it be certified to the Auditor of Public Accounts Kentucky that this Court allows to **William Simpson** eighty five pence for attending one day travelling twenty four miles and two ferriages, Also **Thomas Hutson** ninety seven pence for attending one day travelling thirty miles and two ferriages

Also **William Hutson** eighty nine pence for attending one day travelling twenty six miles and two ferriages, and **Peter Sullins**, eighty nine pence for attending one day travelling twenty six miles and two ferriages as Witness's for the Commonwealth against **John Daniel** Indicted for forgery

– **Robertson Burge** Plt
against In Case
**David Clark** Deft

This day came the parties aforesaid by their attornies, and thereupon came also a Jury, to wit, **John Bustard, Drewry Clark, Hugh Adams, Thomas Green, Zachariah Jones, John Blacklidge, Robert Hudson, William Hail, Daniel Matthews, Samuel Hays, Jeremiah Dungins & John Fitzpatrick** who being elected tryed and sworn the truth to speak upon the Issue Joined Afterwards the Defendant by his Counsil moved the Court, to direct the [page 392] Jury sworn in this Case to find as in Case of a nonsuit, for this that the Plaintiff has failed to support his Declaration herein &c. After hearing the arguments of Counsil on both sides the Court was divided in Opinion &c And afterwards one of the Jurors, to wit, **John Bustard**, by the Consent of the Parties was withdrawn by the Court & the Cause is continued until the next Term of this Court

– **Justis & Galey** Plts
against In Debt
**James Anderson** Deft

This day came the parties aforesaid by their attornies, and by their mutual Consent, all matters and differences between them respecting this suit is refered to the arbitration and final determination of **Robert Modrel, & Joseph Erwin** Esqrs whose award or the award of either of them together with an umpire by them chosen in case of their disagreement, be made the Judgment of the Court and the same is Ordered accordingly

– **Jesse Richardson** Plt

against In Case
**Aaron Lawson** Deft

On the motion of the Defendant who first made Oath a Greeably to an Act of the General Assembly Kentucky in such Cases made and provided, Therefore it is Ordered that the clerk indorse on the Writ Issued on this present day herein directing the Shff to take appearance Bail of said Deft in the sum of two hundred and fifty Dollars

– Ordered that the Court be adjourned until Tomorrow morning nine OClock

**John Prather**

[page 393] At a Circuit Court continued and held for Pulaski Circuit at the Courthouse of Pulaski County in Sommerset on Tuesday the 25 day of April 1809

Present the same Judges as yesterday

– **John Scrimiger** Plt
against In Trespass Assault & Battery
**John & William Burton** Defts

This day came the parties aforesaid by their attornies, and upon the motion of the Plaintiff by his attorney who moved the Court to set a side the award of the Arbitration returned herein yesterday, and entered as the Judgment of this Court which motion after hearing the arguments of the Counsil of both parties is ordered to be sustained and It is further Ordered that a former Order of this Court refering all matters in difference between said Parties to certain referees be set a side, and the cause is continued until the next Term of this Court

– **Benjamin Sloane** Plt
against In Covenant
**John Gwin** Deft

Ordered that this suit be continued until the next Term of this Court and that the Plaintiff recover against the said Defendant his Costs by him about his suit relative to said Continuance expended

– **Speed & Richardson** Plts
against In Case
**George McWhorter** Deft

This day came the Plaintiffs by their attornies, and thereupon came also a Jury, to wit, **James Taylor, George Allcorn, James Griffin, Frances Clear, Drewry Clark, John Cundiff, James Hainey, Drewry Lee, Isaac Ingram, Morgan Williams, William Barrow** & **John Reynolds** who were sworn well and truly to enquire what Damages the Plaintiffs hath sustained in the premises upon their Oaths do say that the Plaintiffs hath sustained Damage by Occasion thereof to forty pounds [page 394] besides their Costs It is therefore Considered by the Court that the Plaintiff recover against the said Defendant their Damages aforesaid by the Jurors in their Verdict aforesaid assessed and their Costs by them about their suit in this behalf expended and the said Defendant in mercy &c.

– **Samuel Burton** Plt
against
**William Stringer** Deft

– **Samuel Matthews** Plt
against In Case
**Benjamin Gwin** Deft

This day came the parties aforesaid by their attornies and upon the motion of the Defendant by his attorney who moved the Court for a Dismissel of this cause the Plaintiff having removed himself without the State of Kentucky, and has failed to enter Security for Costs agreeable to an act of Assembly of the state aforesaid in such cases made and provided, after hearing the Arguments of Counsil on both sides It is Ordered by the Court that the motion be sustained, and that the said Defendant recover against the Plaintiff his Costs by him about defence in this behalf expended

– **William Thacker** &c Plt

against In Case
**Lewis Whitesides** Deft

Ordered that this suit be Continued until the next Term of this Court

– **Nicholas Gwin** Plt
against In Case
**George McWhorter** Deft
– **George McWhorter** Plt
against In Case
**Nicholas Gwin** Deft

Ordered that these suits be Continued until the next Court for award

[page 395] **John Blair** Ass[ee] Plt
against In Debt
**William Stringer** Deft

**James Griffin**, of Pulaski County came into Court and Justified and undertook for the said Defendant that if he shall be cast in the action aforesaid that he shall satisfy and pay the condemnation of the Court or render his body to Prison in execution for the same or on falure thereof that he the said **James** shall do it for him

– **Edmond Williams** Plt
against In Case
**Robert McAlister** & Others Defts

The Persons appointed to settle all matters and differences between the parties aforesaid herein returned their award in these words and figures following, We the arbitrators appointed by the above Order with the help of Others are of the Opinion from the Testimony to us delivered that the Plaintiffs hath good cause of action, Therefore we are of the Opinion that the Defendant do pay $25 Damage and all lawful Costs. Given under our hands and seals this 14th day of February 1807

**Henry James**
**William Stockstill**
**Moses Runnals**
**Elijah Barns**
**Stephen Tilson**

And the same is made the Judgment of this Court

– The Governor for **Philip A Sublette** Plt
against In Debt
**Nicholas Jasper** Shff & Others Deft

On the motion of the Deft It is Ordered that the Judgment & Writ of Inquiry be set a side and The Defendant by his attorney comes and defends the wrong and Injury when and where &c and says that an execution in favor of **Philip A Sublette** against the estate of **Joseph Campbell**, and **Jeremiah Indgrove** was [page 396] not delivered into the hand of **John Daniel** Deputy Sheriff to the Deft **N Jasper** nor did the said **Daniel** Deputy Shff as afs[d] levy said Execution on a kittle and the corn growin in a corn field the property of said **Campbell & Snellgrove** and of this the Defendants put themselves on the Country and the Defendant for further plea in this behalf say the Plaintiff his action ought not to have and maintain because they say the said **Campbell** nor either of them **Snellgrove** had not in the county of Pulaski any estate to the knowledge of the Defendant **N Jasper** or any of his deputies whereby the Execution in the declaration could have been Served or satisfyed and this they are ready to verify wherefore they pray Judgment &c

**Owsley** for Defts

And whilst the said execution was in the hands of the said Deft **N Jaspers** deputies and the said Plaintiff as to the 1st plea of the Defendant above pleaded, likewise puts himself upon the country And the Plaintiff for Replication to the 2nd plea of the Defendant above pleaded says he ought not to be bared from having and maintaining his action aforesaid by any thing in the said plea contained because he says there was estate of the said **Campbell & Snellgrove** in the County of Pulaski Sufficient to satisfy the execution in the Declaration mentioned as in the said Declaration is alledged and this he prays may be enquired of by the Country and the Deft likewise, Therefore It is commanded the Sheriff that he cause to here Immediately twelve good and lawful men by whom &c and thereupon came also a Jury, to wit, **John West, James Taylor, George Allcorn, Frederick Williams, Drewry Clark, Morgan Williams, John Eastham, William Barrow, James Griffin, John Fitzpatrick, Zachariah Adams,** & **Isaac Ingram** who being elected tryed and sworn the truth to speak upon the Issue Joined upon their Oaths do find their Verdict in these words, we of the Jury do find for the Defendant, therefore It is considered by the Court that the Plaintiff [page 397] take nothing by their bill but for their false Clamour be in mercy &c. and that the said Defendant go hence without day and recover of the Plaintiff his costs by him about his defence in this behalf expended The Plaintiff by Attorney moved the Court Immediately to obtain a new trial herein, which is granted him upon the payment of Costs. And the Cause is Continued until the next Term of this Court

– **Thomas Hutchings** Exors Plt
against In Covenant
**Charles Collyer** Deft
The Same Plt
against In Covenant
The Same Deft
– The Same Plt
against In Covenant
The Same Deft

This day came the parties aforesaid by their attornies, and the Defendant by his Atto moved the Court for a Continuance of the above cases, which was granted him and that the Plaintiff recover against the said Deft his costs by him about his suits relative to said Continuances expended, And on the motion of the Defendant leave is given him to take the Deposition of **Elijah Barns** of Tenessee, before a single Justice of the Peace, by consent

– **Francis Lynch** Plt
against In Trespass Assault & Battery
**Taylor** & **Sargent** Defts

This day came the Parties aforesaid by their attornies, and the Defts by their attorney moved the Court to Dismiss the Plaintiffs action herein against them, alledging that the said Plaintiff had removed himself without the State of Kentucky and failed to give security for Costs as directed by an Act of the General Assembly of the state aforesd in such cases made and provided, which motion after hearing the [page 398] Arguments of Counsil on both sides, and mature deliberation thereon being had It is considered by the Court that the said Motion of the Defendant be sustained, and that the Defts go hence and recover against the Plaintiff their costs by them about their defence in this behalf expended

– **Francis Lynch** Plt
against
**Taylor** & **Sargent** Defts

Be it remembered that the Defendants by their attorney moved the Court to dismiss this suit alledging the Plaintiff had removed out of this state prior to the present Term of this Court, the Plaintiff by his attorney tendered Bond and Sufficient Security in Court for the payment of the all the Costs which have or might arrise, which has been refused by the Defendants and rejected by the Court the Defendants then produced **George Allcorn** as a Witness who swore that he about twelve months ago saw the Plaintiff in Natches, and was informed by the Plaintiff that he had desended the River and was then in the imploy of a certain **James Anderson** of Garrard County Kentucky that he **Allcorn** also swore that since he returned home he had recd a letter from the Pltff had been to Orleans since he had saw him in Natches and had then returned as fair as Natches on his way Home but that he was taken Sick, and that since the Reception of the letter aforesaid he **Allcorn** had received another letter from the Pltff informing him that since his returning he had undertaken to Oversee for some person in Natches for the present Season. and should not return till next fall or winter the Witness also proved the Pltff left all his property in this County as far as he knew which was a Horse and that the Horse is here yet, and that the Plaintiff was a single man, upon which motion and witness the Court refused to receive the Bond with Sufficient Security, and dismissed the suit of the pltff To which opinion of the Court the Pltff by his attorney [page 399] excepts and prays this his bill of exception to be signed sealed and made a part of the Record

Signed **John Prather**
**John James**

– **Andrew Turner**, a Constable of Pulaski County came into Court and exhibited to them, an account of public service performed by him in the execution of his Office which account being examined by the Court was Ordered to be Certified to the Auditor of Public Accounts Kentucky

– **George Smith** Plt
against In Trespass Assault & Battery
**Thomas Hansford** Deft

Ordered that this suit be dismissed by Order of the Plaintiffs attorney

– **Absolem Taylor** Plt
against In Case
**Shaderick Price** Deft

– **Samuel Clark** Plt
against In Case
**Martin Barrier** Deft

Ordered that these suits be continued until the next Term of this Court

– **Nathaniel Forbis** Plt
against In Case
**John Simpson** Deft

On the motion of the Defendant It is Ordered that the Judgment and writ of Inquiry awarded against him in the clerks Office be set a side and the said Defendant by his attorney now comes and defends the Wrong and Injury when and where &c and says he did not assume upon himself in manner and form as the Plaintiff against him in his Declaration herein has alledged, and of this he puts himself upon the Country, and the Plaintiff doth the same likewise therefore let a Jury come here &c and the cause is continued until the next Term of this Court

[page 400] **Philip A Sublette** Assce Plt
against upon Petition
**John Eastham** Deft

Ordered that this suit be dismissed and that the Plaintiff recover against the said Defendant his Costs by him about his suit in this behalf expended, the said Defendant now here in Court as well as the Plaintiff and assented to the same

– **George Lankford** Plt
against In Case
**John Daniel** Deft

This day came the parties aforesaid by their attornies, and It is Ordered that this suit be continued until the next Court. And on the motion of the said Defendant a Dedimus is awarded him to take the Deposition of **Peyton Herring**, of the state of Tennessee before a single Justice of the peace, by Consent, to be read as evidence herein

– **John Thurman** Plt
against upon Petition
**Joseph Erwin** Deft

This day came the parties aforesaid, and by their consent all matters and differences between them respecting this suit is refered to the arbitration and determination of **John Phelps**, **Jonathan Smith**, **John Newby**, and **Edward Prather**, whose award or the award of any three of them be the Judgment of the Court and the same is Ordered accordingly

– **Moses Smith** Plt
against Case

**David Cowen** & ux Defts

This day came the Parties by their attornies and It is Ordered that this suit be dismissed &c. Therefore upon the motion of the Defendant by his attorney Judgment is granted him against [page 401] the Plaintiff for one hundred and fifty weight of Tob° agreeable to an act of the General Assembly Kentucky in such cases made and provided and his Costs by him about his defence in this behalf expended

– **Moses Smith** Plt
against Trespass Vict armis
**Richard Beason** Deft

Dismission, and Judgment for the Deft herein, as in the case last above mentioned

– **William Wood** Plt
against In Case
**James Chappel** Deft

On the motion of the Defendant It is ordered that the Judgment and writ of Inquiry awarded against him in the clerks Office be set a side and the said Defendant by his attorney now comes and defends the wrong and Injury when and where &c and says he is not guilty in manner and form as the Plaintiff in his Declaration herein against him hath declared, and this he prays may be enquired of by the Country and the Plaintiff doth the same likewise, therefore let a Jury come here &c and the cause is continued until the next Court

– **Haratha Burns** &c Plt
against In Trespass Assault and Battery
**Samuel Cloyd** Deft

This day came the parties aforesaid by their attornies, and thereupon cam also a Jury, to wit, **Johnson Sargent, John Jasper, Micajah Cooper, Ambrose Coffee, Marvel Nash, Benjamin Hansford, Jesse Williams, Samuel Hendricks, David Puckett, Joel Whitesides, Hugh Chambers & Jesse Evans** who being elected tryed and sworn the truth to speak upon the Issue Joined upon their Oaths do say that the said Defendant is not guilty in manner and form as the Plaintiff in his Declaration herein against him hath complained, Therefore It is Considered by the Court that the Plaintiff take nothing by his bill but for his false clamour be in [page 402] be in mercy &c and that the Defendant go thereof hence without day and recover against the said Plaintiff his Costs by him about his defence in this behalf expended

– Negroe **Jack** Plt
against In Trespass Assault & Battery
**George Allcorn** Deft

This day came the Parties aforesaid by their attornies, and thereupon came also a Jury, to wit, **Marvel Nash, Johnson Sargent, Micajah Cooper, Benjamin Hansford, Adam Morris, James Taylor, David Puckett, David Evans, Samuel Hendricks, James Eastham, Hugh Chambers & Jesse Williams** who being elected tryed and sworn the truth to speak upon the Issue Joined upon their Oaths do say that the said Defendant is guilty in manner and form as the Plaintiff against him in his Declaration hath declared, and they do find the said Negroe **Jack**, the Plaintiff herein free, and do give him one cent in Damages, therefore It is Considered by the Court that the Plaintiff recover his freedom of the said Defendant together with his Damages aforesaid by the Jurors in their Verdict in form afores^d assessed, and his costs by him about his suit in this behalf expended and the said Defendant may be taken &c

– **John Rogers** Complt
against In Chancery
**Thomas McLaughlin** Deft

This day came the Parties aforesaid by their Counsil, and on the motion of the Complainant by his counsil leave is given him to file an amended Bill herein he having first made Oath to the same And it appearing to the satisfaction of this Court that the said Defendant is not an Inhabitant of the Commonwealth of Kentucky Therefore on the motion of the Complainant by his counsil, It is that unless the said Defendant do appear here on the third day of the next Term of this Court and answer the said Complainants [page 403] amended Bill as filed herein, the same will be taken as Confessed and that a copy of this order be published for two months in some Authorized Paper agreeable to an act of the General Assembly Kentucky in such cases made and provided

– **John Rogers** Complt
against In Chancery
**Thomas McLaughlin** Deft

On the motion of the Parties by their attorneys leave is given to take Depositions before a single Justice of the Peace, to be read as evidence on the trial of this Cause

– Ordered that the Court be adjourned until Tomorrow morning nine OClock

**John Prather**

At a Circuit Court Continued and held for the Pulaski Circuit at the Courthouse of Pulaski County in Sommerset on Wednesday the 26th day of April 1809

Present the Honbl **John Prather & John James** Gent

– On the motion of **William Owens** Esqr It is Ordered that the returns made on the Executions Issued from the Clerks Office of the Pulaski Circuit Court on Replevin bonds, One in the hands of **Charles Collyer** against **Edward White** & Security, another also in the name of **Rebekah Collyer** against same, also **Richard Collyer** against same Also **David Garland** against Same, It is Ordered by the Court that said motions be sustained, and that said Returns be quashed and held at nought, and that the said **Charles Collyer** & Others may proceed to take out new Exons and proceed against said Debts, and their Costs expended in these motions

[page 404] **Tunstall Quarles** Plt
against In Case
**William Griffin** Deft

This day came the Parties aforesaid by their attornies and the said Defendant by his attorney moved the Court to place this cause on the Rule dockett, for this that the capias [ ] Issued herein was not served upon the Defendant thirty days before the return day therein mentioned as appears from the return of the Officer thereon agreeable to an Act of the General Assembly Kentucky in such cases made and provided, after hearing the arguments of counsil and mature deliberation being thereon had, the Court are of Opinion that the said motion of the Deft be Overruled with Costs

– **James Hardgrove** Plt
against upon motion
**Nicholas Jasper** late Shff Deft

It appearing to the Satisfaction of this court that the said Deft has had legal notice of this motion, Therefore on the motion of the plaintiff by his attorney Judgment is granted him against the said Deft for one hundred and eight Dollars sixty five and one half Cents [page 405] with legal Interest thereon from the first day of October One thousand eight hundred and six, and that he recover against the said Defendant his Costs by him relative to this motion expended, Note this Judgment is to have all legal Credit

– **Daniel Hill** Plt
against In Covenant
**John Cundiff** & Others Defts

This day came the parties aforesaid by their attornies, and the Plaintiff by his attorney moved the Court for leave to withdraw his Demurer herein, which was argued and Over ruled at a former Term of this Court and file Replication to the Defendants Pleas, which motion was continued "till this Term, at which Term, to wit, the present Term, after hearing the arguments of Counsil on both sides, and mature deliberation thereon being had It is Ordered that the said motion be sustained, to which Opinion of the Court the Defendants by their Counsil Objected, leave is given to withdraw and file Replications as aforesaid, Demurer withdrawn, and leave to reply, on the payment of costs, and the cause is continued until the next Term of this Court

– **David Walker** Plt
against In Trespass Assault and Battery

**Samuel Devore** Deft

*On the motion of the Deft It is Ordered that the Jud[t] and writ of Inquiry aw[d] against him &[c] be set a side and the said Defendant by his attorney comes and defends the force and Injury when and where &[c] and says the plaintiff his action aforesaid against him ought not to have and maintain because he says that at the time and place in the declaration when and where the Plaintiff hath alledged that he the said Defendant committed the Trespass assault and battery on him the said Plaintiff whereof he complains he the said Plaintiff assaulted him the said Deft and then and there would have beaten him the Defendant had not [page 406] the Defendant then and there instantly in his defence beaten him the Plaintiff which is the same trespass assault and battery in the Plaintiffs declaration mentioned, and this he is ready to verify, wherefore he prays Judgment &[c] and the Plaintiff says he ought not to be bared from having his action aforesaid against the Deft by any thing in his plea above pleaded because he says that the Defendant made the Trespass Assault and battery in the declaration mentioned of his own proper injury without such cause as in his said Plea is alledged and this he prays may be enquired of by the Country and the Defendant likewise Therefore let a Jury come here &[c] and the cause is continued until the next Term of this Court

* and the said Deft by his attorney comes and defends the wrong and Injury when and where &[c] and says he is not guilty in manner and form as the Plaintiff against him hath declared and of this he puts himself upon the Country, and the Plaintiff doth the same likewise

– **Allin Cocks** Plt

against In Case

**Thomas Fox** Deft

This day came the Parties aforesaid by their attornies and by Consent leave is given the Plaintiff to file his Declaration herein And on the motion of the Defendant It is Ordered that the Judgment and writ of Inquiry awarded against him in the Clerks Office be set a side, and the said Defendant in his proper person comes &[c] &[c] & saith the plaintiff his action aforesaid Ought not to have and maintain and that the Court should not retain Jurisdiction of said Cause because he saith that the Goods and chattles, to wit, the cow and calf beast in the said plaintiffs declaration mentioned was not of the Value of $20 as alledged by said Plaintiff but was only worth 10 Dollars being a sum under five pounds [page 407] and was properly cognizable before a Justice of the Peace, and not in the Circuit Court, and this he is ready to verify wherefore he prays Judgment of the Court whether they will retain further Jurisdiction & that the same be abated &[c] And the plaintiff saith that he ought not to be bared from having and maintaining his action aforesaid against the Defendant aforesaid by any thing contained in his plea to the Jurisdiction of the Court because he says that the matters and things therein contained are insufficient & neither is he bound by the law of the land to answer thereto and this he is ready to verify wherefore he prays Judgment &[c]. after hearing the arguments of Counsil on both sides and the matters of law arrising upon the Plaintiffs Demure to the Defendants plea being argued, and mature deliberation being thereon had it seems to the Court that the law is in favour of the Plaintiff, and that his Demurer be sustained, and that the Cause be enquired of by a Jury &[c] and the said Deft for further plea herein says he is not guilty in manner and form as the Plaintiff against him in is Declaration has alledged, and of this he puts himself upon the Country and the Plaintiff doth the same likewise Therefore it is commanded the Sheriff that he cause to come here Immediately twelve good and lawful men by whom &[c] and thereupon came also a Jury, to wit, **Benjamin Black, James Eastham** Junr, **John Fitzpatrick, David Puckett, Jesse Evans, George Humphreys, John Reynolds, Henry Garner, William Denham, William Bland, Edward Cooper & Aaron Doss**, who being elected tryed and sworn the truth to speak upon the Issue Joined upon their Oaths do say that the said Defendant is not guilty in manner and form as the Plaintiff against him hath declared, as in pleading he hath alledged It is therefore Considered by the Court that the Plaintiff take nothing by his bill but for his false clamour be in mercy &[c]. and that the Deft go hence without day and recover of the said Pltff his Costs by him about his defence in this behalf expended

[page 408] **Andrew Evans** Pltff

against upon motion, notice of this motion being proven in Court

**William Hays** Deft

Therefore on the motion of the Plaintiff Judgment is granted him against the said Defendant for one hundred and fourteen Dollars _____ it being the amount of a Judgment obtained against the said **Andrew Evans** in the Pulaski Circuit Court as the security of said **William Hays**, by **James Hambleton**, with legal Interest thereon from the 25th day of August 1807 until paid, and that he recover his Costs herein expended

– **Frederick Reperdon** Complt
against In Chancery
**Joseph Casky** Deft

whereas at the October Term of this Court in the year 1806 **Andrew Cowen Jonathan Smith** & **Robert Modrel** who were appointed Commissioners herein returned into Court their report which was entered of record and by which report it appeard that they had failed to make a conveyance to the Purchaser of the land in the mortgage mentioned and which was sold, whereupon the Court [ ] a further decree, giving the said Commissioners until the end of the next Term of the Court then next ensuing to make the said conveyance, but it now appearing to this court that the said Commissioners have neglected to make said conveyance agreeable to the before [ ] decrees, wherefore it is further decreed and ordered that the said Commissioners have until the end of this term to make the said Conveyance which they do by assigning two hundred acres out of Certificate No 3 granted by the County Court of Pulaski County at their April Term 1801 to **Joseph Casky** to be taken out of that part of the Certificate as described in said Mortgage and conveying to the purchaser all the rights [page 409] title and Interest either in law or equity which the said **Joseph Casky** had into and to the Certificate and land before mentioned on the 26th day of June 1804 the time the mortgage was made by **Casky** to **Reperdon** which is decreed and ordered accordingly

**John Prather**
**John James**

– **Elias Earle** Plt
against upon Petition
**William Stringer** Deft

This day came as well the Plaintiff by his attorney as the said defendant in his proper person who says he cannot gainsay the Plaintiffs action against him for thirty two Dollars thirty seven and half cents the Debt in the Petition herein mentioned, with legal Interest thereon from the 25th day of December 1801 until paid & Costs, and said Defendant in mercy &c Note this Judgment is confessed with the reservation of Equity

– **John Faulkner** Plt
against upon Petition
**Samuel Carson** Deft

– **George Helm** Plt
against Same
**John Dickson** Deft

– **Benjamin Bainbridge** Plt
against Same
**James Burton** Deft

– **Joel Matthews** Plt
against Same
**George Allcorn** Deft

Ordered that these Petitions be Dismissed by Order of the Plaintiffs

– **Philip A Sublette** Assee Plt
against upon Petition
**Joseph Porter** Deft

This day came the Plaintiff by his attorney, and the Sheriff having returned the Process executed herein and by failing to appear [page 410] tho solemnly called Therefore on the motion of the Plaintiff by his attorney a Writ of Inquiry is awarded him herein &c and It is ordered that the

Sheriff cause to come here Immediately twelve good and lawful men by whom &c to enquire what Damages the plaintiff hath sustained &c and thereupon came also a Jury, to wit, **Marvel Nash**, **Dudley Ware**, **James Sloan**, **John West**, **John Zachary**, **William Hunt**, **John McCullough**, **John Gibson**, **George Dungings**, **Daniel Hill**, **Nathan Turner** & **Thomas Addison** who were sworn well and truly to enquire what Damages the Plaintiff hath sustained in the premises upon their oaths do find for the Plaintiff the Debt in the Petition mentioned, and they do assess his Damages by Occasion of the detension thereof to one cent, besides his costs It is therefore Considered by the Court that the Plaintiff recover against the said Defendant twenty pounds fifteen shillings the said Debt in the Petition mentioned with legal Interest thereon from the 20th day of July 1807 until paid Damages & Costs and the said Deft in mercy &c

– Pulaski County Court Plt
against upon Petition
**Newby** & **Doss** Deft

The same Jury sworn herein and the same procedings had as in the above case (of **Sublette** Assee against **Porter**) therefore it is Considered by the Court that the Plaintiff recover against the said Defendant the sum of fifty six Dollars the Debt in the Declaration mentioned with legal Interest thereon from the 23rd day of March 1808 until paid Damages & Costs and the said Deft in mercy &c Note fifty four Dollars of this Judgment is for the benefit of **Robertson Burge** as pr endorsement upon the Original note filed in this Case with Interest thereon from 29 day of September 1808

[page 411] Pulaski County Court Plt
against upon Petition
**John Newby** & **Erwin** Deft

The same Jury sworn herein and like proceedings had as in the case **Sublette** Assee against **Porter**, therefore it is Considered by the Court that the Plaintiff recover against the said Defendant the sum of twenty one Dollars the Debt in the Declaration mentioned, with legal Interest from the 28th day of November 1807 until paid Damages & Costs, and the said Deft in mercy

– **Foster** & **Hay** Plts
against upon Petition
**William Stringer** Deft

The same Jury sworn herein & and like proceedings had as in the case (**Sublette** Assee against **Porter**) therefore It is considered by the Court that the Plaintiff recover against the said Defendant the sum of eleven pounds three shillings and three pence, the Debt in the Declaration mentioned with legal Interest thereon from the twenty first day of January one thousand eight hundred and eight until paid Damages & Costs and the said Defendant in mercy &c

– the Same Plts
against upon Petition
**John McWhorter** Deft

The same Jury sworn herein &c and like proceedings had in the case, **Sublette** Assee against **Porter**, Therefore It is Considered by the Court that the Plaintiff recover against the said Defendant the sum of twenty six Dollars and fifteen cents the Debt in the declaration mentioned with legal Interest thereon from the twentieth day of January one thousand eight hundred and eight until paid Damages & Costs and the said Defendant in mercy &c

[page 412] **Philip A Sublette** Assee Plt
against upon Petition
**Stephen Condry**

The same Jury sworn herein, and like Proceedings had as on the case **Sublette** Assee vs **Porter** Therefore It is considered by the Court that the Plaintiff recover against the said Defendant the sum of eleven Pounds thirteen Shillings and two pence the Debt in the Declaration mentioned with legal Interest thereon from the twentyfourth day of December one thousand eight hundred and seven until paid Damages & Costs, and the said Defendant in mercy &c

– The Same Plt

against upon Petition
**Henry Francis** Deft

The same Jury sworn and like proceedings had herein as in the case **Sublette** Ass[ee] against **Joseph Porter**, Therefore It Considered by the Court that the Plaintiff recover against the said Defendant the sum of ninety Dollars the Debt in the Declaration mentioned with legal Interest thereon from the first day of February one thousand eight hundred and seven until paid Damages & Costs and the said Deft in mercy &[c] Note this Judgment is to have credit for forty Dollars thirty seven and one half Cents paid on the thirtieth day of April one thousand eight hundred and eight

– The Same Plt
against upon Petition
**Johnson Sargent** Deft

The same Jury sworn and like proceedings had herein, as in the case **Sublette** Ass[ee] vs **Porter**, therefore It is considered by the Court that the Plaintiff recover against the said Defendant the sum of Seventeen pounds thirteen shillings and four pence the Debt in the Declaration mentioned with legal Interest thereon from the twenty eighth [page 413] day of December one thousand eight hundred and seven until paid Damages & Costs and the said Defendant in mercy &[c]

– **James Doran & Co** Plt
against upon Petition
**William Stringer** Deft

The same Jury sworn, and like proceedings had herein as in the case **Sublette** Ass[ee] against **Porter**, Therefore It is Considered by the Court that the Plaintiff recover against the said Defendant the sum of thirty Dollars the Debt in the Declaration mentioned with legal Interest thereon from the 25[th] day of July 1807 until paid Damages & Costs and the said Defendant in mercy &[c]

Note this Judgment is to have credit for fifteen Dollars paid on the 15[th] day of December 1807 as p[r] credit in the original note herein

– **James Slone** Ass[ee] Plt
against upon Petition
**John McWhorter** Deft

The same Jury sworn and like proceedings had herein as in the case **Sublette** Ass[ee] against **Porter**, therefore It is considered by the Court that the Plaintiff recover against the said Defendant the sum of twenty Dollars and nine cents the Debt in the Petition mentioned with legal Interest thereon from the sixth day of January one thousand eight hundred and eight until paid Damages & Costs, and the said Deft in mercy &[c]

– **James Doran & Co** Plt
against upon Petition
**James Montgomery** Deft

The same Jury sworn, and like Proceedings had herein as in the case **Sublette** Ass[ee] vs **Porter** Therefore It is considered by the Court that the Plaintiff recover against the said Defendant the sum of twenty two Dollars It being the Debt in the Petition herein mentioned [page 414] with legal Interest thereon from the twenty sixth day of May One thousand eight hundred and seven until paid Damages & costs and the said Defendant in mercy &[c]

– **James Doran & Co** Plt
against upon Petition
**John Simpson** Deft

The same Jury sworn, and like Proceedings had herein as in the case **Sublette** against **Porter**, therefore It is considered by the Court that the Plaintiff recover against the said Defendant the sum of eight pounds twelve shillings and ten pence the Debt in the Petition with legal Interest thereon from the twenty eighth day of December one thousand eight hundred and seven until paid Damages and Costs and the said Deft in mercy &[c] But to be credited for six shillings

– **Aaron Doss** Plt
against upon Petition
**John McWhorter** & **Garner** Defts

The same Jury sworn, and like proceedings had herein as in the case **Sublette** against **Porter** Therefore It is considered by the Court that the Plaintiff recover against the said Defendant the sum of twenty two pounds thirteen shillings, the Debt in the Petition mentioned with legal Interest thereon from the thirtieth day of September one thousand eight hundred and seven until paid Damages and costs and the said Defendant in mercy &c. Note this Judgment is to have credit for eight Dollars paid on the 30th day of September 1807 as appears from an endorsement on the note &c

– **John Faulkner** Plt
against upon Petition
**John Newby** Deft

The same Jury sworn, and like proceedings had herein (as in the case **Sublette** Assee against **Porter**) therefore It is considered by the Court that the Plaintiff recover against the said Defendant [page 415] the sum of One hundred Dollars It being the Debt in the Petition mentioned, with legal Interest thereon from the twenty eighth day of June One thousand eight hundred and eight until paid Damages & Costs, and the said Defendant in mercy &c

– **Robert Wray** Plt
against upon Petition
**George Allcorn** Deft

The same Jury sworn, and like Proceedings had herein (as in the case **Sublette** Assee against **Porter**) Therefore It is considered by the Court that the Plaintiff recover against the said Defendant the sum of twenty one Dollars and sixty six sents the Debt in the Petition herein mentioned with legal Interest thereon from the first day of May one thousand eight hundred and eight until paid Damages & Costs and the said Defendant in mercy &c

– **James T Worthington** Plt
against upon Petition
Joseph Camp Deft

The same Jury sworn and like Proceedings had herein (as in the case **Sublette** Assee against **Porter**) Therefore It is considered by the Court that the Plaintiff recover against the said Defendant the sum of Seventy and half Dollars. It being the Debt in the Petition mentioned with legal Interest thereon from the first day of September one thousand eight hundred and eight until paid Damages and Costs and the said Defendant in mercy &c

– **Jesse Williams** Plt
against upon Petition
**Alexander Crawford** Deft

The same Jury sworn and like proceedings had herein (as in the case **Sublette** Assee against **Porter**) therefore It is Considered by the Court that the Plaintiff recover against the said Defendant the sum of twenty six Dollars four shillings the Debt in the Petition mentioned with legal Interest thereon from the first day of March One thousand eight hundred [page 416] and eight until paid Damages and Costs and the said Defendant in mercy &c

– **Henry Francis** Plt
against upon Petition
**Robertson Burge** Deft

Ordered that this Petition be Dismissed

– **Stephen Wilkerson** Plt
against upon Petition
**Allcorn** & **Meek** Defts

This day came as well the Plaintiff by his attorney as the said Defendants in their proper person, who say they cannot gainsay the Plaintiffs action against them for fifty six Dollars the Debt in the Petition herein mentioned therefore with the assent of the Plaintiff, It is considered by the Court that the Plaintiff recover against the said Defts the sum confessed as aforesaid with legal Interest thereon from the eleventh day of September one thousand eight hundred and seven until paid & costs and the said Defts in mercy &c this Judgment is confessed with the reservation of

Equity and to have a credit for four Dollars as p^r^ credit on the note &c

– **James Griffin** Plt
against upon Petition
**George Allcorn** Deft

This day came as well the Plaintiff by his attorney as the said Deft in his proper person, who acknowledges the Plaintiffs action against him for seventy Dollars and one shilling the Debt in the Petition herein mentioned Therefore with the assent of the Plaintiff It is considered by the Court that the Plaintiff recover against the said Defendant the sum ack[d] as afores[d] with legal Interest thereon from the first day of May one thousand eight hundred and eight until paid & Costs and the said Deft in mercy &c

[page 417] **Abraham Price** Plt
against upon Petition
**George Allcorn** Deft

This day came the parties aforesaid by their attornies, and the said Defendant saith he cannot gainsay the Plaintiffs action against him for ninety four Dollars the Debt in the Petition herein mentioned Therefore with the assent of the Plaintiff It is considered by the Court that the Plaintiff recover against the said Deft the said Debt in the Declaration mentioned with legal Interest thereon from the nineteenth day of October one thousand eight hundred and eight until paid & Costs and the said Defendant in mercy &c. Note this Judgment is confessed with the reservation of Equity

– Ordered that the Court be adjourned until Tomorrow morning nine OClock

**John Prather**

At a Circuit Court continued and held for the Pulaski Circuit at the Courthouse of Pulaski County in Sommerset on Thursday the 27th day of April 1809

Present the Hon[bl] **John Prather & John James** Gent

– **Samuel Dennis** Complt
against In Chancery
**William Evans** Deft

This day came the Complainant by his attorney and produced to the Court a copy of their Order made in this cause at their October Term 1807 against the before named **William Evans** as an absent Defendant, which order, from the certificate of **John Nowell** Editor of the Informant printed in Danville, thereto annexed, it appears that the said order has been published in the Informant printed in Danville two months successively [page 418] agreeable to the law & the tenor of said order Whereupon the said **William Evans** having failed to enter his appearance herein agreeable to the rules of this court and the Court being sufficiently with the Complainants proofs produced herein Do order & decree that the said bill be taken as confessed against the said Defendant But for reasons appearing to this Court they do further order, that the said cause be continued untill the next Term of this Court, for [ ] further order & decree to be [ ] therein as they shall deem just & equitable which is decreed & ordered accordingly

**John Prather**
**John James**

– **Tunstall Quarles** Plt
against In Case
**William Griffin** Deft

This day came the plaintiff by his attorney and on his motion It is ordered that this suit be dismissed

– **Peter Chew** Ass[ce] Plt
against upon Petition
**James Davis** & **Ambrose Coffee** Defts

This day came the parties aforesaid by their attornies (except the Deft **Davis**, who from the return of the Sheriff on the copy of the Petition & Summons Issued from the Clerks Office herein has not been served with a process &c Therefore on the motion of the Plaintiff by his attorney It is ordered that this cause abate as to said **Davis**, And the said Defendant **Coffee** Comes and defends the wrong and Injury when & where & craves Oyer of the Writing Obligatory, Summons & Petition which was read to him, the Commonwealth of Kentucky &c [ ] the Petition & Summons and saith that the plaintiff his action [page 419] against him Ought not to have and maintain because he says the matter & things therein Contained are insufficient & neither is he bound by the law of the land to answer thereto, and this he is ready to Verify wherefore he prays Judgment &c & agreeably to the act of General Assembly assigns the following Causes of Demurer to wit, 1st there is a variance between the Petition & Summons Issued thereon in [ ]ing the assignments upon the Writing Obligatory 2nd The Petition does not deduce the title of the Plaintiff by reciting the usual assigns & Assee in commencing the deduction of the claim, whereby the Plaintiff became possessed of the Writing Obligatory 3rd the plaintiff states his claim by note of the Deft when it is by bond 4th that it is altogether defective in form and substance, And after hearing the arguments of Counsil on both sides as to the Defendants Demurer aforesaid, and the matters of law arrising &c It is ordered by the court that the said Demurer be over ruled, and that the cause be enquired into by a Jury &c And the said deft saith the Plaintiff his action against him Ought not to have and maintain because he says that on the ___ day of ____ to wit, after writing Obligatory became due he payed and discharged the writing Obligatory in the Petition mentioned to the Plt and this he is ready to verify wherefore he prays Judgment &c and the Plaintiff by his attorney for Replication to the plea of the Deft says that he Ought not to be bared of his action by reason of any thing set forth by said Deft in his plea because he says that the said Defendant hath not paid the Debt in the Declaration mentioned as the said Deft in pleading hath alledged but that he doth aver the same &c and this he prays may be enquired of by the Country, and the Deft likewise, therefore it is commanded the sheriff that he cause to come here Immediately twelve good and lawful men by whom &c and thereupon came also a Jury, to wit, **William Boyd, John Boyd, John West, James Boyd, William Denham, Nicholas Jasper** Senr, **Stephen Hail, Samuel King, Absolem Dodson, Andrew Wolverton, William Addison** & **Thomas Vanhook** who being elected tryed and sworn the truth to speak upon the Issue Joined upon their [page 420] Oaths do find for the Plaintiff four hundred Dollars the Debt in the Petition herein mentioned and do assess his Damages by Occasion of the detension thereof to one Cent besides his Costs It is therefore considered by the Court that the Plaintiff recover against the said Defendant, the said four hundred Dollars the Debt in the Petition mentioned as aforesaid together with his Damages aforesaid by the Jurors in their Verdict aforesaid assessed and his Costs by him about his suit in this behalf expended, and the said Defendant in mercy &c. Note this Judgment is to be discharged by the payment of four hundred Dollars, with legal Interest on two hundred Dollars thereof from the first day of October One thousand eight hundred and seven, and the remaining two hundred Dollars to bare Interest from the twenty fifth day of December in the year last above mentioned until paid and Costs And to have credit for ten Dollars paid on the fourth day of April, one thousand eight hundred and eight

– **John January** Plt
against upon Petition
**William Newland** Deft

Ordered that this suit be discontinued by order of the Plaintiff

– **Maclure Bridie & Co** Plt
against In Debt
**John Warren** Deft

This day came the Plaintiff by his attorney, and the Defendant being called but came not, made default & therefore on the motion of the Plaintiff by his attorney Judgment is awarded him against the said Defendant and **William Nolin** who is returned as his appearance Bail herein for the Deft in the Declaration mentioned, and his Costs by him about his suit in this behalf expended and the said Defendant in mercy &c

Note this Judgment is to be discharged by the payment of forty two pounds one shilling and eight pence with Interest thereon to be computed after the rate of six pr centum pr annum from [page 421] the twenty ninth day of July one thousand seven hundred and ninety nine until paid & Costs

– **John Lease** Plt
against In Case
**P A Sublette** Deft

– **John McWhorter** Plt
against In Covenant
**Robertson Burge** Deft

– **Samuel Dennis** Plt
against In Covenant
**James Anderson** Deft

– **Tunstall Quarles** Plt
against Trespass
**Thomas Fox** Deft

– **David E Matthews** Plt
against In Trespass Assault & Battery
**Washington Redmon** Deft

Ordered that these suits be continued until the next Term of this Court

– **James Doran & Co** Plt
against In Covenant
**George W Saunders** Deft

This day came the Plaintiff by his attorney and thereupon came also a Jury, to wit, **William Boyd, John Boyd, John West, James Boyd, William Denham, Nicholas Jasper** Senr, **Stephen Hail, Samuel King, Absolem Dodson, Andrew Wolverton, William Addison** & **Thomas Vanhook**, who were sworn well and truly to enquire what damages the Plaintiff hath sustained in the premises upon their Oaths say that the Plaintiff hath sustained Damage by Occasion thereof to fourteen pounds fifteen shillings besides his Costs It is therefore [page 422] Therefore It is considered by the Court that the Plaintiff recover against the said Defendant his damages aforesaid by the Jurors in their Verdict aforesaid in form aforesaid assessed, and his costs by him about his suit in this behalf expended and the said Defendant in mercy &c

– **Thomas Addison** by **William Addison** Plt
against In Trespass Assault and Battery
**Stephen Hail** & Als Deft

On the motion of the Defendants It is ordered that the Judgment and Writ of Inquiry awarded against them in the Clerks Office be set a side and the said Defendants by their attorney now comes and defends the wrong and Injury when and where &c and says they are not Guilty in manner and form as the Plaintiff against them hath declared and this they pray may be enquired of by the Country, and the Plaintiff saith the same likewise, and the said Defendants for further plea herein saith that at the time and in the Declaration mentioned also and where the Plaintiff hath alledged that the said Defendants Committed the Trespass Assault and Battery on him the said Plaintiff whereof he complains he the said Plaintiff assaulted them and the said Defendants and then and there, would have beaten them the said Defendants had not the Defendants, then and there instantly in their defence beaten him the plt, which is the same Trespass assault and Battery in the Plaintiffs Declaration mentioned, and this they are ready to verify wherefore they pray Judgment &c and the plt says he ought not to be bared from having his action afsd against the Defts by any thing in their plea above pleaded because he says that the said Deft made the Trespass Assault and Battery in the Declaration mentioned of their own proper Injury without such cause as in their plea is alledged and this he prays may be inquired of by the Country and the Deft likewise therefore let a Jury come here &c

and the Cause is continued until the next Court

– **William Hays** Assee Plt
against In Covenant

**Philip A Sublette** Deft

This day came the Parties aforesaid by their attornies, and It is agreed by the said Parties that this suit be dismissed, and that the Plaintiff recover against the said Defendant his Costs by him about his suit in this behalf expended and the said Defendant in mercy &c

– **William Stringer** for **Cornelius Doolin** Plt
against In Covenant
**John Stringer** &c Defts

This day came the Plaintiff by his attorney and thereupon came also a Jury, to wit, **Drewry Clark**, **David Puckett**, **James Eastham** Junr, **Francis Clare**, **Isaac Hays**, **Stephen Hail**, **William Hunt**, **James Cox**, **Nathan Turner**, **Aaron Doss**, **Zachariah Roy**, and **Asa Dodson** who were sworn well and truly to enquire what Damages the Plaintiff hath sustained in the premises upon their Oaths do say that the Plaintiff hath sustained Damage by Occasion thereof to forty Dollars besides his Costs It is therefore considered by the Court that the Plaintiff recover against the said Defendant his Damages aforesaid by the Jurors in their Verdict aforesaid in form aforesaid assessed and his Costs by him about his suit in this behalf expended and the said Defendant in mercy &c

– **Vincent Garner** Plt
against In Case
**John Colvin** Deft

This day came the Plaintiff by his attorney and on his motion It is ordered that this suit be Dismissed

[page 424] **Stephen Mayfield** Plt
against In Case
**Stephen Condry** Deft

On the motion of the Defendant It is ordered that the Judgment and writ of Inquiry awarded against him in the Clerks Office be set a side and the said Defendant by his attorney now comes and defends the wrong and Injury when and where &c and says he is not Guilty in manner and form as the Plaintiff against him in his Declaration herein hath declared, and this he prays may be enquired of by the Country, and the Plaintiff doth the same likewise, therefore let a Jury come here &c and the cause is continued until the next Term of this Court, and It is Ordered that leave be given the said parties to take Depositions Generally before a single Justice of the Peace without the state of Kentucky

– **John Hardwick** Plt
against In Trespass Assault & Battery
**Moses Turpen** Deft

This day came the Plaintiff by his attorney, and thereupon came also a Jury, to wit, **Drewry Clark**, **David Puckett**, **James Eastham** Junr, **Francis Clear**, **Isaac Hays**, **Stephen Hail**, **William Hunt**, **James Cox**, **Nathan Turner**, **Aaron Doss**, **Zachariah Roy** and **Asa Dodson**, who were sworn well and truly to enquire what Damage the Plaintiff hath sustained in the premises upon their Oaths do say that the Plaintiff hath sustained Damage by Occasion thereof to One Cent besides his Costs It is therefore considered by the Court that the Plaintiff recover against the said Defendant his Damages aforesaid by the Jurors in their Verdict aforesaid assessed and his Costs by him about his suit in this behalf expended, and the said Defendant may be taken &c

[page 425a - inserted sheet] **Obediah Phelps** Plt
against In Case
**William Stringer** Deft

This day came as well the Plaintiff by his attorney as the said Defendant in his proper person, who says he cannot gainsay acknowledged the Plaintiffs action against him for fifty five Dollars, together with Interest thereon to be computed after the rate of six per centum per from the first day of December, one thousand eight hundred and seven until paid. Therefore with assent of the Plaintiff, It is considered by the Court that the Plaintiff recover against the said Defendant the sum of fifty five dollars with Interest thereon from the first day of December one thousand eight hundred and seven assessed as aforesaid, and his Costs by him about his suit in this behalf expended

& the said Defendant in mercy &c

[page 425] Ordered that the Court be adjourned until Tomorrow morning nine OClock

**John Prather**

At a Circuit Court Continued and held for the Pulaski Circuit at the Courthouse of Pulaski County in Sommerset on the 28th day of April 1809

Present the Honorable **John Prather** & **John James** Gentlemen

– **John Evans** Plt
against upon a Writ of Scirafacies
**John Collyer** Deft

for the Deft to show cause why the said Plaintiff may not have his execution against him for thirty five Dollars with legal Interest thereon from the twenty Eighth day of February One thousand eight hundred and three, and eight Dollars Seventy four and one half Cent for his Costs in that behalf expended, Obtained by the Plaintiff against the Defendant, This day came the Plaintiff by his attorney and the Sheriff having returned that he had executed the Plaintiffs said Writ on the Defendant, and he failing to appear, therefore on the motion Plt by his attorney It is ordered that the Judgment and Writ of Inquiry awarded against the said Defendant in the Clerks Office be waved, And It is considered by the Court that the Plaintiff may have his execution against the said Defendant for the sums as before mentioned herein, and that the Plaintiff recover against the said Defendant his costs by him in this behalf expended, and the said Defendant in mercy &c

– **Jesse Chapple** Plt
against In Case
**William Lynch** Deft

– **Obediah Phelps** Plt
against In Case
**William Stringer** Deft

[page 426 ] **Samuel Burton** Plt
against In Case
**William Stringer** Deft

– **Jacobs** & **McGuire** Plts
against In Chancery
**Clark** & **English** Defts

Ordered that these suits be continued until the next Term of this Court

– **John Brooks** Complt
against In Chancery
**Mark Evans** Deft

This day came the parties aforesaid by their Counsil and It is Ordered that leave be given to take Depositions Generally before a single Justice of the Peace, and Commissions awarded

– **James Birny** by Gov Plt
against In Debt
**Nicholas Jasper** Shff &c Defts

On the motion of the Defendants It is ordered that the Judgment and writ of Inquiry awarded against him in the Clerks Office be set a side and the said Defts by their Attorney come and defend the wrong and Injury, when and where &c. And say the Plaintiff his action aforesaid ought not to have and maintain, because they say that the said **John Daniel**, Deputy Sheriff for the Defendant **N Jasper**, did not wilfully, neglegently & fraudulently permit the said **William J Sally** and **William Ursery** In the Declaration mentioned, to replevy the Debt In the Declaration mentioned, nor did the said Deputy Sheriff take from the [page 427] said **Sally** and **Ursery**, Insufficient Security, in replevying said Debt in the Declaration mentioned, But the said **Daniel** did faithfully and diligently execute his office of Deputy Sheriff in the taking Security in the Replevying the Debt in the Declaration mentioned and of this they put themselves upon the Country

**Owsley** for Defendant

And the Plaintiff likewise

S **Daviess & Montgomery** Att[o] for the Pltf

And the Cause is continued till the next Court

– **Daniel McIlvey** by Governor Pltf
against In Debt
**Nicholas Jasper** &[c] Defendants

On the motion of the Defendants It is ordered that the Judgment and writ of enquiry awarded against them In the Clerks office be set aside and the said Defendants by their Attorney come and Say the Pltf his action aforesaid ought not to have and maintain because they say the said **Elihu Sanders** at the time of his Executing the Replevy bond in the Declaration mentioned was not a person of Indigent and entirely unable to pay the amount of the Execution in said Declaration mentioned to the knowledge of the said **John Daniel** Deputy sheriff, for the Defendant **Nicholas Jasper** Sheriff of Pulaski county nor might the same be known to the said **John Daniel** or any other person [page 428] using due diligence to ascertain the same and of this they put themselves upon the Country

**Owsley** for Defendants

And the Plaintiff likewise

S **Daviess & Montgomery** for Pltf

And the cause is continued untill the next Term of this Court

– **Edward Flowers** Plt
against upon a Scirafacias
**Henry Francis** Deft

This day came the Plaintiff by his attorney, and upon his motion It is Ordered that the Judgment and writ of Inquiary awarded the said Deft in the Clerks Office, be waved, therefore on the motion of the Plaintiff by his attorney Judgment is granted him against the said Defendant for six Dollars forty three and one half cents for his Costs, yet remaining unpaid of a former Judgment, and his costs by him about his suit in this behalf expended and the said Defendant in mercy &[c]

– **Ralph Williams** Plt
against upon a Scirafacias
**Thomas Green** Deft

This day came the Plaintiff by his attorney, and on his motion It is ordered that the Judgment and writ of Inquiry awarded against the said Defendant in the clerks Office be waved, therefore it is considered by the Court that the Plaintiff may have his Execution against the said Defendant for five dollars sixty six and one half cents as mentioned in the said Scirafacias, and his Costs by him about his suit in this behalf expended and the said Defendant in mercy &[c]

– **Jesse Richardson & Thomas Owsley** Complt
against In Chancery
the Heirs and legal Representatives of **James Christy** Dec[d]

[page 429] This day came the Complainants aforesaid by their Counsil and the names and places of residence of said Defendants being unknown Therefore on the motion of the complainants by their Counsil It is Ordered that the said Defendants do enter their appearance herein on the third day of the next July Term of this Court and answer the complainants Bill or upon their falure the same will be taken as confessed against them, and further that a copy of this Order be published for two months successively in the Political Thetor printed in Lancaster Kentucky, according to an act of the General Assembly of the state aforesaid in such cases made and provided

– **George Allcorn** Plt
against In Covenant
**Robert Sawyers** Deft

– The Same Plt
against The Same
The Same Deft

**James Norflette**, of Pulaski County came into Court and undertook for the said Defendant in the actions aforesaid that if he shall be cast in them that he shall satisfy and pay the condemnation of the Court or render his body to Prison in execution for the same or on falure thereof that the said **James** shall do it for him

– **Frederick Williams** Plt
against
**William Brooks** Deft

This day came the Plaintiff by his attorney, and on his motion It is ordered that this suit be continued until the next Term of this Court

– **Washington Redmon** Ass$^{ee}$ Plt
against In Covenant
**Alexander Crawford** Deft

This day came the Plaintiff by his attorney and thereupon came [page 430] also a Jury, to wit, **William Hunt, William Humphreys, Pall Garner, John Jasper, Samuel Stout, Mashack Cundiff, Henry Garner, John Brooks, William Woodson, William Hays, John Evans** & **Stephen Hail** who being sworn well and truly to enquire what Damage the Plaintiff hath sustained in the premises upon their Oaths do say that the plaintiff hath sustained damage by Occasion thereof to One hundred Dollars besides his Costs It is therefore considered by the Court that the Plaintiff recover against the said Defendant his Damages aforesaid by the Jurors in their Verdict aforesaid assessed and his Costs by him about his suit in this behalf expended, and the said Defendant in mercy &$^{c}$.

– **Tunstall Quarles** Junr Plt
against In Case
**William Stringer** Deft

This day came the Plaintiff by his attorney, who produced and filed his Declaration herein, and the Defendant appeared in proper person and agreed that Judgment may be entered against him for five hundred and twenty one Dollars and fifty three Cents in Damages therefore with the assent of the Plaintiff It is considered by the court that the plaintiff recover against the said Defendant his Damages agreed by the Defendant as aforesaid and his costs by him about his suit in this behalf expended and the said Deft in mercy &$^{c}$ And the Plaintiff here in Court acknowledges satisfaction of the Judgment aforesaid, the said Defendant agreeing & hereby transferring any damages or money which he may [ ]gth recover against **William Griffin** by an action to be brought for the plaintiff **Tunstall Quarles's** benefit against the said **William Griffin** upon or relative to his assignment mentioned in the Declaration in this cause of a note on **Spencer Griffin** for Horses [page 431]

– **William Owens** a Constable of Pulaski County exhibited an account of Public Service performed by him in the execution of his Office, which account being examined by the Court, was Ordered to be Certified to the Auditor of Public Accounts Kentucky

– **John Jasper** Plt
against In Case
**Francis Day** Deft

This day came the Plaintiff by his attorney and thereupon came also a Jury, to wit, **William Hunt, William Humphreys, Pall Garner, Sam$^{l}$ Stout, Mashack Cundiff, Henry Garner, John Brooks, William Woodson, William Hays, John Evans, Stephen Hail**, & **John West**, who was sworn well and truly to enquire what Damage the Plaintiff hath sustained in the premises upon their Oaths do say that the Plaintiff hath sustained Damages by Occasion thereof to eighty Dollars besides his costs It is therefore Considered by the court that the plaintiff recover against the said Defendant the damages aforesaid by the Jurors in their Verdict aforesaid in form aforesaid assessed and his Costs by him about his suit in this behalf expended and the said Defendant in mercy &$^{c}$

– **Washington Redmon** Plt
against In Covenant
**Edward Williams** Deft

This day came the Plaintiff by his attorney, and thereupon came also a Jury, to wit, **John**

**Evans**, **Pall Garner**, **Stephen Hail**, **John West**, **William Hunt**, **William Woodson**, **William Hays**, **William Humphreys**, **Samuel Stout**, **Mashack Cundiff**, **William Denham** & **John Brooks**, who was sworn well and truly to enquire what Damage the Plaintiff hath sustained in the premises upon their Oaths do say that the Plaintiff hath sustained Damage by Occasion thereof to two hundred eighty seven Dollars and fifty Cents besides his Costs It is therefore Considered by the Court that the Plaintiff recover against [page 432] the said Defendant his Damages aforesaid by the Jurors in their Verdict aforesaid assessed and his costs by him about his suit in this behalf expended and the said Defendant in mercy &c

– **Frederick Williams**, one of the Guard, Summoned for the safe keeping and conveying **John Dickson**, charged with felony exhibits to the Court, an Account of his service rendered therein, which account being examined by the Court, was ordered to be Certified to the Auditor of Public Accounts Kentucky

– On the motion of **Randolph Alexander**, who made satisfactory proof to this Court, that he holds two Certificates, covering one and the same tract of land, to wit, one of said Certificates Number 438 Granted by the Court of Commissioners at Standford for one hundred and twenty five acres of second rate land, bearing date on the fourteenth day of August One thousand seven hundred and ninety eight, which he holds as Assignee of **Robert Whitehead**, The other certificate Granted by the County Court of Pulaski County to said **Randolph Alexander**, in his own proper name granted him at their July Term One thousand eight hundred and two No 365 for one hundred and twenty Acres of land, the proof being satisfactory to the Court as aforesaid It is ordered that the said claims be combined and reduced to one; and the same is Ordered to be Certified to the Register and also to the Auditor agreeable to an Act of the General Assembly Kentucky in such cases made and provided

– Ordered that the Court be adjourned until tomorrow morning nine OClock

**John Prather**

[page 433] At a Circuit Court Continued and held for the Pulaski Circuit at the Courthouse of Pulaski County in Sommerset on Saturday the 29th day of April 1809

Present the Honorable, **John Prather** & **John James** Gentlemen

– Ordered that it be Certified to the County Court of Pulaski County that this Court allows to **Tunstall Quarles** Esqr as their Commonwealths attorney, the sum of One hundred dollars for services performed in the execution of his Office for the last year Preceding the fourth Monday in October One thousand eight hundred and eight

– Ordered that It be Certified to the Auditor of public accounts that this Court allows to **William Fox**, as their Clerk the sum of thirty Dollars for Public Services performed by him in the Execution of his Office for the last year Preceeding the fourth Monday in October One thousand eight hundred and eight

– The Clk exhibited to the Court an account of stationary as stated therein furnished for the use of his Office for the last year preceeding the fourth Monday in October one thousand eight hundred and eight which account being examined and approved of by the Court, was Ordered to be Certified to the Auditor of Public Accounts Kentucky

– **Enoch Fleming** Plt
against In Case
**Hugh Logan** Deft

Ordered that this suit be continued until the next Term of this Court

– **James Fletcher** Plt
against In Covenant
**Henry Francis** Deft

This day came the Plaintiff by his attorney, and the said Defendant being called but came not, Therefore It is Commanded the Sheriff that he cause to come here Immediately twelve good and [page 434] lawful men by whom &c and thereupon came also a Jury, to wit, **Nathan Turner**, **Aaron Doss**, **William Hunt**, **Thomas Addison**, **Asa Roy**, **Gillam Hopper**, **William Denham**,

**Washington Redmon, Arther B Nash, William Hail, Peter Sallee** & **Thomas Vanhook** who were sworn well and truly to enquire what Damages the Plaintiff hath sustained in the Premises upon their Oaths do say that the Plaintiff hath sustained Damage by Occasion thereof to One hundred and sixty six Dollars and fifty Cents besides his costs It is therefore Considered by the court that the Plaintiff recover against the said Defendant the Damages aforesaid by the Jurors in their Verdict aforesaid assessed and his Costs by him about his suit in this behalf expended and the said Defendant in mercy &c

– **Gilham Hopper** Plt
against In Trespass Assault & Battery
**John Mayfield** & Al[s] Deft

On the motion of the Defendants It is Ordered that the Judgment and writ of Inquiry awarded against them in the Clerks Office be set a side and the said Defendants by their attorney now comes and defends the wrong and Injury when and where &c and says they are not guilty in manner and form as the Plaintiff against him hath declared and of this he prays may be enquired of by the Country and the plaintiff doth the same likewise, and leave is given the Defendant to put in the plea of con assault Demessne at the next Term of this Court to which Term this Cause is Continued

– **Isaac Anderson** Plt
against In Debt
**Ann Anderson** Deft

This day came the Plaintiff by his attorney, and on his motion It is Ordered that this suit be remanded to the Rule Dockett for proceedings to be had thereon, the Dismission as taken herein in the Clerks Office is ordered to be set a side

[page 435] It is Ordered by the Court, that the Several Office Judgments and Dismissions taken in the Clerks Office in Common law cases, such as have not been prior to this Order been set a side, be confirmed &c

– **George Allcorn** Plt
against In Covenant
**Robert Sawyers** Deft

This day came the Parties aforesaid by their attornies, and the said Defendant says he cannot gainsay the Plaintiffs action against him for sixteen pounds Therefore with the assent of the Plaintiff It is Considered by the Court that the Plaintiff recover against the said Defendant the acknowledged sum as aforesaid together with legal Interest thereon from the first day of March one thousand eight hundred and eight until paid, and his Costs by him about his suit in this behalf expended and the said Defendant in mercy &c Note this Judgment is confessed with the reservation of Equity and Execution to be staid until the next Term of this Court

– The Same Plt
against In Covenant
The Same Deft

This day came the Parties aforesaid by their attornies, and the said Defendant says he cannot gainsay the Plaintiffs action against him for sixteen pounds therefore It is Considered by the Court with the Assent of the Plaintiff, that he recover against the said Defendant the sum acknowledged as aforesaid with legal Interest thereon from the first day of January one thousand eight hundred and eight until paid, and his Costs by him about his suit in this behalf expended and the said Defendant in mercy &c Note this Judgment is Confessed with the reservation of Equity and Execution to be staid until the next Term of this Court

[page 436] **James Kincaid** Plt
against In Ejectment
**Charles Collyer** Deft

On the motion of the Defendant it is Ordered that the Judgment and Writ of Inquiry awarded against him in the Clerks Office be set a side and the said Defendant by his attorney now comes and Defends the wrong and Injury when and where &c and says that he is in no wise Guilty of the Trespass an Ejectment in the Declaration mentioned as the Plaintiff against him in his Declaration herein hath declared and this he prays may be enquired of by the Country, and the Plaintiff doth the same likewise, therefore let a Jury come here &c

– **James Kincaid** Plt
against In Ejectment
**Joseph Camp** Deft

On the motion of the Defendant It is Ordered that the Judgment and Writ of Enquiry awarded against him in the Clerks Office be set a side and the said Defendant by his attorney now comes and defends the wrong and Injury when and where &c and says that he is in no wise guilty of the Trespass and Ejectment in the Declaration herein mentioned as the Plaintiff against him has declared, and this he prays may one enquired of by the Country and the Plaintiff doth the same likewise, therefore let a Jury come here &c

– The Same Plt
against In Ejectment
**Moses Cummins** Deft

On the motion of the Defendant It is Ordered that the Judgment and Writ of Inquiry awarded against him in the Clerks Office be set a side and the said Defendant by his attorney now comes and defends the wrong and Injury when and where & and says he is not guilty of the Trespass and Ejectment in the Declaration mentioned as the Plaintiff therein against him hath declared and of this he prays may be enquired of by the country and the Plaintiff doth the same likewise

[page 437] **James Kincaid** Plt
against In Ejectment
**Samuel Elder** Deft

On the motion of the Defendant It is ordered that the judgment and writ of Inquiry awarded against him in the Clerks Office be set a side and the said Defendant by his attorney now comes and defends the wrong and Injury when and where &c and says he is not guilty of the Trespass and Ejectment in the declaration mentioned as the Plaintiff against him in his Declaration herein hath declared, and this he prays may be enquired of by the Country, and the Plaintiff doth the same likewise therefore let a Jury come here &c

– **James Kincaid** Plt
against In Ejectment
**Borter Garrett** Deft

On the motion of the Defendant It is Ordered that the Judgment and writ of Inquiry awarded against him in the clerks Office be set a side and the said Defendant by his attorney now comes and defends the wrong and Injury when and where &c and says that he is in no wise guilty of the Trespass an Ejectment in the Declaration herein mentioned, as the Plaintiff against him hath complained, and this he prays may be enquired of by the country, and the Plaintiff doth the same likewise, therefore let a Jury come here &c

– **James Kincaid** Plt
against In Ejectment
**Zachariah Denny** Deft

On the motion of the Defendant It is Ordered that the Judgment and writ of Inquiry awarded against him in the Clerks Office be set a side and the said Defendant by his attorney now comes and defends the wrong and Injury when and where &c and says he is in no wise guilty of the Trespass and Ejectment in the Declaration mentioned as the Plaintiff against him [page 438] hath declared, and this he prays may be enquired of by the Country and the Plaintiff doth the same likewise therefore let a Jury come here &c

– **James Kincaid** Plt
against In Ejectment
**John Collyer** Deft

On the motion of the Defendant It Ordered that the Judgment and writ of inquiry awarded against him in the clerks Office be set a side and the said Defendant by his attorney now comes and defends the wrong and Injury when and where &c and says that he is in no wise guilty of the Trespass and Ejectment in manner and form as the Plaintiff in his Declaration herein against him hath declared, and this he prays may be enquired of by the Country and the Plaintiff doth the same likewise therefore let a Jury come here &c

– **James Kincaid** Plt
against In Ejectment
**John McCullough** Deft

On the motion of the Defendant it is ordered that the Judgment and writ of Inquiry awarded against him in the Clerks Office be set a side and the said Defendant by his attorney now comes and defends the wrong and Injury when and where &c and says that he is in no wise Guilty of the Trespass and Ejectment in the Declaration mentioned in manner and form as the Plaintiff therein against him hath declared, and this he prays may be enquired of by the Country and the Plaintiff doth the same likewise, therefore let a jury come here &c

– **James Kincaid** Plt
against In Ejectment
**Charles Collyer** Deft

– The Same Plt
against The Same
**Moses Cummins** Deft

[page 439] **James Kincaid** Plt
against In Ejectment
**Joseph Camp** Deft

– The Same Plt
against In Ejectment
**Samuel Elder** Deft

– The Same Plt
against In Ejectment
**Borter Garrett** Deft

– The Same Plt
against In Ejectment
**Zachariah Denny** Deft

– The Same Plt
against In Ejectment
**John Collyer** Deft

– The Same Plt
against In Ejectment
**John McCullough** Deft

This day came the Parties aforesaid by their attornies, And on motion an Order of Survey is awarded herein, directed to **Thomas Whites** who is Ordered to go on the land in controversy between the aforesaid parties on the ___ day of ____ next if fair if not then on the next fair day and then and there survey and lay off the same as either party would have it, having regard to all Deeds and Other evidence that may be produced report all matters of fact specially before the day of hearing to the Clerks Office, And it is further Ordered that the said **Thomas Whites** do ascertain the variation of the magnetic needles from the true meridian Counting the degrees of Variation from the south end of the needle and report such Variation and its Bearing with the line established by act of Assembly as the line of the reserved military lands and It is further agreed by the parties and Ordered by the court that three Platts [page 440] and Certificates of Survey shall be deemed Sufficient in the whole of the Cases aforesaid, and shall be used in each, and the said Causes are continued until the next term of this Court

– On the Application of **Joab Garton**, who produced satisfactory Proof to this Court that he holds two Certificates covering in part the same tract of land, to wit, one of the said Certificates granted by the Court of Commissioners No 27 for two hundred acres of second rate land which he holds as Ass[ee] of **John Evans**, the other Certificate granted by the County Court of Pulaski County No 707 at their October Term 1804 for One hundred and fifty acres of land which he states he also holds by assignment from said **John Evans** One hundred acres of the land is covered and taken by the claim herein first above mentioned granted by the Court of Commissioners as aforesaid, the said Proof being satisfactory to the Court, It is Ordered that the said claims be combined and reduced into one so far as it respects the Interferance of the One hundred acres afores[d] and the same is Ordered to be Certified to the Register and also to the Auditor agreeably to an Act of the General Assembly Kentucky in such cases made and provided

– **Robert McClure** & others Heirs and representative of **Arther McClure** & **Francis McClure** Deceased Complainants
against In Chancery
**Robert Modrel** & wife Defendants

This day came the Parties aforesaid by their attornies, and the Defendant moved the Court to set a side the Judgment taken in the Clerks Office herein taking the said Complainants Bill professed, and for leave to file their answers to which the Complainants by their counsil Objects and after hearing the arguments of Counsil, It is ordered by the Court that said [page 441] the Judgment aforesaid be set a side, and leave to file answers which is done Accordingly, and It is further Ordered that this Cause be remanded to the Rules Dockett &[c]

– On the motion of **Edward Williams** an Injunction is granted him to stay all further proceedings on ninety four Dollars and fifty Cents it being part of a Judgment Obtained against him before this Court yesterday by **Washington Redmon**, the said **Williams** made Oath to his Bill filed herein in Court, and It is Ordered that he enter into bond in the Clerks Office of this Court in the penalty of one hundred and ninety eight Dollars, within twenty days, with **Frederick Williams** his security conditioned as the law directs

– Ordered that the Court be adjourned until Monday morning next and then to meet at nine OClock

**John Prather**

At a Circuit Court Continued and held for the Pulaski Circuit at the Courthouse of Pulaski County in Sommerset on Monday the first day of May 1809

Present the Honourable **John Prather**, & **John James** Gentlemen

– **George Helms** Plt
against In Covenant
**George Allcorn** Deft

This day came as well the Plaintiff by his attorney as the Defendant in his Proper Person who says he cannot gainsay the Plaintiffs action against him for sixty two Dollars, therefore with the assent of the Plaintiff It is considered by the Court that the Plaintiff recover against the said Defendant, the sum of sixty two Dollars confessed as aforesaid, and his Costs by him about his suit in this behalf expended [page 442] and the said Defendant in mercy &[c]

– **George Helms** Ass[ee] Plt
against In Debt
**Philip A Sublette** Deft

This day came the Plaintiff by his attorney, and the said Parties aforesaid by their attornies and the said Defendant says he cannot gainsay the Plaintiffs action against him for sixty pounds eighteen shillings & nine pence the Debt in the Declaration mentioned, therefore with the assent of the Plaintiff it is considered by the Court that the Plaintiff recover against the said Defendant the said sixty pounds eighteen shillings and nine pence with legal Interest thereon from the fifteenth day of July One thousand eight hundred and eight until paid and Costs and the said Defendant in mercy &[c]. Note this Judgment is Confessed with the reservation of Equity

– **Nathaniel Bruce** Plt
against In Trespass Vict armis

**William Hill** & others Deft

On the motion of the Defendants by their attornies It is Ordered that the Judgment and writ of Inquiry awarded against him in the Clerks Office be set a side and the said Defendants by their attornies now comes and defends the wrong and Injury when and where &c and says that they are not guilty in manner and form as the Plaintiff against them in his Declaration hath declared, and this they pray may be enquired of by the Country and the Plaintiff doth the same likewise Therefore let a Jury come here &c and the cause is continued until the next term of this Court

– The Same Plt
against In Trespass Assault & Battery
The Same Defts

On the motion of the Defendants It is ordered that the Judgment [page 443] and writ of Inquiry awarded against them in the Clerks Office be set a side and the said Defendants by their attornies now comes and defends the wrong and Injury when and where &c and say they are not guilty in manner and form as the Plaintiff against him hath declared and this they pray may be enquired of by the Country and the Plaintiff doth the same likewise therefore let a Jury come here &c and the cause is continued until the next Term of this Court

– **Asa Roy** Plt
against In Covenant
**James Johnson** Deft

This day came the Plaintiff by his attorney and upon his motion it is ordered that this suit be Dismissed

– **Henry Givin** by **Porter** Plt
against In Trespass Assault and Battery
**William Hill** Deft

On the motion of the Defendant It is Ordered that the Judgment and writ of Inquiry awarded against him in the Clerks Office be set a side and the said Defendant by his attorney now comes and defends the wrong and Injury when and where &c and says that at the time and in the Declaration mentioned when and where the Plaintiff hath alledged that the said Deft committed the Trespass Assault and Battery on him the said Plaintiff whereof he complains, he the said Plaintiff assaulted him, and the said Plaintff then and there would have beaten him the said Deft, had not the Defendant instantly in his defense beaten him the said Plaintiff, which is the same Trespass assault and Battery in the Plaintiffs Declaration mentioned and this he is ready to verify wherefore he prays Judgment &c and the plaintiff says he Ought not to be bared from having his action afores[d] against the said Defendant by any thing in his plea above pleaded because he says that the said Defendant made the Trespass Assault and Battery in the Declaration mentioned of his own proper Injury without such cause as in his plea is alledged, and this he prays may be enquired of by the Country and the said Defendant likewise therefore It is Commanded the Sheriff that he cause to come here Immediately [page 444] twelve good and lawful men by whom and & and thereupon came Also a Jury, to wit, **John Blacklidge, Samuel Hendricks, Lambert White, Benjamin Hansford, John West, John Jasper, Richard Walter, Moses Reynolds, Richard Barns, William Boyd, Jesse Evans & Drewry Clark** who being elected tryed and sworn the truth to speak upon the Issue Joined upon their Oaths do say that the Plaintiff did not first assault the Defendant, as in pleading herein he hath alledged, and they do assess the Plaintiffs Damages by Occasion thereof to one Cent besides his Costs It is therefore Considered by the Court that the Plaintiff recover against the said Defendant his damages afores[d] by the Jurors in their Verdict aforesaid assessed and his Costs by him about his suit in this behalf expended and the said Defendant may be taken &c

– **William Hill** Plt
against In Debt
**William Blane** Deft

This day came as well the Plaintiff by his attorney as the said Deft in his proper person who says he cannot gainsay the Plaintiffs action against him for the debt in the Declaration mentioned, therefore with the assent of the Plaintiff It is considered by the court that the Plaintiff recover against the said Defendant ____________ it being the amount in said Declaration mentioned and his costs by him about his suit in this behalf expended and the said Defendant in mercy &c Note this Judgment is confessed with the reservation of Equity

– **Alexander Crawford** Plt
against In Case
**Jesse Williams** Deft

On the motion of the Defendant It is Ordered that the Judgment and writ of Inquiry awarded against him in the Clerks Office be set a side and the said Defendant by his attorney now comes and defends the wrong and Injury when and where &c and says he is not Guilty in manner and form as the Plaintiff against him [page 445] hath in his Declaration hath declared, and this he prays may be enquired of by the Country and the Plaintiff doth the same likewise. Therefore let a Jury come here &c and the cause is continued until the next Court

– **John Blair** Assee Plt
against In Debt
**William Stringer** Deft

The Defendant having given Special Bail herein, therefore on his motion It is Ordered that the Judgment taken in the Clerks Office herein against the said Deft be set a side and the said Deft by his Attorney now comes and defends the wrong and Injury when and where &c and says that he hath well and truly paid the Debt in the Declaration mentioned and of this he puts himself upon the Country and the Plaintiff doth the same likewise, therefore let a Jury come here &c, Afterwards upon the motion of the Plaintiff It is Ordered that the Issue made up in this Cause be waved, and It is Ordered that the Plaintiff recover against the said Defendant the sum of sixty five Dollars the Debt in the Declaration mentioned with legal Interest thereon from the first day of May one thousand eight hundred and eight until paid & Costs and the said Defendant in mercy &c.

– On the motion of **William Blane** to Obtain an Injunction to stay all further Proceedings in a Judgment Obtained against him before this court on this present day by **William Hill**, the said **Blaine** having filed his Bill, herein and made Oath to the same in Court, It is therefore considered by the Court that an Injunction be granted to the Complainant agreeable to the prayer of this his Bill, and that he enter into Bond in the Clerks Office within twenty Days in the sum of one hundred Dollars with **William Cooper** his security conditioned as the law directs

[page 446] **John Smith** Plt
against In Case
**Aaron Doss** Deft

This day came the Plaintiff by his attorney and on his motion It is ordd that this suit be dismissed

– **John Beard** Complt
against In Chancery
**George W Saunders & Benjamin Burch** Defts

The Parties now appeared by Counsil & a Jury was thereupon empannelled & sworn to enquire what is the Value of the 228 acres & 12 Poles of land pursuant to the interlocutary decree herein Viz **Benjamin Black, David Puckett, Thomas Hale, Absolem Dodson, Asa Dodson, John Fitzpatrick, John Cowan, David Evans, Richard Blacklidge, William Hansford, Joseph N Dodson & Smith Williams**, who upon their Oaths do say that the said 228 acres and 12 poles of land is of the value of $285 whereupon it is decreed and ordered that the complainant, **John Beard** do recover against the Defendants **George W Saunders & Benjamin Burch**, the said sum of two hundred and eighty five dollars & the Costs of suit to be [ ] by the Clerk, and that he may Immediately, have execution therefore, and it appearing to the satisfaction of the Court, that the said Defendants have failed to Convey the one hundred and seventy acres and three quarters & eight poles of land pursuant to the former decree herein, wherefore it is further and finally decreed & ordered that **Jesse Richardson & Henry James** be appointed Commissioners on the part of the said Defts and they do further at the request of the said Complainant or his attorney, convey to the said Complainant his heirs &c with claim of General Warranty the said 171 and three quarters acres

and eight poles of land
[page 447] **John Logan** Plt
against In Covenant
**William Stringer** Deft

This day came as well the plaintiff by his attorney, as the said Deft in his proper person who acknowledges the Plaintiffs action against him for twenty pounds twelve shillings and eleven pence with Interest therefore with the assent of the Plaintiff It is considered by the Court that the Plaintiff recover against the said Defendant the sum acknowledged as aforesaid with legal Interest thereon from the twenty fifth day of August One thousand eight hundred and eight until paid & costs and the said Defendant in mercy &c.

– **Alexander Montgomery** Plt
against In Covenant
**Joseph Porter** Deft

Ordered that this suit be continued until the next Term of this Court

– **Tunstall Quarles** Plt
against In Debt
**Jimmey Cundiff** Deft

This day came the Plaintiff by his attorney, and the Defendant being called but came not, and the Shff having returned the writ herein Executed, Therefore on the motion of the Plaintiff by his attorney Judgment is granted him against the said Defendant and **John Cundiff** his appearance Bail, for the sum of thirty three pounds, the Debt in the Declaration mentioned with legal Interest thereon from the twentieth day of November One thousand eight hundred and eight, until paid & Costs and the said Defendant in mercy &c

– **James Lastley** Plt
against In Covenant
**John Newby** Deft

This day came the Plaintiff by his attorney and thereupon came also a Jury, to wit, **William Blane, William Hainey, William Cooper, George Dougherty** junr, **Adam Crawford, George Allcorn,** [page 448] **Isaac Muse, George Cooper, George Dougherty** Senr, **Jesse Sutton, Charles Hays** & **Hugh Logan** who were sworn well and truly to enquire what Damages the Plaintiff hath sustained in the Premises upon their Oaths do say that the Plaintiff hath sustained Damage by Occasion thereof to thirty eight Dollars and twenty five Cents besides his Costs It is therefore considered by the Court that the Plaintiff recover against the said Defendant his Damages aforesaid by the Jurors in their Verdict aforesaid assessed and his Costs by him about his suit in this behalf expended and the said Defendant in mercy &c

– **Andrew Crockett** Plt
against In Covenant
**Washington Redmon** & **John McWhorter** Defts

This day came the Plaintiff by his attorney and the Shff having returned the process executed herein executed on the Defendant **Redmon**, and not on the other Defendant **McWhorter**, It is therefore ordered that this cause abate as to said Defendant **McWhorter**, and on the motion of the plaintiff by his attorney a Writ of Inquiry is awarded herein therefore it is Commanded the Sheriff that he cause to come here Immediately twelve good and lawful men by whom &c and thereupon came also a Jury, to wit, **William Blane, William Hainey, William Cooper, George Dougherty** Junr, **Adam Crawford, George Allcorn, Isaac Muse, George Cooper, George Dougherty** Senr, **Jesse Sutton, Charles H[ ]y,** & **Hugh Logan** who were sworn well and truly to enquire what Damage the Plaintiff hath sustained in the premises upon their Oaths do say that the Plaintiff hath sustained Damage by Occasion thereof to nineteen pounds seventeen shillings and eight pence besides his costs It is therefore [page 449] Considered by the Court that the Plaintiff recover against the said Defendant his Damages aforesaid by the Jurors in their Verdict afores[d] and his costs by him about his suit in this behalf expended and the said Defendant in mercy &c

– **John Newby** Plt

against In Trespass Assault and Battery
**William Hill** Deft

The defendant by his attorney appears and moved the Court to quash the Bail bond taken herein, which motion was sustained by the Court And the said Defendant by his attorney now comes and defends the wrong and Injury when and where &c and saith he is not guilty in manner and form as the Plaintiff against him in his Declaration herein hath declared and this he prays may be enquired of by the Country and the Plaintiff doth same likewise. Therefore let a Jury come here &c and the cause is continued until the next Term of this Court

– **Joseph Porter** Plt
against In Trespass Vict armis
**William Hill** Deft

This day came the parties aforesaid by their attornies, and the writ Issued in this case being returned by the Sheriff as [ ] agreeably to an Act of Assembly, in such cases made and provided, the said Defendant by his attorney comes and defends the wrong and Injury when and where &c and says he is not guilty in manner and form as the Plaintiff against him in his Declaration herein hath complained, and this he prays may be enquired of by the country and the Plaintiff likewise therefore it is commanded the sheriff that he cause to come here Immediately twelve good and lawful men by whom &c and thereupon came also a Jury to wit, **Isaac Muse**, **Richard Barns**, **John Cowen**, **Anderson Nunnaly**, **John Dollahide**, **James Griffin**, **George Dougherty** Junr, **Stephen Sawyers**, **Absolem Dodson**, **George Dougherty** Senr, **John Griffin** & **Cornelius Dollihide** who being elected tried and sworn the truth to speak upon the Issue Joined upon their Oaths do say that the [page 450] said Defendant is not Guilty in manner and form as the Plaintiff against him hath complained, therefore it is Considered by the Court that the Plaintiff take nothing by his bill but for his false clamour be in mercy &c and that the Defendant recover his costs &c

– On the application of **Cornelius Dollihide** who made satisfactory proof to this Court, that he has two claims to one and the same tract of land, or at best the said two claims materially Interfere as follows, to wit, 1st he holds by a Certificate No 296 granted by the Court of Commissioners for one hundred and fifty acres of second rate land bearing date the 11th day of August one thousand seven hundred and ninety eight which he holds as Assee of **Richard Beason**, the other claim he holds under a Certificate granted him in his Own name by the County Court of Pulaski County at their February Term One thousand eight hundred and six No 962 for one hundred and sixty two acres of land under which last mentioned claim he has obtained a patent, the proof being satisfactory as aforesaid It is ordered that the said claims be combined and reduced into one as far as it respects the interferance of said claims, and the same is Ordered to be Certified to the Register and also to the Auditor Agreeably to an Act of the General Assembly Kentucky in such cases made and provided

– **William Finley** Plt
against In Covenant
**Robertson Burge** Deft

**Joseph Erwin** of Pulaski County came into Court and undertook for the said Defendant that if he shall be cast in the action aforesaid that he shall satisfy and pay the condemnation of the Court or render his body to prison in execution for the same or on falure thereof that he the said [page 452] **Joseph** shall do it for him, and the said Defendant by his attorney now comes and defends the wrong and Injury when and where &c and craves Oyer of the bill of sale in the Declaration mentioned which read as follows ( here insert bill of sale ) and says the Plaintiff his action aforesaid Ought not to have and maintain because he says the said negro Woman **Anna** in the Declaration mentioned was sick at the time of the sale and delivery of said Negro by the Deft to the Plaintiff, and long before that time [ ] and labouring under an old and Confirmed disease commonly called the Phthispick, and of this he puts himself upon the Country, and the Plaintiff likewise, and the cause is Continued till next Term of this Court at the Plaintiffs Costs

– Ordered that the Court be adjourned until Tomorrow morning nine OClock

**John Prather**

At a Circuit Court Continued and held for the Pulaski Circuit at the Courthouse of Pulaski County in Sommerset on the Tuesday the 2nd day of May 1809

Present **John Prather** & **John James** Gent

– **John Fitzgerald** Complt
against In Chancery
**James S Davis** &c Deft

This day came the parties aforesaid by their attornies, and the said Defendant by his attorney moved the Court, that the Complt should give Counter Security in the Injunction Obtained herein, which motion was sustained by the Court, the present security appearing to be Insufficient, and It is Considered that said Counter Security be given on the first day of the next Term of this Court, Otherwise the said Injunction will stand or be considered as dissolved & the Cause is continued

[page 452] **Joseph Porter** Plt
against In Trespass Vict armis
**William Hill** Deft

This day came the parties aforesaid by their attornies, and on the motion of the Plaintiff by his attorney to obtain a new trial on the Verdict of the Jury and Judgment herein Obtained against him yesterday by said Defendant for Costs, on the Grounds of said Verdict being contrary to evidence, which motion was overruled the Court being divided in opinion, to which the Plaintiff by his attorney Objects, and files his Bill of exception thereto in these words, Be it remembered that on the trial of this cause, the Plaintiff proved that whilst he had the Possession and Occupancy of a House in the town of Somerset, Pulaski County of the Value of $60 that the said House was consumed in ashes by fire in which was burnt the Cabinet and House Joiner Tools of the Plaintiff of the value of $200 and also a Beaureau of the Value of $20 and several other articles the Plaintiff proved by several Witnesses the enmity of the Deft towards the Plaintiff, and one Witness swore, that **William Mills** the evening preceeding the burning of the House & Tools in a conversation respecting some property taken by **Andrew Turner** a Constable by the direction of the Plaintiff **Joseph Porter** to satisfy an execution against said **Porter** & **William Stringer**, and which property was claimed by the Defendant **Hill**, and which property **Hill** had violently taken from the Possession of said **Stringer**, Observed that he had taken the course directed by three Lawyers namely **Tunstall Quarles**, **Thomas Montgomery**, & **William Logan** [page 453] that as to **Turner**, he had sworn he would not sue him and as to **Porter**, it was not worth while to sue him he had heard something about his having land in Tennissee but he knew nothing of that, and he had nothing here but his Tools, and damn him he shall not have them long, the Witness who swore to the facts last mentioned was the wife of **William Stringer** & upon being interrogated said she was angry with the Deft **Hill**, for taking the property aforesaid and the Deft **Hill** acknowledged in Court that he had never received such advise from **Quarles** or **Montgomery** but had from **Logan**, and that was as much as he had told the Witness, It was also proven that the day after the House was burnt the Defendant denied making any such threats and said any Person who would say he did told a damed lye, and it was Proven that the Defendant sometime after acknowledged to **John Daniel** who was not sworn nor present at the Trial and who alledged he heard such threats from the Defendant, that he **Hill** had made use of some such expression but that he ment the Tools of the Plaintiff would be taken and sold to pay his Debts, the Clerk of the Court was called who swore he knew of no Judgments against the Plaintiff at the time the House was burnt But two executions in the hands of **William Owens** a Constable to the amount of not exceeding 20 Dollars and the executions were against **Porter** the Plaintiff as Security for **William Stringer**, whose property was then under execution to satisfy said execution and was afterwards sold to satisfy said Executions, **William Owens** the Constable was then called on he stated he always considered Mr **Porter** good for any sum that came into his hands for to Collect, and had never refused the Plaintiff as Security in any Case when he might offer himself as Security, a Mr **Turner** was introduced who swore that he had previous to the House Burning an Execution for about $10 against the Plaintiff but that it was Replevied by **Porter** the Plaintiff previous to the day on which the house was burnt, that [page 454] all the witnesses went to prove that the Plaintiff was solvent and no execution was ever returned against him no property found it was proved that there was no fire in the House for two or three days previous to its being burnt and on the evening preceding it being burnt it was proved there was no fire in the House it was proved the Plaintiff was not in Town the upon the night the House was burnt but being convenient in the neighborhood got the alarm and came to the House whilst it was in flames and then observed he thought the Deft burnt it but on the next morning after hearing the Deft Solemnly deny it the Plaintiff observed he c[ ] some of the family of **William Stringer** for burning his House and supposed the Deft did not burn his House but sometime thereafter from hearing more of the Circumstances he the Plaintiff observed the Deft must certainly be the man who done the mischief and brought suit against him, the Deft then heard by a certain **John Eastham** that he **Eastham** on the night the House was burnt, was at **Hills** the Deft that he **Eastham** lay down before the fire having been drinking and before he lay down he saw the Deft go to bed, [ ] **Eastham** took a nap of sleep he awoke and went up stairs and went to Bed to a Certain **William Denham**, and after lying some time talking to the said **Denham** he heard a roaring of fire he rose up and looked out and discovered the House on fire he run down stairs in [ ] to **Hills** Bed and called **Hill** then shook him and then again shook him told him the House was on fire **Hill** rose as one surprised ran down in his shirt Tail with the said **Eastham** and **Denham** to the fire but the House was so fair consumed as no relief could be given in extinguishing the fire, **W^m^ D**[ ] said he was at the Deft House the same night and saw the Deft go to bed and he **Denham** was a sleep but **Eastham** coming to bed to him awoke him after lying some time **Eastham** [ ] the fire he got up gave the alarm run down and [ ] wake **Hill**, the House was so fair consumed as the fire could not be extinguished, The Deft proved by **Lambert White** a Constable in [ ] hands there was an [ ] that he had applyd to the Deft a short time previous to said House being burnt to know where he could find the property of the Plaintiffs so as to lay said Execution upon it that the Deft mentioned the plaintiffs tools but enquired of the said **White** whether they were Subject to an Execution **White** informed him that they were, the Deft proved by **Aaron Lawson** that the next Sunday after the House was burnt that the plaintiff told him that he had been disposed to believe the Deft for burning his House, but he did not now, altho some people wished him to do so, this was the whole of the evidence upon which the Jury after retiring from the bar sometime returned a Verdict for the Deft and the attornies for the plt moved the Court to grant a new trial alledging the Verdict was contrary to evidence which motion of the Plt the court Over ruled and refused to grant a new trial to which Opinion of the Court the plaintiff by his attorney excepts & prays this his Bill of exception to be signed and made a part of the record the Court being divided

**John Prather**
**John James**

[page 455] **Joseph Horner** for the benifit of **Thomas Kennedy** Plt
against upon motion
**Bazil Meek** Shff Deft

This day came the plaintiff by his attorney as well as the said Deft in his Proper Person And It is mutually agreed between them that this motion be continued until the third day of the next Term of this Court and the same is ordered accordingly

– **Henry Willis** Plt
against In Trespass Assault & Battery
**Washington Redmon** Deft

– **Andrew Cowen** Complt
against In Chancery
**Tunstall Quarles** Deft

Ordered that these suits be Continued until the next Term of this Court

– **Whitley** & **Wyatt** Plt
against In Debt
**John McWhorter** Deft

This day came the Plaintiffs by their attorney, and the capias [ ] Issued herein being returned executed by the Sheriff agreeably to an Act of Assembly in such cases made and provided, and the said Defendant failing to appear tho solemnly called, therefore on the motion of the Plaintiff by his attorney a writ of Inquiry is awarded him herein. Therefore it is commanded the Sheriff that he cause to come here Immediately twelve good and lawful men by whom &c and thereupon came also a Jury to wit, **Samuel Hendricks, William Boyd, William Humphreys, John Mills, Ichabud Blacklidge, George Humphreys, Benjamin Harris, Samuel King, William Hunt, Gilham Hopper, William Stringer** & **Aaron Lawson** who were sworn well and truly to enquire what damage the Plaintiff hath sustained in the Premises upon their Oath [page 456] do find for the Plaintiff the Debt in the Declaration herein mentioned and do assess his Damages by Occasion of the detension thereof to one Cent besides his Costs It is therefore Considered by the Court that the Plaintiff recover against the said Defendant the sum of forty two Dollars & twenty five Cents the Debt in the Declaration mentioned with legal Interest thereon from the first day of April One thousand eight hundred and eight until paid Damages & Costs and the said Deft in mercy &c.

– **James Hardgrove** Assee Plt
against In Covenant
**Stephen Condry** Deft

This day came the Plaintiff by his attorney, and the same Proceedings had thereon, and the same Jury sworn herein as in the case (**Wyatt** & **Whitley** against **John McWhorter**) who were sworn well and truly to enquire what Damage the Plaintiff hath sustained in the premises upon their Oaths do say that the Plaintiff hath sustained Damage by Occasion thereof to one hundred Dollars besides his Costs It is therefore Considered by the court that the Plaintiff recover against the said Defendant his Damages aforesaid by the Jurors in their Verdict aforesaid assessed and his Costs by him about his suit in this behalf expended and the said Defendant in mercy &c.

– The Commonwealth Plt
against upon an Indictment for forgery
**John Daniel** Deft

This day came the attorney for the Commonwealth and upon his motion It is Ordered that a Capias Issue [page 457] herein against the said **Daniel** returnable to the first day of the next Term of this, and the Clerk is directed to endorse thereon that Bail is required in the sum of two thousand Dollars, And It is further Ordered that a scirafacias Issue on the Recognizance against said **Daniel** & securities who were bound therein for his appearance here on the first day of this present Term to answer the said Indictment, the said Recognizance being forfeited &c &c.

– **Morgan Williams** Plt
against upon motion
**Bazil Meek** Shff Deft

notice of this motion being acknowledged by the Defendant and by his counsil came in for tryal on this day the said Defendant acknowledges Judgment against [ ] herein for one hundred and eighty Dollars with legal Interest thereon from the twelfth day of June One thousand eight hundred and six, until paid & the costs of his motion, Note this Judgment is to have all legal credits

– Ord that it be certified to the auditor of Public accounts Kentucky that this Court allows to **Henry James** the sum of one hundred dollars for keeping and maintaining **John Barns** a person of unsound mind for the last year preceeding the fourth Monday in October one thousand eight hundred and eight

– Ordered that the Court be adjourned until Court in Course

**John Prather**

At a Circuit Court held for the Pulaski Circuit at the Courthouse of Pulaski County in Somerset on Monday the 24th day of July 1809

Present the Honbl **Christo Thompkins, John Prather,** & **John James** Gentlemen
[page 458] A Grandjury was sworn for the Pulaski Circuit, to wit, **Henry Francis** foreman, **Joseph Lewis, Samuel Hendricks, Thomas Vanhook, John Preston,** Charles Neal, **Saborn Hail, Benjamin Harris, Thomas Reed, John Evans, Obediah Phelps, Drewry Lee, David Roper,**

**George Evans**, **William Addison**, **David Puckett**, **Cornelious Dollihide** & Henry Farmer who after receiving their charge retired to consider of their Presentments
– The Commonwealth
against upon Presentment
**William Denham** Deft
– The Commonwealth
against Same
**John Cowen** Deft
– The Commonwealth
against Same
**John Ingram** Deft

This day came as well the said Defendants by their attorney as the attorney for the Commonwealth, and after hearing the arguments of Counsil on both sides and mature deliberation being thereon had It is Ordered that the said Presentments be quashed, for informality &[c]

– **George W Saunders** Plt
against In Trespass Assault & Battery
**John Griffin** Deft
– **George W Saunders** & ux Plt
against In Trespass Vict armis
**John Griffin**
[page 459] **John Griffin** & County Plt
against In Debt
**George W Saunders** Deft
– **John Griffin** Plt
against In Trespass Assault and Battery
**George W Saunders** & ux Deft

This day came the Parties aforesaid by their attornies, and upon their motion It is Ordered that these suits be dismissed they agreed

– **Robertson Burge** Plt
against In Case
**David Clark** Deft

This day came the parties aforesaid by their attornies and on the motion of the Plaintiff by his attorney It is Ordered that this suit be continued until the next term of this Court at the Plaintiffs Costs and that the said Defendant recover against the Plaintiff his costs by him about his defence relative to said Continuance expended

– **Thomas McGuire** Plt
against In Debt
**English** & **Clark** Defts

Ordered that this suit be dismissed for want of prosecution

– **Nicholas Gwin** Plt
against In Case
**George McWhorter** Deft
– **George McWhorter** Plt
against In Case
**Nicholas Gwin** Deft

This day came the parties aforesaid by their attornies, and on [page 460] motion it is agreed that these suits be Dismissed

– **Andrew Cowen** Complt
against In Chancery
**Tunstall Quarles** Deft

Ordered that this suit be continued until the next Term of this Court

– **John Rogers** Complt

against In Chancery
**Thomas McLaughlin** Deft

This day came the parties aforesaid by their attornies, and it is Ordered that this suit be continued until the next Term of this Court, and leave is given to take Depositions

– The Grandjury returned into Court and made the following presentments, to wit, The Commonwealth against **William Hill** upon an Indictment, a true Bill

**Henry Francis** foreman of the Grand jury

Also an Indictment, the Commonwealth against **Zachariah Eastham**, a true Bill

**Henry Francis** foreman of the Grand jury

Also an Indictment, The Commonwealth against Marvel Nash Junr & **David Dutton**, a true Bill

**Henry Francis** foreman of the Grandjury

The Commonwealth of Kentucky Pulaski County & Circuit, to wit, the Grandjury good and lawful men of the body of the County of Pulaski, Circuit aforesaid, in the name and by the authority of the Commonwealth of Kentucky upon their Oaths [page 461] present that **Ichabud Blacklidge** labourer of the County and Circuit aforesaid did on the Second day of May One thousand eight hundred and nine, did profanely swear two Oaths in the following words, to wit, you are a God damed liar in the Town of Somerset in the House of **Wil Sallee**, contrary to the statute in that case made and provided, and against the peace and Dignity of this Commonwealth of Kentucky upon the Information of **Samuel Hendricson**, and **David Puckett**, both of the grand jury and residents of Pulaski County

**Henry Francis** foreman of the Grand jury

– The Commonwealth Plt
against upon an Indictment for Felony
**William Hill** Deft

This day came as well the attorney for the Commonwealth as the said Defendant by his attorney and the Sheriff having returned a pannel of the Venire Summoned herein agreeably to an Act of the General Assembly Kentucky in such cases made and provided and the said Defendant moved the Court to quash the array which was objected to by the attorney on the part of the Commonwealth, therefore It is Ordered that a Venirafacias D[ ] be awarded herein directed to the high Sheriff of Pulaski County commanding him to summon a legal Jury to appear before this Court on this present day to [ ] between the Commonwealth and said Defendant, **William Hill** upon his trial &c which was Issued accordingly

[page 462] **Joseph Casky** Plt
against In Case
**John January** Deft

This day this Opinion and Decree of the Court of Appeals being produced in Court, and Ordered to be entered of Record as follows, to wit

State of Kentucky Court of Appeals Office June 17th 1808

**Joseph Casky** Plt
against upon a writ of Error to reverse a Judgment of the Pulaski Circuit Court
**John January** Deft

This day came the parties aforesaid by their attornies, and the arguments of Counsil being heard but the Court not being sufficiently advised thereof took time &c and afterwards, to wit, on the 18th day of June in the year aforesaid, the Court being now sufficiently advised of and concerning the Premises delivered in the following Opinion, to wit, this is an application for this Court to Correct the decision of the Pulaski Circuit Court in refusing to grant a new Trial on the Ground the Verdict being Contrary to evidence, The whole evidence is spread upon the record by a Bill of exception signed and sealed by the Court, the power of granting or causing a new trial to be granted after it has been refused by the Court before whom the cause was tried, Ought to be very cautiously and circumspectly exercised by this Court we cannot see the evidence in all its minutia as it has appeared before that Court, and therefore we will not grant a new trial unless the Verdict clearly appears to be contrary to the evidence and flagrantly unjust such seems to us to be the case in the present instance, the Bill of exceptions stated that the Plaintiff proved eighty one pounds of his account by several witnesses the Defendants whole account pleaded as a [ ] amounted but to [page 463] Sixty odd pounds; so that if the whole of it had been proved which was not done there would still be a clear ballance in favour of the Plaintiff and yet the Jury found a verdict for the Defendant, this could not possibly be right, unless the Plaintiffs witnesses were not worthy of credit which is not pretended; or unless the Jury were justified in their Verdict, by the Settlement attempted to be [ ] on the part of the Defendant, The evidences show clearly there was no final settlement made between the parties, but only an ineffectual attempt to make a Settlement, and even if a Settlement had been made as there was nothing to settle but their mutual accounts exhibited, if it appears that any Gross mistake had been made in the settlement it ought not to have been concluded, We are therefore of Opinion that the Circuit Court erred in refusing to grant a new trial and in giving Judgment against the Plaintiff on the verdict, on the subject of the other errors assigned it will only be necessary to add the award is illegal on its face so that it ought not to be made the Judgment of the Court, and that it would be in Vain for us now to require that the award should heretofore be brought before the Court below for the purpose of doing only that which has been already done nor do we think the setting a side the Order of rep[ ] ought to be regarded, both parties having afterwards appeared and made up pleadings in this cause without any exceptions having been taken or Objections made, Wherefore it is Considered that the Judgment aforesaid be reversed annuled and set a side and that the Verdict of the Jury be also set a side, and the cause remanded to the said Circuit Court, with directions to place it again on the Issue Docket for a new trial to be had between the Parties and that the Defendant in error pay to the Plaintiff his costs in this behalf expended which is ordered to be Certified to the said Circuit Court of Pulaski County

A Copy teste Achilles Snead CCA

[page 464] And it is ordered by this Court that the Cause be placed on their Issue Docket

– **John Scrimiger** Plt
against In Trespass Assault & Battery
**John & William Burton** Deft

– **William Thacker** &c Plt
against In Case
**Lewis Whitesides** Deft

This day the Plaintiffs in the above cases was solemnly called but came not, neither are suits further prosecuted, Therefore on the motion of the said Defendants by their attornies It is Considered by the Court that the Plaintiffs be non suited, and that the Defendants go hence without day and recover of the Plaintiffs their Costs by them about their defence in this behalf expended

– **John Fitzgerald** Complt
against In Chancery
**James S Davis** Deft

This day came the Parties aforesaid by Attornies and this cause came on for hearing on the face of the Bill and answer, the Court took time to deliver in their Decree &c

– **John Rogers** Complt
against In Chancery
**Thomas McLaughlin** Deft

This day came the Complainant by his counsil, and the said Defendant having failed to answer the Complainants amended filed herein, and It appearing to the satisfaction of this Court that the said Defendant is not an Inhabitant of the Commonwealth of Kentucky, Therefore on the motion of the Complainant by his Counsil It is Ordered that the said Defendant do appear here on the third day of the next [page 465] October Term of this Court, answer the Complainants amended Bill, or upon falure thereof the same will be taken as Confessed against him, and further that a Copy of this Order be Published for two months Successively in the Political Theator, printed in Lancaster Kentucky, according to an act of the General assembly Kentucky in such case made and provided

– The Commonwealth
against upon Indictment

**William Hill** Deft

The said **William Hill** who stands bound to appear here before the Judges of the Pulaski Circuit Court on the first day of their present July Term of the Court aforesaid, which is this present day, to answer a Certain felony whereof he is Accused appeared according to the Condition of his Recognizance, and the Grandjury having returned the Indictment against him a true Bill, and the said **William Hill** now at the Bar in the Custody of the Sheriff, and thereof arraigned, and pleaded not Guilty to the Indictment, and for his Trial puts himself upon god and his country, and the Attorney for the Commonwealth, and Pulaski Circuit likewise, whereupon came also a Jury, to wit, **John Jones, William Mayfield, Samuel Allin, Edward White, John Fitzpatrick, William Herrin, John Jasper, Stewart Clark,** John Gragg, **Thomas Clark, Daniel McKinsey** & **Thomas Hail,** who being elected tried and sworn the truth of and upon the premises to speak, and having heard the evidence, and the arguments of Counsil, upon both sides upon their Oaths do say that the said **William Hill** is not guilty and proclamation being made as the manner is and nothing further appearing, or being alledged against him, It is therefore Considered by the Court that he be acquited of the charges aforesaid, and go thereof hence without day

[page 466] Ordered that the Grand jury Impanneled and sworn for Pulaski County, on this present day, be adjourned until Tomorrow morning ten OClock, and then to meet again

– **John Eastham,** a affrayer, being brought into Court, and sufficient evidence being produced to the Court It is ordered that the said **Eastham** be bound to his good behavior for one year and a day whereupon the said **John Eastham** being called upon to give Security for his good behaviour for the Term aforesaid, when the said **Eastham** refused, whereupon the said **Eastham** is Ordered to Jail, and there to remain until he be discharged by due Course of law

– Ordered that the Court be adjourned until Tomorrow morning nine OClock

**Christ^o Tompkins**

At a Circuit Court continued and held for the Pulaski Circuit at the Courthouse of Pulaski County in Sommerset on Tuesday the 25th day of July 1809

Present the Hon^bl **Christ^o Tompkins** & **John James** Gentlemen

– **Charles Collyer** Plt
against upon motion to quash an Ex^on Issued herein
**Edward White** & **James Price** Defts

after hearing the arguments of Counsils on both sides, It is Ordered that the motion of the said Defendants motion be Overruled with Costs

– **Benjamin Sloane** Plt
against In Covenant
**John Gwin** Deft

This day came the parties aforesaid by their attornies, and It is agreed that this cause be continued until the next Term [page 467] of this Court, at the Defendants Costs

– **Tunstall Quarles** Plt
against In Trespass
**Thomas Fox** Deft

This day came the parties aforesaid by their attornies, and It is ordered that this suit be Dismissed it being agreed

– Present **John Prather** Esq^r

– **Thomas Hutchings** Ex^or Plt
against In Covenant
**Charles Collyer** Deft

Ordered that this suit be continued until the next Term of this Court at the Defendants costs

– **Stephen Mayfield** Plt
against In Case
**Stephen Condry** Deft

This day came the Parties aforesaid by their attornies, and by consent this cause is Continued until the next Term of this Court at the Plaintiffs Costs. Therefore on the motion of the Plaintiff a Dedimus is awarded him to take Depositions without the state of Kentucky before a single Justice of the Peace

– The Grand jury sworn and adjourned, for Pulaski County on yesterday to meet on this day, met according to adjournment, and having nothing further to present were discharged by the Court, And It is Ordered that the delinquents be Summoned, and that a Capias Issue in the case the Commonwealth against **Zachariah Eastham** against whom it was pr[ ] to the Grand jury a Bill of Indictment and upon which the Grand jury returned a true Bill, and endorse a [ ] Caps that bail is req[d] in the sum of $500 and [ ] security or securities in the like sum

[page 468] **John Fitzgerald** Complt
against In chancery
**James S Davis** Deft

The Court now be sufficiently advised &[c] delivered in the following written Decree, to wit, This cause came on to be heard on the 24[th] day of July 1809 and having heard the Bill answer and other exhibits in this cause filed and the Court being now sufficiently advised in the Premises do order and Decree that the Injunction herein Obtained be desolved and the Bill dismissed and that the Defendant **Davis** have the benifit of his Judgment at law and also that the Defendant recover of the Complainant ten per centum upon the amount injoined in this cause, and It is further Decreed and Ordered that the Defendant recover of the Complainant his cost by him in the defence of this cause expended

– **Absolem Taylor** Plt
against In Case
**Shaderick Price**

This day came the Plaintiff by his attorney, and on his motion It is Ordered that this Cause be continued until the next Term of this Court

– **Samuel Clark** Plt
against In Case
**Martin Barrier** Deft

This day came the parties aforesaid by their attornies and by their Consent It is Ordered that this cause be Continued until the next Term of this Court

[page 469] **Michael Weaver** Plt
against In Case
**William Woodson** Deft

**Seaton Lee** of Pulaski County came into Court and Justified, and undertook for the said Defendant that if he shall be cast in the action aforesaid that he shall satisfy and pay the condemnation of the Court or render his body to prison in execution for the same, or on falure thereof that he the said **Seaton Lee** shall do it for him

– **William Wood** Plt
against In Case
**James Chappel** Deft

This day came the Deft aforesaid by his attorney, and the Plaintiff tho solemnly called came not, and he having failed to prosecute his suit further It is Ordered by the Court that the Plaintiff be non suited therefore on the Motion of the Defendant by his attorney it is considered by the court that the Defendant go hence & recover against the Plaintiff his costs by him about his defense in this behalf expended

– **John Femister** Plt
against In Case
**Daniel Adams** Deft

This day the Plaintiff, being solemnly came not but made Default and having failed to prosecute his suit further. It is ordered that he be non suited &[c].

– **Thomas Hutchings** Ex[ors] Plt
against In Covenant (next case)

**Charles Collyer**

The Defendant having entered Special Bail herein, It is Ordered that the Judgment and Writ of Inquiry awarded against him in the Clerks Office be set a side and the said Deft by his attornies now comes and defends the wrong and injury when and where &c and for the plea in [page 470] this behalf saith that the Plaintiff their action aforesaid against him Ought not to have or maintain because he saith that on the ___ day of _____ 1805 at the state of Kentucky and Circuit of Pulaski it was agreed between the Plaintiffs and Defendant that the 400 Gallons of whisky in the writing Obligatory in the Declaration mentioned, should be discharged by the payment of Horses at their value upon a day which was fixed upon between said parties and which Horses was to be received by the Plaintiffs of the Deft at the House of **John McCullough** in the Circuit aforesaid and the Deft doth aver that pursuant to said agreement he did upon the Day which he and the Plaintiffs had agreed upon as aforesaid alledged at the House of the said **John McCullough** as aforesaid with a sufficient number of Horses to have discharged the aforesaid 400 Gallons of Whisky and was then and there ready to have discharged the same if the Plaintiff had attended to receive the same, and this he is ready to verify wherefore he prays Judgment &c

**Owens** & **Davis** attorneys for Deft

and for further plea in this behalf with the Plaintiff their action aforesaid against them ought not to have or maintain because he with [ ] the writing Obligatory in the Declaration mentioned for the 400 gallons of whisky therein specified was given by the Deft to the said Plaintiffs in part pay of a tract or parcel of land purchased by the Deft of the Plaintiffs Exors as aforesaid lying and being in the County of Pulaski and Circuit aforesaid on a Branch of Brush Creek containing nineteen hundred sixty two and a half acres of land for which land the Plaintiff [ ] as aforesaid executed a bond for the Conveyance of the same by Deed with a special warranter which bond bears date the 9th day of February 1805 and [ ] to the Court shown by which [page 471] it appears the Plaintiff was bound to make said Deed of Conveyance to the Deft within a reasonable time after being called on by the Defendant **Charles** and the Defendant doth aver that previous to the Plaintiff [ ] out their original Writ in this cause, to wit, on the ___ day of ____ 1806 at the State and Circuit aforesaid he did demand of the Pltffs Exors to make a Deed of Conveyance as aforesaid within a reasonable time thereafter to the land afsd which the Plaintiff failed to comply with, and still doth fail and which conveyance of the land afsd by the Pltffs to the Deft as aforesaid was to be performed by the Pltffs before this Deft was bound to pay the whisky aforesaid, and this he is ready to verify wherefore he prays Judgment &c

**Owens** & **Davis** attornies for Deft

And the Defendant for further plea in this behalf saith that the Plaintiffs their action aforesaid against them Ought not to have or maintain because he saith that the writing Obligatory in the Declaration mentioned was executed by the Deft to the Plaintiffs and the whisky therein contained was for and in part Consideration of a tract of land sold by the Pltffs Exors as aforesaid to the Deft containing nineteen hundred sixty two and a half acres lying and being in the state of Kentucky and County of Pulaski which land the Pltffs was to convey to the Deft, within a reasonable time after being called on by the said Deft, and the Deft doth aver that the Plaintiffs are unable to make a good and sufficient Title to the said land agreeable to the Terms of said [ ], the same being covered by interfering claims superior in dignity, to wit, the claim of a certain **James Kincaid**, and this he is ready to verify [page 472] wherefore he prays Judgment &c

**Owens** & **Davis** attornies for Deft

And the Pltffs say that they ought not to be bared from having and maintaining their action aforesaid by any thing in the 1st & 2d pleas of the Defendants above pleaded Because they say that the said pleas and the matters therein contained are not sufficient in law to bar the Pltffs of their said action neither are they bound by the law of the land in any manner to answer thereto, and this they are ready to verify whereupon they pray Judgment &c

**Quarles** & **Montgomery** attornies for Pltff

And the Deft says that his said pleas above pleaded and the matters therein contained are sufficient in law to bar the Pltffs action aforesaid all which matters and things the Deft is ready to verify wherefore and because this Plaintiff have refused to receive the said Verification he prays Judgment &c

**Davis**

And the said Plaintiffs for Replication to the 3rd plea of the Deft above pleaded says they ought not to be bared from having and maintaining their action aforesaid against the said Deft because they say that the Title of **James Kincaid** is not superior to the Title of their Testator and this pray may be enquired of by the Country and the Deft likewise and the said Pltff craves Oyer of the bond for the conveyance of the land in the 2d plea of the Deft mentioned and which they say ought not to be bared from having and maintaining their action aforesaid by any thing in the said plea contained because they say that the [page 473] payment of whisky in the Covenant mentioned was not to be defered until after the conveyance of the said tract of land and this they pray may be enquired of by the Country and the Deft likewise, Demurers argued and first plea adjudged bad, Second good, Replication to the third and second pleas of the Deft and Joinders (**Charles Collyer** at the suit of **Hutchings** Exors Be it remembered that upon the trial this cause the Deft appeared to prove by **John McCullough** as witness for him that the claim of **James Kincaid** as is set forth in this Defendants 3rd plead covered a part of the land as purchased of the Pltffs as he was informed which evidence going to the Jury the Pltffs by their Counsil Objects and the Court sustained their Objection to which Opinion of the Court the Deft by his counsil excepts and tenders this his bill of exceptions, and prays that the same may be signed Sealed and recorded, the witness aforesaid stated he knew nothing about the said interference of his own knowledge but only from Information

**Christ Tompkins**
**John Prather**
**John James**

It is ordered the Sheriff that he cause to come here Immediately twelve good and lawful men by whom &c and thereupon came also a Jury, to wit, **Washington Redmon, John Jasper, Willis Embry, John Boyd** Senr, **Thomas Banks, Martin True, Samuel King, John Cundiff, James Boyd, William Boyd, James Eastham** junr & **Anderson Nunnaley**, who being elected tried and sworn the truth to speak upon the Issue Joined upon their Oaths do find for [page 474] the Plaintiff sixty pounds in Damages besides their Costs It is therefore Considered by the Court that the Plaintiff recover against the said Defendant their Damages aforesaid by the Jurors in form aforesaid assessed, and their Costs by them about this suit in this behalf expended, and the said Defendant in mercy &c

– **Thomas Hutchings** Exors Plts
against In Covenant (3rd Case)
**Charles Collyer** Deft

This day came the parties aforesaid by their attornies, and the same pleading being had herein Verbatim, and the same Jury sworn as in the 2d case between said parties last above mentioned, to wit, **Washington Redmon, John Jasper, Willis Embry, John Boyd** senr, **Thomas Banks, Martin True, Samuel King, John Cundiff, James Boyd, William Boyd, James Eastham** Junr & **Anderson Nunnaly**, who being elected tried and sworn the truth to speak upon the Issues Joined upon their Oaths do find for the Plaintiffs twenty eight pounds four shillings and two pence in Damages, besides their costs. It is therefore Considered by the Court that the Plaintiff recover against the said Deft their Damages aforesaid by the Jurors in their Verdict in form aforesaid assessed and their Costs by them about their suit in this behalf expended and the said Defendant in mercy &c

– **Nathaniel Forbis** Plt
against In Case
**John Simpson** Deft

[page 475] **David Walker** Plt
against In Trespass Assault & Battery
**Samuel Devore** Deft

– **George Lankford** Plt

against In Case
**John Daniel** Deft

This day came the parties aforesaid by their attornies and by their mutual consent these causes are continued until the next Term

– **Micajah Cooper** Plt
against In Case
**Johnson Sargent** Deft

This day came the Plaintiff by his attorney and upon his motion It is ordered that this suit be Dism[d] at the Plaintiffs Costs

– **Samuel Dennis** Plt
against In Covenant
**James Anderson** Deft

Ordered that this suit be continued until the next Term of this Court

– **Moses Justis** & **Galey** Plts
against In Debt
**James Anderson** Deft

This day came the parties aforesaid by their attornies, and by consent It is ordered that a former Order of this Court for the appointment of jurors herein be set a side and the cause continued until the next Term of this Court and leave is given to take Depositions without this state before a single justice of the peace

[page 476] **Daniel Hill** Plt
against In Covenant
**John Cundiff** & Others Defts

The Plaintiff by his attorney says he ought not to be bared or precluded from having and maintaining his action, by reason of any thing by the Defendants in their plea first above pleaded because he says the Deed of Covenant in the declaration mentioned was not executed by the Defendant In consideration of two tracts of land lying in Pulaski County, sold by the Plaintiff to the Defendant **John Cundiff**, But the Plaintiff avers the said Deed of Covenant was executed by the Defendant In consideration of one tract of land lying in Pulaski County on which tract of land there was due for tax the Commonwealth of Kentucky from the Plaintiff the sum of fourteen cents six mills for which the said tract of land since the Commencement of the action of the Plt against the Deft, to wit, on ____ day of _____ the said arrears of Tax was sold by the Sheriff of Pulaski County and the Plt avers that he afterwards, to wit, on the 13[th] day of November 1807 did redeem the said tract of land from the sale aforesaid according to the law in such cases made and provided, which will appear by the receipt of the auditor of Public accounts now to the Court ready to be shown and this the Plt is ready to verify wherefore he prays Judgment &[c] and the Plt for Replication to the second plea by the Deft above pleaded says he Ought not to be bared or precluded from having and maintaining his action aforesaid Because he says the Deed of covenant in the Declaration mentioned was not executed by the Defendants In consideration of two tracts of land lying in Pulaski County sold by the Plt to the Deft **John Cundiff** but that the said Deed of Covenant was executed by the Deft In consideration of one [page 477] tract of land lying in Pulaski containing 217 acres the Title papers of which was to be transferred by the Plt to the Deft **John Cundiff** and the Pltff avers he did on the ___ day of ____ Transfer the title papers to the Deft **John Cundiff** according to the true intent and meaning of the Contract and agreement of the Plt and the Deft **John Cundiff**, and of this he prays may be inquired of by the Country

**Davis** & **Owsley** for Plt

And the Deft likewise

**Quarles** &[c] attornies for Deft

and the said Defendant says that the Replication of the Plaintiff to his first plea herein & the matters therein contained are not Sufficient in law for the Plaintiff to have and maintain his action aforesaid against the Deft, neither is he in any manner bound by the law of the land to answer thereto, and this he is ready to verify wherefore he prays Judgment &[c]

**Montgomery Quarles** & **Logan** attornies for the Deft
This day came the Parties aforesaid by their attornies, and the Defts Demurer to the Plaintiffs Replication to the first plea of the Deft herein being argued by the Counsil on both sides, It is considered by the Court that the law is for the Plaintiff, It is therefore ordered that the said Demurer be Over ruled, &c, and to be enquired of by a Jury. Therefore It is Commanded the Sheriff that he cause to come here Immediately twelve good and lawful men by whom &c and thereupon came also a Jury, to wit, **William Blain, Joseph Sargent, Jesse Williams, James Condry, Christ**o **Clonch, Charles Rusk, Owen Adkins, William Cooper, John Boyd, Richard Blacklidge, Jeremiah Boone** & **Asa McKinsey,** who being elected tried and [page 478] sworn the truth to speak upon the Issue Joined upon their Oaths do find for the Plaintiff two hundred twenty seven Dollars and eighty five Cents, in Damages besides his Costs. It is therefore Considered by the Court that the Plaintiff recover against the said Defendant his Damages aforesaid by the Jurors in their Verdict in form aforesaid assessed and his Costs by him about his suit in this behalf expended and the said Defendant in mercy &c

– **Gilham Hopper** Plt
against In Trespass Assault and Battery
**John Mayfield** & Als Deft

This day came the parties aforesaid by their attornies, and the Deft **John Mayfield** acknowledges the Plaintiffs action or damages against him for ten Dollars. therefore with the assent of the Plaintiff It is considered by the Court that the Plaintiff recover against the said **John Mayfield** the Damages acknowledged aforesaid, and his Costs by him about his suit in this behalf expended and the said Defendant may be taken &c

– **Thomas Addison** by **William Addison** his next friend &c Plts
against In Trespass Assault & Battery
**Stephen Hail** & Others Defts

This day came the parties aforesaid by their attornies, and thereupon came also a Jury, to wit, **Thomas Dollihide, John Kelly, David Evans, Smith Williams, James Cox, Thomas Pascall, Hugh Logan, Joseph Erwin, James Campbell, Seaton Lee, Samuel Hendricks** and **Henry Farmer**, who being elected tried and sworn the truth to speak upon the Issue Joined upon their Oaths do say that the said Defendants are not Guilty of the Trespass Assault and Battery in manner and [page 479] form as the Plaintiff in his Declaration herein against them hath complained, It is therefore considered by the Court that the Plaintiff take nothing by his Bill but for his false clamour be in mercy &c and that the Defendants go hence and recover of the Plaintiff their Costs by them about their defence in this behalf expended &c

– **John McWhorter** Assee Plt
against In Covenant
**Robertson Burge** Deft

This day came the parties aforesaid by their attornies, and it is agreed that any thing may be given in evidence herein under any legal plea, therefore It is commanded the Sheriff that he cause to come here Immediately twelve good and lawful men by whom &c and thereupon came also a Jury to wit, **Benjamin Hansford, Thomas Hail, Benjamin Harris, Joseph Crain, John Boyd, James Boyd, George Cooper, Edward White, Andrew Campbell, James McM[ ], Stephen Hail,** & **John Gibson** who being elected tried and sworn the truth to speak upon the Issue Joined upon their Oaths do say that the said Deft hath well and truly kept and performed the several Covenants in the writing mentioned on his part as in pleading he has alledged, and hath not broken the same in manner and form as the Plaintiff in his Declaration against him hath complained It is therefore Considered by the Court that the Plaintiff take nothing by his bill but for his false clamor be in mercy &c and that the Defendant go hence and recover his Costs by him about his Defence in this behalf expended

– **David E Matthews** Plt
against In Trespass assault and Battery
**Washington Redmon** Deft

[page 480] On the motion of the Defendant it is Ordered that the Judgment and writ of Inquiry awarded against him in the Clerks Office be set a side and the said Defendant by his attorney now comes and defends the wrong and Injury when and where &c and says that he is not Guilty in manner and form as the Plaintiff against him hath declared, and this he prays may be enquired of by the Country and the Plaintiff doth the same likewise and the said Deft for further plea herein says that at the time and in the Declaration mentioned when and where the Plaintiff hath alledged that the Deft committed the Trespass assault & Battery upon the said Plt by the said Plts assault him and there would have beaten him the said Defendant had not the said Deft then and there Instantly in his defence beaten the Plt which is the same Trespass Assault and Battery in the Plaintiffs Declaration mentioned and this he is ready to verify wherefore he prays Judgment &c. And the Plt says he ought not to be bared from having his action afsd against the said Deft by any thing in the plea above pleaded because he says the said Deft made the Trespass assault and Battery in the Declaration mentioned of his own proper Injury without such cause as in his plea is alledged and this he prays may be enquired of by the County and the Deft likewise, therefore it is Commanded the Sheriff that he cause to come here Immediately twelve good and lawful men by whom &c and thereupon came a Jury, to wit, **Benjamin Th[ ]**, **William Boyd**, **Aaron Doss**, **Francis Clear**, **Ephraim Haines**, **John West**, **Reubin Scott**, **James Ratekin**, **George Dougherty**, **John Hill**, **Lambert White**, and **James Eastham** who being elected tried and sworn the truth to speak upon the Issue Joined upon their Oaths do say that the said Deft is guilty of the Trespass assault and Battery in the Declaration mentioned, as the Plaintiff therein hath complained and they do assess the Plaintiffs Damages by Occasion thereof to one cent besides his Costs. It is therefore Considered by the [page 481] Court that the Plaintiff recover against the said Deft his Damages aforesaid by the Jurors in their Verdict aforesaid assessed and his costs by him about his suit in this behalf expended and the said Deft may be taken

– On the motion of **Edward White**, who presented his Bill in Court and made Oath to the same, an Injunction is granted him to stay all further proceeding on four Judgments Obtained against him said **White** and **James Price** as his security &c in the name of **Charles Collyer** & others, as specified in said Bill, at common Law in the Pulaski Circuit Court, on the said **Whites** entering into Bond in the Clerks Office with **John McCullough & Ephraim Haines** or either of them his security in the penalty of $60 conditioned as the law directs

– **Philip A Sublette** &c Sct
against In Detinue
**John Daniel** Deft

This day the Opinion and Decree of the Court of Appeals was produced in Court in these words State of Kentucky Sct Court of Appeals Office June 16th 1809

**John Daniel** Appellant
against upon an Appeal from a Judgment of the Pulaski Circuit Court
**Edward Prather & Philip A Sublette** Appellees

The Court being now sufficiently advised of and concerning the premises [note: a second hand begins, much more difficult to read] delivered the following opinion, to wit, This was an action of Detinue for a Negro girl to which the appellant who was Deft in the action below pleaded non Detinet and Issue was thereupon Joined by the plaintiff were appellees in this Court [page 482] The Jury sworn to try the Issue returned the Verdict that the sd Defendant doth detain the Negro girl **Matilda** in the declaration mentioned in maner and form as the Plaintiffs therein against him hath Complained and do find for the plaintiff the sd Negro girl **Matilda** if she may be had and if she may not be had the sum of $200 her value in damages. The Judgment of the Court thereon is in the words following, to wit, It is therefore Considered by the Plaintiff recover against the said Defendant the said negro girl **Matilda** if she may be had and if she may not be had the sum of $200 her Value in damages by the Jurors in their Verdict afsd assessed and their Costs in this behalf expended and the Defendant &c

The Deft moved the Court for a new trial alledging the Verdict was contrary to Law and evidence and that three of the Jurors were in favor of finding for the defendant and offered to produce the affidavit of the said three Jurors and the affidavit of other Jurors of the Jurors who were in favor of finding for the plaintiff to prove that the s[d] three Jurors were in favor of finding for the Deft that they were induced to submit to the Verdict as returned under the impression and belief that a majority was to govern them in finding a Verdict and this information was procured from the Jurors shortly after being Discharged the Court overruled the motion and the Deft excepted thereto

The errors assigned are 1[st] that the writ is Defective it does not state the Value of the negro girl and is [ ] whereas it should have been [ ] [page 483] Sheriff 2[nd] the Declaration varies from the writ in alledging that the s[d] girl is of the value of $[ ] 3[rd] the Verdict is defective in not finding as to the whole issue by the Issue Joined they were bound to find as to the detention of the negro and if the Deft detained her the damages the plaintiff had sustained by the detention they have only found as to the detention without any finding as to damages as to the detention 4[th] The Court below erred in refusing to permit the affidavit of the Jurors to be used as stated in the bill of exceptions 5[th] the Court below erred in overruling the motion for a new trial on the Case stated in the bill of exceptions The direction of the writ to the [ ] may be come in some cases not only proper but indesfencibly necessary for the interest of the [ ] the subject of the Controversy or his relation to one of the parties where the writ is so directed and the propriety of it is not questioned in the Court below and made to appear upon the record this Court must presume that circumstances existed which made the direction to the Coroner [?] proper but this as well as the omission to state in the writ the Value of the negro girl are objections giving only to the abatement of the writ and to [ ] the deft after having appeared and pleaded in chief in bar of the action would violate the established order of pleading These Objections to the writ as well as that taken in the second error assigned to the variance between the writ and declaration are silenced by the Verdict as to the objection taken to the Verdict for not having found damages for the detention of the negro does not appear to comport with common sense that such an objection should be in the mouth of Deft [ink smeared] [page 484] Damages were found but where the plaintiff goes for a specific thing as in Debt and detinue their damages being merely an accessary the Verdict and Judgment may be for the principal thing without its [ ] and if such Judgments is given it would not appear reasonable that the Deft should object because the Plaintiff had not also recovered damages against him but admitting that the objection lay at Common Law it seems to the Court to be covered by the statute of 1799 The Cause has been evidently tried upon its merits and the Judgment may be plead in bar to any other action for the same cause and in such cases the statute has prohibited an appeal or writ of errors The 4[th] error presents to the Court a question that they have repeatedly decided and offer to produce affidavits as a grown for a action for a new trial cannot be sufficient to authorize the granting the motion on the cases both **Conroy** and **Wickliff** against **Payne** decided at this time the facts upon which the motion is allowed should always be made out by proof produced to the Court or by the admissions of the adverse party and the Court ought never to be required to give an opinion upon a [ ] case There is no dificulty in deciding the question arising upon the fifth error assigned the evidence exhibited in the bill of exceptions is not alledged to be the whole evidence in the Cause and if it was the weight of it, is too nearly balanced to have authorized the Court to grant a new trial Wherefore it is Considered by the Court that the Judgments afs[d] be affirmed that appelles may proceed to have the benefit of the same in the Court below and recover of the appellant [ ] damages [page 485] on the amount thereof according to the statute in such cases made and provided which is ordered to be certified to the s[d] Circuit Court

[note: Will Fox resumes writing] Ordered that the Court be adjourned until Tomorrow morning nine OClock

**Christ[o] Tompkins**

At a Circuit Court Continued and held for the Pulaski Circuit at the Courthouse of Pulaski County in Somerset on Wednesday the 27[th] day of July 1809

Present the Hon[bl] **Christopher Tompkins** & **John James** Gent

– **Jeremiah Stone** Plt

against In Case

**Robert Stubblefield** & **Thomas Nedry** Defts
The Defendant **Nedry** by his attorney moved the court to discharge him on Confinement, for defects appearing from the affidavit upon the back of the capias Issued herein upon which bail was directed to be taken, therefore It is ordered that the said **Nedry** be discharged from his Confinement

– **William Horner** for the benifit of **Thomas Kennedy** Plt
against upon motion now brought on his motion continued from the last Term
**Bazil Meek** late Shff Deft
against the Defendant Late Sheriff of Pulaski County & exhibited the following notice of this motion _______________ Mr **Bazil Meek** late Sheriff of Pulaski County Kentucky take notice that on the 10th day of the present April Term of the Circuit Court for the County of Pulaski aforesaid I will move said Court for a Judgment against you for the money [page 486] collected by **John Daniel** your deputy by Virtue of an execution issued on a Replevy bond, on the 17th day of April in the year 1808 returnable to the May Rule day ensuing, issued in the name of **William Horner** Senior against **Spencer Griffin** & **Drewry Lee** his security, endorsed for the benifit of **Thomas Kennedy**, the amount of which your said Deputy collected & hath refused and failed to pay over, altho requested to do so at the House of **William Fox**, his place of residence in the county aforesaid, on the 4th Monday in July in the year aforesaid I will also at the same time move the same Court for Judgment against you for the fifteen per centum, per annum, interest allowed by law to be computed from the return day of said execution until paid April the 24th day A.D. 1809
**William Horner** Senr for **Thomas Kennedy**, by **Thomas Montgomery** Pltffs atto
upon which was made the following endorsement Viz, I acknowledge Service of the within notice this 24th day of April 1809
**Bazil Meek**
Teste **Tho: Montgomery**
And the said **Bazil Meek** being present here in Court made an Objection to the said motion, and it appearing to the Court, that the motion could not have been sooner made against the said Sheriff because no Court was holden in Pulaski County after the return day of the execution in the notice aforesaid mentioned until the last Term of this Court, whereupon on hearing the motion aforesaid and all things relative thereto It is considered by the Court that the said **William Horner** for the benifit of **Thomas Kennedy** recover against the said **Bazil Meek** the sum of ninety eight Dollars and thirty eight [page 487] cents the amount of the execution Including Interest with Interest on the said sum after the rate of fifteen percentum per annum from the 2nd Monday next succeeding the 4th Monday in May 1808 until paid & also the Costs incurred by the plaintiff in prosecuting this motion and the said Deft in mercy &c

– Present **John Prather** Gent

– **Jesse Chapple** Plt
against In Case
**William Lynch** Deft
Ordered that this suit be continued until the next Term of this Court

– **William Beard** Complt
against In Chancery
**Hiram Geons** Admors Defts

– **John McWhorter** Plt
against In Covenant
**John Spencer** Deft

– **William Bradley** Plt
against In Covenant
**Elijah Henley** Deft

– The Same Plt
against In Covenant
The Same Deft

– **William Sprowl** Plt
against In Covenant
**Moses Francis** Deft
– **Limoledge Stringer** Plt
against In Debt
**William & David Clark** Deft
[page 488] **John Cundiff** Ass[ee] Plt
against In Debt
**George A Allin** Deft
– **Pamela Stringer** &[c] Plt
against In Case
**William Hill** & ux Deft
– **Michael Lease** Plt
against In Debt
**David Busters** Ex[ors] Deft
– The Same Plt
against In Case
The Same Deft
– **Jesse Richardson** Plt
against In Case
**Aaron Lawson** Deft
– **George Allcorn** Plt
against In Case
**John Barns** Deft
– **George Humphreys** &[c] Plt
against In Covenant
**James Griffin** deft
– **John Rogers** Plt
against In Covenant
**Samuel Tindal** Deft

The above cases, having been Dismissed & upon the Rules taken in the Clerks of this Court It is therefore Ordered by the Court that the said Dismissions &[c] be confirmed and made the Judgment of the Court agreeably to an act of [page 489] the General Assembly Kentucky in such cases made and provided

– **John Thurmon** Plt
against upon Petition
**Joseph Erwin** Deft

This day came the parties aforesaid by their attornies, and by consent it is Ordered that a former Order of this Court refering all matters and differences between the said Parties relative to this suit be set a side and the Cause is continued until the next Term of this court, It appearing to the satisfaction of the Court that the referees aforesaid had refused to act on the case

– **Drewry Lee** & **John Faulkner** Plts
against upon Petition
**John Newby, Nicholas Jasper, Jonathan Swift** & **John Griffin** Defts

This day came the Plaintiffs by their attorney and it appearing to the satisfaction of this Court that the Defendants has been duly Served with a Copy of the Plaintiffs Petition and Summons Issued herein, and the said Defendants being solemnly called but came not Therefore on the motion of the Plaintiffs by their attorney It is Considered by the Court that the Plaintiffs recover against the said Defendants the sum of two hundred Dollars current money of Kentucky the Debt in the Petition herein mentioned, with Interest thereon to be computed after the rate of six per centum per annum from the twenty fifth day of July One thousand eight hundred and eight until paid & costs by him about their suit in this behalf expended and the said Defendants in mercy &[c]

[page 490] **Henry Francis** Plt
against upon Petition
**Robertson Burge** Deft

This day came the Plaintiff by his attorney, and It appearing to the Satisfaction of this Court that the Defendant has been duly Served with a copy of the Plaintiffs Petition & Summons herein and the said Defendant being solomnly called but came not but made default, Therefore on the Plaintiff by his attorney It is considered by the Court that the Plaintiff recover against the said Defendant the sum of three hundred Dollars the Debt in the Petition herein mentioned, with legal Interest thereon from the fourth day of June 1808 until paid & Costs to be computed after the rate of six per centum per annum. But to be credited by the sum of one hundred and Seven Dollars paid on the twenty sixth day of September 1808 Also to have credit for one hundred and fifty eight Dollars paid on the ninth day of May one thousand eight hundred and nine

– The Commonwealth Plt
against upon Indictment
**John Daniel** Deft

The Defendant by **Thomas Montgomery** his attorney was this day about to move to quash the Indictment to which the attorney for the Commonwealth Objected, for this that the said Defendant has failed to appear in person and having forfeited his Recognizance, in failing to appear before this Court at their last Term, agreeablly to the Condition of this said Recognizance and the arguments of Counsil being heard, It is Ordered that the said Objection stand until a further day for consideration

[page 491] **James Kincaid** Plt
against In Ejectment
**Charles Collyer** Deft

– The Same Plt
against Same
**Moses Cummins** Deft

– The Same Plt
against Same
**Joseph Camp** Deft

– The Same Plt
against Same
**Samuel Elder** Deft

– The Same Plt
against Same
**Bortre Garrett** Deft

– The Same Plt
against Same
**Zachariah Denny** Deft

– The Same Plt
against Same
**John Collyer** Deft

– The Same Plt
against Same
**John McCullough** Deft

This day came the Parties aforesaid by their attornies and the plaintiff by his attorney moved the Court to have the aforesaid causes Continued until the next Term of this court, which motion was Objected to by the Defendants Counsils, after hearing from the Counsil on both sides [page 492] and mature deliberation being thereon had, It is Ordered by the Court that the said Cause be continued until the next Term of this Court and that the said Defendant recover of the said Plaintiff their Costs by them about their defence relative to said Continuance expended, to which opinion of the Court the Defendant by their attornies excepts, and files their Bill of exceptions, which being first signed by the Court was Ordered to be entered of Record as follows, Be it remembered that upon this suit being called the Plaintiff by his attorney moved the Court for an continuance of this cause, and support of the motion the said **Kincaid** appeared in Court and swore that he was not ready for trial not having had executed a Survey in this cause and alledged as a reason for his not having the Survey executed that he in conversation with **Thomas Montgomery** his attorney at the last Term of this Court understood from said Attorney he would transmit information to him the said **Kincaid**, what would be necessary for him to have done against the Court if any thing to prepare for trial and that he has never received any Information from his attorney until during this Court at this place and that he relying upon receiving such information has failed to have the Survey executed not knowing it was necessary the attorney **Montgomery** then made his statement in Court which was received by the Deft as upon Oath that he had given such information as sworn by the Plt above to him at the last Term of this Court, which said motion of the plt by his attorney was sustained by the Court and the Cause Continued the said **Thomas Montgomery** stated to the Court that [page 493] In the conversation refered to as passing between him and his client he told said **James Kincaid** that he did not know what course the Deft would take, that if he confessed Judgment at law with a reservation of equity which was the most usual course nothing would be necessary to be done by said **Kincaid** between that time and the present Term, but that if he plead he would Obtained an Order of Survey and inform him thereof by writing, and said **Montgomery** stated further that he had no direct Opportunity of writing to said **Kincaid** to his knowledge that he had expected to have seen him at Knox Circuit Court about the first of this Instant but said **Kincaid** was not there It appears to the Court that said **Kincaid** resides in Pulaski County about 16 or 18 miles from the Courthouse, to which opinion in continuing the said Cause, the Deft by his attorney excepts and prays this his bill of exceptions to be signed sealed and made a part of the Record

**Christ Tompkins**
**John Prather**
**John James**

On the motion of the Plaintiff by his attorney an Order of Survey is awarded him herein directed to **Thomas Whites**, who is to go on the land in Controversy between the aforesaid parties on the ___ day of ___ next if fair if not then on the next fair Day and then and there Survey and lay off the same as [page 494] either party would have it having regard to all Deeds and other evidences that may be produced report all matters of fact specially before the day of hearing to the Clerks Office and it is further Ordered that the said **Thomas White** do ascertain the variation of the magnetic needle from the true meridian counting the degrees of Variation and its bearing with the line established by Act of Assembly as the line of the reserved Military lands, and it is further agreed by the parties and Ordered by the Court, that three plats and Certificates shall be deemed sufficient in the whole of the cases aforesaid, and shall be used as such

– **James Doran & Co** Plts
against In Debt
**Nathaniel Forbis** Deft

This day came the Plaintiff by his attorney, and the Defendant being solemnly called came not, but made default, Therefore on the motion of the Plaintiffs by his attorney, Judgment is awarded him against the said Deft & Sampson Vanhoosen, who is returned herein as the Defendants appearance Bail, for seven pounds one shilling and three pence, the Debt in the Declaration mentioned, with Interest thereon to be computed at the rate of six per centum per annum from the 28th day of April 1807 until paid & Costs and the said Deft in mercy &c

[page 495] **Thomas Jacob & Thomas McGuire** Complt
against In Chancery
**Thomas Clark & Charles English** Deft

This day came the parties aforesaid by their attorney, and the Defendants Demurer to the Complainants Bill, as filed herein being argued, and mature deliberation thereon had, It is Ordered that the said Demurer be sustained, that the Complainants Injunction be desolved, that the said Defendants may have the benifit of their Judgment at law, that the Bill of the Complainants be

Dismissed, and the Defendants recover of the complainants the ten per centum Damages on the Debt & interest up to the time which was enjoined, and that the Complainants pay unto the said Defendants their Costs by them in this behalf expended

– **Obediah Phelps** Plt
against In Case
**William Stringer** Deft

This day came the Plaintiff by his attorney, and the Deft being called but came not, Therefore It is Commanded the Sheriff that he caused to come here Immediately twelve good and lawful men by whom &c and thereupon came also a Jury, to wit, **Samuel King, John Evans, Edward Cooper, William Camp, Greenberry Middleton, James Campbell, John Charter, James Kincaid, John McCullough, John Ping, William Carr** and **John Williams**, who were sworn well and truly to enquire what Damages the Plaintiff hath sustained in the Premises upon their Oaths do say that the Plaintiff hath sustained Damages by Occasion thereof to fifty Dollars besides his costs It is therefore Considered by the Court that the Plaintiff recover against the said Defendant [page 496] his Damages aforesaid by the Jurors their Verdict in form assessed and his Costs by him about the suit in this behalf expended and the said Defendant in mercy &c

– **James Binnay** by Governor Plt
against In Debt
**Nicholas Jasper** Shff &c Deft

This day came the parties aforesaid by their attornies and thereupon came also a Jury, to wit, **Edward Cooper, James Taylor, James Gun, John Fitzpatrick, Christo Clonch, Johnson Sargent, Drewry Clark, Thomas Addy, Aaron Doss, Samuel Crow, John Hughes & John Charter** who being elected tried and sworn the truth to speak upon the Issue Joined upon their Oaths returned their verdict in these words, (we of the Jury find for the Defendants It is therefore Considered by the Court that the Plaintiff take nothing by his bill but for his false clamor be in mercy &c and that the Deft go hence without day and recover of the Plaintiff their Costs by them about their defence in this behalf expended

– **James Hardgrove** Plt
against In Debt
**Henry Francis** Deft

**George Allcorn**, of Pulaski County came into Court and justifd and undertook for the said Deft that if he shall be cast in the action aforesaid that he shall satisfy and pay the condemnation of the Court or render his body to prison in execution for the same or on falure thereof that he the said **George Allcorn** shall do it for him

– **Frederick Williams** Plt
against In Covenant
**William Brooks** Deft

This day came the Plaintiff by his attorney, and on his motion It is Ordered that this suit be Dismissed

[page 497] **Daniel McIlvey** by Gov Plt
against In Debt
**Nicholas Jasper** Shff &c Defts

This day came the Parties aforesaid by their attornies and thereupon came also a Jury, to wit, **Frederick Williams, Francis Clear, John Camp, William Barns, George Dungings, Daniel Lewis, Thomas G[ ], Zack Steadham, John Long, John Weaver, Henry Garner, & Henry Farmer**, who being elected tried and sworn the truth to speak upon the Issue Joined upon their Oaths returned their Verdict in these words (we of the Jury find for the Defends, therefore It is considered by the Court that the Plaintiff take nothing by his bill but for his false clamor be in mercy &c and that the Defendants go hence and recover of the Plaintiff their Costs by them about their defence in this behalf expended,

Be It remembered that upon the trial of this cause the Plaintiff offered in evidence the Commissioners Book of the year 1805 and 1806 to prove the property of the security **Elihu**

**Sanders** in the Replevin Bond, refered to in the Pleadings in this cause, to the production of which Books as evidence the Defendant by their attorney objected, which Objection was Over ruled and the Books received as evidence the Court being of the opinion they might be presumptive tho not conclusive evidence of said **Elihu's** Property, to which opinion of the Court on Over ruling the Objection and receiving the evidence aforesaid the Defts by their Attorney excepts and prays this his bill of exceptions to be signed Sealed and made a part of the Record

**Christopher Tompkins**

– Ordered that the Court be adjourned until Tomorrow morning nine OClock

**Christ Tompkins**

[page 498] At a Circuit Court Continued and held for the Pulaski Circuit at the Courthouse of Pulaski County in Sommerset on Thursday the 28th day of July 1809

Present the Honbl **Christo Tompkins & John Prather** Gent

– **Daniel McIlvey**, by Governor Plt
against In Debt
**Nicholas Jasper** Shff & Deft

This day came the Parties aforesaid by their attornies, and the Plaintiff by his attorney moved the Court for a new trial herein on the Verdict of the Jury and Judgment rendered yesterday, after hearing the arguments of Counsil on both sides, and mature deliberation thereon being had, It is considered by the Court that the said motion be Over ruled, To which Opinion of the court the Plaintiff by his attorney excepts, and files his Bill of exception in the words following Be it remembered that on the trial of this Cause which happened at the July Term of the Pulaski Circuit Court 1809. the plaintiff on his part [ ] as evidence to show the probable insufficiency of **Elihu Sanders** as security in the Replevin bond in the declaration mentioned the Commissioners Book for Pulaski County for the year 1805 by which it appears the said **Elihu** entered 200 acres of 3rd rate land plus two Horses and the Commissioners Book for the year 1806 by which it appeared he entered 4 Horses only the Plaintiff also introduced Sundry persons as Witnesses one of which **Joseph Erwine**, swore that he lived in six or seven miles of **Elihu Sanders** was acquainted with him knew of no property which he owned that he was a single man and that he would not have been Willing to have received him as security in the Replevy bond [page 499] In the Declaration mentioned or for such sum: another witness **Samuel Irvins**, swore the same with respect to receiving the said **Saunders** as security but stated further that he has seen him riding different Horses at different times which he claimed, **John McCullough** another witness swore he lived within three miles of where the said **Elihu Saunders**, generally resided that he had known him for many years that he always considered him a very poor man, that he was a Single man and that he would not have been willing to have received him as security for any sum _____ **Reynolds** another witness swore he was acquainted with **Elihu Saunders** lived within three miles of him that he had no family, lived sometimes with one relative and at other times with others that he never knew of him having but one horse & believes he would have known of other property if he had owned any such and that he would not have been willing to have received him as security for such sum as is mentioned in the Replevy bond; and upon being Interrogated declared he heard **John Ping** as witness sworn for the Deft say on the day of the trial that he would not have been willing to have received **Elihu Saunders** as security for the sum mentioned in the replevin bond another witness **William Griffin** said he lived within three miles of the said **Saunders** that he only knew of his having one Horse and supposed if he had others he would have known of them and that he would not have received him as security for the sum mentioned in the Replevin bond, that he never was at his place of residence this was the evidence adduced on the part of the Pltff in addition to the Sheriff returns of the said **Saunders** having left the state which was also proved [page 500] by the witnesses to have happened in the month of March or April 1807 on the part of the Defendant _____ **Stringer** was Introduced, who swore that in 1805 **Elihu Saunders** claimed 200 acres of land in Pulaski County and had two Horses in Possession but knew nothing of his property in the year 1806, **John Ping** another witness swore on the part of the Deft, at first declared he knew nothing about the subjects in question or words tantamount, but on being interrogated declared that about the date of the Replevy bond said **E Saunders** either had a trade of 200 acres of land and two Horses or if he had sold the land three Horses that the said three Horses were of the value of sixty three pounds but upon being interrogated to know whether the said Horses would have brought the amount of the Replevy Bond at a Sheriffs sale he equivocated and finally said they would not know but that Horses would not sell [ ]for near as much as they would then and that the Valuation stated by him was not with a view to that kind of sale or words tantamount; and upon being asked whether he had not on the day of the Trial and before he was sworn told one of the attornies of the Plaintiff that he would not have received the said **Saunders** as security for the sum Replevied by him he declared he did not recollect to have said so but now upon being asked by the Defendants Counsil he said he would have received him for such sum **Elijah Saunders** also swore on the part of the Deft, swore **Elihu Saunders** at the date of the Replevin Bond had three Horses of the Value of two hundred Dollars that he left the state in March or April 1807 after executing the Replevin Bond, and at the time of executing the bond **Elihu Saunders** had no Intension of leaving [page 501] the State that he did not know whether the Horses would have produced the sum mentioned in the Replevin bond at the Sheriffs sale or not, the sheriff returns on two executions in these words (Viz) executed on two tracts of land and sold on the fifteenth day of June for One dollar and Sheriffs Costs, and the Defendants both removed out of this state before the date of the execution

**John Daniel** DS for **Bazil Meek**

Executed on **George W Saunders** and delivered in Jail to the Jailor but the other Defendant not found

**John Daniel** DS for **Bazil Meek**

was read it was also that the said **Elihu Saunders** was sometime out of this state but that his place of his residence was in this County for the Term of twelve years past and at the time of executing the Replevy Bond he lived with his Brother **Elijah Saunders** in this County and was making a crop with him, and all the witness interviewed by the Plaintiff Stated that **Elihu Sanders** at the time of executing the Replevy bond, might have been possessed of Property for any thing they new that they had never [ ] any enquiry or examination as to his property, the foregoing as all the evidence adduced and upon such evidence the Jury found a verdict for the Deft, whereupon the plaintiffs attorney moved for a new trial upon the ground that the Verdict was against & without evidence to Justify it but which motion was overruled by the Court to which Opinion of the Court the Pltffs excepts & prays that this his Bill of exceptions may be signed [page 502] Sealed and entered of Record

**Christopher Tompkins**
**John Prather**

– **James Binney** by Governor Plt
against In Debt
**Nicholas Jasper** Shff &c Defts

This day came the parties aforesaid by their attornies, and on the motion of the Plaintiff by his attorney, to obtain a new trial herein on the Verdict of the Jury and Judgment rendered in this cause on yesterday, After hearing the arguments of Counsil on both sides and mature deliberation thereon being had, It is Ordered by the Court that the said motion be Over ruled, (and leave given to file exceptions to the Opinion of the Court

– **Tunstall Quarles** Complt
against In Chancery
**John Prather** & Others Deft

This day came the parties by their Counsil, and leave to amend the Bill herein, making **James Montgomery** of Wayne County a Defendant thereto

– The Commonwealth Plt
against upon Presentment
**Ichabud Blacklidge** Deft

This day came as well the attorney for the Commonwealth, as the said Defendant by his attorney, who moved the Court to quash the presentment of the Grandjury herein, for certain defects appearing on the face of it, after hearing the arguments of the Counsil and mature deliberation being thereon had, the Court being divided in Opinion, therefore the motion of the said Defendant [page 503] is overruled, this motion was taken up by the Consent of the attorney for the Commonwealth, as also the Deft

– **Nathaniel Bruce** Plt
against In Trespass Vict armis
**William Hill, George Humphreys, William Humphreys, John Eastham** and **James Alderson** Defts

This day came the parties aforesaid by their attornies, and thereupon came also a Jury, to wit, **Benjamin Harris, Frederick Williams, Andrew Turner, James McMin, Alexander Crawford, Isaac Mayfield** junr, **George Dougherty** junr, **William Mayfield, Smith Williams, John Nailor, William Lynch** & **David Fain** who being elected tried and sworn the truth to speak upon the Issue Joined upon their Oaths do find the Defendants **William Hill, James Alderson** & **John Eastham** guilty of the Trespass &c in the Declaration herein mentioned in manner and form as the Plaintiff against them hath complained, and do assess the Plaintiffs Damages by Occasion thereof to two hundred Dollars besides his Costs. and do find the other Defendants **George Humphreys** & **William Humphreys** not Guilty, Therefore It is considered by the Court that the Plaintiff recover against the said Defendants **William Hill, James Alderson** & **John Eastham**, his Damages aforesaid by the Jurors in their Verdict in form aforesaid assessed. and his Costs by him about his suit in this behalf expended and the said Defendants may be taken and that the Other Defendants, to wit, **George** & **William Humphreys**, go hence and recover their Costs by them about their defence in this behalf expended

– Ordered that **Samuel King** be fined in the sum of two Dollars for a Certain Contempt Offered to this Court, on this present day, when sitting in their Judicial capacity, by making a noise, the said Contempt having taken place within the walls of the Courthouse of Pulaski County, and he the said **King** now here present before the Court, and that he pay costs and may be taken &c.

[page 504] **Henry Willis** Plt
against In Trespass Assault & Battery
**Washington Redmon** Deft

This day came the parties aforesaid in proper person, and on their motion It is ordered that this suit be Dismissed at the Defendants Costs, by Consent, therefore It is Ordered that the Plaintiff recover against the said Defendant his costs by him about his suit in this behalf expended &c.

– Ordered that the Court be adjourned until Tomorrow morning nine OClock

**Christ° Tompkins**

At a Circuit Court Continued and held for the Pulaski Circuit at the Courthouse of Pulaski County in Somerset on Friday the 29th day of July 1809

Present the Honbl **Christopher Tompkins, John Prather,** & **John James** Gent

– **Tunstall Quarles** Complt
against In Chancery
**John Prather, James Montgomery** & Als Defts

This day came the Defendants **Prather** and **Montgomery**, filed their answers and made Oath to the same in Court. And on the motion of the Defendants, and upon the prayer of their [ ] It is Ordered that **John W** & **Abijah Hunt** be made Defts to this suit and by the consent of the parties herein this cause is to be removed to the Garrard Circuit Court Kentucky for further Prosecuting to be had thereon

– **Nathaniel Bruce** Plt
against In Trespass vict armis
**William Hill, James Alderson** & **John Eastham** Defts

[page 505] Be it remembered that upon the trial of this cause and Issue the Jury retired from the barr the plt by his Counsil moved to Court to direct the Jury that they could not sever the

Damages as to the Defendants they found jointly guilty, but the Verdict must be joint, which motion was Opposed by the Defendants Counsel, the Court thereupon read from 2nd Bacons abridgement page (8) the Jury cannot regularly assess several damages for one Trespass with which the Defendants are jointly charged, by the Plaintiffs suit or Declaration, for though in fact one was more malicious, and did greater wrong that the Other, yet all coming to do an unlawful act, the act of one is the act of all the parties present Also from 1st Espenass [?] page 419 & 20, the following passages (In a suit action of Trespass where the Jury find the Defendants jointly guilty, they cannot sever the Damages according to the degrees of guilt: and therefore where in the Common Pleas the Plaintiffs in this action were declared against Jointly, and a Verdict against one for one shilling, and against the Other for forty shillings, and Judgment was entered up Accordingly; is error. brought into the Kings Bench, the Judgment was reversed, as the rule first laid down seems to apply only where the finding is joint, and that the Jury may find them severally Guilty as to part, and not guilty as to part, and assess Damages severally, and directed the Jury that the said Passages was law, and that they were to be Governed accordingly, to which opinion of the Court the Defendants by their Counsil excepts and tenders their Bill of exceptions and prays that the same may be Signed, Sealed and enroled; The Court more over instructed the Jury that they were at liberty if they thought the evidence Justified it, to acquit some of the defendants & find others guilty

**Christopher Tompkins**
**John Prather**

[marginal note] (A) But in Trespass if one Deft is found Guilty at one time and the Other at another time, several Damages may be [ ]

[page 506] **Enoch Fleming** Plt
against In Case
**Hugh Logan** Deft

This day came the parties aforesaid by their attornies, and by their Consent this cause is continued until the next Term of this Court

– **Nathaniel Bruce** Plt
against In Trespass, Assault & Battery
**William Hill** & Others Defts

This day came the parties aforesaid by their attornies, and on motion It is Ordered that this cause be Continued until the next Term of this Court, at the Plaintiffs Costs, and that the Deft recover their costs by them relative to this continuance expended

– **William Griffin** Plt
against In Case
**William Stringer** Deft

Upon this day the Defendant by his attorney, moved the Court to Dismiss this suit, upon the ground that the Plaintiff since the initiation thereof, has removed himself & family out of & from the State of Kentucky which fact of removal the defendant was tending with competent Proof in Court, to establish and Offered the evidence thereof but the Plaintiffs counsil then offered Sufficient security for in the Costs in said suit to which the Counsil of the Defendant Objected, but the Court Overruled the motion to Dismiss the suit upon the Plaintiff giving Security for Cost, to which Opinion of the Court the Defendant by his attorney excepts and prays that this his bill of exception may be Signed & Sealed by the Court

**Christopher Tompkins**
**John Prather**
**John James**

The above exceptions are by the Court Ordered to be entered of Record

[page 507] **Alexander Crawford** Plt
against In Case
**Jesse Williams** Deft

On the motion of the Defendant It is Ordered that the Judgment and Writ of Inquiry awarded against him in the Clerks Office be set a side and the said Defendant by his attorney now comes and defends the wrong and Injury when and where &c and says he is not Guilty in manner and form as the Plaintiff in his Declaration herein against him hath declared, and of this he prays may be enquired of by the Country and the Plaintiff doth the same likewise, Therefore let a Jury come here &c and the Cause is Continued until the next Term of this Court at the Plaintiffs Costs, And the Plea of the Defendant aforesaid to be Considered as the filed at the last Term of this Court, by Consent

– **William Findley** Plt
against In Covenant
**Robertson Burge** Deft

This day came the parties aforesaid by their attornies and thereupon came also a Jury, to wit, **John Jasper, William Walden, Micajah Cooper, John West, John Baker, John Baker, James Gisler, Obediah Denham, Parrish Garner, Drury Clark, John McWhorter** & **James Eastham** who being elected tried and sworn the truth to speak upon the Issue Joined upon their Oaths do say, we of the Jury find for the Plaintiff & assess his Damages by Occasion thereof to One hundred Dollars besides his Costs. It is therefore Considered by the Court that the Plaintiff recover against the said Defendant his Damages aforesaid by the Jurors in their Verdict in form aforesaid assessed and his Costs by him about his suit in this behalf expended and the said Defendant in mercy &c.

[page 508] On the motion of **Samuel Owens** a Constable of Pulaski County who exhibited to this Court an account of Public Services performed by him in the execution of his Office, in the Case Commonwealth against **John Daniel**, which account being examined and Allowed by the Court, a copy of which Order is Ordered to be Certified to the Auditor of Public Accounts Kentucky

– **Michael Weaver** Plt
against In Case
**William Woodson** Deft

This day came the Parties aforesaid by their attornies, and It is Ordered this suit be Dismissed at the Plaintiffs Costs as per a Written Order from the Plaintiff, It is therefore Considered by the Court that the Defendant go hence and recover of the Plaintiff his Costs by him about his defence in this behalf expended

– **James Hardgrove** Plt
against In Debt
**Henry Francis** Deft

The Defendant having entered Special Bail herein Therefore on the motion of the Defendant It is ordered that the Judgment and Writ of Inquiry awarded against him in the Clerks Office be set a side, and the said Defendant by his attorney now comes and defends the wrong and Injury when and where &c and saith he has well and truly paid the Debt in the Declaration mentioned and this he prays may be enquired of by the Country and the Plaintiff doth the same likewise, therefore let a Jury come here &c. Afterward on the motion of the Defendant by his attorney leave is granted him to withdraw his plea herein, and the [page 509] said Defendant says he cannot gainsay the Plaintiffs action against him for one hundred and thirty Dollars the Debt in the Declaration mentioned, therefore with the assent of the plaintiff, It is considered by the Court that the Plaintiff recover against the said Defendant the one hundred and thirty Dollars the Debt in the Declaration mentioned with legal Interest thereon to be computed after the rate of six per centum per annum from the second day of October One thousand eight hundred and eight until paid and Cost and the said Defendant in mercy &c

– **Joseph Herbert** Plt
against In Case
**Jeptha West** Deft

This day came the Plaintiff by his attorney, and on his motion, It is Ordered that this suit be Dismissed

– **Alexander Montgomery** Ass[ee] Plt
against In Covenant
**Joseph Porter** Deft

This day came as well the Plaintiff by his attorney and the said Deft in his proper person who says he cannot gainsay the Plaintiffs action against him for sixty Dollars. therefore with the assent of the Plaintiff It is Considered by the Court that the Plaintiff recover against the said Defendant the sum of sixty Dollars confessed as aforesaid and his Costs by him about his suit in this behalf expended and the said Defendant in mercy &c Note this Judgment is confessed with the reservation of equity, and stay of Execution three months

– **John Newby** Plt
against In Trespass Assault and Battery
**William Hill** Deft

This day came the parties aforesaid by their attornies and thereupon [page 510] came also a Jury, to wit, **George Cooper, Robert Smith, William Camp, W[ ] Camp, John Gibson, James Cooper, Jesse Williams, William Owens, Andrew Cowen, Jacob Blacklidge, Johnson Sargent,** & **Isaac Ingram** who being elected tried and sworn the truth to speak upon the Issue Joined upon their Oaths do find their verdict in these words, we of the Jury find the Deft within mentioned guilty as in the Declaration mentioned and assess the Plaintiffs Damages in consequence thereof to fifteen Dollars besides his Costs. It is therefore considered by the Court that the Plaintiff recover against the said Defendant the Damages aforesaid by the Jurors in their Verdict aforesaid assessed and his Costs by him about his suit in this behalf expended and the said Defendant may be taken &c.

– Ordered that the Court be adjourned until tomorrow morning nine OClock

**Christopher Tompkins**

At a Circuit Court Continued and held for the Pulaski Circuit at the Courthouse of Pulaski County in Somerset on Saturday the 30th day of July 1809

Present the Honbl **Christo Tompkins & John James** Gent

– **William Hill** Assee Plt
against In Covenant
**McGinnis** & **King** Deft

– **Hezekiah Haines** Plt
against In Trespass Assault and Battery
**John Eastham**

Ordered that these suits be continued until the next Term of this Court

[page 511] **Joseph Patterson** Plt
against In Case
**Glover Matthews** & ux Deft

This day came the Plaintiff by his attorney, and It is ordered that this cause be remanded to the Rule docket and an alias capias to Issue against the **Glover Matthews** upon whom it appears the capias has not be executed &c

– Present **John Prather** Gentleman

– **James Beagley** Plt
against In Covenant
**John Smith** Deft

**Jesse Richardson** of Pulaski County came into Court and undertook for the said Deft that if he shall be case in the action aforesaid that he shall satisfy and pay the condemnation of the Court or render his body to Prison in execution for the same, or on falure thereof that he the said **Jesse Richardson** shall do it for him, And the Plaintiff by his attorney this day came, and thereupon came also a Jury, to wit, **Robert Smith, Ichabud Blacklidge, P A Sublette, William Denham, Aaron Lawson, Richard Beam, Johnson Sargent, John Newby, Francis Clear, John Coughron, John Puckett,** & **Vincent Garner**, who were sworn well and truly to enquire what Damages the Plaintiff hath sustained in the premises upon their Oaths do say the Plaintiff hath sustained Damages by Occasion thereof to three hundred and twenty Dollars and twenty five Cents besides his Costs, It is therefore Considered by the Court that the Plaintiff recover against the said Defendant his Damages aforesaid by the Jurors in their Verdict aforesaid in form assessed and his Costs by him about his suit in this behalf expended, and the said Defendant in mercy &c

[page 512] **Micajah Cooper** Plt
against In Trespass vict armis
**James Campbell**

On the motion of the Defendant, It is Ordered that the Judgment and Writ of Inquiry awarded against him in the Clerks Office be set a side, and the said Defendant by his attorney now comes and defends the wrong and Injury when and where &c and says he is not Guilty in manner and form as the Plaintiff in his Declaration herein against him hath declared, and this he prays may be enquired of by the Country and the Plaintiff doth the same likewise, Therefore, It is commanded the Sheriff that he cause to come here Immediately twelve good and lawfull men by whom &c and thereupon came also a Jury, to wit, **Robert Smith, Philip A Sublette, Vincent Garner, Ichabud Blacklidge, John Puckett, William Denham, Aaron Lawson, Richard Beason, Francis Clear, John Evans, Shaderick Harris** & **William Griffin,** who being elected tried and sworn the truth to speak upon the Issue Joined upon their Oaths do find the Deft not Guilty as charged by the Plaintiff in his Declaration herein, It is therefore Considered by the Court that the Plaintiff take nothing by his bill but for his false clamour be in mercy &c and that the Defendant go hence without day and recover against the Plaintiff his costs by him about his defence in this behalf expended

– **James Birney** by Governor Plt
against In Debt
**Nicholas Jasper** Shff &c Deft

[page 513] Be it remembered that after the Jury had returned with their Verdict in this Cause the Pltff by his Counsil moved the Court to set a side said Verdict and grant a new trial upon the ground that the Verdict was contrary to evidence, the Plaintiff to support his cause Introduced a Mortgage executed by **William J Salle** & **Olliver Sallee** to **John** & **James Warren**

[return of the poorer handwriting] This Indenture made and Intered into this 24th day of July in the year 1805 Between **Oliver Sallee** & **William J Sallee** of the one part and **John** [ ] and **James** [ ] of the other part all of the Commonwealth of Kentucky witnesseth that the said **Oliver** and **William** for and in Consideration of the sum of one hundred & eighty six pounds four shillings and four pence to us in hand paid by the said **John** and **James** the receipt whereof is hereby acknowledged have this day ourselves our heirs &c granted bargained & sold allined and Confirmed and by these presents doth grant bargain sell allien and confirm unto the said **John** and **James** their heirs &c two tracts or parcels of ground lying and being in the County of Pulaski and in the town of Somersett containing one half acres each and are known and designated in the plan of said town of Somersett by number thirty five and thirty six, and also 42 acres of land lying and being in the County of Pulaski and bounded as follows, viz, Beginning on the beginning line of **Richard Churchwells** two hundred acre survey at a red oak tree thence down the west fork of Pitmans Creek south 30 East 98 poles to three white oaks thence south 60 W [ ] poles to a walnut and hickory thence with the road leading from Somersett to **Montgomeries** ferry S 24 East 170 poles to the beginning and we the said **Oliver** and **William** doth hereby for ourselves our heirs Executors &c grant bargain sell allien and by these presents doth grant bargain sell allien and confirm unto the said **John** and **James** their heirs &c forever the two lots of ground and the said forty two acres of land together with all and singular the appurtenances and advantages their unto belonging to the said **John** & **James** their heirs assigns Exors [ ] to their only proper use and behoof from us and our heirs and assigns &c for ever and we the said **Oliver** and **William** do hereby for ourselves our heirs Executors &c covenant to and with the said **John** and **James** their heirs assigns &c that we will [ ] [page 514] and forever Defend the afsd two lots of ground and the afsd forty two acres of land with all the appurtenances advantages &c against the claim or Claims of all those Claiming by through or under us our heirs executors &c and against the claim of all persons whatsoever [ ] it is now Clarely to be understood by the presents and by the said **Oliver** & **William** and by the said **John** and **James** that the foregoing deed and conveyance is however subject to the following condition, to wit, that if the said **Oliver** and **William** their heirs executors &c shall well and truly pay unto the said **John** and **James** their heirs executors &c the afsd sum of one hundred and eighty six pounds four shillings and four pence with legal interest thereon from the 23rd day of January 1805 and that on or before the first day of August next insuing the date hereof without fraud or delay there and in that case this Indenture shall void and the foregoing Conveniance shall be of no affect or for either in law or Equity but if the said **Oliver** and **William** shall fail to pay to the said **John & James** or their heirs or certain attorney the aforesaid sum of one hundred and eighty six Pounds four shillings and four pence with legal Interest from the said 23rd day of January 1805 and that on or before the said first day of August next there and in that case the above and foregoing indenture and Conveyance shall be full force and virtue in law and Equity in testimony wherefore the said **Oliver & William Sallee** have hereunto set our hands and affixed our seals the day & year above written

**Oliver Sallee**
**William Sallee**

Kentucky Pulasky Count Sct

I hereby certify that this deed of Mortgage was produced to me as Clerk to the County Court of Pulaski County on the 27th day of July 1805 which was acknowledged by **Oliver Sallee** & **William J Sallee** there to be their act and deed and the same hath been duly recorded in my office

Attest **Will Fox**

[page 515] He also introduced the execution which had issued on the replevin Bond set fourth in the declaration

The Commonwealth of Kentucky to the Sheriff of Pulaski County greeting you are hereby commanded that of the estate of **Wm J Sallee & Oliver Sallee** his security in the replevin bond late of your bailwick you cause to be made the sum of fifty five pounds six shillings which late in the Circuit Court holden for the Pulaski Circuit was adjudged to **James Birney** [ ] also one Dollar and fifty cents for his costs in this behalf expended whereof the said **Sallee** is Convict as appears to us of record and that you have the same before the Judges of the circuit Court aforesaid at the Court house of Pulaski County in Somerset on the second Monday succeeding the fourth Monday in March next to render to the said **James Birney** his Debt and Costs aforesaid and have them their [ ] witness **Will Fox** Clerk of our said Court at the Court house aforesaid the 19th day of February 1806 and in the IXth year of the Commonwealth

**Will Fox**

Memo this Exon is to be Discharged by the payment of thirty one pounds fourteen shillings with legal Interest thereon from the 17th day of September 1805 until paid & Costs & no security to be taken

Attest **Will Fox**

No property Found

**John Daniel** DSPC
For s **Jasper** SPC

The Plaintiff also proved by three witnesses that the said **Oliver Sallee** never resided in the County of Pulaski but that he had been frequently in sd County before and after the date of said replevin bond that a Considerable time previous to the date of sd replevin Bond the said **Oliver** and **William Sallee**, had purchased the property Mortgaged to the [ ] in pardnership that of the [page 516] said property was mortgaged they new of no property which the said **Oliver** possessed except one horse which he had purchased of a Mr **Williams** on [ ] of the value of one hundred Dollars & it was proved that he owned another Horse besides at the same time the Deft produced two witnesses who swore that the said **Oliver Sallee** at the date of the replevin resided in the County of Mercer on Chaplins fork of salt river that he owned at that time and after an ordinary amt of Houshold furnature two horses & the hundred acres of land besides some cattle and hoggs the number of which they did not know but that he generally kept three milk cows neither did they know whether the sd **Oliver Sallee** had the legal title to the land but it was proved that he afterwards sold it [ ] of the witnesses stated that he had heard that he had the legal title that about the same period one of the Defts Witnesses stated that he had heard that the sd **Oliver Sallee** was in Debt one of the Deft Witnesses state that he considered the beforementioned land to be worth $200 and that the other property was worth a greater sum that the amount of the replevin bond This was all the evidence given upon the trial of s[d] Cause but the Court over ruled the motion for a new trial to which opinion of the Court the plaintiff by his Counsil excepts & tinders this his Billl of exceptions & prays that the same may be signed sealed and Enroled.

**Christopher Tompkins**
**John Prather**

[page 517] [Will Fox's hand resumes] **Jesse Richardson** Plt
against In Case
**Aaron Lawson** Deft

On the motion of the Defendant It is Ordered that this suit be continued until the next Term of this Court at the Defendants Costs, therefore on the motion of the Defendant by his attorney leave is given him to take the Deposition of **John Smith** De benessee, also leave is given him to take the Depositions of **Thomas Whitlock, William Finell** & **Samuel Hanly** before a Single Justice of the Peace without the State of Kentucky

–**Samuel McKee** complt
against In Chancery
**John Brown** Deft

– **John Collyer** & **John Preston** Complts
against In Chancery
**John Evans** Deft

– The Commonwealth Plt
against upon Indictment
**John Daniel** Deft

– **Philip A Sublette** by Gov Plt
against In Debt
**Nicholas Jasper** Shff &[c] Defts

[page 518] **Samuel Burton** Plt
against In Case
**William Stringer** Deft

Ordered that this suit be Continued until the next Term of this Court by Consent of Parties

– **Aaron Doss** Plt
against In Covenant
**John Eastham** Deft

This day came the Plaintiff by his attorney, and thereupon came also a Jury, to wit, **Micajah Cooper, Thomas Alexander, William Hays, William Walden, John Gibson, Adonijah Morgan, Johnson Sargent, James Cooper, Thomas Vanhook, Henry Garner, John Coughron** & **Washington Redmon** who were sworn well and truly to enquire what Damages the Plaintiff hath sustained in the premises upon their Oaths do say that the Plaintiff hath sustained Damages by Occasion thereof to eighty eight Dollars besides his Costs. It is therefore Considered by the Court that the Plaintiff recover against the said Defendant his Damages aforesaid by the Jurors in their Verdict in form aforesaid assessed and his Costs by him about his suit in this behalf expended and the said Defendant in mercy &[c].

– **William Stringer** for the benifit of **Tunstall Quarles** Plt
against In Case
**William Griffin** Deft

The Capias [ ] Issued herein being returned by the Officer executed agreeably to an act of the General Assembly Kentucky in such [page 519] cases made and provided, and the said Defendant by his attorney now comes, and defends the wrong and Injury when and where &[c] and says he did not assume upon himself in manner and form as the Plaintiff in his Declaration herein against him hath complained and of this he puts himself upon the Country and the Plaintiff doth the same likewise, Therefore It is Commanded the Sheriff that he cause to come here Immediately twelve good and lawful men by whom &[c] and thereupon came also a Jury, to wit, **Micajah Cooper, Thomas Alexander, William Hays, William Walden, John Gibson, Adonijah Morgan,**

**Johnson Sargent, James Cooper, Thomas Vanhook, Henry Garner, John Coughron**, and **Washington Redmon**, who being elected tried and sworn the truth to speak upon the Issue joined afterwards one of the Jurors by Consent of the Parties, to wit, **Washington Redmon** is withdrawn by the Court and the cause is continued until the next Term of this Court

– **Joseph Patterson** Plt
against In Case
**Grover Matthews** & ux Deft

On the motion of the Plaintiff by his attorney, It is ordered that the Order made at the present Term of this Court remanding this cause to the rule Docket, be set a side and on the motion of the plaintiff this suit is ordered to be Dismissed

[page 520] **Francis Lynch** Plt
against In Trespass Assault & Battery
**Sargent & Taylor** Deft

– **Henry Francis** Plt
against In Case
**John Wood** Deft

Ordered that these suits be Continued until the next Term of this Court by consent

– **Robert Moores** Executrix & Ex^ors Plts
against upon Petition
**James Kincaid** Deft

This day came the Plaintiffs by their attorneys, and the Deft being solemnly called but came Therefore on the motion of the Plt by their attorney Judgment is granted the Plaintiff against the said Defendant for thirty five pounds good and lawful money of Kentucky the Debt in the Petition herein mentioned, with Interest thereon to be computed after the rate of five per centum per annum from the twenty fifth day of December One thousand seven hundred and ninety five until paid & costs.

Note this Judgment is to have credit for nine shillings paid on the twenty eighth day of December One thousand Seven hundred and ninety five Also for fifteen pounds six shillings paid on the 26th day of October One thousand seven hundred and ninety six

– John Doe (ie, **James Thompkins** Plt
against In Ejectment
Richard Roe (~~ie **John Puckett**~~ Deft

It is Ordered by the Court and by the assent of the parties that **John Puckett** be made a Defendant in the place of the now Defendant Richard Roe, and shall Immediately appear to the Plaintiffs action and receive a Declaration in a plea of Trespass and Ejectment of the [page 521] Messuage and lands in question, and Immediately plead thereto not Guilty, and upon the trial of the Issue [ ] lease entry and Ouster and insist upon the Title only, as it is further ordered that if upon the trial of the said Issue a verdict shall be given for the Defendant, and the Plaintiff shall not prosecute his suit upon any other cause, than for not confessing lease entry and Ouster as aforesaid then the lesser of the Plaintiff shall pay Costs if the Plaintiff himself doth not pay them, Whereupon the said Deft comes and defends the force and Injury when and where &c Confesses the lease entry and Ouster in the Declaration supposed, and agrees to Insist upon the title only at the Trial, and he further says, that he is in no wise guilty of Trespass & Ejectment aforesaid, and of this he puteth himself upon the Country, and the Plaintiff likewise therefore It is commanded the Sheriff that he cause to come here Immediately twelve good and lawful men by whom &c and thereupon came also a Jury, to wit, **Edward Cooper, George Williams, Benjamin Harris, Obed Denham, James Campbell, Isaac Muse, Martin True, Hugh Logan, George Allcorn, Henry Francis, Joseph Porter & Isaac Ingram**, who being elected tried and sworn the truth to speak upon the Issue Joined upon their Oaths do find their Verdict in these words, we of the Jury find for the Plaintiff the land in the Declaration mentioned and do assess his Damages thereof to one penny besides his Costs. It is therefore Considered by the Court that the Plaintiff recover against the said Deft his Term yet to come and unexpired of and in the premises in the Declaration mentioned, and his

Damages afs^d by the Jurors in their Verdict aforesaid assessed and his Costs by him about his suit in this behalf expended and the said Deft in mercy &c.

And on the motion [page 522] of the Plaintiff by his attorney the Commonwealth writ of Haberafacias Possessionium be awarded him against the said Deft to cause him to have possession &c

– Ordered that the Court be adjourned until Court in Course

**Christ^o Tompkins**

At a Circuit Court held for Pulaski County at the Courthouse thereof in Somerset on Monday the 23rd day of October 1809

Present the Honourable **Christ^o Tompkins, John Prather & John James** Gentlemen

– A Grandjury was sworn for Pulaski County, to wit, **John McCullough** foreman, **Stephen Tilson, Jeremiah Stone, Andrew Davidson, William Walden, John Baker, Thomas Hail, Andrew Jasper, Daniel Waddle, John Cowen, Asa Dodson, David McKinsey, Thomas Reed, William Griffin, Frederick Kinser, Edward Cooper, Thomas Thompson, Isaac Muse & John Stotts,** who having received their charge retired to consider of their presentments

– The Commonwealth Plt
against upon Indictment
**David Dutton & Marvel Nash** Defts

This day came as well the attorney for the Commonwealth as the said Defendant **David Dutton** by his attorney, who defends the wrong and Injury when and where &c and says the Commonwealth the prosecution ought not to have and maintain because he says on the ___ day of ___ in the Circuit aforesaid he was properly and legally tried before a Justice of the peace and jury and was acquited for the same charge [page 523] set forth in the Indictment by the Justices of the peace, and a Jury and which will appear by a copy of the record now ready to be shown to the Court this he is ready to verify wherefore he prays Judgment &c

**Letcher** for Deft

And the Commonwealth by her attorney **T Quarles** Junr saith that she ought not to be bared from having and maintaining her action against the said Defendant by any thing in their special plea in here pleaded because the Commonwealth saith that the matters and things therein contained are insufficient and neither is she bound by the law of the land, to answer thereto, and this she is ready, wherefore she prays Judgment &c

**Quarles** att^o for Commonwealth

After hearing the arguments of Counsel on both sides, and the matters of law arrising in the Demurer to the Defendants Plea, It seems to the Court that the law is for the Defendant. It is therefore Ordered that the Demurer be Over ruled & that the Defendants plea be sustained, and that he be discharged from further prosecution, And as to the other Defendant **Marvel Nash** who being called came not. It is commanded the sheriff that he cause to come here Immediately twelve good and lawful men by whom &c. to enquire what Damages the Commonwealth has sustained in the premises, and thereupon came a Jury to wit, **Isaac Hays, John Ashley, Thomas Dollihide, Thomas Pascal, Thomas Muse, Richard Walters, Jesse Williams, Amassa Spencer, James Kerr, David Evans, Jesse Evans, & Thomas Smith** upon their Oaths do say we of the Jury do find for the Commonwealth against **Marvel Nash** Seven Dollars and a half as a fine besides Costs It is therefore considered by the Court that the said defendant **Marvel Nash**, do make his fine to the Commonwealth by the payment of $7 ½ the Damages by the Jurors in their Verdict aforesaid assessed, and also the Costs of his Prosecution, and the said **Nash** may be taken &c.

[page 524] **Charles Scott** Governor of Kentucky Plt
against upon a Scifas &c
**Joseph Porter, William Lynch** & others Defts

and the said Defendants by their attorney comes and defends the wrong and Injury when & where &c and craves oyer of the recognizance upon which the writ of scirafacias herein is prosecuted and it is read to them in these words viz, whereupon the said **John Daniel**, Deputy Shff as aforesaid together with **George Allcorn, William Lynch, Joseph Porter, Francis Clear, William J Sallee, James Whitesides, John Jasper, Thomas Simpson**, acknowledged themselves Indebted to **Charles Scott** Esq[r] Governor of this Commonwealth and his Successors that is to say the said **John Daniel** in the sum of $250 and the said **George Allcorn, William Lynch, Joseph Porter, Francis Clear, William J Sallee, James Whitesides, John Jasper** and **Thomas Simpson** in the sums of $31.25 Costs [ ] to be levied of their several and respective lands and tenements goods and chattles to the use of the said Commonwealth, in case the said **John Daniel** shall fail to appear personally before the Circuit Court holden for the Pulaski Circuit at the Courthouse of Pulaski county in the Town of Somerset on the first day of the next Term of this said Circuit Court to be holden in this present Instant, and then and there to answer an Indictment to be pressed to the Grand jury against the said **John Daniel** for the Offense aforesaid, whereof he the said **John Daniel** stands charged, and shall not depart without the leave of said Court, then this recognizance to be Void Otherwise to remain in full force and Virtue in law Acknowled this 17[th] day of April 1809 In presence of the Court

**John Daniel**
**Geo: Allcorn**
**William Lynch**
**Joseph Porter**
**Francis Clear**
**W[m] J Sallee**
**James Whitesides**
**John Jasper**
**Thomas Simpson**

[page 525] And they also crave oyer of the writ of scirafacias and It is read to them in these words, Viz, The Commonwealth of Kentucky to the Sheriff of Pulaski County greeting whereas **George Allcorn, William Lynch, Joseph Porter, Francis Clear, William J Sallee, James Whitesides, John Jasper** & **Thomas Simpson** on the seventeenth day of April One thousand eight hundred and nine, before an examining Court held for the County aforesaid before the three of the Senior Justice of the Peace for said County recognized and acknowledged themselves Indebted to **Charles Scott** Esq[r] Governor of the Commonwealth of Kentucky in the sum of thirty one Dollars and twenty five cents to be levied of their several and respective lands and tenements goods and chattles to the use of the said Commonwealth to be Void on these conditions that **John Daniel**, Deputy sheriff of the County aforesaid charged with forgery, should appear before the Judges of the Pulaski Circuit Court at the Courthouse of the County aforesaid in the Town of Somerset on the first day of their next Term to be holden in the then present Instant, and then and there, answer to an Indictment to be Pressed to the Grandjury against him the said **John Daniel** for the Offence aforesaid and as Specified in said Indictment whereof he the said **John Daniel** stands charged and not to depart from thence without the leave of said Court, and whereas on the fourth Monday in April one thousand eight hundred and nine being the 24[th] day of the said Instant and the first day of the Pulaski Circuit court, to which the said **Daniel** was bound to appear as aforesaid the said **John Daniel** was solemnly called but came not, we therefore command you, that by good and lawful men of your bailiwick you make known to the said **George Allcorn, William Lynch, Joseph Porter, Francis Clear, William J Sallee, James Whitesides, John Jasper** & **Thomas Simpson** that they be and appear before the Honourable the Judges of the Circuit court aforesaid at the Courthouse of the County aforesaid in the Town of Somerset on the first day of their next July Term, to shew cause if any they can why their [page 526] said recognizance shall not be forfeited, and that they make their fine to the Commonwealth agreeable to the Terms of their said recognizance If to them it shall seem expedient to do so, and further to do and receive what ever said Court shall in that part consider, and having then the names of these, by [ ] to them you shall make known, and this writ witness **William Fox** clerk of Our said Court at the Courthouse aforesaid the 20[th] day of May 1809 and in the 17[th] year of the Commonwealth aforesaid

**Will Fox**

and the said recognizance and scirafacias being read and heard the said Defendants say the Plaintiff the Governor his action aforesaid against them ought not to have and maintain because they say the said recognizance and writ of scirafacias and the matters therein contained are not sufficient for the Plaintiffs aforesaid action aforesaid to have and maintain neither are they bound by the law of the land in any manner to answer thereto and this they are ready to verify wherefore they pray Judgment &c

**Tho: Montgomery** Att° for Deft

And the Plaintiff says that the recognizance & writ aforesaid are good and sufficient in the law for the Plaintiff aforesaid his action aforesaid to have and maintain all of which [ ] the Plaintiff is ready to verify whereupon & because the Defendants have wholly to receive such Verifications or make answer thereto the Plaintiff prays Judgment &c

**T Quarles** att° for Pltff

– The Commonwealth Plt
against upon Presentment
**Ichabud Blacklidge** Deft

This day came as well the attorney for the Commonwealth, as the said Defendant by his attorney, and being fully heard It is Considered by the Court that the said Defendant do make his fine with the Commonwealth by the payment of ten shillings, for two profane Oaths, and also the [page 527] Costs of this prosecution and may be taken &c.

– **Hezekiah Haines** Plt
against In Trespass Assault & Battery
**John Eastham** Deft

This day came the Parties aforesaid, and by their consent, It is Ordered that this suit be Dismissed at the Defendants Costs

– **Robertson Burge** Plt
against In Case
**David Clark** Deft

This day came the parties aforesaid by their attornies, and thereupon came also a Jury, to wit, **James Noflet, Aaron Vanhook, Edward White, Thomas Nedry, James Ashbrook, William Blair, Adam Morris, Robert Smith, David Puckett, Begley Hart, Hansford Price, & John Waddle** who being elected tried and sworn the truth to speak upon the Issue Joined, afterwards the Defendant by his attorney moved the Court to direct the Jury to find as in case of a non suit which motion after hearing the arguments of Counsel was sustained in part, and the Jurors upon their Oaths do say that the said Defendant is not Guilty in manner and form as the plaintiff in his Declaration herein against him hath Declared. It is therefore Considered by the Court that the plaintiff take nothing by his bill but for his false clamor be in mercy &c and that the Defendant go hence without day and recover against the Plaintiff his Costs by him about his defence in this behalf expended

– The Grandjury returned into Court and Indictment the Commonwealth against **John McWhorter** a true Bill

**John McCullough** foreman of the Grand jury

[page 528] Also an Indictment The Commonwealth against **Jonathan Addison** a true Bill

**John McCullough** foreman of the Grand jury

Also made the following Presentments, The Commonwealth of Kentucky Pulaski County Circuit & Sct The Grand Jurors Good and lawful men of the body of Pulaski County and Circuit aforesaid in the name and by the authority of the Commonwealth of Kentucky upon their Oaths present **George Rayburn** labourer, of the County and circuit aforesaid for [ ] swearing three Oaths in the following words by God at the plantation of **David Waddle**, in the County aforesaid and within the Jurisdiction of the Pulaski Circuit and on the twentieth day of October in the year of Our lord, One thousand eight hundred and nine Contrary to the statute in that case made and provided and against the peace and dignity of the Commonwealth of Kentucky upon the information of **Daniel Waddle**, and **John Cowen**, both of the Grand jury, and residents of Pulaski County

**John McCullough** foreman of the Grand jury

– The Commonwealth Plt
against
**John McWhorter** Deft

The Defendant who stands bound by a recognizance to appear here before the judges of this Court, on the first day of the Present Term failed to appear according to the conditions of his said recognizance, tho solemnly called

– The Commonwealth
against
**Jonathan Addison**

Same Order

[page 529] **Benjamin Sloane** Plt
against In Covenant
**John Gwin** Deft

The Defendant having entered special Bail herein, Therefore on his motion It is Ordered that the Judgment and writ of Inquiry awarded against him in the Clerks Office be set aside and the said Defendant by his Attorney now comes and defends the wrong and Injury when and where &c and says the Plaintiff his action aforesaid against him ought not to have and maintain because he says he has well and truly kept and performed the several Covenants in the writing mentioned on his part and this he is ready to verify, wherefore he prays Judgment &c. And the Plaintiff by his attorney says he Ought not to bared or precluded from having and maintaining his action aforesaid against the Defendant aforesaid for any thing in the Defendants plea above pleaded because he says the said Defendant hath not well and truly kept and performed the Several covenants in the writing mentioned on his part as in pleading he had alledged, and this he prays may be enquired of by the Country and the Defendant doth likewise, and leave to give special matter in evidence as per written agreement, Therefore It is commanded the sheriff that he cause to come here Immediately twelve good and lawful men by whom &c and thereupon came also a Jury, to wit, **Hugh Chambers, Thomas Dollihide, Thomas Pascal, Richard Walters, David Dutton, Jeremiah Boone, Andrew Keller, James Philips, Samuel Meek, William Boyd, Henry James** & **Stephen Condry** who being elected tried and sworn the truth to speak upon the Issue Joined upon their Oaths do say that the said Defendant has not well and truly kept and performed the several Covenants in the writing mentioned on his part as in pleading he hath alledged, but hath broken the same in manner and form as the Plaintiff in his Declaration herein against him has Declared [page 530] and they do assess the Plaintiffs Damages Inconsequence thereof to two hundred Dollars besides his Costs It is therefore Considered by the Court that the Plaintiff recover against the said Defendant his Damages aforesaid by the Jurors in their Verdict aforesaid in form aforesaid assessed and his Costs by him about his suit in this behalf expended and the said Defendant in mercy &c.

– **Jesse Wauldridge** Assce Plt
against In Covenant
**James Philips** Deft

**Samuel Meek** of Pulaski County came into Court (and Justified) and undertook for the said Defendant that if he shall be cast in the action aforesaid that he shall satisfy and pay the condemnation of the Court or render his body to prison in execution for the same or on falure thereof that he the said **Samuel Meek** shall do it for him

– Ordered that the Court be adjourned until Tomorrow morning nine OClock

**Christopher Tompkins**

At a Circuit Court Continued and held for the Pulaski Circuit at the Courthouse of Pulaski County in Somerset on Tuesday the 24th day of October 1809

Present the Honbl **Christo Tompkins** Gent

– **Charles Scott**, Governor of Kentucky Plt
vs upon a writ of Scire facias

**Joseph Porter**, **William Lynch** & others Defts

This day came the parties aforesaid by their attornies when the arguments of the Counsel on the matters of law arrising on the Demurer of [page 531] the Defendants to the recognizance & Writ of Scira Facias herein were heard, and on due consideration being had it is the opinion of the Court that the recognizance herein is void & that the law is consequently for the Defts Therefore it is considered by the Court that the Pltff take nothing by his writ & recognizance and that the Defendants go thereof without day

– Present **John Prather** Esq[r]

– **Justis** & **Galy** Plt
against In Debt
**James Anderson** Deft

This day Came the Parties aforesaid by their attornies, and by their consent this Cause is continued until the next Term of this Court

– **Philip A Sublette**, by Governor Plt
against In Debt
**Nicholas Jasper** Shff &[c] Deft

This day came the parties aforesaid by their attornies, and It is Ordered that this suit be Continued until the next Term of this court at the Defendants costs

– **Thomas Hutchings** Ex[ors] Plt
against In Covenant
**Charles Collyer** Deft

This day came the parties aforesaid by their attornies, and It is Ordered that this suit be continued until the next Term of this Court at the Plaintiffs Costs

– **Absolom Taylor** Plt
against In Case
**Shaderick Price** Deft

This day came the Plaintiff by his attorney, and the Defendant being Called but came not, therefore It is Commanded the Sheriff [page 532] that he cause to come here Immediately twelve good and lawful men by whom &[c] and thereupon came also a Jury, to wit, **Thomas Whites, Amasa Spencer, James Kerr, Nathaniel Brown, Martin True, William Zachary, Andrew Kellar, George Mc[ ], Thomas Barlow, William Hunt, Enoch H[ ]** & **James Eastham** who were sworn well and truly to enquire what Damages the Plaintiff hath sustained in the Premises upon their Oaths do say that the plaintiff hath sustained in the premises upon their Oaths do say that the Plaintiff hath sustained Damage by Occasion thereof to one cent besides his Costs It is therefore Considered by the Court that the Plaintiff recover against the said Defendant his Damages aforesaid by the Jurors in their Verdict aforesaid assessed and his Costs by him about his suit in this behalf expended and the said Deft in mercy &[c]

– **Samuel Clark** Plt
against In Case
**Martin Barrier** Deft

The Plaintiff being Called but came not made default therefore his suit not further prosecuted

– **David Walker** Plt
against In Trespass Assault & Battery
**Samuel Devore**

Same Order

– **Jesse Chapple** Plt
against In Case
**William Lynch** Deft

Same Order

– **Samuel Benton** Plt
against In Case

**William Stringer** Deft
[page 533] Same Order
– **George Lankford** Plt
against In Case
**John Daniel** Deft

This day came the Parties aforesaid by their attornies, and by consent this Cause is continued until the next Term of this Court at the Plaintiffs cost

– **Nathaniel Forbis** Plt
against In Case
**John Simpson** Deft

This day came the Parties aforesaid by their attornies and by Consent this Cause is Continued until the next Term of this Court

– **Samuel Dennis** Plt
against In Covenant
**James Anderson** Deft

**Joseph Porter** of Pulaski County came into Court and undertook for the said Defendant that if he shall be cast in the action aforesaid that he shall satisfy and pay the condemnation of the Court or render his body to Prison in execution for the same or on falure thereof that he the said **Joseph Porter** shall do it for him, and It is Ordered that the Judgment and writ of Inquiry awarded against the said Deft in the Clerks Office be set a side, and the said Defendant by his attorney now comes and defends the wrong and Injury when and where &c and says that he has well and truly kept and performed the several covenants in the writing mentioned on his part & of this he prays may be enquired of by the Country and the pltff likewise therefore let a Jury come here &c And the right of trial being [page 534] waved It is ordered that this cause be Continued until the next Term of this Court

– **Stephen Mayfield** Plt
against In Case
**Stephen Condry**

This day came the parties aforesaid by their attornies, and the Plaintiff being called came not but made default Therefore neither is his suit further Prosecuted, And on the motion of the Deft by his attorney It is considered by the Court that he recover against the Plaintiff one hundred and fifty pounds of Tob° agreeably to an Act of the General Assembly Kentucky in such cases made and provided and that the Defendant recover against the Plaintiff his Costs by him about this defence in this behalf expended

– **Joseph Casky** Plt
against In Case
**John January** Deft

This day came the parties aforesaid by their attornies, and It is Ordered that this Cause be Continued until the next Term of this Court at the Plaintiffs Costs. And on the motion of the Plaintiff by his attorney a Commission is a warded him to take Depositions Generally without the State of Kentucky before a single Justice of the Peace

– **James Kincaid** Plt
vs In Ejectment
**Charles Collyer** Deft
– The Same Plt
vs Same
**Moses Cunningham** Deft
[page 535] **James Kincaid** Plt
vs In Ejectment
**Joseph Camp** Deft
– The Same Plt
vs Same

**Samuel Elder** Deft
– The Same Plt
vs Same
**Borter Garrett** Deft
– The Same Plt
vs Same
**Zachariah Denny** Deft
– The Same Plt
vs Same
**John Collyer** Deft
– The Same Plt
vs Same
**John McCullough** Deft

This day came the parties aforesaid by their attornies, and by their consent, their Causes are continued until the next Term of this court and by Consent leave given to take Depositions Generally, to be had in chief, and leave to amend the Survey by Complainant, by laying down any other Object that he may deem necessary

– **Enoch Fleming** Plt
against In Case
**Hugh Logan** Deft

On the motion of the Deft It is Ordered that the Judment [page 536] and writ of Inquiry awarded against him in the Clerks Office be set a side and the said Defendant by his attorney now comes and defends the wrong and Injury when and where &c and says he did not assume upon himself in manner and form as the Plaintiff in his Declaration herein against him has complained and of this he prays may be enquired of by the Country, and the Plaintiff doth the same likewise, therefore let a Jury come here &c and the cause is continued until the next Term of this Court at the defendants Costs

– **Nathaniel Bruce** Plt
vs In Trespass Assault & Battery
**William Hill** & Others Defts

Ordered that this suit be Continued until the next Term of this Court at the Plaintiffs costs

– **Alexander Crawford** Plt
against In Case
**Jesse Williams**

This day came the parties aforesaid by their attornies, and thereupon came also a Jury, to wit, **James Taylor, John Fitzpatrick, Richard Walter, Jeremiah Boone, Marvel Nash, Richard Blacklidge, Edward White, Absolem Dodson, Aaron Harris, John Mayfield, James Griffin** and **John Gragg**, who being elected tried and sworn the truth to speak upon the Issue Joined upon their Oaths do say that the said Defendant is not Guilty in manner and form as the Plaintiff in his Declaration herein hath Declared. It is therefore considered by the court that the Plaintiff take nothing by his bill but for his false clamour be in mercy &c and that the Defendant go hence without day & recover of the Plaintiff his Costs by him about his defence in this behalf expended

[page 537] Present **John James** Esqr

– **William Hill** Assee Plt
vs In Covenant
**McGinnis & King** Defts

**Robert Smith**, of Pulaski County, came into Court and justified and undertook for the said Defendants that if they shall be cast in the actions aforesaid that they shall satisfy and pay the condemnation of the Court or render their bodies to prison in execution for the same or on falure thereof that he the said **Robert Smith** shall do it for them, and the said Defendants by their attorney come and defend the wrong & Injury when and where &c and crave oyer of the writing Obligatory in the Declaration mentioned, which being seen and to them read they say that the

Plaintiff his action aforesaid against them ought not to have or maintain because they say that a certain **Robert Smith** sued out an attachment against the Estate of the said **Thomas Mayfield** the Obligee of said note for the sum of eight Dollars and sixty three cents which attachment was Obtained from a certain **Joseph Erwine**, a Justice of the Peace for the County of Pulaski who had full power and authority to Issue the same and which process required these Defendants to be Summoned as Garnishees to answer how much they owed to the said **Thomas Mayfield** which process being served on these Defendants and they appearing before the said **Joseph Erwin** Justice as aforesaid upon the day upon which they were summoned to appear and having at that time no notice of said Writing Obligatory in the Declaration mentioned being assigned to the pltff or any one else they did upon Oath answer and say that they owed the said **Thomas Mayfield** the thirty five Dollars in Cattle as in said Writing Obligatory Set forth whereupon the said **Joseph Erwine** Justice of the Peace for the County of Pulaski [page 538] as aforesaid and who was holding pleas of and concerning the attachment aforesaid entered Judgment in favour of the said **Smith** against the said **Mayfield** for the sum of $8..63 and one Dollar and twenty five Cents Costs and did thereupon Condemn in the hands of these Defendants the aforesaid $35 in Cattle, and ordered **Lambert White**, Constable of Pulaski County to make sale of the same, or so much thereof as would be Sufficient to satisfy the Judgment and Costs aforesaid, and the said **White**, Constable as aforesaid In pursuance of said Judgment and Order of sale did receive the thirty five Dollars in Cattle which is contained in said writing obligatory in the Declaration mentioned, and so sell the same in satisfaction of the Judgment and costs aforesaid and this they are ready to verify wherefore they pray Judgment &c

**Sam[l] Davis** att[o] for Deft

And the Plaintiff by his attorney saith that his action aforesaid against the Defendants, he ought not to be bar from having and maintaining because he saith that the plea of the Deft aforesaid is not sufficient in law to bar the said Plaintiff of his action aforesaid wherefore the said Plaintiff prays Judgment of the plea &c

**R Garth** for Pltff

And the said Defendants by their attorney saith that the Plaintiff his action aforesaid against them ought not to have and maintain because they say their plea as above pleaded is sufficient in law to bar the plaintiffs of his action aforesaid against them wherefore they pray Judgment &c

**S Davis** for Deft

The Plaintiffs Demurer to the Deft plea being argued the Court took time

[page 539] **Jesse Richardson** Plt
vs In Case
**Aaron Lawson** Deft

This day came the parties aforesaid by their attornies, and the said Defendant by his attorney moved the Court to discharge the appearance bail taken herein, after hearing the arguments of Counsil on both sides and mature deliberation thereon being had It ordered by the Court that the said motion be Over ruled, Be It remembered that a motion was made to the Court to discharge the appearance bail upon the Grounds that no Affidavit in writing was filed at the time of the Ordering bail in this cause but the Court refused to discharge the bail to which opinion of the Court the Defendant by his counsil excepts and tenders this his bill of exceptions, and prays that the same by be Signed Sealed and enroled

**Christopher Tompkins**
**John Prather**
**John James**

**Andrew Evans**, of Pulaski County came into Court and undertook for the said Defendant that if he shall be cast in the action aforesaid that he shall satisfy and pay the condemnation of the Court or render his body to prison in execution for the same or on falure thereof that he the said **Andrew Evans** shall do it for him, On the motion of the said Defendant It is ordered that the Judgment and Writ of Inquiry awarded against him in the Clerks Office be set a side, And the Defendant comes & defends the wrong and Injury when &c and says that the plaintiff afs[d] his action aforesaid thereof against him Ought not to have and maintain because he says that the said Declaration & the matters and things in the same Contained are not sufficient in law for the said Plaintiff to have and maintain his said actions therein, neither is he bound by the law of the land in any manner to answer thereto, whereupon for [ ] of a sufficient Declaration in this behalf he prays Judgment &c

**Davis & Taul** for Deft

[page 540] And the said Plaintiff by his attorney says he ought not to be bared from having & maintaining his said action against the Defendant because he says that his said Declaration and the matters and things therein contained are sufficient in law: whereupon he prays Judgment of the Demurer &c

**Owsley** and **Logan** for Pltff

– **Samuel McKee** Complt
vs In Chancery
**John Brown** Deft
– **Andrew Cowen** Complt
vs Same
**Tunstall Quarles** Deft

This day came the Parties aforesaid by their attornies, and by their consent It is Ordered that these causes be continued until the next Term of this Court

– The Grandjury again returned into Court the following presentments, to wit,

[second hand] The Commonwealth of Kentucky Pulaski County and Circuit Sct

The Grand Jurors good and lawfull men composed of the body of the County of Pulaski and Circuit aforesaid In the name and by the authority of the Commonwealth of Kentucky upon their Oths present **John Griffin** labourer for profanely swearing an oath in the following words, to wit, I will be God damed on the twenty third day of October in the year of our lord one thousand Eight hundred and nine in the town of Somerset in the County of Pulaski and within the Jurisdiction of the Pulaski Circuit Court Contrary to the form of the Statute in that case made and provided and against the peace and dignity of the Commonwealth of Kentucky upon the information of **Daniel Waddle** and **Isaac Muse** both of the grand Jury & residents of Pulaski County

**John McCullough** foreman of the grand Jury

[page 541] The Commonwealth of Kentucky Pulaski County and Circuit Sct

The Grand Jurors good and Lawful men composed of the body of the County of Pulaski & Circuit aforesaid in the name and by the authority of the Commonwealth of Kentucky upon their oath present **Andrew Russel** laborer **Willis Embray** laborer of the County and Circuit aforesaid for unlawfully gambling at cards at the house of **Vincent Garner** in the town of Somerset in the County of Pulaski and within the Jurisdiction of the Pulaski Circuit on the twenty third day of October in the year of our Lord one thousand eight hundred and nine Contrary to the Statute in that case made & provided and against the peace and dignity of the Commonwealth of Kentucky upon the information of **William Boyd** a resident of Pulaski County and not one of the Grand Jury

**John McCullough** foreman of the Grand Jury

The Commonwealth of Kentucky Pulaski County and Circuit Sct

The Grand Jury Good and lawful men Composed of the body of the County of Pulaski and Circuit aforesaid in the name & by the authority of the Commonwealth of Kentucky upon their Oaths present **William Burton** laborer of the County of Pulaski for retailing spiritous liquor, to wit, one pint of Brandy on the twenty third day of October in the year of our lord, one thousand eight hundred and nine in the Town of Somerset in the County of Pulaski and within the Jurisdiction of the Pulaski Circuit Court Contrary to the statute in that Case made and [page 542] provided & against the peace and dignity of the Commonwealth of Kentucky upon the information of **Isaac Muse** & **Andrew Davidson** both of the Grand Jury and residents of Pulaski County

**John McCullough** foreman of the Grand Jury

[Will Fox's hand resumes] The Grand jury having nothing further to present were discharged by the Court, and Delinquents Ordered to be Summoned

– Ordered that the Court be adjourned until tomorrow morning nine OClock

At a Circuit Court Continued and held for the Pulaski Circuit at the Courthouse of the County of Pulaski in Somerset on Wednesday the 25th day of October 1809

Present the Honorable **Christ° Tompkins, John James, & John Prather** Gent

– The Commonwealth Plt
vs upon an Indictment
**Marvel Nash** Deft

This day came as well the attorney for the Commonwealth as the said Defendant by his attorney, who comes and says that Judgment in the Verdict of the Jury herein ought to be stayed and arrested for the following causes, Viz, 1st Because there is no prosecutor set down at the foot of the Indictment [page 543] 2nd Because the Defendant was not present at the trial of the Indictment, 3rd Because the said Defendant was not served with legal process to compell his appearnce

**Tho: Montgomery** Att° for Deft

After hearing the arguments of counsils, Errors adjudged good and ordered to be sustained by the Court, and that the Defendant go hence &c

– **Jesse Richardson** Plt
vs In Case
**Aaron Lawson** Deft

This day came the parties aforesaid by their attornies, when the arguments of Counsil on the matters of law arrising on the Defendants Demurer to the Plaintiffs Declaration were heard, and mature deliberation thereon being had It is Considered by the Court that the said Demurer be overruled, Therefore on the motion of the Defendant by his attorney leave is given him to withdraw his said Demurer. And the Deft having entered special bail herein on his motion It is Ordered that the Judgment and writ of Inquiry awarded against him in the Clerks Office be set a side and the said Deft by his attorney now comes and defends the wrong and Injury where and where, and says he is not Guilty in manner and form as the plaintiff in his Declaration herein against him has declared and this he prays may be enquired of by the Country and the Plaintiff doth the same likewise, and the Deft for further plea herein says the Plaintiff his action aforesaid against him Ought not to have and maintain because he says that he was justifiable in Imposing the charges in the Declaration mentioned in as much as the charges said in the Declaration to have been made by the Deft on the Pltff &c are true and not false & this he is ready to verify: wherefore he prays Judgment & &c

**Davis & Taul** for Deft

[page 544] The Plaintiff by his attorney says he ought not to be bared or precluded from having and maintaining his action aforesaid by reason of any thing in the plea of the Deft last pleaded because he says that the charges Imposed upon the Plaintiff by the Defendant as stated in the Declaration is not true, and this the Plaintiff prays may be enquired of by the Country

**Logan & Owsley** for Pltff

And the Defendant likewise, And on the motion of the Deft by his attorney It is Ordered that this suit be continued until the next Term of this Court at his the said Defendants Costs

– **Isaac Anderson** Plt
vs In Debt
**Ann Anderson** Deft

**Thomas Vanhook** of Pulaski County came into Court and undertook for the said Defendant that if she shall be cast in the action aforesaid that he shall satisfy and pay the condemnation of the Court or render her body to prison in execution for the same or on falure thereof that he the said **Thomas Vanhook** shall do it for her, and on motion It is Ordered that the Judgment awarded against the said Defendant in the clerks Office be set a side and the said Deft by her attorney now comes and defends the wrong and Injury when and where &c and says that she has well and truly paid the Debt in the Declaration mentioned and this she prays may be enquired of by the Country and the Plaintiff likewise, therefore let a Jury come here &c and the right of trial being waved, It is ordered that the cause be continued until the next Term of this Court, And it is Ordered

that the Plaintiff give security for Costs herein before the next Term of this Court, or on failing so to do his suit will be dismissed It appearing to the Court that the Pltff is not a resident of Kentucky
[page 545] **Jacob Vanhorner** Plt
vs In Case
**Douglas Sinclear** Deft

This day came as well the Plaintiff by his attorney, as the said Deft in his proper person, and by Consent this suit is ordered to be dismissed at the Deft Costs

– **William Hill** Ass[ee]
vs In Covenant
**McGinnis** & **King** Defts

This day came the parties aforesaid by their attornies, and It is Ordered that this suit be continued until the next Term of this Court

**John Thurmon** Plt
vs upon Petition
**Joseph Erwine** Deft

and the Defendant comes and defends the wrong and Injury where and when &[c] and craves Oyer of the petition and the writing Obligatory recited therein which are read to him in the following words, Know all &[c] and saith the Plaintiff his action against him Ought not to have because he says that the writing Obligatory aforesaid was executed for and Inconsequence of the purchase of a tract of land lying in the County of Pulaski containing 200 acres and that the plaintiff shewed him a certain boundary within the limits of which a large quantity of land laid, to wit, ___ acres of a good quality and possessing advantages of being level with timber and &[c] alledging that it was within the aforesaid tract of land of 200 acres when in truth it was entirely out of the boundary aforesaid of 200 a[s] and this he is ready to verify and the Defendant avers that the land shewed to the Defendant lying without the boundary of the aforesaid 200 acres Induced him to execute the writing Obligatory afores[d] wherefore he prays [page 546] Judgement &[c]

**Quarles** P Defendant

And the Plaintiff by his attorney says he ought not to be bared or precluded from having and maintaining his action aforesaid by reason of any thing in the plea of the Deft pleaded because he says he did not show to the Defendant different land than that sold by the Plaintiff to the Deft as the Consideration of the note in the Petition mentioned and this he prays may be enquired of by the Country

**Owsley** for Pltff

And the Defendant likewise, therefore It is commanded the Sheriff that he cause to come here Immediately twelve good and lawful men by whom &[c] and thereupon came also a Jury, to wit, **George Modrel, Aaron Sargent, Richard Walter, Drewry Clark, William Sinclear** [?], **James Griffin, William Zachary, Stephen Feilds, Thomas Vanhook, Samuel Owens, William Griffin** & **John Dick** who being elected tried and sworn the truth to speak upon the Issue Joined upon their Oaths returned their Verdict in these words, to wit, we of the Jury find for the Plaintiff the Debt in the Petition mentioned and one cent in Damages besides his Costs It is therefore Considered by the Court that the Plaintiff recover against the said Defendant one hundred pounds the Debt in the Petition aforesaid mentioned with legal Interest thereupon from the first day of December 1805 until paid together with his Damages aforesaid by the Jurors in their Verdict aforesaid assessed and his Costs by him about his suit in this behalf expended and the said Deft in mercy &[c] Note this Judgment is to have credit for One hundred dollars paid on the 27[th] day of February 1807 Also for four Dollars paid on the 11[th] day of February 1808 as p[r] Credits given the back of the note
[page 547] **William Stringer** for **Quarles** Plt
vs In Case
**William Griffin** Deft

On the motion of the Plaintiff by his attorney It is ordered that this Cause be Continued until the next Term of this Court at the Plaintiffs Costs

– **Francis Lynch** Plt

vs In Trespass Assault & Battery
**Taylor** & **Sargent** Deft

By Consent this Cause is Continued until the next Term of this Court at the Defendants Costs

– **Henry Francis** Plt
vs In Case
**John Wood** Deft

This day came the Plaintiff by his attorney, and the Defendant being solemnly called came not, therefore on the motion of the Plaintiff by his attorney It is Ordered that the Sheriff cause to come here Immediately twelve good and lawful men by whom &c and thereupon came a Jury, to wit, **George Modrel, Aaron Sargent, Richard Walters, Drewry Clark, Stephen Fields, William Sinclear, Samuel Owens, Henry Farmer, John Fitzpatrick, James Price, Thomas Vanhook** & **John Dick** who were sworn well and truly to enquire what damage the plaintiff hath sustained in the premises upon their Oaths do say that the Pltff hath sustained Damage by Occasion thereof to $308 besides his Costs It is therefore Considered by the Court that the Plaintiff recover against the said Defendant his Damages aforesaid by the Jurors in their Verdict aforesaid assessed and his Costs by him [page 548] about his suit in this behalf expended and the said Defendant may be taken &c

– **Alexander** & **William Porter** Plts
vs
**William Hays** Deft

On Motion It is Ordered that this suit be continued until the next Term of this Court

– **Jesse Wouldridge** Assee Plt
vs In Covenant
**James Philips** Deft

This day came the Plaintiff by his attorney and the Deft being called but came not, therefore on the motion of the Plaintiff by his attorney It is Commanded the Sheriff that he cause to come here Immediately twelve good and lawful men by whom &c and thereupon came also a Jury, to wit, **Stephen Richardson, John Westerman, Thomas Reed, Thomas Hail, David Puckett, Isaac Muse, William Cooper, William Griffin, George Humphreys, Samuel Hendricks, Nathan Meek** & **William Blair** who were sworn well and truly to enquire what Damage the Plaintiff hath sustained in the premises upon their Oaths do find their Verdict in these words, to wit, we of the Jury find for the Plaintiff seventeen pounds in Damages It is therefore Considered by the Court that the Plaintiff recover of the said Deft his Damages aforesaid by the Jurors in their Verdict aforesaid assessed and his costs by him about his suit in this behalf expended and the said Defendant in mercy &c

[page 549] **James Clark** Plt
vs In Case
**David Evans** & ux Defts

On the motion of the Defendant It is ordered that the Judgment and writ of Inquiry awarded against them in the Clerks Office be set a side and the said Defendants by their attorney now Comes and defends the wrong and Injury when and where &c and say that they are not Guilty in manner and form as the Plaintiff against them hath Declared and this they pray may be enquired of by the Country and the Plaintiff doth the same likewise, therefore let a Jury come here &c and the right of Trial being waved It is Ordered that this Cause be continued until the next Term of this Court Note leave to give special matter in evidence

– **William Spears** Plt
vs In Covenant
**Amassa Spencer** Deft

Ordered that this suit be continued until the next Court

– **Jeremiah Stone** Pltff
vs In Case
**Thomas Nedry** Deft

On the motion of the Defendant It is Ordered that [page 550] the Judgment and writ of Inquiry awarded against him in the Clerks Office be set a side and the said Defendant by his attorney now comes and defends the wrong and Injury when and where &c and says he did not assume upon himself in manner and form as the Plaintiff in his Declaration herein hath Declared and of this he prays may be enquired of by the Country and the Plaintiff likewise therefore let a Jury come here &c and the right of trial being waved It is Ordered that this cause be Continued until the next Term of this Court

– **William Hird** by Gov Plt
vs In Debt
**Samuel Owens** & ux Deft

This day came the parties aforesaid by their attornies and on the motion of the Plaintiff by his attorney it Ordered that this suit be remanded to the Rules and leave to amend Decn

– **William Spears** Plt
vs In Covenant
**Amassa Spencer** Deft

**Nathan Meek** of Pulaski County came into Court and Justified and undertook for the said Defendant that if he shall be cast in the action [page 551] aforesaid that he shall satisfy and pay the condemnation of the Court or render his body to prison in execution for the same or on falure thereof that he the said **Nathan** shall do it for him

– The Governor for **Belsha** Plt
vs In Debt
**Bazil Meek** Shff Deft

This day came the Plaintiff by his attorney and thereupon came a Jury, to wit, **George Humphreys, Thomas Hansford, David Puckett, Jeremiah Stone, John Evans, Amassa Spencer, William Cooper, William Owens, David Evans, Hugh Logan, Drewry Clark & John McCullough** who were sworn well and truly to enquire what Damage the Plaintiff hath sustained in the premises upon their Oaths returned their Verdict in these words, to wit, We of the Jury find for the Plaintiff the Debt in the Declaration mentioned to be discharged so far as relates to the Interest of **Zachariah Belsha**, by the payment of £23..8 in Damages besides his Costs, It is therefore Considered by the Court that the Plaintiff recover against the said Deft his Damages aforesaid by the Jurors in their Verdict aforesaid assessed and his Costs by him about his suit in [page 552] this behalf expended and the said Deft in mercy &c

– **John Northrip** Plt
vs In Covenant
**Andrew Russell** Deft

This day came the plaintiff by his attorney and the Deft being called came not Therefore on the motion of the Plaintiff by his attorney It is Commanded the Sheriff that he cause to come here Immediately twelve good and lawful men by whom &c and thereupon came a Jury, to wit, same Jury as in the case **Belsha** by Governor against **Meek** Shff) who being elected tried and sworn well and truly to enquire what Damage the Plaintiff hath sustained in the premises upon their Oaths do say that the Plaintiff has sustained Damage by Occasion thereof to twenty Dollars besides his Costs. It is therefore Considered by the Court that the Plaintiff recover against the said Defendant his damages afsd by the Jurors in their Verdict aforesaid assessed & his Costs by him about his suit in this behalf expended and the said Deft in mercy &c

[page 553] **Washington Redmon** Plt
vs In Case
**Tunstall Quarles** Deft

On the motion of the Defendant It is Ordered that the Judgment and writ of Inquiry awarded against him in the Clerks Office be set a side, and the said Deft by his attorney comes and defends the wrong and Injury when and where &c and says the Plaintiff his action aforesaid against him Ought not to have and maintain because he says he is not Guilty of speaking the slanderous words in the Declaration mentioned, and of this he puteth himself upon the Country and the

Plaintiff likewise

**Montgomery** for Pltff

And the said Deft for further plea in this behalf saith confessing the speaking the word in the Declaration charged, the Pltff his action aforesaid against him Ought not to have and maintain because he says the said Pltff did commit wilfull & corrupt Perjury in the County of Pulaski when giving evidence on the trial of an action of Trespass assault and battery in this Circuit Court for the County aforesaid between **John Newby** Pltff and **William Hill** Deft in a point material in the Issue between the parties aforesaid [page 554] in the Action Aforesaid and this he is ready to verify wherefore he prays Judgment &c

**Montgomery** Atto for the Pltff

And the Pltff by his attorney says he ought not to be bared from having & maintaining his action aforesaid by any thing in the sd plea of the Deft above pleaded because he says the did not commit wilfull & corrupt perjury as in the said plea mentioned and this he prays may be enquired of by the Country

**Davis** for Pltff
**Montgomery** for Deft

Therefore It is Commanded the sheriff that he cause to come here Immediately twelve good and lawful men by whom &c and thereupon came also a Jury, to wit, **Thomas Hail**, **Jeremiah Stone**, **John Evans**, **Amassa Spencer**, **William Cooper**, **John McCullough**, **John Fitzpatrick**, **Hugh Logan**, **William Blair**, **George Modrel**, **David Evans**, & **Joseph Lewis** who being elected tried and sworn the truth to speak upon the Issue Joined Afterward one of the Jurors, to wit, **Joseph Lewis**, by Consent was withdrawn & the cause continued until the next Term of this Court

[page 555] **Francis Lynch** Plt
vs In Trespass assault & Battery
**Taylor** & **Sargent** Deft

By consent of parties It is Ordered that an Ord made continuing this cause till the next Term of this Court be set a side, and by Consent of said parties all matters if difference between them relative to this suit is refered to the arbitration and determination of **Martin Turpin**, **John Phelps**, **Drewry Lee** & **Andrew Owens** whose awd or the award of any three of them be made the Judgment of the Court, and in case of disagreement, said referees to chose a fifth person and the same is ordered accordingly, and the said referees may return their award to this Present Term or the next Term of this Court

– **Francis Stephens** Plt
vs In Case
**Bendin** & **Barns** Defts

– **William Davis** Assee Plt
vs In Debt
**Larue** & **Waters** Deft

– **Thomas Hail** Plt
vs In Case
**Polly Parker** Deft

[page 556] **James Hardgrove** Assee Plt
vs In Debt
**James Montgomery** &c Defts

– **William Barrow** Plt
vs In Debt
**George Allcorn** Deft

It is ordered by the Court that the several Dismissions, and Judgments taken in the Clerks Office in the above cases be confirmed and made the Judgment of the Court

– **John Puckett** Plt
vs In Trespass assault & Battery
**John Phelps**

This day came the parties aforesaid and It is Ordered that this cause be Continued until the next Term of this Court by Consent

– **John Patton** Ass[ee] Plt
vs In Debt
**William Zachary** Deft

This day came as well the Plaintiff by his attorney as the said Deft in his proper person who says he cannot gainsay the plaintiffs action against him for nineteen Dollars the Debt in the Declaration herein mentioned, therefore with the assent of the plaintiff It is considered [page 557] by the Court that the Plaintiff recover against the said Deft his Debt aforesaid together with legal Interest thereon from the 6[th] day of July 1809 until paid & costs and the said Deft in mercy &[c]

– **Isaac Muse** Plt
vs In Trespass Assault & Battery
**William Burton** Deft

This day came the parties aforesaid, and by consent It is Ordered that this suit be dismissed at the Defts Costs

– **William Hudson** & **John Patton** Plts
vs In Debt
**Joseph Porter** Deft

This day came as well the Plaintiffs by their attorney as the said Deft in his proper person, who says he cannot gainsay the plaintiffs action against him for the Debt in the Declaration mentioned therefore with the assent of the plaintiffs It is Considered by the Court that the plaintiffs recover against the said Defendant eight pounds four shillings and Seven pence the Debt in the Declaration afores[d] mentioned with legal Interest thereon from 24 of August 1808 until paid [page 558] and Costs and the said Defendant in mercy &[c]

– **James Anderson** Plt
vs In Debt
**Smith** & **William Hill** Defts

This day Came the Pltff by his attorney and on his motion It is ordered that his suit abate as to the Deft **Smith**, the process herein not being served on him, and the other Deft **William Hill** called but came not, therefore on the motion of the Plaintiff by his attorney It is commanded the Sheriff that he cause to come here Immediately twelve good and lawful men by whom &[c] and thereupon came a Jury, to wit, **Philip A Sublette, Drewry Clark, Thomas Pascall, Nicholas Jasper** Junr, **Thomas Dollihide, Hansford Price, Hugh Chambers, Adonijah Morgan, Christ[o] Clonch, Thomas Hail, Jeremiah Dungans,** & **James Price**, who were sworn well and truly to enquire what Damages the Plaintiffs hath sustained in the premises upon their Oaths do find for the Plaintiff the Debt in the Declaration mentioned do assess his Damages Inconsequences of the Detention thereof to one Cent besides his Costs It is [page 559] therefore Considered by the Court that the Plaintiff recover against the said Deft one hundred and Seventy Dollars the Debt in said Declaration mentioned together with legal Interest thereon from the first day of September One thousand eight hundred and nine until paid & Costs as well as his Damages afores[d] by the Jurors in their Verdict aforesaid assessed, and the said Deft in mercy &[c]

– **James Hear** Plt
vs upon Petition
**Nathan Meek** Deft

This day came the Plaintiff by his attorney and the Deft being called but came not therefore on the motion of the Pltff by his attorney It is ordered that the shff cause to come here Immediately twelve good and lawful men by whom &[c] and thereupon came a Jury, to wit, (the same Jury as in the case of **Anderson** vs **Hill** &[c]) who were sworn well and truly to enquire what Damage the plaintiff hath sustained in the premises upon their Oaths returned their verdict in these words, We of the Jury find for the Pltff the Debt in the [page 560] within Petition mentioned and assess his Damages by Occasion of the detention thereof to one cent exclusive of Interest, and the same is made the Judgment of the Court

Note this Judgment is to be discharged by the payment of £5..13..7½ with legal Interest thereon from the first day of March 1809 until paid & Costs and the said Defendant in mercy &c

– **Willis Embry** Assee Plt
vs upon Petition
**Andrew Campbell** & **Robert Modrel** Defts

This day came the Pltff by his attorney and on his motion It is Ord that this suit abate as to the Deft **Campbell** he having not been served with the proper process, And the other Deft **Robt Modrel** called but came not, on the motion of the Pltff by his attorney It ordered that the Sheriff cause to come here Immediately twelve good and lawful men by whom &c and thereupon came also a Jury, to wit, same Jury as in the case **Anderson** vs **Hill**) who were [page 561] sworn well and truly to enquire what Damages the Plaintiff hath sustained in the premises returned their verdict in these words we of the Jury find for the Pltff the Debt in the Petition mentioned and one cent in Damages, It is therefore considered by the Court that the Plaintiff recover against the said Deft eighty Dollars the Debt in said Petition mentioned with legal Interest thereon from the first day of October 1809 until paid & Costs, and the said Deft in mercy &c

– **John Arnold** Plt
vs upon Petition
**Andrew Davidson** Deft

This day came the Plaintiff by his attorney and the Deft being called but came not therefore on the mo of the Pltff &c (same proceedings had and same Jury as in the case last above mentioned) who were sworn well and truly to enquire what Damage the Plaintiff hath sustained in the premises upon their Oaths returned their Verdict in these words, to wit, We of the Jury find for the Pltff the Debt in the Petition mentioned & one cent in Damages, and It is Ordered that the same be made the [page 562] Judgment of the Court, Note this Judgment is to be discharged by the payment of One hundred and ninety five Dollars with legal Interest thereon from the tenth day of April 1807 But to have credit for forty dollars paid April 22d 1809

– **Enoch Hume** Assee Plt
vs upon Petition
**Dollarhide** & **Gibson** Defts

Same Jury and like proceedings had as in the case last above mentioned, and returned their Verdict herein in these words, to wit, we of the Jury find for the Pltff the Debt in the Petition mentioned & one cent in Damages. and It is ordered that the same be made the Judgment of the Court and the Deft in mercy &c

Note this Judgment is to be discharged by the payment fourteen pounds eight shillings, with legal Interest thereon from the 5th day of May One thousand eight hundred and eight until paid & Costs but to have credit for 20/ paid &c

– **Reubin Scott** for the benifit of **Alexander Montgomery** Plt
vs In Covn
**Ezekiel Montgomery** & **Jenning Cundiff** Defts

This day came the Plaintiff by his attorney and the capias not having been served on the Deft [page 563] **Montgomery** herein, It is Ordered that this suit abate as to sd Deft **Montgomery**, and the Other Deft **Cundiff** being called came not therefore on the motion of the Plaintiff by his attorney It is commanded the sheriff that he cause to come here Immediately twelve good and lawful men by whom &c and thereupon came also a Jury to wit, (same Jury as in the case last above mentioned) who were sworn well and truly to enquire what Damages the plaintiff hath sustained in the premises upon their Oaths do say the Plaintiff hath sustained Damage by Occasion thereof to forty three Dollars and ten cents besides his costs It is therefore Considered by the Court that the Plaintiff recover against the said Deft his Damages aforesaid by the Jurors in their verdict aforesaid assessed and his Costs by him about his suit in this behalf expended and the said Deft in mercy &c

– **Joseph Patterson** Plt
vs Trespass Vict armis
**Nancy Matthews** & als Defts

This day came the plaintiff by his attorney and on his motion It is Ordered that [page 564] this cause be remanded to the Rule Dockette & alias awarded on Deft Nathaniel Wi[ ]

– **William Spears** Plt
vs In Covenant
**Amassa Spencer** Deft

On the motion of the Plaintiff by his attorney leave is given him to take the Deposition of **Benjamin Adair**, De benesse

– **John Rogers** Complt
vs In Chancery
**Thomas McLaughlin** Deft

This day came the parties aforesaid by their Attornies, and It is ordered that this cause be continued until the next Term of this court and leave is given to take Depositions Generally by consent

– **William Stringer** for the benifit of **John Newby** Plt
vs In Covenant
**Thomas Woosley** Deft

**James McKinsey** of Pulaski County came into Court and Justified, and undertook for the said Deft that if he shall be cast in the action aforesaid that he shall satisfy and pay the condemnation of the Court or render his body to prison in execution for the same or on falure thereof that he the said **James McKinsey** shall do it for him

[page 565] On the motion of **May Hixon** who produced in Court a writing which was sworn to by **Thomas Vanhook** & **Rob[t] Smith** as to her late husband **Matthew Hixon** Dec[d] having resided on a certain tract of land d[o]. It is ordered that the said writing be certified agreeably to an act of the General Assembly Kentucky in such cases made and provided

– **John Taylor** Ass[ee] Plt
vs In Covenant
**Thomas Woosley** & Al[s] Defts

**Joshua Woosly**, of Pulaski County came into Court and Justified and undertook for the said Deft **Thomas Woosly**, that if he shall be cast in the action aforesaid that he shall satisfy and pay the condemnation of the Court or render his body to prison in execution for the same or on falure thereof that he the said **Joshua** shall do it for him

– **Zachariah Johnston** Plt
vs In Case
**Joseph Lewis** Deft

This day came the parties aforesaid, and by Consent leave is given the plaintiff to take Depositions before a single Justice of the Peace without the state of Kentucky to be had as evidence herein and Dedimus awarded

[page 566] Ordered that the Court be adjourned until Tomorrow morning nine OClock

**Christopher Tompkins**

At a Circuit Court Continued and held for the Pulaski Circuit at the Courthouse of Pulaski County in Somerset on Thursday the 26[th] day of October 1809

Present the Honorable **Christ[o] Tompkins, John Prather & John James** Gent

– On motion of **Philip A Sublette** who came into Court and acknowledged himself Justly Indebted to **John Patton** Ass[ee] in the sum of Twenty six Dollars and ninety two Cents, as p[r] note filed, with stay of Execution six months, and with the assent of the s[d] **Patton**, It is therefore Considered by the Court that the said **Patton** recover against the said **Sublette**, the sum Confessed as aforesaid and his Costs by him in this behalf expended &[c]

– **John Thurman** Plt
vs upon Petition
**Joseph Erwine** Deft

On the motion of the Defendant by his attorney a new trial is awarded him on the Verdict

of the Jury and Judgment Obtained [page 567] herein yesterday, on the said Defendants paying Costs [ ] the cause is continued until the next Term of this Court
– **John Collyer** & **John Preston** Plt
vs In Chancery
**John Evans** Deft

This day came the parties aforesaid by their attornies and by consent this cause is continued until the next Term of this Court
– **John Brooks** Complt
vs In Chancery
**Mark Evans** Deft

This day came the Complainant by his attorney, and on hearing the Bill, answer and sundry Depositions and mature deliberation thereon had It is Ordered and Decreed that the Injunction prayed in the Complainants bill be made perpetual bar to the said **John Brooks** against the said **Mark Evans** at Common law agreeable to the prayer of the said Bill, and It is further considered that the Complainant recover against the said Deft his Costs by him in this behalf expended
– **Francis Lynch** Plt
vs In Trespass assault & Battery
**Taylor** and **Sargent** Deft

[page 568] The Persons to whom all matters and differences is refered between the parties aforesaid returned their award in these words following, to wit, In Obedience to an order made by the Honorable, the Circuit Judges of Pulaski Circuit Court &c whereas **Francis Lynch** Plaintiff and **James Taylor** & **Sargent** Deft we the referees find for the Plaintiff vs **Sargent** one cent Damage and **Taylor** acquitted Given under our hands and seals this 25th day of Oct 1809

**John Phelps**
**Drewry Lee**
**Andrew Cowen**

And the same is made the Judgment of the Court
– The Commonwealth Plt
vs upon Indictment
**John Daniel** Deft
– The Commonwealth Plt
vs Same
**Zachariah Eastham** Deft

This day came the attorney for the commonwealth an on his motion It is Ordd that an Als Caps be awarded against each of the above Defendants
[page 569] The Commonwealth
vs upon an Indictment
**John McWhorter**

On the motion of the attorney for the Commonwealth It is ordered that a Capias Issue herein against the said Deft with an endorsement therein directing that said Deft shall be held to Bail in the sum of $1,500, and one or two good Securities in a like sum, and It is ordered that a scifs Issue on the forfeited recognizance against the said **McWhorters** Securities
– The Same Plt
vs Same
**Jonathan Addison** Deft

On the motion of the attorney for the Commonwealth It is ordered that a capias Issue herein against the said Deft with an endorsement thereon directing that the said Deft shall be held to Bail in the sum of $300, and one or two good securities in a like sum, and that a scifa Issue herein as in the case Cmmth vs **McWhorter**
– **Bazil Meek**, late Sheriff of Pulaski County, exhibited to the Court an Account for public Services performed by him in the execution of his Office [page 570] the amount of which is $14..51 which being examined by the Court was Ordered to be Certified to the Auditor of Public Accts

– **Ralph Williams**, Shff of Pulaski County exhibited to the Court a similar account for $19..77 which is Ordered to be Certif[d] as above
– Ordered that it be certified to the County Court of Pulaski County that this Court allows to **Tunstall Quarles** Esq[r] as their Commonwealths att[o] the sum of One hundred and twenty Dollars, for his services in the execution of his Office for the last year preceeding this day
– **Edward Prather**, exhibited an account for guarding **Dickson** the amount of which is $1..43 which account being examined and filed is Ordered to be certify[d] to the auditor of Public Accounts
– **William G Cowen**, one of the Guard over the above named **Dickson** exhibited an acc[t] the amount of which is $1..72 which account being examined by the Court and filed is ordered to be Certified to the auditor of Public Accounts
– **William Fox** clerk of this Court exhibited to the Court an account for stationery & Record Books furnished [page 571] by him for the use of his Office for the last year preceeding the fourth Monday in this present Instant the amount of which is $29..00 which being ex[d] by the Court was ordered to be Certify[d] to the Auditor of Public Accounts
– **John January**, Jailor exhibited an account for eighteen days service attending on the Court at their April, July & this Present October Term in this year for which he is allowed one Dollar p[r] which is ordered to be Certified to the Auditor of Public accounts
– Ordered that it be certified to the auditor of public acc[ts] that this Court allows to **William Fox** as their clerk for [ ] services performed by him in the Execution of his Office for the last year preceeding the fourth Monday in this present Instant the sum of $30..00
– Ordered that **Joseph Porter** & **Tunstall Quarles** Gent be appointed to examine the clerks of this court or Circuit and make report to the next Term of this Court the situation thereof &[c]
– Ordered that it be Certified to the auditor of public Accounts that this Court allows to **Henry James**, the keeper of **John Barns**, a person of unsound mind the sum of $100, for keeping and maintaining [page 572] said **Barns** for the last year preceeding this day
– **Andrew Cowen** Complt
vs In Chancery
**Tunstall Quarles** Deft

This day came the parties aforesaid by their Counsel and by Consent it is Ordered that the Order Continuing this Cause until the next Term of this court be set a side, And the land in the bill mentioned Descend to the Complt and by consent each party to pay his own Costs
– **John Chesney** Complt
vs In Chancery
**Tunstall Quarles** Deft

This day came the parties aforesaid by their Counsil and by consent the land in the bill of the Complt mentioned is Decend to the Complt, and Deft to pay all the Costs (except ten Dollars by agreement between the parties afores[d]
– Ordered that the Court be adjourned until Court in Course

**Christopher Tompkins**

# Index

www.ingramcontent.com/pod-product-compliance
Lightning Source LLC
Chambersburg PA
CBHW032043040426
42334CB00038B/370
* 9 7 8 0 8 9 3 0 8 8 9 2 7 *